PROPHETIC ENCOUNTERS

Prophetic Encounters

Religion and the American Radical Tradition

DAN MCKANAN

Beacon Press
BOSTON

Beacon Press
25 Beacon Street
Boston, Massachusetts 02108-2892
www.beacon.org

Beacon Press books
are published under the auspices of
the Unitarian Universalist Association of Congregations.

14 13 12 11   8 7 6 5 4 3 2 1

This book is printed on acid-free paper that meets the uncoated paper ANSI/NISO
specifications for permanence as revised in 1992.

Text design and composition by Wilsted & Taylor Publishing Services

Library of Congress Cataloging-in-Publication Data

McKanan, Dan
  Prophetic encounters : religion and the American radical tradition /
by Daniel Patrick McKanan.
       p. cm.
  Includes bibliographical references (p.   ) and index.
  ISBN 978-0-8070-1315-1 (hardcover : alk. paper)
    1. Religion and politics—United States—History. 2. Ideology—Religious aspects—
History. I. Title.
  BL2525.M3925 2011
  211'.40973—dc22   2011012350

CONTENTS

Everyone needs a history, especially those who seek to change the future. When radical activists confront the entrenched legacy of racism and sexism in both our institutions and our textbooks, we are tempted to imagine that all history supports the status quo. In an era in which prominent representatives of American Christianity are outspoken in their support of reactionary politics, it is easy to imagine that the history of religion is doubly conservative. But there have always been American radicals—and those radicals have always drawn strength from their diverse faiths, Christian and Jewish, pagan and Buddhist, orthodox and humanist. To forget our predecessors' work is not only to risk repeating their mistakes, it is to lose their wisdom and inspiration. And so, as we organize our neighborhoods or march on Washington, we must tell the stories of the cloud of witnesses who came before us. To encounter them is to discover the human sources of radical faith.

On August 11, 1841, Frederick Douglass made his first public speech at a convention in Nantucket. The prospect of addressing white people, Douglass would later recall, was "a severe cross" because he still "felt myself a slave." Yet the act of speaking proved to be liberating for Douglass and revelatory for his audience. "I spoke but a few moments," Douglass wrote in his autobiography, "when I felt a degree of freedom." The antislavery editor William Lloyd Garrison, for his part, reported that "I think I never hated slavery so intensely as at that moment. Certainly, my perception of the enormous outrage which is inflicted by it, on the godlike nature of its victims, was rendered far more clear than ever." For both men, their meeting was an encounter with the divine, and they retained a sense of its religious power long after their personal paths diverged. Thirty years later, Douglass mused that it was only through his encounters with other radicals that he could "get any glimpses of God anywhere."[1]

Echoes of this sentiment can be heard in every American movement for social transformation. A century after Garrison met Douglass, a radical journalist named Dorothy Day found herself longing to encounter the "poor and oppressed" immigrants, whom she regarded as "collectively the new Messiah." Noticing that most immigrants were Roman Catholics, she joined the church, but soon missed the militant idealism of her socialist past. Why, she wondered, could not Catholicism also gather "bands of men and women together" for social change? Day launched a national network of farms and households where pious Catholics, committed radicals, and the desperately poor encountered one another as they fed the hungry, comforted the afflicted, and afflicted the comfortable.[2]

A similar hunger for encounter brought several feminists together in a California storefront in the 1970s. They had already had their consciousness raised, but they yearned to tap more deeply into the womanpower that, they believed, had inspired ancient worship of the goddess and the medieval healing practices that were stigmatized as witchcraft. Their conversation about magic became a ritual, as the women "took hands, and started breathing together." Realizing that "a circle had been cast," they anointed themselves, kissed, and began chanting the names of ancient goddesses, entreating them to "pour out your light and your radiance upon us. . . . Shine! Shine! Shine!" As the energy subsided, they chose a coven name, Compost, thus reassuring themselves that "whatever magic brings, it will not take away our ability to laugh at ourselves." They also realized that magic could empower them to change the world. Coven leader Starhawk introduced their Spiral Dance at a massive demonstration against a nuclear power plant, and soon pagan-inspired rituals were an integral part of direct action campaigns against war, environmental destruction, and globalization.[3]

The empowering encounters of William Lloyd Garrison, Frederick Douglass, Dorothy Day, and Starhawk stand in a tradition that has gone by many names. Some would call it the path of the prophets. Others speak of the "American radical tradition" or simply "the Left." It is the tradition of abolitionists who called on their neighbors to immediately renounce the sin of slavery, of feminists who recognized patriarchy as itself a form of slavery, of socialists who labored to build a "cooperative commonwealth," and of pacifists who saw war as the ultimate affront to humanity.

What holds this tradition together is the experience I have tried to encapsulate in my opening vignettes. When human beings encounter one another deeply, in the midst of their struggles for freedom and equality and community, prophetic power is unleashed. This is power to denounce, to condemn those who would "grind the faces of the poor into the dust," in the words of Isaiah. It is also power to *announce*—to proclaim God's Kingdom that will be realized here on earth, the beloved community of black and white and brown together, the new society within the shell of the old. Prophetic power enables people to speak boldly in the face of brickbats and bludgeons and fire hoses. It empowers them to tell new stories and build new communities. Because interpersonal encounters are the source of this power, their place within radicalism is analogous to the role of divine revelation within traditional Christianity, Judaism, or Islam. For this reason, I describe them as *prophetic* encounters.

By placing prophetic encounters at the heart of my story, I hope to share three guiding insights about the American radical tradition. First of all, it *is* a tradition. Too often we remember abolitionism or feminism or socialism as self-contained "movements" that emerged in response to particular social problems and disappeared when those problems were overcome or changed form. Such memories obscure the way in which activists of each generation have built alliances and drawn inspiration, religious convictions, and strategies from those who have gone before. Garrison and Douglass were as eloquent in denouncing the sin of sexism as the sin of slavery, and they helped to inspire the pacifists and socialists of their day. They also pioneered activist tactics that have lasted for centuries. Garrison used his imprisonment for libeling a slave trader to raise awareness of his cause, while Douglass repeatedly refused to leave segregated railway cars until he was expelled by force; Dorothy Day and Starhawk were among the thousands who followed in their footsteps, facing arrest for refusing to participate in civil defense drills or for disrupting the 1999 World Trade Organization meeting in Seattle. One scarcely needs seven degrees of separation to trace the personal connections among the four: Garrison's grandson was among the founders of the pacifist Fellowship of Reconciliation, which worked with the Catholic Worker movement to sponsor the civil defense protests and Vietnam-era draft-card burnings; the first man to go to prison for draft-card burning would later marry Starhawk. Though the Left has not always been one big happy family, even in its divisions and rancor it has been a family.

Second, religious ideas, institutions, and practices have always been intertwined with radical activism. American radicals drew inspiration from religious communities as diverse as Frederick Douglass's African Methodist Episcopal Church, Dorothy Day's Roman Catholicism, and Starhawk's neopaganism. It is common nowadays to speak of a "religious Left" that is distinct from secular radicalism, or to suggest that the prophetic tradition possesses a wisdom lacking in both the "religious Right" and the "secular Left." Such formulations fail to do justice to the spirituality of even the most seemingly "unchurched" radicals. Many of the most bitter critics of the churches have been people of deep personal faith, inspired by the example of Jesus driving the moneychangers from the temple, while those who have tried to separate radical causes from religious language have often hoped to make room for persons of divergent theologies. Though Dorothy Day's orthodox Catholic piety was far removed from the dogmatic materialism of the Communist Party, it is not possible to draw a line that neatly separates religious from secular radicals.

Indeed—and this is my third guiding insight—leftist activism is almost a form of religion. It occupies much of the same psychological and sociological space. People are drawn to religious communities and radical organizations in order to connect their daily routines to a more transcendent vision of heaven, salvation, or a new society. Both religion and radicalism offer individuals powerful new identities—as "children of God" or "class-conscious workers" or "New Negros." In order to extend this power, radicals build organizations—social reform societies, utopian communities, third parties—that have many churchlike qualities. Radicals come together to sing hymns and hear sermons, often gathering on Sunday morning; they articulate their defining beliefs and excommunicate those who dissent; their marches are like pilgrimages and their "line-crossing" in civil disobedience like a ritual of initiation. Radicalism is more like a religion than like mainstream political traditions, which suspend questions of transcendence in order to reconcile competing interests and build electorally viable coalitions.

To say that radicalism is almost a form of religion is not to deny the tension between the two but to explain it. Radicals seek to live in relation to a better world that might exist here on earth in the future; most conventionally religious people orient their lives to realities beyond this world. While radicals achieve empowered identities through interpersonal encounters, most religions offer a new identity through encounter with spiritual beings. (The major exception, religious humanism, has rarely clashed with the Left.) As a result, the relationship between the Left and conventional religiosity has the volatility of sibling rivalry. Some radicals find their religious and radical commitments to be mutually reinforcing; others come to see their cause as the true church. Many American leftists have, from time to time, found themselves in both of these postures. The tensions run deep and should not be dismissed as a matter of secularist prejudice.

I will return to these three guiding insights—the Left is a tradition, the Left is thoroughly intertwined with religion, the Left is itself analogous to religion—throughout this book. Before entering into my narrative, it may be helpful to define some terms. I use "Left" and "radicalism" interchangeably to designate a tradition of social movements and organizations that seek to extend the values of liberty, equality, solidarity, and peace. These values are rooted in the American and French revolutions of the late eighteenth century, and American radicalism in particular is defined by its twofold relationship to the heritage of 1776. On the one hand, American radicals place themselves in the legacy of the Revolution. Taking pride in America, they imitate the rhetoric of the Declaration of Independence and hope to persuade all Americans to join their cause. On the other hand, American leftists are radically dissatisfied with the Revolution's institutional heritage. They refuse to believe that American structures of political democracy will inevitably lead to greater liberty, equality, and solidarity. And they refuse to worry that present agitation will undermine past gains. American radicalism has included movements to end slavery; to include people of all races, genders, and sexualities fully in the national community; to build a cooperative or socialist economy; and to limit or end war and violence.

American radicalism as I have defined it excludes incremental forms of progressivism that are more concerned with *preserving* the institutions of the Revolution than with *extending* its values; my definition excludes as well as separatist movements that renounce American ideals. Neither Abraham Lincoln nor Franklin Delano Roosevelt, neither Marcus Garvey nor Elijah Muhammad were truly American radicals by my definition, though Garvey and Muhammad were radicals of another stripe. This is not to suggest that true leftists must hold themselves aloof from such people. The Left has learned from Garvey's and Muhammad's passionate devotion to their people, and it has often embraced tactical separatism as a way of empowering people for sustained struggle. Similarly, the Left's critique of institutions does not preclude fruitful dialogue with persons who support those institutions. True radicals have never been comfortable within the two-party system of American politics, but some have worked to nudge the parties to more radical ground. Others have cheered from the sidelines when men like Lincoln and Roosevelt embraced elements of their agenda.

In arguing that American radicalism constitutes a sustained tradition with a two-hundred-year history, I do not mean to suggest that it is sealed off from other traditions. Radicalism has always had transatlantic and global dimensions, though limitations of space preclude more than glancing acknowledgment of those. American radicals were inspired by the European revolutions of 1830, 1848, and 1917, and by the global anticolonialism of the 1950s and 1960s, just as partisans of those causes drew strength from the "spirit of 1776."

Similarly, radicals hold multiple allegiances—to specific religious traditions, to their crafts or professions, to their ethnic communities. To say that Dorothy Day was part of the radical tradition, heir to the legacy of Garrison and Douglass, is not to deny that she was also part of the Catholic tradition and heir to the legacy of Thomas Aquinas and Thérèse of Lisieux. Unlike Catholicism, radicalism has lacked a continuous institutional framework to help preserve a consciousness of tradition. As a result, it is easy to imagine that Catholicism was the *only* tradition that shaped Day's activism in a profound way, or that the black church was the only tradition informing Martin Luther King Jr. My task is to correct this impression by tracing the contours of the tradition all radicals shared, not to diminish the contributions of other traditions.

My view of the Left as a tradition does not deny the presence of deep divisions among radicals. Radicals have maintained a sense of shared identity in part by arguing about the best way to promote liberty, equality, and solidarity. Pacifists and revolutionaries repeatedly squared off over the question of whether nonviolent suffering or holy violence was the best way to change institutions. When anarchists and Marxists split over the role of the state in bringing about a cooperative commonwealth, they echoed a nineteenth-century debate between nonvoting Garrisonians who believed that the U.S. Constitution was inherently proslavery and Liberty Party members who countered that its antislavery potential needed only to be unleashed. Other radical debates focused on the value of small-scale utopian experiments, the merits of single-issue organizing versus comprehensive programs of reform, and the best way to reconcile the tensions among liberty, equality, and solidarity. A persistent and bitter debate concerned the family: was it better understood as yet another oppressive institution or as a sacred gift threatened by unjust institutions? Debates over how the Left should interact with mainstream religion also shaped radicalism. These debates contributed to bitter feelings and organizational schisms, but could not bring the conversation to an end. Dorothy Day had strong positions on all the issues I just listed, and she recognized Fidel Castro as a comrade even though his views were diametrically opposed to hers. Given the scope of this book, I will devote more space to the debate over religion than to the others, but all would be of vital importance in a comprehensive history of American radicalism.

As I have defined it, radicalism is concerned with relationships among people, rather than with human connections to spiritual realities or the material world. The Left as such is not committed to any particular understanding of God or spirits, nor does it prescribe specific practices of diet, dress, or sexual behavior. Yet in practice it is rarely possible to separate human relationships from spiritual and material realities. For many activists, radical commitment has been unthinkable apart from belief in God, or from communication with the spirits of the deceased, or from the practice of free love or abstinence from alcohol. At specific historical moments, certain correlations have been almost ubiquitous on the left: it would be almost as difficult to find an 1840s radical who opposed the temperance movement as a 1990s leftist who opposed recycling. My narrative will thus intersect with the stories of temperance and environmentalism as well as of such religious movements as Quakerism, Universalism, and Spiritualism. But I make no claim to tell the whole stories of such movements, and I insist that none of them has ever been *entirely* identified with American radicalism.

Like "radicalism," the term "religion" is notoriously difficult to define. I use it in two senses, corresponding roughly to my second and third guiding insights. On the one hand, I sometimes define religion as whatever people say it is—practices, institutions, and ideas that are conventionally labeled religious. Thus, I will track the intertwining between radicalism and such practices as Sunday morning worship, such organizations as the United Methodist Church, and such ideas as the claim that all people are created in God's image.

On the other hand, I take religion to include all practices, ideas, and institutions that connect people to what Paul Tillich called "ultimate concern," providing a frame of reference that reaches beyond pragmatic adjustment to the here and now. It is in this sense that I describe radicalism as almost a form of religion, echoing Socialist leader Norman Thomas's observation that there is an "implicit religion of radicalism," since a "high order of faith" is required to hope that ordinary people can make the world anew. Accordingly, I will unpack the ways in which attending a rally or protecting a fugitive slave constitute religious practice and the ways in which radical groups parallel church structures. It is important to stress, though, that radicalism's "ultimate concern" is not ultimate or transcendent in quite the same way as most religious claims to ultimacy. Radical hope transcends the institutions of present-day society, but it does not transcend the laws of physical or human nature. It looks to the future, not to heaven. Though the same could be said of a few traditions that are conventionally labeled religious, radicalism is best described as a sibling of religion rather than a form of religion. Like most siblings, the two have interacted in both constructive and combative ways.[4]

A few "ideal types" may illustrate the diverse interactions between religion and radicalism. First, some radicals have been comfortable members of mainstream religious communities. For them, revelatory experiences of interpersonal encounter confirmed the truths of biblical revelation. The most famous "religious radicals" fall into this camp: Dorothy Day, John Brown, Martin Luther King Jr. Because these radicals presented their sociopolitical vision in widely shared religious categories, they often succeeded in building mass movements and sometimes, for pragmatic reasons, gained the support of radicals who did not share their religious commitments. Some studies of the "religious Left" focus exclusively on persons in this group, even suggesting that their motives were incommensurable with those of their "secular" counterparts. But such a distinction would divide Day, Brown, and King from many of their most intimate allies.

A second group of leftists espoused ideals rooted in mainstream religion but harshly criticized religious institutions. For them, churches and synagogues had betrayed their defining principles, just as had the American government. William Lloyd Garrison exemplified this type when he urged abolitionists to "come out" of all existing churches. Ironically, many who found him excessively anticlerical ultimately followed a similar path, organizing splinter denominations to avoid compromise with proslavery "churchianity." Here we see one reason why it is difficult to distinguish the religious and the secular Left: the line between self-critical believer and critical unbeliever is in the eye of the beholder.

A third type of radical, only superficially similar to Garrison, argued that religion in general is intrinsically opposed to freedom, equality, and solidarity. Typically, there were two lines of reasoning here. One saw the priesthood as the original oppressive class: a group of unproductive exploiters who manipulated people's fears in order to gain power over them and thus paved the way for slaveholders and capitalists. The other saw belief in heaven as a distraction from the work of building heaven on earth. Adherents of this viewpoint included the American disciples of Thomas Paine, Robert Owen, and Karl Marx as well as nineteenth-century "Freethinkers" and later "secular humanists." In a sense, they were the classic "secular leftists"—and yet of all radicals they were most inclined to re-create the social forms of religion. They denied classical doctrines with as much dogmatism as the orthodox affirmed them, and they sponsored local communities that often gathered on Sunday mornings to sing hymns and hear speeches.

Another group addressed the problems with mainstream religion by building up alternative spiritual traditions. These people were typically involved in such emerging religious movements as Spiritualism, Theosophy, New Thought, religious humanism, and neopaganism. These movements drew heavily from the radical constituency, though some of their adherents found they had less energy left over for Left causes—provoking complaints of comrades "lost" to "cults" or "fads." Starhawk's example demonstrates that it need not be so: neopaganism has sustained her activism as consistently as Roman Catholicism did for Dorothy Day.

Finally, a significant number of radical leaders actively discouraged religious debate within the organizations they led. This was the position that Susan B. Anthony took in her leadership of the women's suffrage movement, and it was also the approach of the most influential Socialist Party organizer, Morris Hilquit, who in 1908 pushed through a resolution declaring that socialism was "not concerned with religious belief." These folks were the true secularists of the Left, in that they divided religious and sociopolitical concerns into distinct spheres of activity. But their fiercest hostility was directed *not* at the orthodox members of my first group, but rather at the Freethinkers or adherents of new religions. Though they often shared freethinking or unorthodox beliefs, these leaders were determined to build mass movements, and they did not want religious controversy to get in the way.

The history of American radicalism is distorted when observers confuse these positions. Blithe generalizations about the "secular Left" ignore the bitter battles fought between Freethinkers and those wary of theological debate. Likewise, those who complain that faithful Christians have been marginalized by radical anticlericalism fail to see that some of the harshest attacks have come from people who believed they were truer Christians than the clergy they attacked. Even a complex typology obscures the way that radicals move from one position to another over their lifetimes. This is so because of the prophetic power that inheres in radical encounters. If radical activism were a way of putting preexisting faith into action, it would have little impact on the character of activists' faith. But for most radicals, activism is itself a source of revelation. And one cannot see the face of God, or the shape of ultimate reality, without having one's religious identity transformed. My story will often follow the radicals' wayward spiritual pilgrimages.

Just as radicalism has a complex relationship with religion, so it has a fraught connection with institutions of all sorts. Radicals look at existing institutions with suspicion, yet they need some sort of institutional base in order to hold meetings, disseminate information, and preserve a memory of what has worked or failed in the past. Religious institutions have served this purpose well, both because they are inherently oriented to values transcending the here and now and because they enjoy some degree of autonomy from structures of political power. The First Amendment to the U.S. Constitution freed religious institutions (if they chose) to play an ever more important role as social critics. From the radical perspective, the church has always had a double aspect: as relatively autonomous from political and economic institutions, it is an ideal organizing base; as interwoven with those institutions, it is an inevitable target of radical critique.

Throughout the nineteenth century, the congregation or local religious community was the most important organizational base for American radicals. This was partly because some congregations were eager to make use of the new freedom afforded them by the First Amendment, and partly because congregations were where the people were. Far more people were affiliated with congregations than with labor unions or universities—the most important "secular" bases for radicalism in the twentieth century. Congregations gave birth to the voluntary societies, agitating newspapers, experimental communities, and third parties that were unreservedly committed to radicalism. They also paved the way for the gradual radicalization of denominations and seminaries in the twentieth century. All these institutions figure prominently in these pages.

Chronologically, my narrative will highlight both the ways in which radicals passed on their tradition during "conservative" epochs and those rare moments when activists transformed the structures of American society. Paradoxically, conservative times were essential for the development of radicalism *as* a tradition. Veterans of past struggles had the time to be intentional about mentoring new generations of leaders; they also composed narratives that traced the genealogy of the Left. In times of success, by contrast, some leftists emphasized the "newness" of their cause by distinguishing it from past struggles, while others focused on alliances with conventional politics. It is noteworthy that the three greatest victories of the American Left—the abolition of slavery during the Civil War, the enactment of a broad social safety net during the New Deal, and the elimination of formal racial segregation during the civil rights era—were enacted by U.S. presidents who had previously been distrusted and belittled by activists on the left.

Those three victories mark a rough periodization of American radicalism. Each reshuffled the deck of American ideology in a manner similar to, though not as extensive as, the American Revolution itself. The Revolution generated an ideological consensus so broad that it is invoked by both leftists and conservatives; for this reason, it is difficult to extend the radical story back before the Revolution. Neither the Civil War nor the New Deal nor civil rights generated complete consensus. But they blurred the distinction between the Left and the institutional progressivism of politicians whose first commitment was to the preservation of American institutions. When Lincoln and Douglass, Roosevelt and Norman Thomas, MLK and LBJ found themselves in common cause, some radicals moved joyously into the political mainstream, while others retreated to the margins. In their wake, new radical constituencies emerged among those excluded from the fruits of success. Labor activism moved closer to the heart of the Left in the wake of Reconstruction; the black freedom struggle took on new salience in the decades after the New Deal; and feminism revived in the wake of civil rights victories.

The movements associated with these three victories can be correlated with three distinct sorts of "prophetic encounter," illustrated by the three encounters with which I began. The most basic sort of radical encounter is what I will call the "encounter of identity." This takes place when people who lack institutional authority discover their own power by coming together, sharing stories, and claiming a new identity. The experience is much like religious conversion, and it is the greatest source of radical power. This is the sort of encounter experienced by members of the Compost Coven, and it was similarly experienced by the "Working Men" and "Africans" who claimed powerful new identities in the generation after the American Revolution. These two groups launched the American radical tradition, yet because of their minority status neither was able to translate their new identities into social change.

A second sort of encounter exerted more influence in the early nineteenth century. The "personal encounter" bridged the gap between newly empowered groups and persons of inherited privilege by lifting up individual representatives of the former as embodiments of the radical cause. This is what happened when Frederick Douglass met William Lloyd Garrison, and for many of their contemporaries the simple experience of meeting Garrison or Douglass sparked a lifetime of activism. The women's rights movement, which emerged in close association with abolitionism, made women's public speaking its definitive practice, both because it defied gender convention and because it forced audiences to encounter the full humanity of the empowered woman speaker. The testimonials of fugitive slaves were equally important for the antebellum Left. These practices reflected the emphasis on individual testimony characteristic of Protestant revivalism, and they gave rise to a radical theology centered on the idea that every human person mirrored the image of God.

Dorothy Day's desire to meet the "masses" suggests that a more collective form of encounter came to the fore during the decades between the Civil War and the New Deal. With the rise of industrialization and urbanization, radicals came to realize that they needed to meet not just exemplary individuals but society as a whole. They pioneered new practices and institutions, such as the large-scale demonstration and the settlement house. They also embraced a theology that saw both "sin" and "salvation" in social terms, so that the building of a new society was identified with the Christian promise of a Kingdom of God. Like the personal encounters of the abolitionists, these "collective encounters" ultimately derived their power from the encounter of identity. Professional-class activists between the Civil War and Second World War drew inspiration from workers who had empowered themselves through the Knights of Labor, Industrial Workers of the World, or Socialist Party.

Though the encounter of identity was always the most basic source of radical power, it was not visible to the majority of Americans until television coverage of the Montgomery bus boycott revealed the ways in which ordinary Southern blacks had come together to affirm their own dignity and defy Jim Crow. This ushered in a third epoch of triumphant radicalism, as additional groups sought to access the power displayed in Montgomery. For civil rights activists, identity encounters took place in mass meetings that adapted black church preaching and hymns to the cause of freedom; for college students, the encounter of identity made possible resistance to a military draft that threatened to destroy a generation; for feminists, consciousness-raising groups evolved into new forms of religious community, among them the Compost Coven. Encounters of identity gave birth to the multiform tradition of liberation theology, which ascribes special authority to communities of the oppressed.

When we see that religious practices, ideas, and institutions are thoroughly intertwined with the Left, we will be able to tell richer stories from every epoch of American radical history. No single book, of course, can rewrite the history of radicalism. My goal is to highlight important religious threads within the fabric of the Left. In some cases, this will involve correcting popular misperceptions. Many Americans assume that the Communist Party was the major representative of American socialism in the twentieth century, simply because red-baiters painted all radicals as Communists. My narrative will accent the more numerous adherents of the Socialist Party, for many of whom socialism was the best way to live out a Christian or Jewish or humanistic faith. Other emphases reflect the limitations of my own research. I wish I could say more about the personal theologies of grassroots radicals, but in a work of this scope it is easier to track the religious views of leaders than of followers.

In telling the story of religion and radicalism, I recognize that some readers who share a commitment to liberty, equality, and solidarity will not embrace the "Left" and "radical" labels. Some activists who appear in this narrative shared that reluctance. One objection is that these labels imply an oppositional stance that requires one not only to be *for* liberty, equality, and solidarity, but also *against* some other set of values, such as security, order, and property. It implies a dichotomized world in which there is no worth in the ideals espoused by people on the right.

Even though I embrace the "leftist" label, I share that concern. Too often, radicals have failed to honor the best insights of their opponents; too often, the tendency to dichotomous thinking has destroyed radical solidarity. The current threat of ecological catastrophe demands that radicals begin rethinking such conservative values as sustainability, harmony, and restraint. But these concerns should not obscure the fact that, for the past two centuries, most people in the United States who have struggled for liberty, equality, and fraternity have done so in oppositional terms.

Other readers may wonder why I do not have more to say about the "failure" of radicalism. Historians of American socialism, in particular, have often assumed that their main task is to explain why "it didn't happen here." Other movements have their own share of shortcomings. Why couldn't the abolitionists end slavery without a Civil War? Why couldn't they end racism as well as slavery? Why couldn't suffragists and antiracists work together after the Civil War? Why didn't women transform American politics when they started voting? Why was the black freedom struggle so difficult in Northern cities?[5]

Curiously, two common explanations for these failures have to do with religion. On the one hand, interpreters influenced by Marxism often assume that American radicalism has been tainted by the bourgeois idealism of its religious supporters, preventing the rise of a class-based revolutionary tradition. The Garrisonians are blamed for their emphasis on nonviolent moral suasion, the Social Gospelers for alienating the Socialist Party from its base in labor unions. On the other hand, champions of a distinct "religious Left" blame anticlericalism for alienating the pious masses from radical causes.

Such arguments are most convincing if one assumes that the triumph of the Left was the natural outcome of the American story. If radicals didn't succeed, they must have blundered, because history is on the side of justice. Most of the radicals in this book believed something of this sort, so it is pardonable that historians who study them might believe it too. But I would like to leave open the possibility that American radicals failed not because they did something wrong but because they undertook a very difficult task. And I would insist that, this side of the Kingdom of God, every radical movement generates a tangled mix of success and failure.

For this reason, I am less interested in diagnosing the reasons for the failure of radicalism than in identifying the sources of its strength. Those sources are summed up in the words "tradition" and "encounter." Today's radicals have inherited a rich tradition, a heritage of prophetic forebears who struggled against enormous odds, won signal victories, and created a repertoire of practices that we may adapt to the challenges of today. Like those predecessors, we can unleash power through fresh encounters with one another. By telling our stories and sharing our lives, we can glimpse the face of the divine and change the world.

CHAPTER I

The Faith of the Working Men

Among the first American radicals to challenge existing institutions on the basis of the nation's founding ideals were the "Working Men"—artisans of the 1820s who claimed a new identity and a full share of America's democratic inheritance. Pioneering a class-based interpretation of America, the Working Men gained power by reflecting together on "our real condition." Previous generations of workers had "surrender[ed] their rights to the non-productive and accumulating class," but in the enlightened nineteenth century workers could join "the progressive march of improvement" by insisting on the rights enshrined in the Declaration of Independence. They even rewrote the Declaration to inspire resistance to the "oppression and degradation of one class of society" by another.[1]

The Working Men's movement intersected with religion in three ways. First, it relied on local congregations as an organizing base. Many activists gave their first speeches in congregational settings, while others were clergymen or former clergymen. As the movement unfolded it spawned new congregations of its own. Second, its rhetoric was often theological, as advocates quoted prophetic denunciations of those who "grind the faces of the poor," cited biblical prohibitions against usury, and argued that inequality violated providential laws. And third, it urged adherents to look beyond the pleasures of barroom culture and orient their daily lives to the coming earthly millennium of social justice. Yet the movement is usually associated with the "secularism" of the Left.[2]

The reason for this is that the Working Men were aligned with the less visible side of a religious controversy. At the dawn of the nineteenth century, the great fault line in American religion was not the one dividing Protestants from Catholics, for the great wave of Catholic immigration was still in the future. Nor was it between biblical literalists and liberals: most Protestants would not contemplate historical approaches to scripture until midcentury. Instead, the great debate concerned religious establishment: were the social benefits of religion so significant that government had an obligation to fund or encourage it?

Answering yes were the Congregationalist heirs of New England Puritanism, along with their theological cousins, the Presbyterians. When the First Amendment prohibited the federal government from sponsoring religion, these "establishmentarians" followed such leaders as Lyman Beecher in fights to preserve New England's state-level establishments. When those battles were lost, they campaigned for Sabbath-observance laws, voted for explicitly "Christian" political candidates, and created voluntary mission, tract, and Bible societies to perform tasks that might otherwise have been funded by the government.

The "Benevolent Empire" of voluntary societies proved to be a winning strategy. In conjunction with popular revivals, it allowed Presbyterians and Congregationalists to evolve from their inherited Calvinism to a more optimistic "Arminianism," which stressed the capacity of each individual to accept divine grace and live a good life. The empire's soft version of establishment appealed to increasingly prosperous Methodists, Baptists, and Quakers, who had supported the First Amendment but now craved the respectability of informal establishment. To some extent it was also supported by the Unitarians, whose roots were in the established Puritan churches but whose theology was anathema to most other Protestants. By 1840 the Whig Party had captured the loyalties of most churchgoing Protestants by promoting a broadly "evangelical" social vision.

On the "disestablishmentarian" side of the divide was a coalition of people who feared state-sponsored religion. Some were deistic "Freethinkers" who venerated natural law, rejected Christian scripture as an immoral mess of fables, and drew inspiration from the revolutionary hero Thomas Paine. Others were sectarians who feared that government support and revivalistic enthusiasm would melt away the theological distinctiveness of their groups. Significant minorities of Methodists, Baptists, and Quakers resisted their traditions' slide toward social respectability. Midway between the Freethinkers and the sectarians were the Universalists, Christians who accepted the authority of scripture but replaced traditional theology with an insistence that God would ultimately save all people. This position implied skepticism about government-enforced piety, and Universalists took pride in their fierce attacks on the New England establishment.

Most Working Men came from the disestablishmentarian side of this debate, though the exact composition of the movement varied from city to city. Universalists and Freethinkers were often leaders, as were followers of the Quaker teacher Elias Hicks, who insisted on such Quaker "distinctives" as lay ministry, simple lifestyles, and fidelity to the inner light during an era when other Quakers were accommodating their tradition to the revivalist style. The Hicksites were accused by their Orthodox opponents of denying the authority of scripture and the divinity of Christ, and some undoubtedly sympathized with Freethought or Unitarianism. Another sectarian group was the Methodist Protestants, who resisted the authority of bishops within their denomination. All these groups told a similar story about church history: the "primitive" teaching of Jesus had been betrayed when Constantine made Christianity the official religion of the Roman Empire, turning a pure faith into "Babylon the mother of harlots."[3]

This reading of sacred history inspired opposition to concentrated power, whether that power was ecclesial, political, or economic. For artisan radicals, established churches embodied the same "cunning, avarice, and oppressive potency" as political and economic aristocracies, and they moved freely from attacks on private capital to criticisms of "magnificent places of public worship" that "engender[ed] spiritual pride" and created "odious distinctions in society." True religion, from their perspective, was focused "exclusively in the practice of works for ameliorating the condition of suffering humanity." Perceiving the interlocking voluntary associations of the Benevolent Empire as a new establishment, artisans opposed them. They were troubled by the campaign to prohibit mail delivery on Sundays, by temperance societies that condemned poor people's spirits but not rich people's wine, and above all by the call for a "Christian party in politics." Because they were more united in their religious critique than in their religious affirmations, their agenda was perceived as antireligious. And because many white abolitionists had roots in the Benevolent Empire, the Working Men inaugurated a long history of tension between labor and abolitionist radicals.[4]

Working Men and white abolitionists drew their prophetic power from different sorts of encounter. While white abolitionists characteristically encountered representative individuals who personified the cause of freedom, Working Men—like black abolitionists—found power by encountering one another. Men who might once have identified as "carpenters" or "hatters" now claimed a shared identity as "working men" who would fight together against the "drones" who profited without working. Not all artisans embraced this new identity. Some who had experienced revivalist conversion identified with others who had been "saved," regardless of class, while others found meaning and camaraderie at the theater and saloon. Working Men's encounters were neither as widespread nor as widely noticed as those that brought blacks, women, and students together for "consciousness-raising" in the 1960s. But the class-conscious Working Men set a precedent for those encounters as well as for subsequent movements among workers.

Labor organizing was not entirely new in the 1820s. The union and the strike were pioneered in Philadelphia in the 1780s, when journeymen shoemakers and printers organized to defend their traditional privileges. Both groups stopped work to protest wage cuts, and Philadelphia's carpenters subsequently conducted an unsuccessful strike for a ten-hour day. But the prospects for labor radicalism in the early Republic were hampered by the structure of economic life. For most artisans, there was no clear line separating bosses from workers: rather, craftsmen moved through the traditional stages as apprentices, journeymen, and masters. The three groups socialized with one another, and most could aspire to the economic independence enjoyed by their masters.

The situation changed with the invention of the cotton gin and the creation of large mills at Lowell and other river towns. In the 1820s successful masters teamed up with nonartisan investors to expand their shops into factories, blocking the path of advancement for their journeymen. The use of women and children as factory labor depressed wages and increased profits. More Americans sensed that the widening gap between rich and poor threatened democracy, and the journeymen and small masters who occupied the shrinking middle ground rallied in opposition. Though their movement anticipated socialism, their core ideology is better described as "producerist." They believed that labor, manual and mental, was the source of all value and condemned the "nonproducing" classes for depriving workers of the fruits of their labor.

The religious case for producerism was articulated by Thomas Branagan and Cornelius Blatchly around the time of the depression of 1817, when poverty was on everyone's mind. An itinerant Methodist and all-purpose social reformer, Branagan looked at poverty through the lens of theodicy. Rejecting Voltaire's denial of a loving providence and Calvin's portrayal of providence as inscrutable, he insisted that God had given humans sufficient intelligence to achieve happiness. It was "not nature, but man that is to be impeached with the miseries and ills of life." Humanity was particularly to be blamed for having "manufactured a thousand religions, as inhuman as the priests by whom they are administered."[5]

These words encapsulated two themes that future radicals would repeat. On the one hand, Branagan assured his suffering readers that God's justice and power were on their side; on the other, he warned that the official churches rarely sided with God or justice. In a pamphlet attached to one of Branagan's books, the Quaker physician Cornelius Blatchly elaborated the analysis by identifying five obstacles to justice for the poor: interests, rents, duties, inheritances, and "churches established by laws of men." All, he believed, violated biblical principle and natural law. Interests and rents presumed that "wealth should generate more wealth," when in fact "industry and labours are the *sole* causes of the opulence of nations." The biblical prohibition of usury forbade rent as well as interest, and most private wealth was the result of "ancient usurpation." On the question of inheritance, Blatchly called for the estates of all who die in a year to be divided among the "young people" coming of age.[6]

Blatchly painted church establishments with the same brush as economic oppression. Violating Jesus' teaching that "his kingdom was not of this world," they imposed "pecuniary exactions and demands" on the poor, who no longer enjoyed the biblical remedy of the jubilee year. "All national religions," Blatchly concluded, "whether Pagan, Mahomedan, or *Christian* (so called) have been, and naturally must be tyrannies." After documenting the hunger, disease, and warfare suffered by the poor as a result of the five causes, he urged "*christendom* (so called)" to restore the apostles' practice of holding all things in common. Enlisting the support of Swedenborgians and sectarian Methodists in a society for this purpose, he argued that successful communism would be religious, because "all goodness comes only from God."[7]

As he developed his ideas, Blatchly learned of another reformer who had derived similar social principles from different religious convictions. Scottish philanthropist Robert Owen had transformed his father-in-law's cotton-spinning mill into a model village that disavowed child labor, provided day care for working mothers, and offered experiential education to all residents. On the basis of this experience and his reading of Enlightenment texts, Owen articulated a distinctive theory of human nature and a corresponding social program. Building on John Locke's sensationalist epistemology, Owen believed that "the character of man is always formed for him . . . by his predecessors." A bad society created bad individuals, not—as most orthodox Christians assumed—the other way around. Since Owen traced most evils to economic inequality, he concluded that joint ownership—pure communism—would preclude "in the rising generation . . . the miseries which we and our forefathers have experienced." Blatchly attached extracts from Owen's writings to his own manifesto, noting that he hoped Owen would inspire "irreligious people" to form their own communities.[8]

Given Blatchly's use of the term "irreligious," we might identify Owen as a founding father of the "secular Left." Along with Thomas Paine, he was doubtless the progenitor of much that goes by that name. But he was hardly indifferent to religious matters. Owen described his philosophy as a "rational religion" and frequently claimed that observance of this religion would usher in the millennium. He published a volume of "Social Hymns" for gatherings of his followers; one Owenite hymn for children promised a "glorious day" when "pain shall cease, and every tear / Be wiped from every eye." Owen castigated religious systems that fell short of his rational standard: in one speech, he identified private property, traditional marriage, and "absurd and irrational systems of religion" as the "trinity" of evils blocking social progress.[9]

In 1825 Blatchly joined a host of politicians in welcoming Owen to the United States. After a tour of seaboard cities, Owen headed to southwestern Indiana, where he had purchased New Harmony, a domain previously inhabited by German pietists, to demonstrate his social ideals. Here Owen's communistic ideals did battle with his paternalistic habits, and mostly lost: the property was never held in common, and Owen undermined the community by spending most of his time propagandizing off-site. But radicals attracted to the experiment developed practices of experiential education that soon became mainstays of leftist culture. Owen's system of "labor notes"—each good for the fruit of one hour's labor—gave practical expression to producerist ideology. New Harmony was also home to a controversial "Church of Reason" that provided rational religionists with a ritual of their own.

New Harmony evolved in tandem with Nashoba, a Tennessee community for freed slaves founded by another wealthy foreigner, Frances Wright. An orphaned Scottish heiress, Wright was a protégé of the Marquis de Lafayette as well as of Owen, and her plan for Nashoba was in-spired by the success of Haiti's revolution. But it succumbed to the same fate as New Harmony. Wright was not present often enough to shape the community's life, and the juxtaposition of her free-love ideals and her interracial community generated special hostility from the outside.[10]

The collapse of New Harmony, Nashoba, and other Owenite com-munities scattered radical seeds across the landscape. New Harmony's school became a model for the Indiana public school system. Owen's partner, William Maclure, endowed 160 workingmen's libraries in the Midwest. Participant Josiah Warren was sufficiently impressed with the "labor note" system that he came to believe that the equal exchange of labor could replace the collective ownership of property as the basis for a just society; he went on to found several anarchist communities. Other New Harmony members would eventually bring their expe-riences to communities founded on the blueprint of French utopian Charles Fourier.

In the immediate aftermath of New Harmony, Owen's son Robert Dale Owen and Frances Wright relocated the community's paper to New York City, where they renamed it the *Free Inquirer* and used it to promote labor radicalism and religious freedom. Deploring "silence on the subject of religion" as "treason to truth and virtue," they prom-ised to open their pages to "any spirited, well written communication, be it religious or infidel, orthodox or heterodox." Wright used a national speaking tour—the first widely recognized case of a woman addressing mixed audiences in the United States—to plant or revitalize congrega-tions of Freethinkers in Boston, Philadelphia, Wilmington, Providence, and New York City. These congregations attracted hundreds of mem-bers and held Sunday services that might feature readings from Owen's writings, songs from his *Social Hymns,* and talks on topics ranging from the platform of the Working Men's Party to the doctrine of the soul. Hungry for the sort of fellowship enjoyed by conventional Christians, Freethinkers supplemented their weekly lectures with courses on art and science and with Wednesday evening balls that scandalized the or-thodox. They turned the birthday of Thomas Paine into their annual festival.[11]

The proliferation of Freethought congregations coincided with an upsurge of union organizing, especially among urban journeymen. One innovative leader was shoemaker William Heighton. In a series of public addresses at Philadelphia's First Universalist Church, Heighton linked the labor theory of value to Philadelphia workers' sense that they were losing ground in an increasingly prosperous nation. "When we look around us, my fellow workmen, we behold men on every side, enjoying wealth in all its luxuriant profusion . . . while we, comparatively, receive nothing but the crumbs which fall from their tables." The remedy, Heighton argued, was a class consciousness that hearkened back to the spirit of 1776. He asserted that "the working classes of our country" no longer enjoyed the equal rights promised in Jefferson's Declaration. As expressions of class consciousness, he urged workers to join a citywide union federation, educate themselves at the Mechanics' Library Company, and flex their political muscle by voting only for workers and their declared allies.[12]

Heighton regarded the clergy as part of the nonproducing class and urged them instead to imitate "those primitive Christians who had 'all things common'" and "among whom no idle accumulator was allowed to rob the hard toiling producer." Siding with the workers would bear positive fruit, Heighton promised: by attacking the "fountain head" of vice, the clergy could eliminate crime and usher in "the day of manifest glory." But he did not hold out much hope that this would happen. Since clergy were unlikely to join the cause, it was up to the workers to develop "what powers we yet possess of our own to destroy this fatal evil."[13]

It was no accident that Heighton chose First Universalist as the venue for his agitation. The rapidly growing congregation's membership of sixteen hundred was four times that of the Society of Free Enquirers, with which it shared leadership in Philadelphia's labor movement. Under the leadership of Abner Kneeland, First Universalist had sponsored a discussion society in which future labor leaders polished their speaking skills. Shortly before Heighton's speech, Kneeland had left Philadelphia; he eventually defected to Owenite Freethought and served as leader of Boston's Society of Free Enquirers. The minister during Heighton's time, Theophilus Fisk, attracted large audiences with his "sensational topics" and "sensational manner"; a decade later he was in Boston, declaiming against preachers who opposed the ten-hour day. One of Fisk's assistants, Abel Thomas, also wound up in Massachusetts, where he helped launch the *Lowell Offering* for the mill workers.[14]

Universalists and Freethinkers were the most consistent religious supporters of labor, but they were by no means alone. In each city, artisans allied themselves with a different cluster of local congregations.

Wilmington, Delaware, was home to the most "liberal" wing of the Hicksite movement, which had not fully consolidated itself in the late 1820s. The editors of the local Hicksite paper sympathized with temperance and abolition as well as artisan radicalism. Their criticism of "the present system of Christianity" with its "rules, disciplines, creeds, and dogmas," and above all its clergy, "who have ever discovered enemies of God in the friends of mankind," was consistent with traditional Quaker preference for silent worship and lay ministry. But when they refused to attack Robert Dale Owen, other Hicksites accused them of being Freethinkers. By 1831, the most important Working Men leaders in Wilmington were expelled from their Hicksite meeting.[15]

The Methodists also had a wing that sought to preserve sectarian distinctiveness in the face of denominational centralization, and it also produced important labor leaders. Among those who opposed the "connectional" system dominated by bishops were New York's William Stilwell and James Covel. Shortly before they became cofounders of Blatchly's Society for Promoting Communities, Stilwell and Covel were instrumental in the 1820 schism of New York's oldest Methodist congregation, John Street. Their initial objection was to an expensive renovation project that included a carpeted altar, but supporters of the renovation added fuel to the fire by asking the state legislature to support their cause. Declaring that "to seek for legislative aid to enforce the discipline of a church is a step toward popery," Stilwell and Covel persuaded four hundred whites and eight hundred blacks to walk out.[16]

Soon the two racial groups went their separate ways, in part because the African Americans, who formed the African Methodist Episcopal Zion Church, objected to white supremacy but not to bishops. Stilwell's Methodist Society opted for a fully democratic polity in which women enjoyed full voting rights, and in which alcohol, lawsuits, participation in the slave trade, "giving or taking things on unlawful interest," and aggressive war were all prohibited. Stilwell's producerism was evident in his critique of the "grinding tradesman" who violated the Golden Rule by refusing to pay a just wage.[17]

Similar concerns in Baltimore led artisans there to organize a "Union Society" that agitated for lay representation within Methodism and provided "mutual support" for members facing "persecution or maltreatment" in the economic arena. Their advocacy of labor prompted mill-owning Methodists to expel them from their congregations, and the expellees organized an autonomous denomination called the Methodist

Protestants. The work of building a denomination proved to be deradicalizing: eager to gain financial support for their movement, denominational leaders were publicly praising capitalism by the mid-1830s.[18]

Support for labor coincided with the impulse to establish "free-pew" congregations. Since the venerable practice of allowing wealthy church members to rent their own pews reinforced social hierarchies and gave the wealthy disproportionate influence, those who sympathized with the workers often wanted a new system. Lutheran Benjamin Kurtz gathered a free-pew congregation in Baltimore's Trades' Union Hall and edited the staunchly pro-union *Lutheran Observer*. An Episcopalian who identified himself as "No Sectarian" expressed the views of many labor Protestants when he wrote that it was blasphemous for "private property churches" to allow wealthy parishioners to lock their pews as if they could "bar the gates of the kingdom of heaven."[19]

Freethinkers in New York, Universalists in Philadelphia, Hicksites in Wilmington, Methodist Protestants in Baltimore, and free-pew proponents everywhere transformed the Working Men's movement into a network of local parties in the late 1820s. These were the first labor parties in the world, and they briefly enjoyed electoral success. In Philadelphia, Heighton's Mechanics' Union began nominating candidates for local office in 1828. (The label "Working Man's Party" was attached by the media.) They used a technique now known as "fusion," nominating some candidates jointly with the major parties. The results were disappointing in 1828, when Andrew Jackson's coattails swept many Democrats into office. But Jackson's conservative early appointments sparked an artisan backlash, and the Working Men gained a balance of power in Philadelphia's city elections the next year. They achieved similar victories in Albany, Troy, and New York City.

By 1830 the movement faced a question that would bedevil subsequent radical movements: how best to translate popular agitation into policy, when the major parties were dominated by economic elites? In some ways, the moment was propitious. The old Federalism had collapsed, but the "second-party system" pitting Jacksonian Democrats against Whigs had not consolidated. Both nascent parties were eager to attract new constituencies, and the Working Men seemed ripe for the picking. Embracing the artisan slogan of "From Six to Six," Whigs and Democrats signaled support for a ten-hour workday, with two hours scheduled for meals. Unfortunately, the Working Men weren't quite ready for the attention. They had a comprehensive platform of reform but no agreement about priorities. The disciples of Owen stressed education: a national system of boarding schools would separate children from the inegalitarian influences of their parents and prepare the nation for more sweeping economic changes. New Yorker Thomas Skidmore insisted that a "General Division" of inherited property was the indispensable first step. And a more conservative faction publicized Owen's controversial religious and sexual views in hopes of drawing Working Men toward the Whigs.

Ultimately, the lion's share of the artisan vote went to the party of Jackson, who capitalized on artisan fears of economic centralization by making opposition to the Bank of America the centerpiece of his 1832 reelection campaign. The Owenite minister Abner Kneeland was solidly Jacksonian by 1832, as was his erstwhile Universalist brother Orestes Brownson, who shared his social values but not his Freethinking theology. In some ways, the shift of emphasis to the major parties paid off: the 1830s saw the beginnings of a public school system, the abolition of debtor prisons, and the implementation of a ten-hour day for federal employees. But alliance with the Democrats meant that workers became aligned with Southern elites whose top priority was the preservation of slavery. Though radical artisans had been among the first white Americans to speak out against slavery, the two-party system would divide urban workers from African Americans for more than a century to come.

Conflicts within the Working Men's Party also shattered the alliance between Freethinkers and disestablishmentarian Protestants. Opponents of the Owenites made much of their religious and sexual irregularities, lifting up Fanny Wright as a symbol of the threat radicalism posed to the very building blocks of society. The party, declared Lyman Beecher, was an "infidel trumpet-call to all the envious and vicious poor." For decades thereafter, radicals in general and women's rights advocates in particular would feel obliged to disavow "Fanny Wrightism" or else forego any hope of rallying mainstream Protestants to their cause.[20]

Cornelius Blatchly, for one, tried to keep the alliance alive. Insisting that he was no infidel if that "meant one who denies Jesus Christ is God manifest in flesh," Blatchly added that since the Working Men supported the same "inclusive rights and property" as "the very first Christians," perhaps their opponents were the true "infidels." In fact, he went on, the Working Men "disclaim all political and ecclesiastical sectarianism, and even the sectarian party of irreligion," while their critics were introducing narrow religious concerns into politics. Singling out the Jacksonian minister Ezra Stiles Ely, who had called for a "Christian party in politics," Blatchly insisted that "the laboring men" were unfairly opposed by "the priests of orthodoxy," and suggested that benevolent societies that "monopolized the printing of all the Bibles" were scheming to unite church and state and destroy "all our liberties."[21]

While Blatchly hoped to rally primitivist Protestants to Owen's defense, most of his allies chose a different strategy. In 1829, the Working Men of Upper Delaware Ward in Philadelphia insisted that "we disclaim all interference with religious matters, or adherence to Miss Wright's principles." When Heighton's newspaper persisted in polemicizing against Sabbath laws, a reader chastised the editors for "distracting" workers and offending the "best feelings of many of the industrious part of the community." Better, this reader suggested, to oppose not only religious sectarianism but also "that sectarianism that is *anti*-religious." Perhaps taking that advice to heart, by the 1830 election season the editors declared that "those who introduce either the subject of Agrarianism or religion into our political proceedings are the avowed enemies of our righteous cause."[22]

The intent of such declarations was manifestly *not* to discourage mainstream Protestants from connecting their religious values to the labor cause. The Upper Delaware Ward workers cited scripture ("The labourer is worthy of his hire") even as they promised not to interfere with religion. When the *Mechanics' Free Press* urged that religion be kept out of the movement, it blamed "infidels" in particular for bringing it in. By affirming secularism, radical editors hoped to prevent conventional Christians from taking offense at the heterodoxy that was widespread among the movement's most devoted supporters. Party leaders and journal editors censored their own religious convictions for tactical reasons, recognizing that they were out of step with the laborers they hoped to recruit. These hard choices would be repeated by leaders in subsequent radical movements that sought to mobilize a mass constituency.[23]

By the 1830s, artisan energies shifted from third-party politics to attempts to unite diverse trades into broad-based labor federations, with a focus on the campaign for a ten-hour day. More than a dozen cities experienced agitation in 1832. Boston's building and ship-making trades joined a strike initiated by the carpenters. In New Bedford, the five hundred ship caulkers and carpenters who walked off work in protest of long hours compared themselves to "the illustrious sages of '76, struggling to throw off oppression." In Baltimore, an 1833 strike by hatters led to the late emergence of a local Working Men's Party. The female mill workers of Lowell, Massachusetts, began organizing in 1834, and a year later a cluster of Boston activists gained national attention with their calls for a national strike for a ten-hour day. In June 1835, twenty thousand Philadelphia workers—women and children as well as journeyman artisans—brought the city to a standstill for a week, prompting concessions from most employers and legal enforcement of the ten-hour day. By 1836, three hundred thousand Americans were union members, a share of the population that would not be matched until the New Deal. The National Trades Union held a loose national network together and saw its president elected to Congress in 1836.[24]

The religious rhetoric of these organizations struck a delicate balance: they espoused a vague Christianity, then asserted their religious neutrality in order to keep the specter of Fanny Wright at bay. The National Trades Union insisted that "the inculcation of any religious or irreligious creeds, constitutes no part of the objects of the Trades Unions." Boston's ten-hour activists described their movement as "the cause of Liberty, the cause of God." The diverse religious currents supporting labor agitation were all on display at Boston's celebration of the Philadelphia general strike, where an elaborate ritual combined Christian, patriotic, and Masonic elements.[25]

In 1837 the cause of labor crashed along with the economy. A speculative bubble, perhaps the consequence of Jackson's anti–Bank of America politics, burst suddenly, causing half the nation's banks to close. Unemployment remained high for five years, giving workers a disadvantage in their clashes with employers. When militant labor organizing finally bounced back in the 1840s, America's radical landscape had been decisively altered by the rise of black and white abolitionism. Though white abolitionists often came from denominations opposed by the Working Men, by 1840 they were deeply disappointed that their churches had not embraced the cause of freedom. The revival of labor radicalism thus came just in time for the diverse currents of American radicalism to begin flowing together.

CHAPTER 2

African Identity and Black Radicalism

While the Working Men were laying one enduring foundation for American radicalism, the organizers of the free African American community laid another. The two groups had much in common. They lived in the same cities—Philadelphia, New York, Boston, Baltimore—and worked in the same artisan trades. Both groups embraced the legacy of the American Revolution, took pride in their participation in that war, and treasured the freedoms it had brought them. Many Northern blacks, in particular, had been emancipated by state statutes passed after the Revolution. And both groups feared that the work of the Revolution was being undone by social elites determined to restore Old World hierarchies. Both were often at odds with the "Benevolent Empire" of voluntary societies created by the heirs of religious establishment. Confronted with new challenges to their freedom, both groups built up power through identity encounters. Just as white laborers claimed a new identity as "Working Men," so their black counterparts found power and solidarity by calling themselves "African."

The word "African," which appeared in the names of the African Society and African Methodist Episcopal Church, signaled the shared identity of all persons of African descent, whether newly emancipated, long free, or still claimed as slaves in the South. The point was clear when Philadelphia blacks gathered in 1817 to rebuke the newly organized American Colonization Society, which proposed to end slavery gradually by expatriating free African Americans to colonies in Africa. "We will never," they resolved, "separate ourselves voluntarily from the slave population of this country; they are our brethren." This vision of racial solidarity was new: throughout the eighteenth century, religious identities had been more prominent than racial ones, and free blacks in the South and the Caribbean sometimes held their own slaves. By 1817, Philadelphia blacks knew that racial prejudice undermined liberty even in the shadow of Independence Hall. Their generously inclusive response inaugurated a half century of agitation against slavery and racism.[1]

By calling themselves "African," the Philadelphians were not renouncing their "American" identity. They had been in North America for as long as their white neighbors; they were "the first successful cultivators of the wilds of America"; they had fought for freedom alongside white patriots. They bristled at the Colonization Society's insinuation that they were a foreign element that could not be integrated. At the same time, they refused to accept any false dichotomy between racial solidarity and full participation in American society. Most of those who repudiated the Colonization Society had walked out of white churches that refused to treat them as fully human. Some were willing to contemplate black-led colonization schemes as a possible response to America's betrayal of its revolutionary values. In their willingness to separate from institutions that had betrayed the Revolution, they affirmed their identity as true American radicals.[2]

They also built on a religious and spiritual tradition that stretched back for centuries. Long before black people claimed their share of the American revolutionary heritage, their faith contributed to the struggle for freedom. Empowered by Islam and indigenous traditions, Africans resisted enslavement in Africa, on the slave ships, and on the shores of Virginia, the Carolinas, and New England. Some eventually found a liberating message at the heart of their oppressors' religion. The God who had heard the cries of the Israelites in Egypt would also hear *their* cries. Baptismal rituals, blended with West African practices of spirit possession, helped Africans feel part of a new community of freedom. By the end of the eighteenth century, independent congregations existed among enslaved Africans in the South and newly freed African Americans throughout the country.

These congregations occupied an ambiguous position with regard to the establishment debate. Like established churches, they identified with their entire community, yet they were ignored or suppressed by political authorities. Like their white neighbors, many African Americans had experienced ecstatic conversion in Baptist or Methodist revivals. But as those denominations gained social respectability, black members were pushed to the margins. With little aid from the Benevolent Empire, black congregations sought to change society by uplifting members of their own community—through literacy and economic self-help—and by challenging the white power structure with petitions, protests, and acts of resistance.

The black church was ideally situated to participate in the emerging American Left. While radicals raised in white Protestant contexts often felt they had to break with their religious roots, black activists could build directly on their inheritance. But black religion was never fully identified with American radicalism. In some contexts, it was more about survival, physical and psychological, than about social change. Intense experiences of conversion or spirit possession gave enslaved Africans a powerful sense of personal worth, but did not always motivate them to take concrete steps to overturn the slave system. In other contexts, forms of black religious radicalism emerged that were not closely tied to the revolutionary values of liberty, equality, and solidarity. The slave rebellions that occurred throughout the eighteenth and early nineteenth centuries were most typically led by charismatic individuals who claimed direct divine sanction for revolt and worked closely with practitioners of folk magic. Nat Turner, whose 1831 revolt coincided with the emergence of a national abolitionist movement, testified that he had enjoyed supernatural signs of a special vocation since childhood, and that his attack on slaveholders was inspired by a heavenly voice that told him Christ had laid down his "yoke" in order that Turner might "take it on and fight against the Serpent."[3]

The story of the African American Left thus begins not with rebels like Turner but with leaders who claimed that they were entitled to a share in the American project, and fought against slavery on the basis of revolutionary values held in common with their white neighbors. This happened dramatically among the free black communities of Boston, New York, Philadelphia, Baltimore, and Charleston. Those communities were led by a national network of religious and political leaders who have been aptly described as "black founders." Their priority was to create institutions that would sustain their people, but they also found time to challenge institutions of white power.[4]

The first "black founder" to create a national network to sustain practices of identity encounter was Boston's Prince Hall. Beginning with his Masonic initiation by British soldiers during the 1775 occupation of Boston and the 1787 chartering of the first specifically African American lodge, Hall extended his vision of an autonomous African Freemasonry to a network of daughter lodges. The Masonic practice of secrecy made it possible for them to circulate rebellious ideas among American cities—including Southern cities where free blacks interacted frequently with their enslaved brothers and sisters—and to learn from comrades involved in Caribbean freedom struggles. Hall was a pioneer of public civil rights activism, petitioning the Massachusetts General Court for gradual emancipation, equal education, and an end to the slave trade. When three free blacks were kidnapped in Boston Harbor and sent to the Caribbean, Hall publicized the incident and turned the tide of Massachusetts opinion against slavery.[5]

The fact that Prince Hall Masonry (as it was known after his death) preceded the founding of the major black denominations—and retained the loyalties of most denominational founders—highlights the religious pluralism that was always a part of the black freedom struggle. Eighteenth- and nineteenth-century Freemasonry was more than a social club for middle-class men who enjoyed wearing funny costumes. It was, rather, an embodiment of cosmopolitan spirituality that linked the wisdom of the ancient world—and, significantly, the wisdom of ancient Africa—to contemporary struggles for social and political freedom.

In the years that Hall was planting Masonry in Boston, Richard Allen and his friends Absalom Jones and James Forten built a parallel set of institutions in Philadelphia. Converted as a teenager by a Methodist itinerant who embodied the movement's early egalitarianism, Allen persuaded his master to draw up an agreement for manumission after a few more years of service. Allen then worked as an itinerant, covering circuits that stretched from New Jersey to Baltimore. Allen's powerful sense of Methodist identity clashed with the marginalized status he experienced in the urban setting of St. George's Church in Philadelphia, where he settled in 1786. In an incident that was incorporated into the sacred story of black religion, Allen and Jones were kneeling in prayer when white trustees forced Jones to his feet, insisting that he move to a newly segregated balcony. Outraged by the violation of the sanctity of prayer and of their own human dignity, they led a walkout of black parishioners. The whites, Allen said, "were no more plagued with us."[6]

Theological differences led the friends to create separate all-black congregations. While Jones's Episcopal congregation accepted the oversight of white bishops, Allen's Bethel Methodist Church resisted the increasingly centralized authority of white Methodism. During these years Allen's friend Bishop Francis Asbury was imposing hierarchical control on what had been a sectarian and egalitarian movement. In order to gain support among white Southerners, Asbury was also backpedaling on his early antislavery convictions. In 1816, Bethel Church joined with similar congregations in Baltimore and elsewhere to create the African Methodist Episcopal denomination, with Allen as presiding bishop. The new church gained the loyalties of Southern congregations, including one in Charleston that was resisting violent suppression. Energetic black founders in other cities created similar networks. The African Methodist Episcopal Zion Church was based in New York City, while Boston's First African Baptist Church inspired a daughter congregation in Albany as well as New York City's Abyssinian Baptist, which would stand for centuries as one of the nation's most influential black congregations.

Methodist, Baptist, Episcopalian, and Presbyterian leaders cooperated in Masonic lodges and a network of mutual-aid societies. Philadelphia's Free African Society provided benefits to widows and orphans and procured a common cemetery for the black community; New York's Manumission Society founded African Free School #2, which trained many leading black abolitionists. Black societies helped persuade the U.S. government to end the slave trade in 1807, and their literacy programs reached free blacks and urban slaves such as Frederick Douglass. In the South, Methodist and Masonic networks made possible Denmark Vesey's slave revolt of 1822, which was partly inspired by Vesey's outrage over the suppression of the Charleston congregation. Black founders also explored the possibility of emigration, especially to the new republic of Haiti, which promised to embody American values more fully than the United States itself.

The American Colonization Society, organized in 1816, promoted a different model of emigration. Related to the benevolent societies dominated by Congregationalists and Presbyterians, it had many slaveholding members but no blacks. The racist implications of its rhetoric were evident to the three thousand African Americans, some free and some enslaved, who gathered at Bethel Church to insist that Allen and other leaders denounce the Colonization Society. The leaders followed where the people led, producing a stirring appeal that affirmed the solidarity of all African Americans and insisted on their right to full participation in American society. It was quoted dozens of times by Frederick Douglass, William Lloyd Garrison, and other leading abolitionists of the 1830s, 1840s, and beyond.

The black abolitionist tradition that emerged in 1816 was renewed in the late 1820s, a period marked both by the fiftieth anniversary of the

American Revolution and by the completion of New York's process of gradual emancipation. It was an auspicious moment for African Americans to take stock of the gap between the American ideals they shared and their lived reality in the United States. In *Freedom's Journal,* the first black-edited newspaper in U.S. history, community leaders called for immediate abolition of slavery and demanded full racial equality in the North. The pairing of these demands defined the tradition known as abolitionism, which was the most authentically radical strand of the broader antislavery movement. While many Americans acknowledged that slavery was in some sense evil, and were willing to abolish it where it was already weak, only abolitionists were willing to risk all American institutions for the sake of the revolutionary ideal of human freedom.[7]

The most articulate early exponent of abolition was the Boston agent of *Freedom's Journal,* a used-clothing dealer named David Walker. Born in North Carolina to a white mother and an enslaved black father, Walker was part of a rising generation of leaders whose sensibilities had been formed by autonomous black congregations. Indeed, Walker's fervent devotion to the legacy of Richard Allen led him to retain his Methodist identity even after his arrival in Boston, where most of his allies were Baptists. Walker led the Massachusetts General Colored Association, a mutual-aid society that openly declared its desire to "unite the colored population" of the entire nation. In his most notable publication, Walker's goal was even more ambitious: he addressed his *Appeal* to "the Coloured Citizens of the World."[8]

The *Appeal*'s effect was to build black power by stimulating encounters of identity among free and enslaved African Americans. While earlier black activists had often addressed the white power structure, Walker spoke directly to his black brothers and sisters, and he did not hesitate to castigate them for insufficient zeal in the cause of freedom. The "coloured people of these United States," he declared, were "the most degraded, wretched, and abject set of beings that ever lived since the world began" as a result of slavery, ignorance, "the preachers of the religion of Jesus Christ," and "the colonizing plan." Any remedy would be the result of concerted black action. While white allies might question Thomas Jefferson's libelous comments about the intellectual inferiority of Africans, few would be convinced until blacks refuted Jefferson themselves. This is why Walker placed such strong emphasis on the struggle against ignorance, and also why he presented violent resistance as one means by which blacks might assert their humanity.[9]

Walker anticipated that the *Appeal* would itself be an instrument of black education and empowerment, and it proved to be so. In his preamble, he urged "all coloured men, women and children" to "procure a copy of this Appeal and read it, or get some one to read it to them," admonishing literate readers to share it with their unlettered sisters and brothers. Mass meetings for this purpose were held in both North and South, and supporters were apprehended by Southern authorities for distributing copies among slaves and fugitives. In December 1830 North Carolina authorities killed sixty armed fugitives who had been inspired by Walker to launch a revolt, and most observers assumed that Walker had also helped inspire Nat Turner's rebellion of 1831.[10]

To Southern officials, Walker's *Appeal* was an incendiary, anti-American document, and many white opponents of slavery agreed. Benjamin Lundy, then the nation's best-known antislavery editor, characterized it as "a labored attempt to rouse the worst passions of human nature," concluding that "religion has nothing at all to do with it." But Lundy failed to see the degree to which Walker was a true American radical, deeply ensconced in the revolutionary tradition. He attacked Jefferson's racism precisely because he venerated Jefferson's "writings for the world." He even reprinted the full Declaration of Independence at the end of the *Appeal,* with a heated comment: "See your Declaration Americans!!!! Do you understand your own language?"[11]

Lundy's view notwithstanding, the religious roots of Walker's abolitionist vision were evident. Integrating biblical allusions and invocations of natural law, Walker "appealed to Heaven" and invoked the doctrine of the *imago dei.* He proclaimed prophetic judgment against the apostasy of the nation, predicting that because God's ears are "continually open to the cries, tears and groans of his oppressed people," a cataclysm would eventually "arrest the progress of the avaricious oppressors." Like subsequent abolitionists, Walker stopped short of advocating insurrection, suggesting instead that God would use violence to end slavery if the whites did not soon repent. "Do you think," he asked white readers, "that our blood is hidden from the Lord?"[12]

Prophetic rhetoric was only one side of the *Appeal*'s religiosity. Walker may have been devoted to God, the Bible, and Richard Allen, but he was unremittingly hostile to mainstream Christianity and, particularly, to the Benevolent Empire of which the Colonization Society was an integral part. In the chapter dedicated to "Our Wretchedness in Consequence of the Preachers of the Religion of Jesus Christ," Walker echoed the Working Men's critique of Constantinian Christianity: the "pure and undefiled religion . . . preached by Jesus Christ . . . is hard to be found in all the earth." Walker insisted that "white Christians" were "ten times more cruel" than their pagan ancestors and that neither Jews, Muslims, nor pagans would be so willing to "*beat a coloured person nearly to death, if they catch him on his knees, supplicating the throne of grace.*" He lashed out at temperance and Sabbath societies for ignoring "the fountain head" of evil, and warned that proslavery missionaries would make their converts "ten times more the children of Hell, than ever they were." He spent eight pages blasting the Whig politician Henry Clay, a colonization proponent who was widely admired by Benevolent Empire Christians, while ignoring the equally proslavery sitting president, Andrew Jackson.[13]

One might wonder why Walker would devote so much space to the racism of the churches while scarcely mentioning the complicity of merchants, industrialists, or white workingmen's associations. In part, Walker's broad indictment of the Benevolent Empire set the stage for his specific attack on the Colonization Society. But this only pushes the question back a step: why did he spend as much time criticizing colonization as slavery itself? One reason lies in the close kinship between religion and radicalism. Walker portrayed the "preachers of Christianity" as the enemy of black liberation because he sensed that a properly preached Christianity—as exemplified by Richard Allen—could be his people's greatest ally. In this regard, he spoke with the same voice as the Working Men.

Yet apparently neither David Walker nor other black abolitionists of his generation actually spoke with the Working Men, who were agitating in the same cities in the late 1820s. One reason for this was that empowering encounters of identity left little room for individuals to claim multiple identities. To claim a primary identity as "African" was, at least implicitly, to downplay the significance of class divisions within the African American community. The fact that Richard Allen and most other black founders were highly successful master craftsmen may have made it difficult for them to align themselves with the cause of the journeymen. On the other side, whiteness was implicit in many laborers' understanding of what it meant to be a "Working Man." The problem was greatest among those workers who aligned themselves with slaveholders in the Democratic Party of Andrew Jackson. But though the Working Men were nominally opposed to slavery, their failure to forge practical alliances with black abolitionists meant that American radicalism in the 1820s flowed in two small streams rather than one large river. And the hostility of both Working Men and black abolitionists to the Benevolent Empire, however justified, limited their capacity to convert middle-class white Christians.[14]

Eleven months after the *Appeal* began shaking the foundations of American racism, David Walker was dead. Slaveholders had put a price on his head, and his friends reasonably concluded that he had been poisoned— though most scholars now believe he died of tuberculosis. *Freedom's Journal* also suffered an early demise, in part because its editor was more open to emigrationist schemes than its readers could tolerate. But their message had not fallen on deaf ears. Soon black abolitionists began meeting in conventions to promote free schools and respond to racist legislation, such as the Ohio policy of expelling free African Americans. A few European Americans, including supporters of the Benevolent Empire, were also paying attention. Beginning in 1830, these activists brought the abolitionist message to a white audience. Drawing on revivalist practices of conversion, they pioneered new forms of encounter between social elites and newly empowered radicals. These encounters would be the next step in the unfolding history of American radicalism.

CHAPTER 3

Encounters with William Lloyd Garrison

William Lloyd Garrison brought the black abolitionist message to the white community with words of fire, promising to melt the icy mountains of slavery and prejudice. In his zealous attacks on proslavery churches, he also embodied the religious tensions inherent in American radicalism. Remembered as both an evangelical and an infidel, Garrison shed Baptist roots to embrace a form of Christian liberalism that verged on Freethought and a radical vision that included antiracism, women's rights, pacifism, and utopian socialism. He pioneered a new form of prophetic encounter that focused less on the shared identity of oppressed groups and more on the individual personality of the activist. By offering *himself* to the cause, Garrison linked the piety of the revivals—which featured personal testimonials of grace—to the radical cause.

Garrison's radical rhetoric was usually in the first person. While William Heighton and David Walker kept their personalities in the background when appealing to "my fellow workmen" or "all coloured men, women and children," Garrison made his own fervor the primary theme of the *Liberator's* inaugural issue. "I *will be*," he promised, "as harsh as truth, and as uncompromising as justice. . . . I do not wish to think, or speak, or write with moderation. . . . I will not equivocate—I will not excuse—I will not retreat a single inch—and I will be heard." Garrison's identification of himself with the abolitionist cause was accepted by friends and foes. Abraham Lincoln may have issued the Emancipation Proclamation, but he spoke for many when he gave the credit for emancipation to "the logic and moral power of Garrison and the antislavery of the people of the country." Garrison succeeded, moreover, in implanting his personality in the memory of subsequent radicals. Prior to Martin Luther King Jr., no other individual appeared so consistently in genealogies of radicalism.[1]

Like many transformative leaders, Garrison habitually confused his own ego with his cause. A champion of nonviolence and free speech, he silenced friends who dared to disagree with him. At one point, Garrison turned on Frederick Douglass with the ferocity he usually reserved for slaveholders. But Garrison's self-absorption allowed him to harness the conversionist energies of revivalism to the cause of institutional change. For radicals touched by Garrison, social transformation flowed from personal encounters with exemplary prophets who made it possible to criticize any and all oppressive institutions. In an age that believed with Ralph Waldo Emerson that "one man is a counterpoise to a city," Garrison positioned himself as that one man.[2]

Ironically, Garrison's reputation as the founder of abolitionism has obscured his real contribution to American radicalism. Garrison borrowed the abolitionist idea from his African American predecessors, but innovated in his personal style and in the way he linked abolition to other causes. He also contributed to the radical tradition through sheer persistence. While many black abolitionists died just as their cause was gaining support among whites, Garrison kept the *Liberator* at the forefront of the movement through continuous publication from 1831 to 1865. Only a handful of radical publications could rival this record, among them Horace Greeley's *Tribune,* Frederick Douglass's *North Star,* and Lucy Stone's *Woman's Journal.* Both Douglass and Stone were protégés of Garrison, and a host of subsequent radical standard-bearers, from the *Nation* to the *Catholic Worker* to *Sojourners,* drew on the *Liberator*'s legacy. Garrison also had the rare good fortune to pioneer a cause that would triumph nationally during his lifetime.

Garrison's abolitionist zeal was matched by his devotion to causes that would not triumph in his lifetime or, indeed, our own. He was the first white abolitionist to challenge Northern racism as forthrightly as Southern slavery, noting in his opening editorial that he had "found contempt more bitter, opposition more active, detraction more relentless, prejudice more stubborn, and apathy more frozen [in New England], than among slave owners themselves." As soon as female abolitionists claimed the right to speak publicly on behalf of the slave, and then on their own behalf, Garrison declared his own commitment to their cause, even at the price of abolitionist unity. An heir to the early peace movements that opposed the War of 1812, Garrison pushed the logic of pacifism to its logical extreme by repudiating governmental coercion in all its forms. And though Garrison refused to equate "wage slavery" with chattel slavery, his in-laws founded one of the era's most egalitarian experiments in utopian socialism.[3]

Garrison also inaugurated a style of activism that can best be described as "agitation." His admirer Elizabeth Cady Stanton defined this approach: "Do all you can," she advised, "*no matter what,* to get people to think on your reform, and then, if the reform is good, it will come about in due season." The radical agitator actively courted offense if it would bring attention to the cause. One of Garrison's tactics that would be emulated by later radicals was casting himself in the role of the martyr. Jailed for libeling a slave trader, Garrison published a full account of his trial and affirmed that "a few white victims must be sacrificed to open the eyes of this nation." These words prepared the way for Henry David Thoreau, for Gandhi (who inherited the Garrisonian legacy via Leo Tolstoy), and for Martin Luther King Jr.[4]

Garrison used harsh rhetoric to provoke proponents of slavery into violent and censorious overreaction, and thus rallied opponents of violence and censorship to join the antislavery cause. He spilled as much ink in attacking moderate opponents of slavery—beginning with the Colonization Society—as in denouncing slaveholding itself. This tactic—perhaps most famously echoed in Malcolm X's criticism of Martin Luther King Jr.—sometimes prodded the moderates to the left and sometimes made it easier for them to gain the support of a less-than-radical public. It engendered esprit de corps among those activists who yearned to be more "ultra" than their neighbors. But it also unleashed schismatic energies that were hard to check. Garrison was ultimately denounced by "no-organization" anarchists who regarded even antislavery societies as a form of tyranny.

Another Garrisonian tactic illuminates the logic of American radicalism. More than any activist before or since, Garrison dramatized the contradiction between America's revolutionary values and its existing institutions. He launched his journal "within sight of Bunker Hill" because he had experienced entrenched opposition to black freedom in the neighborhood of Boston. He was not the first to rewrite the Declaration of Independence as a manifesto for a radical cause—Robert Owen issued a "Declaration of Mental Independence" in 1826 and the Working Men produced their own version in 1829—but he did it *twice,* on behalf of abolition and pacifism. Garrison treated Jefferson's "heaven-attested" Declaration as a revealed text on a par with the Bible, even as he denounced the Constitution as a "covenant with death." The dichotomy signaled that one could be unrelentingly critical of American institutions without ceasing to be fully American.

Garrison also embodied the complex interplay of religion and radicalism. Over the course of his career, he occupied several of the positions I described in the introduction, beginning as a devout revivalist reformer, becoming a critic of the clergy who professed orthodox theology, and eventually attacking the Sabbath, the churches, and the Bible on grounds that differed only slightly from Freethought. Garrison also sympathized with the emerging religious tradition of Spiritualism. The one position he never occupied was that of the secularist who squelches discussion of religious questions in order to shield orthodox radicals from their comrades' heresies.

Garrison's multiple personae enabled him to expand the religious constituency of radicalism. Prior to Garrison, the most significant religious voices on the left were those outside the Benevolent Empire: sectarian opponents of establishment, Freethinking opponents of Christianity, and African Americans relegated to second-class status in white Protestant churches. Though his Baptist roots and Quaker sympathies placed him with the disestablishmentarians, Garrison played a decisive role in bringing the Unitarian and revivalist heirs of New England Puritanism into the radical tradition. He could not testify personally to an orthodox conversion, but he used the revivalist idiom of testimony in a way that appealed to both revivalists and liberals who admired revivalist zeal.

Garrison's religious identity evolved through a series of transformative encounters that began in Newburyport, the Massachusetts seafaring town where he was born in 1805. Garrison's father and brother suffered from alcoholism, creating a family legacy that informed his lifelong commitment to temperance. A more constructive family influence came from his mother, a leader of women's prayer meetings within the Baptist tradition of maritime Canada, where she had grown up. As a young man, Garrison was "a complete Baptist as to the tenets" who attended church and observed the Sabbath even though he had not experienced conversion.[5]

Opting out of his family's seafaring tradition, Garrison apprenticed himself as a printer, working for partisan and reform-oriented journals throughout the 1820s. Though Newburyport's mercantile interests aligned it with the conservative Federalist Party, Federalist journalism nurtured a network of idealistic young printers and editors who would soon transmute middle-class benevolence into social radicalism. Among Garrison's journalistic allies who would become committed abolitionists were the Quaker poet John Greenleaf Whittier; Baptist William Collier, who hired Garrison to write for his *National Philanthropist;* party politician David Lee Child; and Child's assistant Stephen Foster, a future firebrand who allowed Garrison to use the *Massachusetts Journal's* type for the first three issues of the *Liberator.* These friends instilled in Garrison a sense of the interconnectedness of reform causes that was expressed in his editorial vision for the *National Philanthropist.* "The brightest traits in the American character," he wrote there, "will derive their luster, not from the laurels picked from the field of blood . . . but from our exertions to banish war from the earth, to stay the ravages of intemperance . . . to unfetter those who have been enthralled by chains which we have forged."[6]

Garrison's career was transformed by his encounter with Benjamin Lundy, a Baltimore Quaker who came to Boston to raise funds for his new journal, *Genius of Universal Emancipation.* Lundy introduced Garrison to the idea that, because slavery was a sin on the part of the slaveholder and not merely an evil inherent in the social order, masters had an obligation to free their slaves immediately. Impressed with Lundy's account of his personal confrontation with slavery, Garrison accepted the older man's invitation to come to Baltimore and serve as coeditor of the *Genius.*

It soon became apparent that while the two men agreed on principles, they diverged on tactics. Both were opposed to slavery and committed to the full equality of African Americans. But, like his Quaker predecessor John Woolman, Lundy preferred to approach slaveholders with gentle persuasion. He avoided confronting the colonizationists and deplored David Walker's harsh rhetoric. As a natural agitator, by contrast, Garrison stirred up public attention with frontal attacks on slaveholders (regularly featured in a "Black list" of atrocities) and on colonizationists. He praised Walker for his "impassioned and determined spirit," noting that Walker's "injudicious publication" was "warranted by the creed of an independent people." Though these differences spelled an early end to the Garrison Lundy partnership, the younger man was in Baltimore long enough to be transformed by encounters with the city's thriving African American community.[7]

Baltimore in the 1820s was the capital of black America, where the free community of the North interacted most creatively with their enslaved brothers and sisters. It was here that the African Methodist Episcopal Church planted its second most influential congregation, here that African American artisans sustained one of the nation's largest ports while earning their own freedom, here that Frederick Douglass learned to read, experienced Methodist conversion, and began plotting his path to freedom. Garrison met this community at the height of its agitation against the Colonization Society, and he was convinced that blacks were a vital part of the American community. The early *Liberator* featured repeated attacks on Massachusetts's antimiscegenation laws, and Garrison prophetically declared that "the time is to come when all the nations of the earth will intermarry, and all distinctions of color cease to divide mankind."[8]

Garrison's connections with free blacks helped him launch the *Liberator,* whose first subscribers and agents were African American. Garrison spoke to black audiences and featured the words of black activists in his paper. These connections shaped his encounter with two men whom he did not meet face-to-face: David Walker and Nat Turner. The first issue of the *Liberator* appeared about midway between the release of Walker's *Appeal* and Turner's celebrated revolt in Southampton County, Virginia. Although too much of a pacifist to endorse violent rebellion, Garrison insisted that the violence advocated or enacted by Walker and Turner fell far short of the violence inherent in slavery itself. On this basis, he incorporated them into the logic of his jeremiad, which held that massive slave rebellion would be the just consequence if America did not embrace immediate abolition. "It is not for the American people," he insisted, to denounce Walker's *Appeal* "as bloody or monstrous," for Walker embodied the spirit of the Revolution. Nat Turner, he wrote, "deserve[d] no more censure than . . . our fathers in slaughtering the British." And only "IMMEDIATE EMANCIPATION" could save America from the "vengeance of Heaven."[9]

Garrison's sympathy with Walker and Turner may explain the failure of his encounters with Boston's two most prominent preachers, Lyman Beecher and William Ellery Channing. Garrison had once attended services at the churches of both men, who represented the orthodox and Unitarian wings of Massachusetts' religious establishment. Fervent champions of benevolent organizations, Beecher and Channing had inspired Garrison's reform commitments, and the former's congregation hosted one of his early speeches. But when Garrison returned to Boston as an avowed enemy of the Colonization Society, neither man would give him a hearing. The *Liberator* was thus introduced to its Boston neighbors at a hall occupied by Abner Kneeland's Society of Free Enquirers. Kneeland was not really an abolitionist, but his hostility to the Benevolent Empire made him happy for the chance to tweak Beecher and Channing. Garrison's first audience was by no means limited to Freethinkers, however: Channing's assistant and Beecher himself came to hear, as did a cluster of idealistic Unitarians who would become Garrison's most dependable allies.

This circle included Rev. Samuel J. May, the young Unitarian movement's first representative in Connecticut, which was dominated by more conservative Congregationalists; David Child's wife, Lydia Maria Child, one of the nation's most celebrated authors of sentimental fiction; and Channing's parishioner Maria Weston Chapman, a brilliant fund-raiser whose sisters became the bulwark of "Ladies'" antislavery organizing. Garrison offered these disciples a form of revivalist conversion consistent with liberal principles. Brought up in the rational Unitarianism that Emerson had castigated as "corpse-cold," they discovered in Garrison's preaching a way to transform their emotions without sacrificing their reason. Thus May said of his first meeting with Garrison that "my soul was baptized in his spirit," while Lydia Maria Child described the beginnings of abolitionism as a time when "the Holy Spirit did actually descend upon men and women in tongues of flame." Such conversions expanded the circle of American radicalism.[10]

Soon Garrison was building a network of local, regional, and national societies dedicated to the twin propositions that slavery must be abolished immediately (not gradually) and that colonization was a racist denial of human rights. These societies linked people whose economic, racial, and religious differences might otherwise have kept them from encountering one another. In the American Anti-Slavery Society, Garrison met wealthy New York philanthropists Lewis and Arthur Tappan, who were mainstays of the Benevolent Empire, as well as the Quaker hatter Arnold Buffum of Lynn, Massachusetts, and Boston's leading black minister, Thomas Paul, whose youngest son apprenticed at the *Liberator* before attending Dartmouth College.

Ultimately, it was the Quakers—particularly those Hicksite Quakers who sympathized with Unitarianism—who contributed most to Garrison's theological evolution. In 1834 he married Helen Benson, daughter of a family of Connecticut Baptists whose social idealism had led them to Unitarianism via Quakerism. Impressed by the Quaker emphasis on religious inwardness, though not by the distinctive dress and language Quakers used to separate themselves from the world, Garrison confided to his new brother-in-law, "I am growing more and more hostile to outward forms and ceremonies and observances." Another important source of Quaker ideas was Lucretia Mott, the most theologically gifted Hicksite to join the Anti-Slavery Society. A devoted reader of Channing, she stressed the correspondences between his thought and that of leading Quakers. Just as Channing had identified the imago dei with the individual conscience, so Hicks had insisted that true Quakers would value the "inward light" more highly than outward scripture. Garrison credited Mott with liberating him from the "sectarian trammels" of his youth.[11]

Another transformative encounter came in the form of a letter that Garrison received in March 1837. In it, John Humphrey Noyes announced that he had "subscribed my name to an instrument, similar to the Declaration of '76, renouncing all allegiance to the government of the United States, and asserting the title of Jesus Christ to the throne of the world." Part of a circle of revivalists who hoped to attain a state of sinless perfection, Noyes staked out a position that was more sectarian than radical, less interested in transforming the United States than in renouncing it. But he crystallized the ideas toward which Garrison was gravitating. The logic that required withdrawal from association with slavery, Noyes reasoned, should also require him to disassociate from governmental violence. Indeed, he warned, the Anti-Slavery Society might suffer the same fate as the American Colonization Society if it did move to the higher ground of "UNIVERSAL EMANCIPATION FROM SIN."[12]

Garrison took this advice only partly to heart. No matter how many new causes earned his commitment, he never doubted the value of an organization that made freedom for the slave its defining object. Any personal dialogue he might have sustained with Noyes became impossible after Noyes's socialist community at Oneida, New York, embraced the practice of "plural marriage"—anathema to the sexually conventional Garrison. Still, Garrison shared Noyes's assessment of the American government. He had been gravitating toward absolute pacifism since his early editorial days, and had incorporated into the Anti-Slavery Society's Declaration an affirmation that while the Founding Fathers' "principles led them to wage war against their oppressors . . . ours forbid the doing of evil that good might come." Garrison developed these principles in dialogue with Henry Clarke Wright, a former seminarian who had rebelled strongly against orthodox images of divine violence. Together, the two men developed a philosophy of "nonresistance" that repudiated defensive as well as offensive wars, capital punishment, physical chastisement of children, policing, and all governmental coercion.[13]

The influence of Mott, Noyes, and Wright set Garrison on a path that converged with the Freethought critique of institutional religion and the Transcendentalist movement among Unitarians who renounced biblical authority in favor of an intuitive connection with the divine. In 1840 and 1841 he participated in the Chardon Street Convention, a series of gatherings that debated Sabbath observance, ordained ministry, and the institutional church. Garrison proposed resolutions that proclaimed the "true church" to be "independent of all human organizations, creeds, or compacts." At the time, he pitted the Bible as well as the soul against the church and clergy, but years of exegetical debates over slavery gradually convinced him that his commitment to freedom did not depend on biblical sanction. Commenting on an 1845 edition of Thomas Paine's writings, he praised the views of a man he had once imagined to be "a master of iniquity," and eight years later joined in a new convention dedicated to challenging biblical authority. One of Garrison's resolutions there redefined the "Word of God" as a divine witness "before all books."[14]

When Garrison came face-to-face with Frederick Douglass in 1841, his earlier encounters had prepared him to appreciate the revelatory power of meeting another person. His appeal, on that occasion, to the "godlike nature" of Douglass and slavery's other victims was the beginning and end of Garrison's mature theology. Because humanity was created in the image of God, any violation of human freedom or violence against human bodies was an assault on divinity itself. At the same time, the divine law written on every human heart was a surer guide to religious truth than any text or minister. Encounter with the other had become the sole sacrament in Garrison's church.

Garrison's renunciation of his youthful orthodoxy might have limited his capacity to expand the religious constituency of the Left. In the 1820s, as we have seen, radical ideas were only truly at home in those religious communities—sectarians, Universalists, Freethinkers, and African Americans—that stood outside the ecumenical revivalism of the Benevolent Empire. By the middle of his career, Garrison was as far removed from the Benevolent Empire as Elias Hicks or Abner Kneeland,

and many of his allies despaired of his capacity to bridge conservative religion and radical politics. But the decisive work was already accomplished: Garrison's fire had radicalized many people who shared his revivalist roots, some of them holding fast to orthodox theology and others embarked on their own spiritual pilgrimages. Moreover, Garrison was less willing than his Transcendentalist friends to cede his claim to true Christianity. In 1850 the *Liberator* unveiled a new masthead featuring a prominent image of Jesus Christ, glowing in sunlight and declaring, "I come to break the bonds of the oppressor." By claiming Jesus as an ally, American radicalism was positioned to gain adherents of all faiths.[15]

CHAPTER 4

Personifying Radical Abolitionism

For all his gifts, William Lloyd Garrison was not the ideal personifi-
cation of the struggle against racism and sexism, evils that he suffered
only indirectly. His agitating shoes were soon filled by gifted orators
who turned their own persons into object lessons on human freedom.
By speaking of their own struggles for liberty, Sarah Grimké, Angelina
Grimké, Abby Kelley, Frederick Douglass, and Sojourner Truth inspired
in their audiences a new faith in the inherent divinity of human nature.
Their struggles against oppression generated the courage others needed
to stay in the fight.[1]

Two other white men joined Garrison as midwives for this activism.
Though not a radical himself, Charles Grandison Finney set countless
evangelicals on the path to radicalism. A former lawyer who ministered
in the revivalist "Burned-Over District" west of Syracuse as well as in
New York City, Finney created a western, populist version of the Benevolent Empire. Where Lyman Beecher and his friends on the faculty
of Yale Divinity School tried to soften traditional Calvinist teaching
about human depravity, Finney declared forthrightly that humans can
free themselves entirely from sin. Borrowed from the Methodists, this
perfectionist message had a special implication for the Presbyterians and
Congregationalists among whom Finney ministered. Members of these
denominations, who had worked together to plant congregations in upstate New York and Ohio, retained their Puritan forebears' concern
for society as a whole, and they aspired to social as well as individual
perfection. The combination of revivalist fervor and established church
concern for social well-being proved explosive. Finney's disciples were
far more likely to turn radical than other revivalists.

One of those disciples emerged as the model abolitionist speaker.

Raised in New England and converted through Finney's influence, Theodore Dwight Weld enrolled in 1832 at Cincinnati's brand-new Lane Seminary, which was led by Lyman Beecher. Life near the border between slave and free states allowed him to forge transformative friendships with local African Americans who had recently fled enslavement. These encounters in turn inspired a series of debates that persuaded most of his classmates to embrace abolitionism—and earned Weld expulsion from the school. He led thirty-two "Lane Rebels" to Oberlin, which had called Finney as professor of theology. From that base, Weld modeled his method for "abolitionizing" a community on Finney's revivals. Upon arriving in a town, he would speak five, ten, even twenty times in as many venues as possible. Addressing rural communities with few or no African Americans, he dwelt on the horrors of slavery, recounting beatings, brandings, and hunts for fugitives. He appealed to people's emotions, as he was convinced that "if it is not FELT in the very *vital tissues of the spirit,* all the reasoning in the world is a feather thrown against the wind."[2]

As an agent of the American Anti-Slavery Society, Weld emulated Jesus by recruiting a cohort of seventy evangelists to bring these methods to every corner of the nation—or at least of the North, given the reprisals likely to meet antislavery agitators in the South. The young ministers and seminarians who gathered in New York City for training were accompanied by two daughters of a slaveholding Charleston family, Angelina and Sarah Grimké. They had fled to Philadelphia and to Quakerism because of the horror they felt witnessing slavery's violence, and in the city they had transformative encounters with black friends such as Sarah Douglass, who helped them see that interracial friendship was an integral part of the abolitionist cause. Addressing black women in 1838, Angelina noted that "it is only by associating with you that we shall be able to overcome" white prejudice.[3]

At the close of the training, as the rest of "the Seventy" fanned out across the nation, the Grimkés stayed in New York to hone their speaking skills before female audiences and to organize the first Anti-Slavery Convention of American Women, a response to the recently enacted congressional "gag rule" against antislavery petitions. Delegates there made it clear that they did not think the Grimkés should allow their new speaking skills to go unutilized. Women, they declared, had "rights and duties" in "common" with "all moral beings" that were meant to be exercised on behalf of "the cause of the oppressed in our land." Reversing the conventional understanding of woman's sphere, they argued that "the time has come for woman to move in that sphere which Providence has assigned her, and no longer remain satisfied in the circumscribed limits with which corrupt custom and a perverted interpretation of Scripture have encircled her." These words launched the Grimkés on a tour that began in the Quaker stronghold of Lynn, Massachusetts, where five hundred men joined as many women to hear Angelina's first address to an audience of both genders.[4]

The Grimkés were ideal agitators, for their speaking broke a gender taboo. Women were already free to make their living with pen and paper, and were counted among the nation's most popular novelists and poets. Educational opportunities were expanding at single-sex schools such as Mount Holyoke and in the coeducational experiments that began when Oberlin opened its doors to both genders and all races. Yet most Americans assumed that women were private by nature, and that only a sexually licentious woman would expose herself to the public gaze by speaking from lectern or pulpit.

The Grimkés were not the first women to speak publicly to "promiscuous," or mixed-gender, audiences in the United States. Throughout the eighteenth century, female evangelists had helped spread the revivalist gospel. Presenting their preaching as a sign of the impending millennium, these women typically did not assert a general "right" to speak or the perfect equality of women and men. Frances Wright's pugnaciously public lectures in the 1820s, on the other hand, had pointedly asserted women's right to full equality. But since her vision of women's equality included freedom from patriarchal marriage and traditional Christianity, her speaking opened few doors for mainstream Protestant women. Just the opposite: women speakers had to overcome the reflexive charge of "Fanny Wrightism" hurled by male elites.[5]

Abolitionism offered women a new path to a public voice, both by generating a sense of urgency comparable to that of sectarian millennialism and by articulating a discourse of human rights that could be applied to gender as well as race. Since the black abolitionist community had crystallized a decade before white Garrisonianism, it is not surprising that the first female abolitionist lecturer, Maria Stewart, was a member of Boston's African American community. Inspired by David Walker, and perhaps seeking to fill the vacancy left by his death, Stewart gave four public addresses in Boston in the early 1830s, citing the Declaration of Independence and the imago dei as she sought to "fire the breast" of her audience with fervor for "African rights and liberty." Public hostility soon turned her to less controversial forms of activism.[6]

The opposition faced by the Grimkés transformed abolition. This was in part because—as white women working for the American Anti-Slavery Society—they encroached on the territory occupied by the male reformers of the Benevolent Empire, and in part because they refused to back down in the face of opposition. Two months after Angelina's speech in Lynn, the orthodox Congregationalists of Massachusetts issued a "Pastoral Appeal" that reaffirmed the doctrine of separate spheres, asserting that "the power of woman is her dependence. . . . God has ordained her weakness and need of protection." Such words, resting on a selective appeal to biblical authority, had the unintended effect of agitating the issue of women's rights. One future suffragist, Lucy Stone, credited the "Appeal" with her own conversion to the cause. As she listened to it being read from the pulpit, she poked her cousin black and blue in half-suppressed indignation, and later recalled that "if I had ever felt bound to silence by interpretations of Scripture texts or believed that equal rights did not belong to women, that pastoral letter broke my bonds."[7]

Every step Angelina and Sarah Grimké took over the next year added fuel to the fire of agitation. They spoke as part of the antislavery women's campaign to collect a million signatures on petitions asking Congress to end slavery in Washington, D.C. Sarah prepared a series of letters responding to their critics. Her argument was biblical, but not as narrowly millennial as those of her sectarian predecessors. Jesus, she contended, had laid down "grand principles" for his followers in the Sermon on the Mount, and these included a duty of public testimony. Christian duty thus provided a foundation for a sweeping assertion of equal rights: "Men and women were created equal; they are both moral and accountable beings, and whatever is *right* for man to do, is *right* for woman."[8]

The agitation came to a head with two events that took place in Philadelphia in May 1838. The first was the wedding of Angelina Grimké and Theodore Dwight Weld, a service that dramatized the emerging abolitionist understanding of universal human rights. The vows excluded the wife's traditional promise to "obey" her husband, and Weld explained that the mutual authority in marriage is based entirely in love. The unordained William Lloyd Garrison officiated, with white and black ministers offering prayers. Since Quaker discipline forbade marriage to non-Quakers, both sisters accepted expulsion from their meeting. A few days later, Angelina demonstrated that her marriage had not made her into a private woman by addressing the second Anti-Slavery Convention of American Women. As protestors hurled bricks, she thanked God "that the stupid repose of that city had at length been disturbed by the force of the truth."[9]

Such confrontational encounters took a toll, and soon both sisters, as well as Theodore Weld, shifted their energies from public lecturing to writing and editing, childrearing, and eventually leadership of an experimental school at a utopian community. The lecturer who personified the nexus of abolition and women's rights over the next thirty years was the young woman who had first invited the Grimkés to speak in Lynn. Schoolteacher Abby Kelley belonged to Lynn's vibrant community of Quaker Garrisonians, having collected over a thousand signatures on each of four antislavery petitions. One of the Quakers who risked discipline by attending the Grimké-Weld wedding, she gave her own first lecture at the subsequent convention. Kelley preached in a powerful voice on the biblical story of Lazarus the beggar, comparing him to the slaves: "Look! See Him there! We have very long passed by with averted eyes. Ought we not to raise him up?" When she was finished, Theodore Weld congratulated her with a warning: if she did not embark on a lecturing career, "God will smite you!"[10]

Soon elected to leadership positions in the New England Anti-Slavery Society and the New England Non-Resistance Society, Kelley lectured through the orthodox heartland of Connecticut even as clerical opposition to female abolitionists was heating up. She braved comparisons to Fanny Wright and pointed criticism of her own (imagined) sexual behavior. In one town, her initial lectures attracted large audiences while the local minister was out of town, but when she returned for a follow-up, he denounced her as "that woman Jezebel" come "to seduce my servants to commit fornication." At the annual meeting of the Connecticut Anti-Slavery Society, she had a similar confrontation with the minister who had hosted the Grimkés during their stay in New York. When Kelley spoke on behalf of women's "inalienable heaven-derived right" to speak for the slave, he ranted, "I will not submit to PETTICOAT GOVERNMENT. No woman shall ever lord it over me." Clearly, just one woman had the power to agitate the issue of women's rights.[11]

In the 1840s, Kelley embarked on ambitious tours of New York and Ohio, dramatizing the abolitionist cause by traveling with Frederick Douglass as well as the white firebrands Stephen Foster and Parker Pillsbury. Douglass regarded her as the most talented of his companions, praising the way her "wonderful earnestness, her large knowledge and great logical power bore down all opposition . . . though she was pelted with foul eggs and no less foul words." Meanwhile, Foster's personal journey converged with Kelley's. Their marriage grew out of a shared love of agitation. Stephen pioneered the practice of disrupting services at churches that refused to host abolitionist lecturers, rising in the middle of the sermon to launch his own testimony against slavery. He was jailed four times and thrown out of second-story windows twice for this tactic. Once married, they coordinated their dramatizations: on one occasion, as Stephen faced arrest for selling books on the Sabbath, Abby took hold of him and declared that they would not be separated the way enslaved husbands and wives were routinely separated by the masters.[12]

This made for good theater: a sympathetic reporter compared the scene of the two activists "pliant as inanimate carcasses—heavy as sin— meek as lambs—locked in each other's arms" to popular newspaper caricatures. It is hard to know whether such tactics did more harm or good to the cause. But they embodied a distinctive critique of the dominant forms of religion that had emerged in the wake of disestablishment. In one sense, Kelley and Foster presumed an establishmentarian understanding of the local congregation's role. It was not the private domain of either the minister or the congregation but was accountable to society as a whole. At the same time, they insisted that the way to reconstitute true religion was for individuals to imitate Christ and his apostles. When Foster branded the American clergy a "brotherhood of thieves," he echoed Jesus' castigation of religious leaders as a "den of thieves." Practices of this sort inspired Parker Pillsbury to title his history of the movement the *Acts of the Anti-Slavery Apostles*. Even the most seemingly irreligious activism could take on scriptural status by revealing the divine presence in each person.[13]

As Kelley, Foster, and their friends used personal encounters to enrage and inspire Northern audiences, white abolitionists yearned for more transformative encounters with enslaved persons. This yearning took several forms. Eighteenth-century British abolitionists had made frequent use of carved images of a male slave, hands folded in supplication to heaven, with the motto "Am I Not a Man and a Brother?" Appearing ubiquitously, and with feminine variations, in abolitionist publications, the image retained its power to inspire well into the 1830s.

Abolitionists created "Phoenix Societies" and other integrated groups to ensure that the goal of fighting Northern racism would not be lost amid the urgency of combating slavery. Convinced that direct encounters were the best means of dispelling prejudices, William Lloyd Garrison brought four young black Bostonians to Plymouth, New Hampshire, for lectures meant to expose rural whites to "abolition in the *concrete*." Noticing how moved white abolitionists were during visits to her school, black teacher Susan Paul published a sentimental *Memoir* of the life and death of a six-year-old student, hoping that readers could experience a vicarious encounter. And during his service as a conductor on the Underground Railroad, Gerrit Smith introduced the fugitives to such visitors as his young cousin Elizabeth Cady (later Stanton). Presenting "a beautiful quadroon girl, about eighteen years of age," he advised Elizabeth that "you may never have another opportunity of seeing a slave girl face to face, so ask her all you care to know of the system of slavery." He also encouraged the girl herself to turn the visitors into "good abolitionists . . . by telling them the history of your life."[14]

Abolitionists promoted experiments in interracial education to uplift and empower African Americans and to overcome white prejudice. Endorsing the integration of colleges, New York City's leading black minister, Theodore Wright, observed that "even if but few do [enroll], it will have an effect on others. Get two men to love each other . . . and it will make them love the whole class." One short-lived venture was the Noyes Academy in Canaan, New Hampshire, established in 1834 with a student body of twenty-eight whites and eleven blacks and a faculty composed of abolitionist luminaries. Student speakers Henry Highland Garnet and Alexander Crummell wowed the audience at the New Hampshire Anti-Slavery Society's Fourth of July event in 1835, but the resulting publicity inspired a mob to destroy the school. The confrontation was intense and frightening, with students firing shots at their pursuers as they escaped. For Garnet, Crummell, and their friend Samuel Ringgold Ward, it galvanized a sense of commitment that persisted through decades of activism.[15]

These encounters prepared the way for Frederick Douglass's splashy 1841 debut as a "brand new fact"—the first abolitionist lecturer who had escaped, as an adult, from enslavement in the South. Douglass had been raised on Maryland plantations and in Baltimore, where his work in the shipbuilding industry had helped him gain the skills he needed to escape to the North. Douglass experienced Methodist conversion in Baltimore, where an aged "spiritual father" taught him to interpret scripture, assured him that God willed his freedom, and "fanned my already intense love of knowledge into a flame." These gifts equipped Douglass to defy a notorious "Negro Breaker" and plot his escape to freedom.[16]

Soon after Douglass's inaugural speech in Nantucket, Garrison recruited him as an agent for the American Anti-Slavery Society, and he spent the early 1840s touring the country with Abby Kelley, Stephen Foster, and others. Douglass made himself an object lesson on the incoherence of slaveholding ideology: after being introduced "as a *'chattel'*— a *'thing'*—a piece of southern *'property,'* " he astonished audiences with an articulate defense of his own humanity. Douglass's *Narrative*, published in 1845 to refute charges that he was too articulate to have been a slave, inspired imitators who made the fugitive slave narrative one of the most important forms of abolitionist propaganda. By stressing his lifelong love of freedom, Douglass refuted the slaveholding theology that taught that God had created some people for freedom and others for enslavement. Each generation, Douglass insisted, was enslaved anew by human violence, while the "good spirit" of God instilled in him a love of freedom. On this basis, Douglass denounced what he called "slaveholding religion," noting that "the pure, peaceable, and impartial Christianity of Christ" could have nothing to do with "the corrupt, slaveholding, women-whipping, cradle-plundering, partial and hypocritical Christianity of this land."[17]

As Douglass matured, he realized that the task of personifying radical reform was more complicated than it had first appeared. While his white allies believed he could serve abolition best by telling his story, his own "reading and thinking" were pushing him to a more philosophical approach: "It did not entirely satisfy me to *narrate* wrongs; I felt like *denouncing* them." Douglass's trajectory of empowerment, as a fugitive slave, was different from that of the white abolitionist women. For women, the most radical stance was that of public lecturer, for this was the role that patriarchy had most insistently denied them. Fugitive slaves, by contrast, were all too accustomed to being exposed to the public gaze; they could assert their full humanity more effectively by claiming the cultured role of writer and editor. After a tour of Great Britain, Douglass launched his own antislavery newspaper, the *North Star,* in Rochester, New York.[18]

Tragically, this step precipitated Douglass's estrangement from Garrison. To his surprise, the Boston Garrisonians were greatly opposed to his new editorial venture, arguing that he lacked the skills to succeed where many African American predecessors had failed. He located the journal in Rochester to avoid direct competition with the *Liberator,* but as a result he was introduced to a community of abolitionists that did not see eye to eye with Garrison. Gradually, he rethought Garrison's nonresistance and his doctrine that, because the U.S. Constitution was inherently proslavery, abolitionists were obliged to oppose the national government.

These new convictions reflected Douglass's budding friendship with Gerrit Smith, the most generous benefactor of radical causes in upstate New York. The son of a land baron, Smith became a devotee of Charles Grandison Finney while grieving the deaths of his mother and first wife. After his conversion, Smith resolved to "do a little for unhappy Africa and the children that have been torn away from her," which initially meant seeking reconciliation between the Colonization Society and the abolitionists. After an economic panic nearly destroyed his fortune, Smith began encountering African Americans not as objects of benevolence but as teachers and fellow sufferers. "As soon as I came to commune with [the colored man] . . . and in a word to make myself a colored man," he told the American Anti-Slavery Society in 1838, "I saw how crushing and murderous to all the hopes and happiness of our colored brothers is the policy of expelling the colored race from this country." It was with this spirit that Smith greeted Douglass upon the latter's arrival in Rochester, and their circle of friendship, which also included black physician James McCune Smith and white militant John Brown, blossomed into the fullest embodiment of abolitionist ideals in pre–Civil War America. These friendships transformed Douglass's religious commitments, as his Methodist piety gave way to a humanistic faith that derived all religious meaning from experiences of interpersonal encounter.[19]

Douglass's religious pilgrimage was straightforward compared to that of another former slave who embodied the abolitionist cause. Sojourner Truth, who grew up as part of the last generation of persons enslaved in New York State, passed through the notoriously patriarchal commune of the "Prophet Matthias" before aligning herself with abolitionists at the egalitarian Northampton Association. Launching her lecturing career at women's rights conventions in the 1850s, she was the only formerly enslaved woman to sustain such a career. She was also a potent symbol of the way racial and sexual oppression intersected in the lives of black women. In her most famous speech, she objected to patriarchal arguments that suggested women should be protected rather than granted equality. "I have plowed, and planted, and gathered into barns . . . and ar'n't I a woman?" she asked. "I have borne thirteen chilern and seen 'em mos' all sold off into slavery . . . and ar'n't I a woman?" She punctuated her speech by displaying the muscular arms she had developed in slavery, reminding her speakers that the horrors of slavery were there present in the flesh.[20]

The fact that none of the individuals who offered themselves as embodiments of the abolitionist cause emerged from the experience with their original religious convictions intact suggests the religious intensity of personal encounter. People who heard and saw Sojourner Truth, Frederick Douglass, Abby Kelley, and the Grimkés were set on new religious paths as they sought to make theological sense of the power they had experienced in the flesh. But the evolution of abolitionism was more than a matter of individual transformation. Abolitionist organizations were also evolving and, in some cases, dissolving into factions. From the tumult would emerge, by 1848, a more coherent and inclusive radical tradition.

CHAPTER 5

Radicals Fight and Unite

On May 10, 1837, financial panic ended two decades of economic growth, ushering in unemployment and hardship comparable to the Great Depression of the 1930s. The crisis transformed radicalism. Ordinary people lost their faith in existing social institutions and streamed into utopian communities. Abolitionists embraced more "ultra" responses to oppression and began to take the Working Men's critique of capitalism seriously. These developments exacerbated the tension between white abolitionism and the Benevolent Empire from which it emerged, resulting in a bitter threefold division of the Anti-Slavery Society. Not until the rise of the Socialist Party in the twentieth century would one organization again encompass such a broad spectrum of radical sentiment. Yet the divisions themselves drew radicals into a single constituency held together by debate.

The new radicalism was described by Ralph Waldo Emerson, a reluctant radical who inspired others with more activist inclinations. While previous reformers had "all respected something," Emerson noted, the new breed was sounding a "trumpet" that brought everything to judgment. Some Garrisonians moved beyond their master by repudiating the idea of organization as such. Other activists set about creating new and purer sorts of institutions: new political parties, devoted to principle rather than expediency; congregations and denominations that renounced all cooperation with sin; intentional communities that sought to build God's Kingdom on earth. Such experiments gave a generation of activists a foretaste of the social order they hoped to build.[1]

The new radical organizations of the 1840s supplanted the older model of the "benevolent society"—typically a national organization with local chapters, led by a board of directors and staffed by missionary "agents." This model relied on the goodwill of benefactors, and it ran parallel to the platform of the Whig Party, which sought to build a growing economy through federally directed investments coordinated with business elites. Benevolent societies, which appealed to the Congregationalist and Unitarian heirs of the old New England establishment, made existing institutions more humane, but they could not easily accommodate abolitionism's sweeping critique of American racism.

The rending of national organizations began in 1838 when Garrisonian pacifists left the American Peace Society to organize the New England Non-Resistance Society. Garrison hinted at the difference between this society and its predecessors when he described its founding "Declaration" (which he wrote) as the most " 'disorganizing' instrument penned by men." Its signers repudiated defensive wars, individual self-defense, political office holding, and voting for governments "upheld by physical strength." While earlier Christian pacifists had stood aloof from the larger society, Garrisonian nonresistants expressed a cosmopolitan identification with all humanity: "Our country is the world, our countrymen are all mankind." Anticipating "fiery ordeals" and martyrdoms, they predicted that over time their methods would overturn the old society: "It is only the meek who shall inherit the earth."[2]

These nonresistants were hardly meek, and they did not inherit enough funding or supporters to build a national organization. The new society hardened the opposition of religiously conservative abolitionists who had been offended by the female lecturers, and the rival factions squared off at the 1840 antislavery convention in New York City. Both sides tried to pack the convention with their supporters, which meant that 450 Boston Garrisonians crowded aboard a steamboat for a coastal journey that became a radical revival. "There never has been such a mass of *ultraism* afloat," declared Garrison. When participants voted narrowly to seat Abby Kelley on a business committee, the New York City philanthropists Lewis and Arthur Tappan led a walkout of three hundred conservative men who immediately organized the American and Foreign Anti-Slavery Society (AFASS). The split followed denominational lines, with Quakers, Unitarians, and come-outers (who had repudiated formal churches) siding with Garrison even if they did not personally support nonresistance. The AFASS was dominated by orthodox Congregationalists and New School Presbyterians. For the next decade, "Garrisonians" and "Tappanites" pursued rival strategies of religious activism.[3]

The Garrisonians disavowed the mainstream church as "the foe of freedom, humanity and pure religion," and repudiated the federal Constitution for its compromises with slavery. "Secession from the present U.S. government," declared an 1844 resolution, "is the duty of every abolitionist." Few went so far as Nathaniel Rogers, who suggested that even antislavery societies violated the principle of individual freedom. But a version of Rogers's logic was on display at the 1840 gathering of the Friends of Universal Reform. Unlike previous conventions, this gathering was devoted to free speech rather than building up a specific organization. Agrarians and abolitionists, Quakers and "men with beards," mused Emerson, all "seized their moment, if not their *hour* . . . to chide, or pray, or preach, or protest." A similar approach characterized subsequent Garrisonian conventions, allowing a convergence with Emerson's friends the Transcendentalists. Mostly Harvard educated and perched at the fringe of Unitarianism, the Transcendentalists had initially been discomfited by Garrison's extravagant rhetoric, but their devotion to freedom of thought and action made them mainstays of radicalism for the next half century.[4]

Meanwhile, the Tappans' AFASS remained faithful to the original vision of the Benevolent Empire, working closely with the network of interconnected mission and reform societies. It funded schools and congregations for African Americans and helped the kidnapped Africans who had been seized from the Spanish ship *Amistad* return home. It agitated within the major denominations by urging mission societies to refuse contributions from slaveholders and exclude them from mission congregations. When the missionary organizations went no further than to refuse hiring slaveholders as missionaries and affirmed only that slaveholding was an "organic sin" (which meant that individual slaveholders were not necessarily sinners), the Tappanites organized the rival American Missionary Association.[5]

In one sense, Tappanite groups stand outside the story of American radicalism, for their goal was to keep the abolitionist movement from threatening any institutions except slavery. But they were the constant companions of the emerging American Left, the "liberal" side of a left-liberal coalition that would form and dissolve repeatedly over the years. As the largest agency working with liberated African Americans after the Civil War, the American Missionary Association would shape the founding generation of Social Gospelers. It deserves much of the credit for the fact that in the twentieth century the major Protestant denominations would embrace semiradical positions on racial and economic issues.[6]

Many abolitionists, especially outside Boston and New York, were caught between the religious and ideological extremes of Garrison and the Tappans. Theodore Dwight Weld spoke for many when he lamented that the split "crucifies the savior afresh." Gerrit Smith, Frederick Douglass's later ally, resolved to stand "aloof from our National Anti-Slavery Organizations" until his brother abolitionists stopped "torturing and mangling each other." Smith poured his energies into building up a political third party that would be unreservedly committed to the abolitionist cause. Announced in 1839, the Liberty Party nominated former slaveholder James Birney for president in 1840 and 1844, garnering 2 percent of the national total in the latter year. The party drew its most fervent support from westerners who had been converted in Finney's revivals but were often on their way to a liberal religion of humanity.[7]

Many abolitionists feared that political partisanship would corrupt abolition. But in its early incarnation the Liberty Party hardly conformed to the stereotype of political compromise. "A liberty party," wrote one supporter, "must not oppose slavery out of hatred to the master, nor from single love of the slave, nor yet for any mere selfish end," but "for liberty's sake—for the best interests of mankind." The party embraced a novel theory of the Constitution as an antislavery document because the Fifth Amendment's guarantee of "due process" applied to the slaves. Gerrit Smith added a twist: following John Quincy Adams's observation that the government could emancipate slaves during wartime, he pointed out that slaves were already in a state of war against a government that contributed to their enslavement. Such quixotic arguments were neither more nor less radical than Garrisonian disunionism, but they represented a difference in tactics: would the antislavery revolution proceed by dissolving the federal government or by turning governmental powers to dramatically new ends? The same argument would later divide anarchist and communist critics of capitalism.[8]

The Liberty Party evolved alongside a movement of African American conventions that began in Buffalo, New York, just after an 1843 Liberty Party gathering. Presbyterian minister Henry Highland Garnet, whose church was funded by the American Missionary Association, was the primary organizer. Garnet revived the spirit of David Walker by calling for massive slave rebellion: "Brethren arise, arise! Strike for your lives and liberties. . . . Let your motto be resist!" Frederick Douglass, still aligned with Garrison, squashed Garnet's resolution. But Garnet's words anticipated Douglass's own evolution toward a more revolutionary style of activism and prepared the way for John Brown's attempt to spark rebellion at Harpers Ferry in 1859.[9]

Another movement aligned with the Liberty Party has been aptly dubbed "church reform." Launched at an 1838 Christian Union convention held in Syracuse, this movement shared the Garrisonians' opposition to existing denominations but was unwilling to dispense with formal congregations. Church reformers built splinter denominations and freestanding congregations that shared the Liberty Party's devotion to freedom. Their "coming out" was collective rather than individual, just as the party collectively repudiated mainstream politics. The resulting splinters covered a gamut of theologies: Wesleyan Methodists, Free Presbyterians, Franckean Lutherans, and Baptist and Quaker splinter groups. Those with Congregational or New School Presbyterian roots organized "Union" churches that eschewed denominational labels.[10]

These activist congregations spread abolitionist sentiment, pioneered new styles of religious community, and formed many leading radicals. As lay preacher of an Independent Congregational church, John Brown evolved a distinctive theology that blended classical Calvinism with an intense sense of his personal destiny as the instrument of God's sovereignty. At his own Church of Peterboro, Gerrit Smith supported Brown but gravitated toward a liberal theology akin to Transcendentalism. The Unionist congregation in South Butler, New York, broke new ground with its ordinations, selecting African American Samuel Ringgold Ward to serve a predominantly white congregation in 1841, and then making Antoinette Brown (later Blackwell) the first ordained woman in the United States in 1852. But the fervor of church reform congregations made them theologically unstable. Lewis Tappan feared that there was not "religion enough" among them to sustain church discipline, and his fears were confirmed by the trajectories of Antoinette Brown, Gerrit Smith, and most of the Unionists toward a post-Christian spirituality.[11]

The influence of church reform spread east and west from the revivalist areas of New York and Ohio. Silas Hawley, who had attended the Syracuse convention in 1838, planted a congregation in Groton, Massachusetts, on the basis of "primitive unity" and antislavery commitment. His convention on the question of whether the institutional church was human or divine attracted Garrisonians and Transcendentalists as well as revivalists. Amos Phelps, leader of the anti-Garrisonians in Massachusetts, pastored Boston's First Free Congregational Church, founded in 1835 as a bastion of abolitionism. And far to the west of the Burned-Over District, kindred congregations in Grinnell, Iowa, and Topeka, Kansas, preserved their radical traditions for decades, becoming important centers of Social Gospel activism at the end of the century.[12]

Despite their roots in the Benevolent Empire, the church reformers' repudiation of denominational ties set them on a path converging with that of earlier anti–Benevolent Empire congregations. The same was true for those congregations dubbed "free churches" not because they opposed slavery (though many did) but because they rejected the "pew rent" system. Free churches were launched by artisan radicals and by official denominations that hoped to counter the influence of popular Freethought. In 1836 the Unitarians sponsored Orestes Brownson's Society for Christian Union and Progress as an antidote to Abner Kneeland's Society of Free Enquirers. Transcendentalists James Freeman Clarke, William Henry Channing, and Theodore Parker all followed suit with congregations that hoped, in Channing's words, to unite "rich and poor, simple and learned, orthodox and heterodox" in "regard for what is sacred in each other's minds." Parker's 28th Congregational Society, established in 1845, emerged as the era's preeminent radical congregation, with seven thousand congregants representing all factions of radicalism. Even Garrison suspended his come-outer principles to attend services there.[13]

Unitarians had no monopoly on such initiatives. Physician Henry Ingersoll Bowditch organized Boston's Warren Street Chapel during the depression years in order to promote "general improvement of the young of the poor" without the interference of religious dogma. Though it was more a social service than a formal church, the agnostic Bowditch insisted that "no place seemed to me half so sacred." When deacons at his Baptist congregation refused to seat an African American friend of abolitionist Timothy Gilbert, Gilbert launched a Free Church to welcome people of all races and classes while excluding slave owners, liquor dealers, and chronic alcoholics. The congregation shared Tremont Temple with weekday theatricals and political debates. Never as radical in its theology as its politics, Tremont Temple tilted toward fundamentalism in the years after the Civil War, anticipating the modern megachurch as well as the more socially engaged People's Churches that proliferated across the United States between the Civil War and World War II.[14]

These local congregations anchored radicalism while major denominations stood aloof. In the wake of the Panic of 1837, they evolved in parallel with the largest flowering of American intentional communities prior to the 1960s. Far from counseling retreat from the problems of society, these communities inspired broader radical currents. They pioneered new practices of diet and dress that gave American radicals a distinctive culture, provided many radicals their first opportunities for deep encounter across the divides of class and race, and helped launch the careers of the most influential radical journalists and labor organizers of the 1850s. These communities were far from secular: though most repudiated doctrinal boundaries, they couched their missions in millennial terms, declaring their intent to build the Kingdom of God on earth. Many were founded by Protestant ministers who, like the church reformers, hoped their new communities would fulfill the promise of the Revolution.

During these years Emerson observed that there was "not a reading man but has a draft of a new Community in his waistcoat pocket," and several of these clerical schemers connected at Silas Hawley's Groton Convention on Christian Union. The first to turn his vision into reality was a self-educated minister named Adin Ballou, who had passed through the Christian Connection, Universalism, and Unitarianism en route to a position he dubbed "Practical Christianity." This movement blended doctrinal liberalism with a perfectionist standard of practical morality. Intentional community was a way to practice these ideals without the interference of wealthy congregational leaders. "We had gathered a fresh and hitherto unknown species of grape from the primitive Christian vintage," recalled Ballou, and community was the new bottle needed to contain it.[15]

In 1841 the thirty signers of Ballou's "Fraternal Constitution" moved onto a farm near his former congregation in Milford, Massachusetts. The two hundred people who eventually joined Hopedale received free education and nursery care for their children as well as dividends on their labor and their investments in community shares. Women and men shared in the community's democratic governance. Members launched individual and communal businesses, even as they contributed to the larger social reform movement by publishing newspapers, sending out itinerant speakers, and sheltering fugitive slaves. Hopedale was especially central to the work of the New England Non-Resistance Society. Renouncing "the principle of the hermit, and of the monk, and of the

Shaker," Hopedale aspired to reform the world through "continual interchange" with its neighbors.[16]

Those who found Hopedale's model too sectarian preferred Brook Farm, its sister community near Boston. As a young minister, founder George Ripley had despaired of his Boston congregation's ability to heal the "degradation" that surrounded it. Eager to live with others "as a man with men, as a friend, a brother, an equal," Ripley imagined that a progressive school might allow him to use his intellectual gifts with more integrity. Such a school might sustain itself by sponsoring a farm, which in turn could host "a society of educated friends" committed to mental and manual labor. Brook Farm attracted New England's best and brightest. From the Transcendental Club, John Sullivan Dwight signed on as a full member (as did his sister Marianne, a faithful Farmer to the end), while Theodore Parker and Margaret Fuller were steadfast friends of the community.[17]

A third Massachusetts community had close ties to Garrisonian abolition: Northampton Association founder George Benson was Garrison's brother-in-law. Other founders included a struggling silk manufacturer, a prospective Brook Farmer who preferred a community without an identifiable leader, and a former missionary who had converted to Unitarianism under the influence of a Hindu reformer. Unwilling to subscribe to a creed or even a list of moral principles, they agreed on the need for a community that would "rais[e] labor to its true dignity," honor intellectual freedom, and develop "all the capacities of human nature by the union of spiritual, intellectual, and practical attainments."[18]

Hopedalers, Brook Farmers, and Northamptonites believed that elements of individual ownership could be reconciled with economic egalitarianism. This approach dovetailed with the utopian theory of a recently deceased Frenchman whose work was just becoming known on this side of the Atlantic. Charles Fourier had claimed to have scientifically discovered laws of social attraction analogous to the Newtonian law of gravity, though his account of the "divine Social Code" was more esoteric than experimental. Human nature, Fourier taught, is shaped by twelve core passions—for the five physical senses plus friendship, romantic love, parental affection, ambition, group identity, variety, and absorption in an activity—that correspond to the deep structures of the cosmos. In communal "phalanxes" where the passions were properly balanced, he promised, individual interests would harmonize so as to bring about both prosperity and peace.

Fourierist propaganda in the United States was initiated by Albert Brisbane, a businessman's son who returned from a sojourn in France to publish *The Social Destiny of Man* in 1840. Convinced that Fourier's theories could transcend partisan divisions, he published articles in Orestes Brownson's *Boston Quarterly Review* (affiliated with the Democrats) and Horace Greeley's *New York Tribune* (affiliated with the Whigs). Greeley proved the more reliable ally, offering Brisbane a regular column. Fourier's plan attracted enthusiasts from New Jersey to Wisconsin, most of whom ignored Brisbane's warning that a phalanx would not succeed without sufficient capital or the 1,620 members dictated by Fourier. These groups knew little about Fourier's thought and less about agriculture and the laws governing joint stock corporations. After enthusiastic beginnings, most were brought down by heavy mortgages on barren land, by the challenge of bringing strangers together into cooperative association, or by the alluring opportunities of a rebounding economy. Nineteen of twenty-four associations founded during the heyday lasted less than three years.[19]

Brisbane, meanwhile, aspired to build a national organization. He took an important step in this direction when he drew the intellectuals of Brook Farm into the Fourierist orbit. Like Adin Ballou and George Benson, George Ripley had been intrigued but wary when he first encountered Fourier. Other Transcendentalists worried that Fourier relied too much on "a new outward arrangement" to cure "evils which have their root in the soul and heart." Such fears were allayed by William Henry Channing, nephew of the Unitarian founding father, who regarded Fourier as an ally in the project of giving Transcendentalism a social as well as individual dimension. For Channing, the Fourierist slogan of "Universal Unity,—*Unity of Man with God in true religion,—of Man with Man in true society,—of Man with Nature in creative art and industry*" provided the basis for a comprehensive strategy for building heaven on earth. The Brook Farmers soon agreed.[20]

Brook Farm's new constitution clarified the relationship between Fourierism and the larger social reform movement. Their goal was to unite disparate causes in a "universal" reform and move beyond social critique to social reconstruction: "The work we are engaged in is not destruction, but true conservation." The community's newspaper, the *Harbinger,* echoed this vision by promising that the "social reform" achieved in community would speed the "complete emancipation of the enslaved . . . the promotion of genuine temperance, and . . . the elevation of the toiling and downtrodden masses to the inborn rights of humanity." But the work of building a national movement soon sapped the lifeblood out of George Ripley's happy community. As word got out that Fourier encouraged the full expression of sexual as well as other passions, enrollment at Brook Farm's once profitable school declined. A fire destroyed the community's half-finished "phalanstery," or large communal building, and Brook Farmers lost their faith in the immediate applicability of Fourier's ideas. By this time, many had liberated themselves from the conventions of mainstream society, and they moved from the farm into cooperative urban households and new careers as radical journalists or labor organizers.[21]

Lifelong radicals were formed at other Fourierist communities. Wisconsin's Ceresco, which endured six years, grew out of a discussion at a local lyceum and was organized by Warren Chase, a Freethinker who would later become one of the Midwest's most prominent Spiritualist lecturers. The community prospered economically, attracting entrepreneurial frontierspeople, devoted idealists, and single mothers seeking a supportive environment for their families. It broke with Fourierist orthodoxy by honoring the desire of member families to eat meals privately or establish separate households on the periphery of the domain. A similar spirit of experimentation was present at the North American Phalanx, organized in Red Bank, New Jersey, in 1843, by Fourierists who remained in relative prosperity and harmony for twelve years. Though their labor system was indebted to Fourier's model, they refused to build a central phalanstery, preferring gradual growth with as much attention paid to industrial as to residential development. A disagreement over the advisability of starting a church within the community helped launch the rival Raritan Bay Union, which declared itself "unpledged to any social theory as yet presented," attracted Theodore Weld and Angelina Grimké, and creatively integrated people and ideas from Hopedale and the North American Phalanx. All three of these communities eventually folded, in part because they no longer believed the phalanx movement would sweep the nation. But many members remained in place, maintaining informal community ties as they redirected their energies to new radical causes.[22]

As the leading phalanxes modified Fourierist doctrine in response to lived experience, other radicals promoted communal alternatives. In 1843 John A. Collins, previously the general agent of the Massachusetts Anti-Slavery Society, launched a community of pure communism at

Skaneateles, New York. In keeping with the style of Garrisonian ultraism, Collins issued eight "Articles of Belief and Disbelief," ostensibly binding on all community members, that disavowed revealed religion (while admiring the teachings of Jesus insofar as they were "true in themselves"), "governments based upon physical force," private property, and the killing and eating of animals. Then this document was "repudiated by unanimous consent" as inconsistent with anticredal principles. Collins's nonresistant principles left him with little defense against a founding trustee who refused to leave the community even though he opposed Collins on every point. That conflict helped persuade Collins to rethink his principles and close down the community.[23]

Nonresistant principles were linked to a more thoroughgoing anarchism at Modern Times, the Long Island community organized by Josiah Warren, a veteran of the Owenite community at New Harmony. Rather than organizing a joint stock or common stock community, Warren purchased 750 acres of land and sold them at cost to individuals who wanted to live in a neighborhood that honored personal freedom. The community had its own money system of labor notes, but no courts or police. While most Fourierist communities disavowed Fourier's sexual radicalism, Modern Times openly embraced the ideal of "free love," according to which people should be free to dissolve unloving marriages and seek true partnerships with their soul mates.

The most enduring community with its roots in 1840s radicalism was John Humphrey Noyes's Oneida, best known for its practice of "plural marriage" as an antidote to the selfishness Noyes saw as inherent in conventional marriage. Oneida marked the boundary between those utopian experiments that were a vital part of the American radical tradition and more "sectarian" Shakers and Harmonists. Though Noyes maintained an extended dialogue with radical communitarians, his message to them was that the Shakers were right: both the nuclear family and religious pluralism were inimical to true community. This message, coupled with Noyes's autocratic leadership of his own community, kept him out of the radical mainstream.

Radical communities, by contrast, worked alongside more "practical" efforts to change economic structures. Even before Ripley founded Brook Farm, his friend Orestes Brownson sought to reinvigorate Working Men's activism by publishing "The Laboring Classes," a blistering invitation for Christians to identify with the cause of the workers. Like earlier artisan radicals, Brownson rejected a hierarchical priesthood as contrary to "the Christianity of Christ," urging that "no man can enter the Kingdom of God, who does not labor with all zeal and diligence to establish the Kingdom of God on earth." He called for the abolition of national banks, monopolies, and—eventually—inherited wealth. Brownson was one of the first self-avowed Christian thinkers to articulate a social understanding of sin and salvation. Because evil was "inherent in all our social arrangements," he reasoned, it "cannot be cured without a radical change of those arrangements." Such logic was shared by the church reformers and the Fourierists, one of whom noted in 1845 "that we say nothing against individuals; it is merely the false and pernicious system that we attack."[24]

Brownson's views gained in popularity as an improving economy made it easier for workers to demand higher wages and shorter hours. By the 1840s, industrialization was changing the workforce. In such places as Lowell, Massachusetts, water-powered factories employed thousands of women to do work previously performed by skilled craftsmen, and immigrants were pouring into seaport cities. The labor movement faced a choice: would it defend the traditional prerogatives of the skilled crafts or broaden its vision to include all workers?

Lowell's "mill girls" led the way. Shortly after arriving in the city, Sarah Bagley joined an "improvement circle" organized by Universalist minister Abel Thomas, who had come of age in the same Philadelphia congregation that had launched the Working Men's movement. Thomas organized the *Lowell Offering* as a vehicle for mill workers' self-development, and Bagley was one of its most successful contributors. As conditions deteriorated and hours lengthened in the mills, and as the owners gained control of the *Offering,* Bagley was radicalized. She organized the Lowell Female Labor Reform Association and became a vice president of the New England Workingmen's Association, a group whose lead organizer, S. C. Hewitt, was both an artisan and a Universalist minister. Calling for a ten-hour day, these activists adapted revivalist methods to the cause, promising that the "ten hour banner" would bring "the great salvation" to "ev'ry isle and nation."[25]

Throughout the 1840s, the parallel radicalisms of labor and abolition combined and clashed. The process was not easy. William Lloyd Garrison's first reaction to the Working Men's Party—in the inaugural issue of the *Liberator*—had been to call it "criminal . . . to exasperate our mechanics to deeds of violence, to array them under a party banner." Working Men antagonized abolitionists with insensitive allusions to "white slavery" or "wage slavery." When Rhode Island artisans mobilized to extend suffrage to all white men, they met fierce opposition from abolitionists unwilling to exclude blacks.[26]

But this was only one side of the story. Chastised by a reader for his attack on the Working Men, Garrison endorsed the ten-hour day and admitted that employers frequently perpetrated "a robbery of time from the laborers." Theodore Parker preached that the "slave power" of the South and the "money power" of the North worked together to squelch American liberty. Liberty Party papers were even more supportive. On the other side, *Working Man's Advocate* editor George Henry Evans described Nat Turner's cause as just and repudiated racial prejudice on the grounds that "our color is the color of freemen." Both chattel and wage slavery were contrary to American ideals, Evans believed, and he urged Northerners to "set the slaveholders an example, by emancipating the white laborer."[27]

Evans also agitated Gerrit Smith into the brotherhood of labor radicals. In 1844 he sent Smith an article calling him a "Slaveholder" because his landholdings deprived workers of the opportunity for independence. Though Smith replied that "man's right to himself" is "infinitely more important" than his right to the fruits of his labor, he sent a donation—and resolved to redistribute 120,000 acres of land to African Americans, creating his own sort of intentional community. When Smith's neighbors elected him to Congress in 1852, it was on a platform that included the whole roster of causes: immediate abolition, land redistribution, universal suffrage for women as well as blacks, abolition of national wars. Unfortunately, Smith had no plan for converting his ideals into legislation, and he quit in frustration before completing his term.[28]

Meanwhile, the collapse of Fourierism brought radicalized communitarians into the ten-hour cause. Brook Farmer John Allen met some skepticism when he assumed the editorship of the *Voice of Industry,* but he assured readers that he understood that the labor movement derived its power not from any "philosophy of Reform" but from the "cry of indignation" that emanated from factory villages and humble farms. The *Voice,* he promised, would remain "*free* as human thought, benevolent as Christian love."[29]

Church reformers also joined the cause. In Fitchburg, Massachusetts, the "Trinitarian" Third Congregational Society was organized by antislavery and labor activists, and its minister was praised as "one of those men (rare to be found among modern clergy,) who labor for the building up of Christ's kingdom on earth." Other radical congregations grew directly out of the labor movement. K. Arthur Bailey's Church of Humanity taught that capitalism flew in the face of God's plan for all creation "to be the common property of all his children." A general redistribution of land would "make the fair face of this Republic a second Garden of God." Others advocated come-outer religion, urging workers to emulate reformers of all ages who have "left the church, and taken a decided stand against the priests." Lowell's "Sabbath labor Christians" gathered in the streets to worship—and taunt the professional clergy: "While [the workers] have worked for their daily bread, you have prayed for yours."[30]

As the strands of radicalism came together, George Henry Evans launched a new movement for land reform. Stopping short of earlier calls for a redistribution of inherited land and wealth, Evans urged the federal government to eliminate the urban glut of labor by distributing western lands to workers. Evans's appealing invitation to "Vote Yourself a Farm" galvanized a movement, and soon an "Industrial Congress" gathered annually to promote land reform and the ten-hour day. The congress struggled to balance a critique of the mainstream churches with an affirmation of the religious zeal that activists brought to the cause. When one come-outer proposed a motion branding all ministers as "monopolists," it was amended to "to declare *more in sorrow than in anger*" that ministers were "fearfully recreant." Even that language failed to pass, as leaders fretted about alienating the "many religious men engaged in this cause." As before, labor's secularism was motivated by a desire not to offend orthodox Christians.[31]

No one did more to bring the radical streams together than Horace Greeley, whose *New York Tribune* was blossoming into the world's most widely read newspaper. Greeley's biography paralleled that of Garrison. Raised in rural New Hampshire and Vermont, Greeley parlayed his apprenticeship as a printer into an editorial career. He was a temperance man and an admirer of Henry Clay's plan to use tariffs to support nationwide industrial development. Unlike Garrison, Greeley did not shed his early political loyalties as he became radicalized but remained loyal to Clay's Whig Party until its dwindling base folded into the Free Soil and Republican movements. Similarly, Greeley never forsook the Universalist faith he had embraced as a young apprentice, though he also patronized free-pew congregations and the rising Spiritualist movement.

Where Garrison styled himself as an ultra radical, Greeley was a classic "left-liberal" who promoted the exploration of utopian ideas without relinquishing establishment ties. As a loyal Whig, Greeley believed a strong national government would create an umbrella of freedom for artisans, African Americans, women, and utopians. Though those groups never fully trusted him, he publicized them, making the national edition of the *Tribune* a forum for radicals from Maine to Michigan.

In 1848, the *Tribune* was the leading source of information on a wave of European revolutions. Hungarians, Italians, and Slavs rose up against their Austrian overlords; Germans demanded a national parliament; Danes achieved a constitutional monarchy. France's "February Revolution" replaced the monarchy of Louis-Philippe with a Second Republic whose leaders included working-class radicals as well as bourgeois liberals. Following the lead of Louis Blanc, who argued that government should guarantee a "right to work," the radicals employed one hundred thousand people in Paris's National Workshops. Compared to the visions of Owen and Fourier, this was socialism of a new sort, and it prepared the way for Karl Marx's vision of state-sponsored socialism. When more conservative republicans shut down the workshops, radicals took to the barricades but could not stop their government's rightward drift. The drama then shifted to Italy, where Giuseppe Mazzini presided briefly over a "Roman Republic." Not quite a socialist, Mazzini shared Blanc's faith that a strong state was compatible with radicalism. Calling himself a "nationalist," Mazzini taught that the unification of the Italian people would be the first step toward a more cosmopolitan politics and economic democracy. The intervention of the French on behalf of the ousted pope brought an end to his radical experiment.

The *Tribune* stood alone among major American newspapers in celebrating the social as well as the political dimension of 1848. Greeley sent former Brook Farmer Charles Dana to assess the diverse strands of French radicalism and even hired Karl Marx as a correspondent. Though Marx secretly disdained Greeley as incurably bourgeois, he ultimately published 487 articles in the paper. Another mediator between American radicals and the European revolution was Margaret Fuller, the Transcendentalist and pioneering advocate of women's rights who served as the *Tribune*'s literary editor before embarking for Europe. She met Mazzini in London, then participated actively in the Italian struggle. After Mazzini's defeat, she sailed for New York with her new husband and son, but all were killed in a shipwreck just yards from the Long Island coast.[32]

Had she lived, Fuller might have infused the American Left with Transcendentalist spirituality; indeed, women's rights activists hoped she would return home to lead their movement. Instead, 1848 brought a stridently anticlerical cohort of radical émigrés to American shores. Settling in New York City, Saint Louis, and Milwaukee, the German Forty-Eighters revived Missouri's antislavery movement and organized a host of new unions in the North. Those who identified as "liberals" moved easily into the Republican Party; the "radicals" planted the first explicitly Marxist parties in the United States or joined forces with native-born anarchists. More than a half century later, the Socialist Party would achieve its most significant victories in cities and wards influenced by the Forty-Eighters, and New York's Jewish socialists were tutored in Marxism by the Germans who preceded them in the Lower East Side. Because the established churches of Europe had opposed the 1848 revolutions, these exiles were generally antagonistic to religion as such and aligned themselves with the Freethought tradition of Paine, Owen, and Wright. In the disestablished United States, though, they inevitably worked alongside revivalists, Transcendentalists, and adherents of the newly fledged Spiritualist movement.[33]

The *Tribune*'s lasting achievement was that it kept these diverse viewpoints in a single conversation. Neither the theological differences between Forty-Eighters and revivalists, nor the constitutional debate between Garrisonians and the Liberty Party, nor the mutual distrust between abolitionists and artisans could keep radicals apart when all turned to the same newspaper for the news of the day. And so the American radicals of 1848 became a single tradition. People who had tasted a new institutional future in free churches and utopian communities worked together to revolutionize American society as a whole.

Of course, the old debates did not disappear. If radicalism was a single tradition, it was still multiple organizations, and those organizations proposed divergent paths to the new world they all imagined. In the next four chapters, I will trace four trajectories of American radicalism, each of which received a significant impetus around 1848. The impressive showing of the new Free Soil Party in the 1848 presidential election brought some radicals into mainstream politics. Dramatic manifestations purporting to be caused by the spirits of the dead provided a new religious framework for radicals who had broken with conventional churches. The Seneca Falls convention of 1848 freed the women's rights movement from its abolitionist roots. And the labor movement took on a new religious vocabulary around 1848, claiming that Jesus himself had been a class-conscious worker. Distinct but never fully separate from one another, these radical currents flowed through the upheaval of the Civil War and persisted through the conservative decades of the Gilded Age.

CHAPTER 6

Confronting the Slave Power

"Free Soil, Free Speech, Free Labor and Free Men." The Free Soil Party's campaign slogan demonstrated that mainstream politicians hoped to capture the radical constituency that had crystallized in 1848. Bringing Liberty Party supporters together with former Democrats and Whigs who had become disgusted with the slaveholders' dominance of politics, the Free Soil Party was far from radical. "Free Soil" meant keeping slavery out of the West but not ending it in the South; it also meant distributing federal lands as homesteads but not breaking up private land monopolies. "Free Speech" signaled opposition to the "gag rule" that prevented abolitionist petitions from being read in Congress, but it did not imply endorsement of the content of those petitions. "Free Labor" left ambiguous the party's stance toward "wage slavery." And "Free Men" connoted white males: the party would not push for the full inclusion of either women or African Americans in American politics.[1]

Nevertheless, neither Free Soil nor the Republican Party that succeeded it in the 1850s could have emerged apart from radicalism. Abolitionist agitation had provoked a Southern backlash that taught Northerners to fear "Slave Power" aggressions. The idea that slave owners were undermining American democracy gained currency as a result of the Mexican War and annexation of Texas, the Fugitive Slave Law of 1850 (which required federal officers to assist slave owners in capturing fugitives), and the Kansas-Nebraska Act of 1854 (which allowed slavery to expand to any western territory whose residents supported it). For decades the major parties had sought to keep slavery out of the national debate; when it emerged on center stage, the parties disintegrated. The sectional crisis also splintered denominations with a national constituency: Northern and Southern Methodists went their separate ways in 1844 and Baptists in 1845. Tellingly, these splits were initiated by Southerners angered by mild antislavery policies; no major denomination embraced the abolitionist agenda.

For radicals, the moment was rife with irony. In 1830 William Lloyd Garrison had located the *Liberator* in Boston because black abolitionists had persuaded him that Northern racism was nearly as evil as Southern slavery. Interracial encounter and work against racism in all its forms were integral to the abolitionist project. But abolitionism gave rise to a broader antislavery movement of white Northerners who had never encountered their black neighbors and had no desire to do so. The situation posed challenging questions. Could abolitionists work with people who were antislavery but not committed to racial equality? Should they work for compromises, such as limitations on the expansion of slavery in the territories, that might lead to the eventual collapse of the slave system? Or was it better to take more radical ground in the hope of sparking revolutionary change?

Such questions arise whenever radical agitation creates a moment of national crisis, and the challenges of the 1850s foreshadowed those that would crop up in the 1930s and 1960s. In all three decades, a significant number of radicals committed themselves to explicit programs of revolutionary action, reasoning that old institutions were on the verge of collapse. At the same time, radicals of each decade were courted by mainstream politicians who hoped that the support of a new constituency would allow them to emerge triumphant from political realignment. Once that realignment was complete, many radicals—including many of the most professedly revolutionary—would find themselves within the political establishment, while others would revert to earlier positions of marginality.

The revolutionary hopes of post-1848 abolitionists took two forms. Garrisonians, convinced that the only appropriate revolution would be a nonviolent one, argued that the best way to end slavery was for the free North to sever ties with the South and with a federal government controlled by the Slave Power. Underlying Garrison's slogan of "no union with slaveholders" was his view of the Constitution as a proslavery document. On the other side, Gerrit Smith and the radical remnant of the Liberty Party hoped that their antislavery interpretation of the Constitution would provide a basis for federal action against slavery in the South. This view underscored the sacred character of the nation, making militant action against slavery the highest form of patriotism.[2]

The debate over the Constitution did not prevent abolitionists from joining together in increasingly revolutionary action against slavery. Conductors on the Underground Railroad risked the violence of slave catchers by guiding brave souls to freedom in Canada. Black and white radicals organized "vigilance committees" that interfered with slave catchers' attempts to restore fugitives to the South. In 1842 Boston's Vigilance Committee mobilized hundreds of activists to prevent a fugitive named George Latimer from being returned to slavery. It then persuaded the state legislature to pass the Latimer Law, which forbade state officials from cooperating in attempts to apprehend fugitives.

The Fugitive Slave Law was an attempt to undo the Latimer Law by requiring federal officials and courts to cooperate with slave catchers, but its effect was to ratchet up the cycle of agitation. A reinvigorated Vigilance Committee rescued Shadrach Minkins from Boston's Federal Court House in 1851, then failed in similar attempts on behalf of Thomas Sims and Anthony Burns. Thomas Wentworth Higginson, Transcendentalist minister of Worcester's Free Church, became a radical hero when he was injured in the latter struggle. Riding a current of popular support, Higginson and his comrades escaped punishment, even though one courthouse guard had died as a result. A few months later, Rev. Jermain Loguen of Syracuse, himself a fugitive from slavery, achieved similar notoriety for his role in the successful rescue of a fugitive known as Jerry. That rescue relied on the combined strength of twenty-five hundred activists, drawn from both Garrisonian and Liberty Party camps.

While abolitionists were storming courthouses, their Northern neighbors were defecting from the Whig and Democratic parties to support Free Soil and Republicanism. In these parties they were joined by a moderate faction of the Liberty Party that followed such pragmatic activists as Salmon Chase of Ohio. An Episcopalian who was convinced that slavery was a sin, Chase had a theory of the Constitution that contrasted with those of both Garrison and Smith. For him, the Constitution was antislavery only to the extent that it prevented the federal government from directly upholding slavery or allowing it in territories under direct federal control. Slavery in the South could not be constitutionally abolished, but it would wither away once the Slave Power lost its hold on the federal government. This theory appealed to those Northerners who were more concerned about preserving the Union than about slavery. But it was too compromising for those abolitionists who had already broken with the mainstream denominations over slavery. While most of the Liberty Party vote shifted to Free Soil in 1848, church reformers supported Gerrit Smith's Liberty League and the series of radical parties that followed it.

Though Free Soil seemed like a compromise to long-standing radicals, it created space for moderate adherents of the mainline churches to inch their way toward radicalism. The most famous activists to follow this path were Harriet Beecher Stowe and her brother, Henry Ward Beecher. As children of Lyman Beecher, they were heirs to the tradition of quasi-established Protestantism that the Working Men had denounced in the 1820s. But they were as distressed by the Fugitive Slave Law as their neighbors. Stowe's response was to pen a novel, serialized in the *National Era* (soon to become one of the most influential Republican organs), that traced the escape of a family of fugitives and the martyrdom of the Christlike slave who helped them.

In some respects, *Uncle Tom's Cabin* was a step backward. Like earlier abolitionists, Stowe assumed that personal encounters between blacks and whites would translate into common action against slavery. But instead of a realistic picture of interracial alliance, she offered the exaggerated self-sacrifice of Uncle Tom and the colonizationist dreams of her other black hero. At the same time, Stowe amplified the apocalypticism of earlier abolitionists, affirming that "every nation that carries in its bosom great and unredressed injustice has in it the elements of this last convulsion." She linked the American struggle against slavery to the "mustering among the masses, the world over"—a hint that this daughter of the Protestant establishment sympathized with the European Left.[5]

The revolutionary struggle for freedom continued in the fields of Kansas. After the Kansas-Nebraska Act extended to the settlers of new territories the right to decide whether they would allow slavery, abolitionists organized emigration societies to ensure that the Kansas vote would go the right way. Proslavery sympathizers were doing the same thing, and on several occasions the two groups clashed violently. The call went out for activists to send guns as well as settlers to the West, and Henry Ward Beecher joined in so vehemently that the guns came to be known as Beecher's Bibles.

At the heart of the Kansas struggle was John Brown, an ardent Calvinist who had lived in Gerrit Smith's colony of former slaves before joining his sons in Kansas. Brown's ethos of racial solidarity was accompanied by a zest for action and a deep belief that "without the shedding of blood there is no remission of sin." Brown interpreted this to include the violent shedding of other people's blood as well as the sacrifice of his own life, and in keeping with those views, he and his sons killed five proslavery settlers in cold blood in 1856. This "Pottawatomie Massacre"—the details of which were not clearly established until years later—made Brown notorious and helped him organize sympathizers for bigger things.[4]

Virtually everyone who commented on Brown noted his apparent orthodoxy. "John Brown is almost the only radical abolitionist I have ever known who was not more or less radical in religious matters also," observed Thomas Wentworth Higginson. "His theology was Puritan, like his practice." This was perhaps overstated. Brown was an active participant in the church reform movement of upstate New York, serving as the lay minister of a congregation he had organized. Like others who had broken from the mainline churches, Brown espoused perfectionism rather than the Puritan understanding of human depravity, and he summarized his theology by appealing to the Golden Rule and the Declaration of Independence, noting that they "both mean the same thing." Brown was probably not as theologically liberal as his friends Gerrit Smith and Frederick Douglass, and he was more devoted to the text of the Old Testament and the theology of sacrifice than most abolitionists. And his alleged orthodoxy was a useful propagandistic tool in the hands of radicals who had left the mainstream churches but hoped to recruit ordinary Christians to their cause.[5]

This became more evident when Brown turned his attention from Kansas to the South. The irony that African Americans had little role in the Kansans' struggle against the Slave Power was not lost on Brown, who drew up plans for a more direct attack on slavery. Brown's attempts to recruit fellow soldiers and wealthy benefactors met with mixed success. Frederick Douglass, always ambivalent about the connection between violence and liberation, sympathized but declined to participate. Gerrit Smith promised funds, and in this he was joined by Theodore Parker and others in the Transcendentalist circle. Brown then led twenty-one supporters in an attack on the federal arsenal at Harpers Ferry, Virginia, hoping to obtain sufficient arms to establish an independent republic of fugitive blacks in the Appalachians. Instead, he saw most of his supporters shot down; he and the others were captured, convicted of treason, and executed six weeks later. In a final testament, Brown affirmed that "I, John Brown, am now quite *certain* that the crimes of this *guilty, land: will* never be purged *away;* but with Blood."[6]

Brown was acclaimed as a martyr and, for some, a new Christ. One *Liberator* reader predicted that "after fifty years we should find Brown churches all over the South," and Henry C. Wright affirmed that while Christ had been a "dead failure" at freeing the slaves, the nation would "be saved . . . by the blood of John Brown." Appeals to redemptive bloodshed offended Adin Ballou and a few others, but Garrison insisted that it was possible to admire Brown's action while remaining personally nonresistant. Echoing his earlier assessment of Nat Turner, Garrison urged devotees of "Concord, Lexington and Bunker Hill" to pay greater honor to Brown, for "if we are justified in striking a blow for freedom, when the question is one of a threepenny tax on tea, then, I say, they are a thousand times more justified, when it is to save fathers, mothers, wives and children from the slave-coffle and the auction-block."[7]

The Southern attack on Fort Sumter, and the creation of the Confederacy of slaveholding states, turned the radical imagination toward violence and the Republican imagination toward radicalism. Less than two years after John Brown had treasonously attacked a federal armory, soldiers bearing the insignia of the national government were marching into battle singing that Brown's "soul was marching on." Brown's prediction that the sins of the nation would be purged away by blood took on new meaning on April 14, 1865, when John Wilkes Booth shot Abraham Lincoln at Ford's Theater in Washington, D.C. Recognized as a martyr who had died for freedom on Good Friday, Lincoln was given credit as the "Liberator" who had ended slavery by signing the Emancipation Proclamation. It was easy, at the close of the Civil War, to forget Lincoln's sympathy for colonization or his often-declared desire to preserve the Union, with or without slavery. It was easy, too, to forget that Lincoln's presidency would not have been possible without the interracial activism of 1830s and 1840s abolitionism, which in turn built on the self-empowering activities of the first black abolitionists. Lacking such memories, the Republican Party would soon leave its radical roots behind.

Abolitionists faced a crossroads at war's end. After secretary of state William Seward announced the ratification of the Thirteenth Amendment, abolishing slavery throughout the United States, William Lloyd Garrison declared his life's work finished. Once the most "ultra" of multi-issue radicals, Garrison shut down the *Liberator* because it would be fitting for "its existence to cover the historic period of the great struggle," even though there was still "a mighty work of enlightenment and regeneration yet to be accomplished at the South." Garrison was not uninterested in this work; indeed, as soon as the final *Liberator* rolled from the press he headed out to a freedmen's relief meeting. But he brought a new spirit to this work, for the end of slavery had restored his faith in American institutions. He was now less a radical than an institutional liberal, content to allow the Republican establishment to pursue justice at its own pace.[8]

In the newly organized Freedman's Bureau, Garrisonians worked alongside former adversaries to build schools and colleges in the South. The American Missionary Association joined in this work, and the children of abolitionists streamed south to serve at such places as Fisk, Atlanta University, and Tuskegee. Sometimes forgetting the struggle against white racism that had led Garrison to plant the *Liberator* in Boston, many reformers came to assume that only a process of education stretching over generations would prepare African Americans for full citizenship. Others embraced new theories of "scientific" racism that taught that the intellectual capabilities of the children of Africa would never match those of Europeans. The implication was that white-dominated social structures did not need to change, and so the cause of racial uplift was shorn of its radicalism. By accepting the gradualist vision, Booker T. Washington eventually became the most admired black man in America.

Other abolitionists saw things differently. Though Garrison would have liked to close the Anti-Slavery Society as well as the *Liberator,* Wendell Phillips kept it alive until the Fourteenth and Fifteenth amendments—guaranteeing citizenship and male voting rights to people of all races—had been ratified. For the rest of his life, Phillips maintained a busy schedule of agitation on behalf of women's rights, temperance, and the labor movement. Many veteran abolitionists joined Phillips in the campaign for an eight-hour day.

Adin Ballou followed yet another path, holding so fast to his long-standing pacifist commitments that he lost connection to the broader radical community. During the final decades of his life, he continued to serve the Hopedale parish as minister and preserved the memory of his community through historical writings. He also corresponded with Leo Tolstoy, who would eventually hand down the ideals of radical nonresistance to a new generation of peace-loving activists. But pacifism remained marginal to the radical tradition during the final decades of the nineteenth century.

For black abolitionists, Reconstruction provided opportunities to move into politics. Twenty-three were sent to Congress by Southern districts whose white voters had been disenfranchised for their support of the Confederacy. As the most famous African American in the nation, Frederick Douglass was appointed to a series of posts, beginning with the presidency of the Freedman's Savings Bank and culminating with his service as consul general in Haiti between 1889 and 1891. A sought-after lecturer, Douglass inspired all who hoped to keep the abolitionist legacy alive.

Garrison, Phillips, Ballou, and Douglass found very different ways of remaining faithful to their earlier ideals. Likewise, the Republican Party as a whole gradually returned to its own original vision, which prized national unity above all else and saw slavery as an obstacle to white freedom rather than as a violation of the human dignity of those who were enslaved. The thirst for national unity would lead the Republicans to abandon the cause of Reconstruction in 1877, allowing white Southerners to purge blacks from their state governments, impose rigid segregation, and enforce the new regime with lynchings and terrorist violence. With the rise of organized labor, moreover, the Republicans' economic vision shifted to the right, so that the party of Lincoln became the inveterate foe of radicalism. But radicals in those years could draw strength from other institutions and traditions that emerged in the wake of 1848—most importantly on a cluster of new religious movements, on two vigorous associations for women's suffrage, and on the expanding labor movement.

CHAPTER 7

New Religions for Radicalism

By 1848 thousands of Americans had broken with inherited institutions. Neither church nor state, neither private property nor the family could be taken for granted. All might be challenged in the name of liberty, equality, and community. Some activists had claimed new identities as Working Men or African Americans; some had been transformed by personal encounters with Frederick Douglass or Abby Kelley. Some had felt a thrill of defiance by disrupting church services; others had tasted the Kingdom of God at Hopedale or Brook Farm. These newly minted radicals were ready to rebuild the social order, and for many this also meant rethinking the spiritual universe.

This rethinking followed many paths. Revivalist radicals became Freethinkers; liberal Transcendentalists became Roman Catholics; activists who had rejected all creeds clung to the authority of the Bible. Radicals were at the forefront of some of the most popular new religious movements of the nineteenth century, including Spiritualism, New Thought, and Theosophy. Others gravitated to an eclectic religious liberalism. Most spiritual pilgrimages were shaped by the sibling rivalry between religion and radicalism, as participation in radical movements kindled spiritual fires while engendering dissatisfaction with the complicity of the old churches. Perhaps, many imagined, it was possible to create a new "church" that would be in harmony with a radical future.

New religions born in the nineteenth century supported radical causes into the twentieth. But spiritual ferment was a mixed blessing for American radicalism. It takes work to create a new religion, and those who made Spiritualism or New Thought their first priority sometimes had less time for fighting slavery or capitalism. As radicals aged, many discovered hungers that sociopolitical radicalism alone could not fulfill. They wanted new ways of relating to other people, but they also yearned for healthier bodies or for transformative encounters with angels or the souls of lost loved ones. Some came to believe that changes at the material or spiritual level—finding the perfect diet or tapping cosmic energies with a perpetual motion machine—would render the hard work of social transformation unnecessary.

One trajectory led from revivalism through the abolitionist critique of churchly conservatism to a thorough questioning of biblical inspiration, ministerial authority, and even the idea of religion itself. William Lloyd Garrison led the way by abandoning most of his youthful religious beliefs, though he never relinquished faith in Jesus' liberating gospel. His nonresistant ally Henry Clarke Wright went a step further by trading orthodox Calvinism in for faith in human nature. Henceforth, he declared, "anthropology shall be my theology. The science of man is the science of God." The "church reform" radicals who had once recoiled from Garrisonian "infidelity" were only a step behind in their spiritual evolution. In the 1850s Gerrit Smith preached a religion of humanity from the pulpit of the Union Church he founded in Peterboro, affirming that "the religion of all holy hearts" was one regardless of labels. Most of the Liberty Party's founders came to agree.[1]

It was a short step from Wright's and Smith's religion of humanity to full identification with the Freethought movement. Though most who took that step had been raised as Christians, it is noteworthy that the most prominent Freethinker within the early women's rights movement was a rabbi's daughter. Raised in Poland, Ernestine Rose had rebelled as a child against the rigidity of her father's religion; after moving to England, she embraced Owenite socialism. In the United States from 1836 to 1869, she played a leading role in early women's rights conventions, and in the struggle for married women's property rights in New York. She relished confrontation with biblical conservatives, telling one in 1856 that the "living, breathing, thinking, feeling, acting revelation manifested in the nature of woman" was "older than all books," and that "whether it was written by nature or by nature's God, matters not."[2]

An organizational genius of the Freethought revival was Elizur Wright Jr., originally a revivalist abolitionist who was caught in the middle of Garrison's fight with the Tappans. Wright supported women's rights in principle, but believed that linking abolition to any less popular cause would betray the slaves. He was as frustrated with the conservative churches as was Garrison, and his attacks on "holier than thou clergy" alienated him from the Tappans and the Liberty Party. By 1846 Wright was championing a "sisterhood of reforms"—abolition, communitarian socialism, the eight-hour day, free land, immigrant rights, and an end to capital punishment—in conjunction with a rejection of otherworldly religion. "Christianity itself is a total failure," he wrote, "so far as it is a plan of saving souls for a future life without saving souls and bodies for this." Wright eschewed God-language in favor of a stress on scientific rationality. "I don't believe in the God of books," he confided to a friend in 1860. "I don't believe in anything but facts appreciated by some degree of evidence."[3]

Meanwhile, some of Wright's comrades in church reform laid foundations for twentieth-century fundamentalism. More than a few were caught up in the fervor surrounding William Miller's prophecy that Jesus would return to earth by 1844 and usher in the millennium without human assistance, even though this teaching contradicted radicals' faith in the human capacity to build God's Kingdom. Other church reformers turned their energies to the postbellum religious movement known as Holiness. This built on the idea that it is possible for individual Christians to achieve not only "justification," or forgiveness, but also "sanctification," or a state of freedom from sin. The quest for social holiness had led revivalists to radicalism, but after the Civil War the emphasis shifted to markers of personal purity, such as abstention from drinking and dancing. The Wesleyan Methodists, largest of the church reform denominations, formally endorsed the theology of Holiness, and soon they also joined the fight against historical approaches to the Bible and social understandings of sin and salvation.

A more surprising turn toward orthodoxy was taken by radical Unitarians. As Garrisonian abolition converged with Transcendentalism, several Brook Farmers converted to Roman Catholicism—among them cofounder Sophia Ripley and Isaac Hecker, who went on to organize the Paulist Fathers. Both were influenced by Orestes Brownson, whose 1844 embrace of Catholicism was the last step in one of the most convoluted religious pilgrimages in U.S. history. Repudiating his earlier radicalism, Brownson argued that reform movements were incomplete and intolerable rivals to the one true Church, whose responsibility it was to ensure social justice. "Either God has established the Church as the medium of the good he designs us to receive or to work out, or he has not," reasoned Brownson—and human organizations could not substitute for God's Church.[4]

The secularism of Elizur Wright, the piety of the Holiness movement, and the Catholicism of Orestes Brownson all denied the religiosity inherent in radical activism—the first by refusing the category of religion outright, the others by restricting what counted as "true" religion. Radicals who found such a step too wrenching had a promising alternative in Spiritualism, a tradition that was born among two radical circles in the late 1840s. The more famous story took place among the Progressive Friends, Hicksites whose loyalty to Garrisonianism made them unwilling to follow traditional strictures against cooperation with non-Quakers. Around the same time that leaders Amy and Isaac Post helped organize the Seneca Falls women's rights convention, they became aware of fascinating phenomena experienced by their teenaged neighbors, Kate and Margaret Fox. The Fox sisters could call forth mysterious rappings, which they interpreted as messages from the spirits of the dead. Their séances attracted curiosity seekers, bereaved parents and spouses, people hoping for a more empirically grounded spirituality, and radicals hoping that spirit allies would join their cause—as they usually did. By 1850 the sisters were in New York City, conducting séances for the radical intelligentsia under the patronage of Horace Greeley.[5]

A few years earlier, another teenager, Andrew Jackson Davis, amazed Universalist ministers with his practice of clairvoyant healing and his claim to be in touch with the spirit of Emmanuel Swedenborg. Swedenborg's message for the nineteenth century, apparently, was one of radical reform. Davis's "harmonial" philosophy promised to replace supernatural religion with a "theology of nature." Since natural law applied to society and spirituality as well as to physics and biology, this meant "expos[ing] and denounc[ing] wrong wherever found, and inculcat[ing] a thorough Reform and reorganization of society." Davis devoted one-third of his first book to a Fourierist-inflected account of the social implications of the principle that "man is a microcosm, or a combined expression of all the perfections contained in the divine essence." The two Spiritualist strands converged when Davis met with the Fox sisters, offered a qualified endorsement of their practice, and married Mary Fenn Love, whose work organizing the 1853 New York State Woman's Rights Convention allied her with Elizabeth Cady Stanton and Susan B. Anthony.[6]

It was no accident that the Fox sisters and Andrew Jackson Davis first shared their powers with radical activists. These clairvoyant youngsters offered an experience of encounter not unlike what abolitionists felt when they heard Frederick Douglass or Abby Kelley speak. The séance offered two encounters at the same time: one with the medium, who seemed to embody the sacred potential of all humanity, and one with the spirits. Spiritualism also offered radicals a broad philosophy of freedom. A commitment to the divine potential of each person linked the seemingly disparate struggles against Calvinism, chattel and wage slavery, and governmental coercion. One Spiritualist explained that social transformation required firm opposition to the unnatural institutions of conventional society, which "can only produce a feverish and ghastly imitation of life." "Political institutions" were "engines of oppression" and mainstream churches promoted spiritual "*disease,* alternately consuming the soul with intensest fires—and anon—driving it, shivering, away from God." The Spiritualist alternative was not "irreligious. . . . We labor, not to preserve the old form in which religion *has been* enshrined, but to lay hold of the risen Divinity that has gone out of it."[7]

Spiritualists coupled the Freethinkers' radical critique of the churches with a more satisfying spiritual experience. Only "free and unrestricted inquiry," explained Davis, could liberate humankind from the "prison of sectarian darkness." But the result would be not a disenchanted material world but one in which a heavenly host of teaching spirits were accessible. Spiritualism's self-understanding as a scientific religion that asked for nothing to be accepted on authority was plausible enough to persuade even the inveterate Freethinkers Robert and Robert Dale Owen.[8]

Spiritualism made a special contribution to women's rights, which grew up alongside it in the abolitionist strongholds of western New York and northern Ohio. Throughout the 1850s, the majority of women engaged in public speaking were Spiritualists, some of whom spoke only in a clairvoyant trance. Though the practice of trance speaking partly reinforced stereotypes of feminine passivity, trance lecturers often gained the courage to speak in their own voices, and many were quite radical in their understanding of women's rights. They espoused socialism, anarchism, and critiques of the traditional family in the years after the Civil War, even as other activists turned to a narrower focus on suffrage.[9]

Spiritualism helped radicals assert a fully American identity as they challenged American institutions. Many of the most radical spirit messages came from the Founding Fathers, including an abolitionized George Washington, who told Isaac Post that he hoped to "loose every fetter, so that the oppressor will see the necessity of loosening the binds that fasten him to his bondman, as well as his bondman to him." Andrew Jackson and John Calhoun joined Washington's chorus of repentant slaveholders. Like Working Men, Garrisonians, and women's rights activists, Andrew Jackson Davis interpreted the Declaration of Independence as a religious text and composed his own declaration of the liberation of the "inward Deity."[10]

Another Spiritualist who communed with the spirits of the founders was John Murray Spear, a former Universalist minister with a long résumé as an ultraist reformer. With his brother Charles, he had pioneered ministry among prisoners and was a zealous opponent of capital punishment. As a Spiritualist, he conveyed messages from a "Congress of Spirits" who urged him to gather a community at Kiantone, New York, where he strove to perfect such spiritual technologies as a perpetual motion machine. Spear's communitarian impulse was shared by Thomas Lake Harris, another ex-Universalist, who joined a group of ex Millerites in organizing a commune on the basis of direction from spirits. Though Harris eventually disavowed the idea that mediums could "become our spiritual leaders," he never abandoned socialist principle. His Brotherhood of New Life, formed in New York and transplanted to California, inspired some leaders of twentieth-century socialism. Spiritualist tendencies were also present at virtually every 1840s community that survived into the 1850s, including Ceresco and the North American Phalanx, Hopedale and Modern Times.[11]

It is hard to say whether Spiritualism was, on balance, good or bad for radicalism. Like the Holiness movement, Spiritualism took a form of religious experience associated with radicalism and made it an end in itself. Adin Ballou, himself a committed Spiritualist, was disgusted by Spear's quest for perpetual motion, observing that the "mountains" of injustice would not be "removed by spirits in a moment" but only "by the shovelful, through the sustaining power of willingly industrious, ever persevering faith." Other Spiritualists found their encounters with spirits so emotionally satisfying that they lost interest in encountering flesh and blood humans of different races or classes. Many mediums received spirit messages from Native Americans, but few joined in solidarity with the communities fending off genocide in the 1860s and 1870s. Once an ardent abolitionist, Andrew Jackson Davis later accepted the view that the races had been created separately, and that Caucasians were a "spirit race" destined for world mastery. When two mediums were granted a spiritual tour of Mars in 1869, they found four races there that corresponded to the racial hierarchy at home, providing a celestial sanction for segregation.[12]

Other Spiritualists devoted their best energies to building up Spiritualism rather than radicalism. The process of "denominational" consolidation led leaders to downplay radicalism, disavowing free love and distancing themselves from socialism. Fortunately for the radical causes that Spiritualists supported, the movement never fully coalesced as a denomination. Most typically, Spiritualists gathered in homes for séances or attended stand-alone lectures and camp meetings.

Tensions between Spiritualism and radicalism came to the surface at the Rutland Free Convention of 1858, which featured both religious and sociopolitical radicalism. The largest group in attendance, Spiritualists engaged in a heated public debate with Freethinkers Parker Pillsbury and Ernestine Rose. Some said that Spiritualism was the "foundation" for all forms of social reform; Pillsbury and Rose cast it as a distraction. But Andrew Jackson Davis took the middle ground. Spiritualism, he argued, was *not* a foundation but a door into the larger cause of human betterment; he personally had come to Rutland not to promote Spiritualism but to help "all the interests of benighted and oppressed humanity . . . find a voice." In keeping with Davis's sentiments, individual Spiritualists remained at the forefront of radical movements through the end of the nineteenth century.[13]

After the Civil War, the Spiritualist pattern of emergence from a radical milieu, alliance with radical causes, and undercutting of radical energies was repeated for the new traditions of Theosophy and New Thought. The former was created by a transatlantic circle of religious liberals who were fascinated by the esoteric traditions of the East. In 1875 the lapsed Spiritualist Henry Steel Olcott joined Russian immigrant Madame Helena Blavatsky and Irish immigrant William Q. Judge in organizing a Theosophical Society to explore ancient wisdom; after founding a network of local societies in the United States, they moved to an international headquarters in India. Blavatsky claimed to be in contact with a society of spiritual "Masters" or "Mahatmas," though her massive *Isis Unveiled* was indebted more to Western Hermeticism than to Buddhist or Hindu teachings. Theosophy substituted ancient wisdom for the democratic community of spirits, while retaining Spiritualism's positive view of human nature and devotion to "brotherhood." The first of the Theosophical Society's three objectives was "to form the nucleus of a Universal Brotherhood of Humanity, without distinction of race, colour, or creed."[14]

The impulse to join with others in pursuing human brotherhood was sometimes undercut by organizational prerogatives. Theosophists were first to try to implement the socialist vision of Edward Bellamy's *Looking Backward,* but they drew back for fear of becoming implicated in partisan politics. When the society split after Blavatsky's death in 1891, radical women took the lead of both factions. The result was a cluster of Theosophical communes founded between 1897 and the 1920s, all of which aspired to transcend the war between labor and capital but contributed only tangentially to the broader socialist movement.[15]

New Thought, also born after the Civil War, was based on healing practices that had gained popularity earlier. Just as Charles Fourier had tried to apply a Newtonian logic to the "attractions" governing society, so his contemporary Franz Mesmer had tried to heal patients by manipulating their inherent "animal magnetism." Homeopathy, phrenology, and the Graham diet similarly appealed to radicals who were questioning conventional wisdom in medicine as well as society. Among the American healers who drew on most of these practices was Phineas Quimby, and virtually all of the leading figures of New Thought were in the lineage of his teaching. The most famous was Mary Baker Eddy, whose authoritarian style and rigid distinction between divine and human powers made Christian Science unappealing to radicals. But Eddy's rivals and rebellious students built a distinct and much looser movement. Popularized in Ralph Waldo Trine's *In Tune with the Infinite,* New Thought held that anyone could achieve personal and social health by "opening" to his or her "oneness" with "Infinite Life." On this basis, New Thought adherents aspired to divinize humanity.[16]

Like Spiritualism, New Thought was committed to women's rights because so many of its healers were women. The students of Chicago's Emma Curtis Hopkins were especially likely to be involved in the National Woman Suffrage Association—a logical outcome given that Hopkins taught that the old epochs of the Father and the Son were about to give way to the new era of the "Holy Mother," whom she identified with the Holy Spirit of Christianity. The *Woman's Tribune,* edited by Hopkins's student Clara Colby, was the most enduring newspaper aligned with Elizabeth Cady Stanton's radical wing of the suffrage movement.[17]

New Thought also had a close affinity with socialism. Believing in the divine unity of humanity, New Thought adherents rejected Social Darwinist theories of competition. In Boston, New York, Denver, and San Francisco, they organized homeless shelters, day nurseries, and settlement houses. Editor Benjamin Flower built the *Arena* into one of the nation's most influential outlets for both radicalism and New Thought, and a New Thought paper called *Social Ethics* did double duty as the official Socialist paper of Kansas. Ralph Waldo Trine was a devout Socialist, and another party member declared confidently that "all the great men and women of the world have believed in what we call New Thought."[18]

Like Spiritualism, Theosophy and New Thought appealed to radicals but did not necessarily enrich the radical tradition. They could be all consuming, prompting radical leaders to mourn the "loss" of a valued comrade to Theosophical or New Thought fervor. Each was inclined to identify its own cause as all encompassing and other reforms as partial. And each movement had manifestations that were opposed to radical ideals. Just as some Spiritualists espoused racism by the 1870s, so many New Thought practitioners in the early decades of the twentieth century began applying the principles of mental healing to the pursuit of individual wealth. One friend of Eugene Debs even penned a guide to *The Science of Getting Rich,* opening a fountain of self-help spirituality that continues to flow a century later.[19]

Radicalism found steadier if less fervent support from traditions that espoused a free search for religious meaning without presupposing any specific result. After the Civil War the alliance between Garrisonians and Transcendentalists took fragile institutional form in the Free Religious Association (FRA), which functioned as the left wing of Unitarianism and as a freestanding discussion group. The brainchild of young Unitarian ministers who dreamed of a "spiritual anti-slavery society," the FRA opened its doors to Lucretia Mott, Robert Dale Owen, and the founders of Reform Judaism. Its priority was making room for post-Christian and scientific spiritualities within Unitarianism, but plenty of time was available for politics. Founder Francis Abbot explained, "We have a new gospel to proclaim . . . the gospel of faith in man carried out to its extremest consequences." Wendell Phillips was more pointed, noting that religion was "corrupt" because it existed within a "capital-punishment, pro-slavery, fourteen-hours-a-day, woman-under-the-heel society."[20]

Free Religionists and Freethinkers briefly came together in the National Liberal League, an organization committed to "total separation of church and state." At its 1877 national congress, the league responded to the new conservatism of the Republican Party by calling for a "Conscience Party" to fight for separation of church and state (against calls for a constitutional amendment making the United States a Christian nation), women's suffrage, protection of African American rights, and expanded public education. The result might have been a unified left-liberal movement had not the league immediately fractured over the Comstock Law, which gave Christian conservative Anthony Comstock sweeping powers to prosecute purveyors of "obscene" literature. When Comstock singled out a free-love treatise by anarchist Ezra Heywood for special attack, Freethinker Elizur Wright paid his bail—even though he personally was faithfully married. But most Free Religionists in the league were unwilling to jeopardize their other causes by attaching them to one so controversial. Free Religion's social vision was also compromised by its unwillingness to sponsor its own projects for concrete social betterment.[21]

Free Religious ideals found an organizationally minded champion in the person of Jenkin Lloyd Jones. Child of Welsh immigrants, Jones came of age in the Union army, an experience that turned him into both a pacifist and a devotee of Abraham Lincoln. As mission secretary of the Western Unitarian Conference, Jones fostered a tradition that was more radical than its Boston headquarters. He also expanded the ranks of the Midwestern Unitarian ministry to include a remarkable sisterhood of Iowa women. Jones's large congregation in Chicago provided social services and sponsored forums on radical causes. He achieved national prominence as an opponent of the Spanish-American War, the Philippine occupation, and—in his final days—World War I. Though Jones's efforts gradually expanded the theological boundaries of Unitarianism, his impatience led him to organize the Congress of Liberal Religion, which aspired to create the all-inclusive Church of Humanity.

By that time the constituency of religious liberals was not limited to persons with Christian roots. Isaac Wise and other German Jewish rabbis created a Reform movement that saw the ethical vision of the prophets, rather than precise adherence to ritual law, as the heart of Judaism. The example of the prophets led Chicago's Emil Hirsch and New York's Stephen Wise to work closely with Christian and post-Christian reformers on issues of peace, economic justice, and rights for African Americans. Also in New York City, a rabbi's son named Felix Adler took the further step of divorcing ethical religion from any belief in God whatsoever. Convinced that a community could be held together by good works rather than doctrinal belief, Adler made both practical social work and political advocacy integral components of the movement he called

Ethical Culture—and resigned the presidency of the Free Religious Association because of its unwillingness to do the same. Ethical Culture sponsored a free kindergarten, a program of visiting nurses, and a cluster of model tenements; by the beginning of the twentieth century Adler was perhaps the nation's foremost opponent of child labor. Though Ethical Culture was open to people of all ethnicities, it also influenced Reform Judaism through the work of Abraham Cronbach, a professor at Reform's Hebrew Union College who taught that social work was a way of honoring the divinity inherent in all humanity.[22]

Such liberal traditions provided steady support for radicals, but they were never subsumed within radicalism. Deeply intellectual, their adherents often assumed that the spread of science would ameliorate social ills without revolutionary upheaval. At a time when the Republican establishment was retreating from its founding idealism and American universities were wielding "science" as a weapon against immigrants and minorities, members of all these movements courageously insisted that evolutionary science need not entail the Social Darwinist claim that unfettered capitalist competition was the engine of human progress. The real key to evolution was cooperation, they insisted, and on this basis they forged a progressive "new liberalism" that would inspire and ally itself with the most important radical movements of the twentieth century. The new liberalism also drew on contemporary currents of European philosophy, theology, and political thought.[23]

The new liberal constituency included Protestants who were gravitating toward the theology that had characterized Unitarianism and Universalism before they began breaking free of Christian moorings. What distinguished "progressively orthodox" Protestants was their historical sensibility. They believed that Christian truth emerged organically over the course of centuries, and might develop further in the future. Old creeds were not false, but they were culturally specific; in the modern age they could be read symbolically rather than literally. Horace Bushnell articulated these views in sophisticated form, while Henry Ward Beecher and other "princes of the pulpit" translated them into accessible sermons that attracted thousands in America's metropolises. Neither man was a radical. "Progressivism" as they understood it was almost the opposite of radicalism, a strategy for preserving social institutions threatened by extremes both right and left. But they prepared the way for significant alliances between "mainline" Protestantism and the Left.

Ironically, that process began when adherents of the new theology faced charges of heresy from their denominations. Some were Bible professors at seminaries, and their professorial colleagues took their side in the resulting heresy trials. As a result, Union Seminary in New York City cut its ties with the Presbyterian denomination and Vanderbilt University broke with the Methodists. The resulting independence made both Union and Vanderbilt's Divinity School appealing settings for scholars who held radical political views as well as liberal understandings of the Bible. At the same time, autonomy did not prevent them from training denominational ministers, but instead broadened their influence to touch multiple denominations. With a handful of other schools that did not break with their denominations, Union and Vanderbilt infused radical ideals into the Protestant clergy.

Some charismatic ministers who faced heresy trials persuaded congregants to follow them out of their denominations. Some of the "People's Churches" that resulted were the most consistently radical religious institutions in the United States after the Civil War. Typically, they abolished pew rents, eschewed theological boundaries, and made the pursuit of a better society their basis of unity. Most provided social services to persons living in their vicinity and replaced Sunday evening services with forums that brought the public into conversation with activists. People's Churches could be extremely large, if only ephemerally so, with sanctuaries seating thousands.

Though a Methodist congregation in Boston was first to call itself People's Church, the pattern was set by Indianapolis's Plymouth Church in 1877, when pastor Oscar Carlton McCulloch declared his desire to "make this church a People's College." He replaced a theologically conservative creed with a constitution that declared the congregation's goals to be "public worship of God, weekly renewal of religious sympathies and affections, mutual acquaintance and assistance, and the alleviation by physical and spiritual means of poverty, ignorance, misery, vice and crime." Then Chicago's Hiram Thomas resigned a Methodist pulpit rather than face a heresy trial, and organized a People's Church that promised to provide a place where "strangers and those without a religious home" could unite in "the great law and duty of love to God and man." Underscoring its commitment to religious liberalism, the congregation promised to "require no theological tests," noting, "We think and let think." Saint Paul's People's Church was also launched by a renegade Methodist, Samuel G. Smith, who preached the "wild, free theology of the West" and later taught sociology at the University of Minnesota. Between 1887 and the beginning of World War I, at least thirty additional People's Churches were launched in locations ranging from New York and Washington to Iowa Falls and Fairmont, West Virginia. Freedom from denominational accountability allowed People's Church pastors to embrace sociopolitical radicalism, though their commitment to freedom of thought typically prevented them from imposing their allegiances wholesale on their congregations.[24]

In the People's Churches, the diverse spiritualities of American radicalism came together. Representatives of Spiritualism, Theosophy, New Thought, Free Religion, Reform Judaism, Ethical Culture, and sometimes even Freethought were welcome in the pulpits and forums of People's Churches, and activists filled the pews. As had been the case from the beginning, American religion at the close of the nineteenth century was most radical when it was most local. But People's Churches also inspired imitation by denominationally affiliated "institutional churches." In the twentieth century, those institutional churches would be at the heart of a radicalizing ecumenical movement, even as some People's Churches provided a religious foundation for the Socialist Party. Before that happened, all the religious traditions described in this chapter would help to sustain two of the most vital radical movements of the late nineteenth century: women's rights and labor.

CHAPTER 8

Women's Rights, Women Ministers, and a Woman's Bible

The women's rights movement was one of the last children of abolitionism to be born, and one of the most successful at preserving its identity after the parent's death. Organized by women a generation younger than William Lloyd Garrison, the movement crystallized at the Seneca Falls Convention of 1848, maintained a low profile during the decade of sectional division and Civil War (when key leaders were absorbed in childrearing), then asserted its autonomy at war's end. As old abolitionists settled into the Republican establishment, women's rights preserved its radical witness for fifty years. It drew on the energies of Spiritualism and New Thought and the organizational heft of Protestant women determined to free the nation from the scourge of liquor. Yet the culminating achievement of women's suffrage in 1920 failed to usher in the hoped-for revolution in gender relations.

The religiosity of the suffragists was epitomized in a poem by Phebe Hanaford, a Universalist minister and suffrage campaigner. Hanaford described a conversation between her predecessors Lucy Stone and Antoinette Brown, classmates at Oberlin. "Can woman reach the pulpit?" Brown asks soulfully. Stone replies skeptically, but God gives "the answer in the wish inspired." Describing Stone's career as an advocate within "State-House domes" and Brown's work in the pulpit, Hanaford concluded that both had answered a divine call:

> Their lives have shown that naught can stay the tide
> Of God's great purpose in its onward flow;
> That where man nobly labors for the race,
> There, too, may woman, at God's summons, go.[1]

Hanaford's poem tells us a few things about the first wave of women's rights. First, it was a continuous tradition in which the founders' memory remained alive from generation to generation. Hanaford treasured the story of Stone and Brown because her own mentor, Olympia Brown—first of dozens of women ordained by Universalists in the nineteenth century—had drawn early courage from Antoinette Brown's example. Second, the poem highlighted the role of friendship in holding this network together. Stone and Brown inspired one another to break free of gender conventions, and when they married the brothers Henry and Samuel Blackwell, they became part of a remarkable family of radicals that also included pioneering physicians Elizabeth and Emily Blackwell. The pattern was repeated by suffragist friends Elizabeth Cady Stanton and Susan B. Anthony, temperance leaders Frances Willard and Anna Gordon, and the remarkable circle of women who made female ministry the norm in Unitarian congregations in turn-of-the-century Iowa. Women's rights advocates were not lonely pioneers but cooperative sisters.[2]

The poem's setting at Oberlin was also significant. Though Lucy Stone and Antoinette Brown came from opposite wings of the abolitionist movement, they met at Oberlin because it was the most radical school open to women. Their divergent religious beliefs led them to organize a literary society to debate whether religion was an "outgrown creed." Brown's decision to pursue graduate ministerial study at Oberlin prompted Stone to fault her for "studying that old musty theology . . . [while] the great *soul* of the *Present,* hungering & thirsting for the bread and water of Life, falters by the wayside." Brown replied, half presciently, that she would be thankful for the "mental discipline" even if she eventually discarded the Bible. She was a true heir to the revivalist energies that led her, like Gerrit Smith and Elizur Wright, on the path to a religion of humanity.[3]

Hanaford was also right to pair the vocations of suffragist lecturing and ordained ministry. Most lecturers were either Quakers with a tradition of lay ministry, liberal Protestant ministers, or Spiritualist leaders. Those who were none of the three—notably, Lucy Stone and Elizabeth Cady Stanton—also saw activism as a sacred vocation. Whether building up local congregations or tearing down the strictures of "man-made religion," women's rights advocates knew that religious as well as political institutions would need to be transformed for "God's great purpose" to be achieved.

As we have seen, Frances Wright was the first widely recognized advocate of women's rights in the United States, but her legacy was the strong association in the public mind among women's rights, socialism, Freethought, and free love. Abolitionism's contribution was to generate sufficient moral zeal in Lucretia Mott, Abby Kelley, and the Grimké sisters to impel them to risk the opprobrium of "Fanny Wrightism" by speaking on behalf of the slave. These women retained their identity as abolitionists first and foremost, so it was up to a younger cohort, many rooted in the radical culture of western New York, to build an autonomous women's rights movement that would outlive the Civil War. This began in Seneca Falls, home to Liberty Party stalwart Henry Stanton and his wife, Elizabeth Cady Stanton, and not far from either Gerrit Smith's Syracuse or Frederick Douglass's Rochester.[4]

The convention itself was not a grand affair; it was attended by only about a hundred people, of whom only Stanton, Douglass, and Lucretia Mott had national reputations. Mott was in town to visit her sister, and a chance meeting inspired Stanton to pull together a convention before the older woman left town. Stanton and others penned a "Declaration of Sentiments," joining previous radicals in finding a patriotic legacy for a radical agenda. This declaration hewed close to the Jeffersonian original, affirming the self-evident truth "that all men and women are created equal" while decrying man's "repeated injuries and usurpations." It played up religious themes more than Jefferson had, faulting "man" for blocking women's ordination and "usurp[ing] the prerogative of Jehovah himself, claiming it as his right to assign for her a sphere of action, when that belongs to her conscience and to her God."[5]

Presented in the local Wesleyan Chapel, the declaration was coupled with resolutions that demolished the prevailing ideology of separate spheres. The participants did not blame God or the Bible for women's oppression, but contended that "corrupt customs and a perverted application of the Scriptures" had kept women from their divinely appointed "sphere." Alluding to the work of the Grimkés and Abby Kelley, they stressed women's duty to "promote every righteous cause by every righteous means," including public speaking. And, in a resolution that even Mott initially opposed, they affirmed "the duty of the women of this country to secure to themselves their sacred right to the elective franchise." This commitment to suffrage anchored women's rights for seventy years. Its shock value made it an effective tool of agitation, putting the new movement on the map. Suffrage lent itself either to single-issue organizing or to multi-issue radicalism, as women's votes could be presented as essential to anything from prohibition of alcohol to a socialist state.[6]

The petitioners recruited Lucy Stone, then an agent of the Massachusetts Anti-Slavery Society, to bring their message to the lecturer circuit. Two years later, Stone helped organize a truly national convention in Worcester, Massachusetts. This event attracted hundreds of speakers and a thousand attendees, as the suffragist constituency had broadened to include Transcendentalists as well as abolitionists. It did not result in a permanent organization, for the emerging practice was to hold free-standing conventions, without formal delegates, as a safeguard for free speech. When one convention voted down a national organization, Mott rejoiced that no "seeds of dissolution" could be sown, while Angelina Grimké Weld affirmed that "we need no external bonds to bind us together, no cumbrous machinery to keep our minds and hearts in unity of purpose and effort."[7]

They did need lecturers, so Lucy Stone quit her abolitionist job to focus on suffrage. Her speeches recruited a wide range of women to the cause, from the wealthy Julia Ward Howe, a fixture of Boston's reforming high society, to a young admirer who wrote in her diary that "Lucy Stone . . . scorns the idea of *asking* rights of man, but says she must boldly assert her own rights, and *take* them in her own strength." Stone persuaded her old friend Antoinette Brown to address the 1850 convention despite Brown's reservations about both women's suffrage and Garrisonianism. This launched a three-year lyceum career, during which Brown came to appreciate the freedom inherent in the lecturer's call. "I am glad to be again free from any connection with anyone in laboring, for I believe with nobody, & I could not work perfectly well with any one." The sentiment sounds Garrisonian, but Brown was more orthodox than her sisters: she persuaded them to open conventions with prayer, but could not convince them that the Bible was free of sexism.[8]

Women's rights activists sustained themselves on the lecture circuit by building an egalitarian culture in which one woman's victories empowered the others. Here they continued the legacy of Margaret Fuller, who had earlier gathered women for "Conversations" that would prepare them for full participation in the public sphere. Fuller's *Woman in the Nineteenth Century* was the fullest argument for women's equality available. While the Grimkés had made their case for full equality on biblical grounds, Fuller expressed a Transcendentalist spirituality in which women's empowerment would allow "the divine energy" to "pervade nature" and bring about "a ravishing harmony of the spheres."[9]

Women's rights advocates also transformed family life. Most excluded sexist elements from their weddings, and Lucy Stone pioneered the practice of retaining her maiden name. Married activists found deep satisfaction in childrearing, though the attitudes of their husbands and their level of wealth made it more or less easy for them to combine this with public activity. An energetic constitution and many servants enabled Elizabeth Cady Stanton to mother seven children while building a movement, despite her husband's ambivalent support. At the other extreme, Abby Kelley and Stephen Foster had an equal marriage and a profound devotion to their one daughter. Kelley cared for her nearly full-time in infancy and during an adolescent medical crisis, but traveled frequently in the intervening years while Stephen served as primary parent.[10]

The pursuit of ordination was integral to the community of radical women, though many ministers' evolving theologies made it difficult for them to sustain long-term pastorates. Antoinette Brown exemplified the difficulties. Her ordination by the Unionist congregation of South Butler, New York, exacerbated the growing gulf between liberal and Holiness currents within the church reform movement. The ordination preacher was Luther Lee, a Wesleyan Methodist whose presence underscored the fact that church reform was the "denominational" context for Brown's ministry. Brown's radical Unitarian friends would have liked to participate but declined, lest their presence call Brown's orthodoxy into doubt. To persuade Gerrit Smith to speak, she assured him that he would be free to "express himself opposed to all ordinations"—at an ordination service!—so long as he "put woman upon the same platform with man." But Brown's heterodoxy led her to leave the congregation within nine months. Sometimes believing "nothing, not even in my own continuous personal existence," she could not offer orthodox responses to child death and other pastoral crises. "Of course I can never again be the *pastor of a Church,*" she wrote to Horace Greeley, "but must be a *preacher for the people.*"[11]

Brown's time in the spiritual wilderness was filled with lecturing and marriage. Though Susan B. Anthony urged her to stop at two children, she had seven, which kept her occupied throughout the Civil War years. While other activists focused on refining their political strategy, she immersed herself in study, eventually publishing a series of books that integrated traditional theodicy with Darwinian science. She also wrote on the benefits of equal marriage, in which the wife would "learn to breathe more strongly" through manual labor and the husband would find "baby-tending and bread-making [to] be most humanizing in their influence." Eventually, Brown followed the Blackwells into the Unitarian Church and sought ministerial fellowship. Describing herself as an adherent of "Rationalism or Natural Religion," she was still nostalgic for the "common beliefs, aims, sympathies" of her revivalist upbringing. She did not directly serve a church until she organized one of her own in Elizabeth, New Jersey, in 1903, where her role was to give a monthly sermon as minister emeritus. By that time, her daughter Florence had followed her into the ministry, though—intriguingly—she chose the Methodist Protestants rather than the Unitarians.[12]

Brown inspired most of the women who entered the ministry after her. Olympia Brown, who was no relation, came next. She was raised among frontier Universalists who relied on Horace Greeley's *Tribune* for news of "Fourierism, Woman's Rights, Dress Reform, Anti-Slavery, Water-cure and all the ideas and theories then new but now either accepted and adopted or exploded and forgotten." Her sense of vocation to the ministry was formed at Mount Holyoke, where she was repelled by the founder's Calvinist theology, and at Unitarian Antioch, where she arranged for a guest sermon by Antoinette Brown, recalling later that "it was the first time I had heard a woman preach, and the sense of victory lifted me up." Eventually she made her way to the Universalist seminary at Saint Lawrence. Though Saint Lawrence's president opposed women's ordination, she was encouraged by his grudging acknowledgment that he would leave the matter "between you and the Great Head of the Church."[13]

Soon after Brown's ordination, the Universalists had more female ministers than any other church, but most forged alliances across denominational lines. Antoinette Brown advised Olympia Brown that while "the time might come when you would find something 'cramping' in all Christian organizations . . . to refuse present cooperation with those who are really with you in belief would be a sad mistake." Anna Howard Shaw, the first woman ordained in the Methodist tradition, was raised by Unitarians, inspired to seek ordination by Universalists, and converted to Methodism on the eve of preaching her first sermon. Like Florence Blackwell, she chose the egalitarian Methodist Protestant Church, rather than the mainstream Methodist Episcopal, for her ministry; like both Antoinette Brown and Olympia Brown, she logged more hours on the lecture circuit than in the pulpit.[14]

By 1880, the United States census listed 165 women ministers with parish jobs. Hundreds more ministered within Spiritualism, New Thought, and Theosophy, and the cause of women's rights was represented by two national suffrage organizations and the massive Women's Christian Temperance Union. These organizations grew out of the wartime experience, which convinced leaders that new structures were needed to translate agitation into policy change. As male abolitionists entered into the activities—and compromises—of the Republican Party, women's rights advocates had three choices. They could continue as agitators, championing a broad vision of human freedom and trusting in the forces of history to translate that vision into policy. This was the approach taken by most Spiritualists. Or women could identify with their Republican brothers, even if that meant subordinating their own cause to that of the former slaves. This was the choice of Lucy Stone and her ordained male allies. Or, most controversially, they could seek independent access to the halls of power through single-issue organizing. This was the path followed by Susan B. Anthony and Elizabeth Cady Stanton.[15]

The choices came to the fore in 1865 and 1866, when the nation debated the Fourteenth Amendment to the Constitution, which would penalize states that refused to enfranchise all "male inhabitants, being twenty-one years of age, and citizens." The failure to link female and black suffrage offended many radicals, as did the introduction of the word "male" into the Constitution. When Wendell Phillips argued that "this hour belongs to the negro," Elizabeth Cady Stanton shot back: "Do you believe the African race is composed entirely of males?" She also, sadly, argued that women should not "stand aside and see 'Sambo' walk into the kingdom first." More diplomatically, Lucy Stone wrote to Abby Kelley Foster that she was opposing the amendment with "tears . . . in my eyes," because she could not leave "my little daughter drowning with no power to help." Foster (whose husband took Stone's side) replied that the threat of racist violence trumped concerns for women's suffrage: "I should look on myself as a monster of selfishness if, while I see my neighbor's daughter treated as a beast . . . I should turn from them to secure my daughter political equality."[16]

For a time, division was avoided through the work of the American Equal Rights Association (AERA), which agitated for voting rights for women, African Americans, and Irish immigrants. Sojourner Truth was among many who signed up for the new group, warning that "if colored men get their rights, and not colored women get theirs, there will be a bad time about it." But Republican refusal to incorporate women's suffrage into either the Fourteenth or Fifteenth Amendment forced politically inclined radicals to take sides. At a New York constitutional convention, Horace Greeley—following the Republican line—argued that only those willing to bear arms in national defense should vote, and Stanton replied that women could hire substitutes, as Greeley himself had done. Kansas voters faced simultaneous referenda on black and female suffrage, and when Republicans campaigned against the latter initiative, Elizabeth Cady Stanton and Olympia Brown allied themselves with a Democrat who opposed black suffrage. Both measures failed, and the results suggest that the factions would have done better by working together: voters who supported one measure tended to vote for the other.[17]

The two sides came to a showdown in May 1869, when Stephen Foster and Frederick Douglass tried to expel Anthony and Stanton from the AERA for their racist arguments. Lucy Stone appealed for unity, arguing, "The woman has an ocean of wrong too deep for any plummet, and the negro, too, has an ocean of wrongs that cannot be fathomed." The convention declined to force Stanton and Anthony out, then passed Henry Blackwell's resolution endorsing the Fifteenth Amendment with "profound regret that Congress has not submitted a parallel amendment for the enfranchisement of women." Neither he nor Lucy Stone was present when delegates gathered two days later to organize the National Woman Suffrage Association (NWSA), which would mobilize specifically for a sixteenth amendment.[18]

It is not clear whether Stanton deliberately excluded Stone from that meeting, but Stone believed it was so and immediately began organizing a rival group. Stone's American Woman Suffrage Association (AWSA) created a left-liberal alliance of Boston Garrisonians and mainstream Republicans. Stone made a strategic choice in pushing Julia Ward Howe—whose husband was a prominent Republican—into a leadership position, though she had little previous commitment to women's rights. Ironically, given her youthful doubts about the value of Christian ministry, Stone cultivated ministerial support, and she counted Transcendentalist Thomas Wentworth Higginson and Congregationalist Henry Ward Beecher among her allies. The AWSA also helped to heal old wounds by bringing Garrison together with rivals Frederick Douglass and Wendell Phillips at an 1873 rally against "Taxation without Representation."

The AWSA's political strategy focused cautiously on state suffrage initiatives rather than agitating for a national amendment. But it had its radical moments. The Fosters frustrated moderate leaders by introducing such resolutions as "they who seek to deprive woman of the ballot are tyrants and despots." (Urged to "have a Christlike spirit," Abby replied that "rebuke of sin was one important exercise of a Christlike spirit.") They also revived a tactic that Lucy Stone had first tried in 1857, refusing to pay their property taxes until women could vote. Abby goaded the local tax collector to auction off the farm on the Fourth of July as "a peculiarly appropriate time for the enforcement of the principle of taxation without representation," and Higginson praised the strategy as "the nearest we can come to 'the blood of the martyrs.'" But it wasn't near enough: the Fosters stayed on their farm, and no mass movement of tax resistance took off.[19]

While the AWSA kept radicals in conversation with Republicans, the NWSA was politically autonomous and avowedly "revolutionary." Stanton's early proposal for an exclusively female organization was rejected, but the NWSA included few men, with Parker Pillsbury the only prominent male organizer. The NWSA's policy priority was the "Susan B. Anthony amendment" to the Constitution, designed to enfranchise women across the nation in a single stroke. Though Stanton and Anthony did not go out of their way to attract religious leaders, their recruits included Universalist minister Augusta Chapin and Universalist minister's wife Mary Livermore, whose wartime work for the Sanitary Commission gave her national stature.

Stanton and Anthony's passion for suffrage was matched by their disdain for Republicanism, and much of their early organizing focused on building an autonomous constituency. One logical ally was the labor movement. In 1868, suffragists and supporters of an eight-hour day contemplated creating a third party together after being spurned by the Democrats. Stanton and Anthony also reached out to a group of female typesetters who had been hired as strikebreakers and then forced out after the strike was settled. The Working Women's Association pressed for women's full participation in the skilled crafts at a time when moderate reformers emphasized women's need for protection from the dangers of the workforce. But it never built a constituency among women in domestic service and the needle trades, and professional women increasingly pushed out its artisan founders. Then Anthony burned her bridge to organized labor by encouraging employers to train new female typographers during a strike, even though the national union had approved a women's local. The Working Women's Association disintegrated, and female typographers lost the gains they had made.[20]

The NWSA was also caught up in Victoria Woodhull's quixotic attempt to unify all radicals. Woodhull and her sister Tennessee Claflin were entrepreneurial radicals who had grown up in the Spiritualist movement, earned a fortune on Wall Street, and provided spiritual and perhaps sexual services to Cornelius Vanderbilt. At the May 1871 meeting of the NWSA, Woodhull launched a presidential candidacy with a startling platform. "If the very next Congress refuse women all the legitimate results of citizenship," she declared, "we shall . . . frame a new constitution and . . . erect a new government. . . . We mean secession, and on a thousand times grander scale than was that of the South. We are plotting revolution." Like previous radicals, Woodhull defended her treason on patriotic grounds: her anticipated government would honor "the better inspirations of our fathers . . . from which they and their sons have so scandalously departed."[21]

Woodhull gained ambiguous endorsements from the NWSA, the Marxist Workingmen's Association, and the American Association of Spiritualists, which also chose her as its president. As Woodhull's scandalous history and outrageous style became known, all but the Spiritualists repudiated her. She then led three hundred supporters into a new group called the National Radical Reformers. Their platform was one of the most consistently radical ever articulated in the United States, calling for universal access to land, an end to monopolies and charters, government oversight of "all public enterprises," guaranteed employment, graduated taxation, abolition of capital punishment, protection of free expression, government representation for minorities, and full equality for women. "The World our Country, to do Good our Religion," declared the Radical Reformers, as they displayed two biblical texts: "What lack I yet? Jesus said unto him, go sell all thou hast, and give to the poor" and "Neither said any that what he possessed was his own, but they had all things common."[22]

Woodhull's project turned tragic when she decided to agitate the question of free love by attacking the nation's most prominent minister—and AWSA leader—Henry Ward Beecher. Woodhull knew

through the grapevine that Beecher had maintained a long-running affair with the wife of a colleague. Inferring that he privately shared her
free-love sentiments, she hoped to goad him to a public declaration.
Instead he denied the charges. Though the evidence was against him,
Beecher prevailed against a lawsuit, while Woodhull spent Election Day
in jail for violating the Comstock Law. Abandoned by almost everyone
but Stanton—who believed that the scandal had "knocked a great blow
at the priesthood"—Woodhull assumed Fanny Wright's old position as
the image of radical infidelity. Conservatives linked her to new ideas in
politics or religion; radicals of every stripe disavowed her; she retreated
to England; and multi-issue agitation became more difficult.[23]

The suffrage groups were soon dwarfed by a more mainstream advocate of women's rights. The Women's Christian Temperance Union
(WCTU) was organized after women in Ohio launched a "crusade"
to shut down the saloons by sending "praying bands" to confront their
owners directly. As similar campaigns swept the nation, pious middle-
class women had their sensibilities about their own capacity to effect
social change transformed. With hundreds of thousands of members, the
WCTU was described as "the feminine Congress of the United States,"
and its long-serving president, Frances Willard, was the most influential
religious social reformer of the postbellum period. Seeking *"to make the
whole world* homelike," Willard promised to "do everything"—exercise
moral suasion, lobby Congress, and even join the cause of women's
suffrage.[24]

Most WCTU members were far from radical. Their goal was to
protect the traditional family from male misbehavior. But Willard's
expansive vision allowed her to ally simultaneously with conservative
politicians—including those eager to censor sexual material or repeal the
separation of church and state—and with suffragists and labor radicals.
Deploying revivalist rhetoric, she explained that a call from "loftier re-
gions" impelled her to "speak for women's ballot as a weapon" against
the "tyranny of drink." She also joined the Knights of Labor, which
excluded alcohol merchants and manufacturers from its membership,
and identified socialism with "applied Christianity" in the pages of the
WCTU's journal.[25]

The WCTU expanded the religious constituency for women's rights
beyond the abolitionist base. As a friend of revivalist Dwight Moody,
Willard had an emotional style that appealed to Methodists and Baptists,
Northerners and Southerners, whites and blacks. This is not to say that

the Union was monolithically "evangelical." A Methodist, Willard was open to historical criticism and passionate about ecumenical cooperation. On the issues that would later divide "liberals" from "evangelicals," she was decidedly liberal. The "Christian" label in the title did not dissuade old come-outers like Abby Kelley Foster from joining. Unitarian Frances Ellen Watkins Harper served as national superintendent of the black division, and Universalist Mary Livermore was founding president of the Massachusetts chapter. The WCTU was a comfortable place for anyone who did not want theological divisions to prevent the coming of a motherly millennium.

It was not comfortable for those who believed women's liberation required an assault on biblical and clerical authority. Several NWSA leaders were convinced that the Bible was uniquely hostile to women's equality. Against Antoinette Brown's biblical argument for women's ordination, Ernestine Rose had countered that the Bible was too contradictory to be taken as authority on anything. When Willard endorsed a "Christian" amendment to the Constitution, Matilda Joslyn Gage replied that Willard's "magnetic force" made her "the most dangerous person upon the American continent today." Perhaps Gage hoped to shake up the WCTU as Garrison had once undermined the Colonization Society, but the more pragmatic Susan B. Anthony would have none of it. She promptly apologized on behalf of the NWSA.[26]

Elizabeth Cady Stanton took Gage's side. As a child, she had been traumatized by a minister who persuaded her that she was a "monster of iniquity" but could not bring her on to conversion, and she subsequently put her faith in "rational ideas based on scientific facts." She credited William Lloyd Garrison with freeing her from "the darkness and gloom of a false theology" and Auguste Comte with introducing her to the "religion of humanity." With her cousin Elizabeth Miller Smith, Stanton devoted six weeks to Theosophical study in 1883, and she learned about New Thought from Clara Colby, a Nebraskan disciple of Emma Curtis Hopkins who edited the *Woman's Tribune*. But she was most at home with Freethought. She and Gage repeatedly introduced NWSA resolutions describing Christian "self-sacrifice and obedience" as "fatal not only to [woman's] vital interests, but . . . to those of the race," or warning against women's "subjugat[ion] by priestcraft." These in turn provoked a backlash from NWSA members who believed it was "enough to undertake to change the National Constitution without undertaking to change the Bible."[27]

When scholars issued a revised edition of the New Testament that did not challenge its sexism, Stanton launched the project that would become her spiritual legacy—the *Woman's Bible,* published in two volumes in the 1890s. Stanton hoped that her Bible would allow women from across the theological spectrum to demonstrate their capacity as biblical exegetes. But few were willing to risk being tarred with Victoria Woodhull infidelity. Mary Livermore warned that the project would provoke "the mad-dog cry of 'atheist,' 'infidel' and 'reviler of holy things.'" Antoinette Brown Blackwell said that her Greek was too rusty and that her study of scientific grounds for immortality was "a thousand fold more important." Undaunted, Stanton listed both Livermore and Willard as contributors when she announced that her Bible would be serialized in the *Woman's Tribune.* Though her real circle of contributors was not broad enough to include the likes of them, it incorporated Universalists, New Thought practitioners, Spiritualists, and Freethinkers.[28]

All contributors agreed that the surface meaning of the Bible was sexist. But while some accented that point, others offered "esoteric" readings that revealed an androgynous religion of humanity beneath the surface. Where Stanton blasted Sarah for her subservience to Abraham and her harsh treatment of Hagar, for example, Clara Colby argued that Sarah and Hagar were allegorical representations of the choice facing each individual woman: "It is an inspiration for woman to-day to stand for her liberty. The bondswoman must be cast out. All that makes for industrial bondage, for sex slavery and humiliation . . . must be cast out from our home, from society, and from our lives." While the New Thinkers hoped their esoteric readings would empower "men and women [to] clasp hands as comrades with a common destiny," Stanton insisted that no interpretive technique could "twist out of the Old or New Testaments a message of justice, liberty or equality."[29]

The *Woman's Bible* had a long afterlife. Rediscovered by feminists in the 1970s, it was hailed as the founding text of feminist biblical critique. But its immediate effect was to shift power to Susan B. Anthony's cautious secularism. The public response was so negative that Clara Colby backed away from serializing the second volume, forcing Stanton to turn to the Freethinking *Boston Investigator.* People's Church minister Alexander Kent, who hosted the suffragists' 1896 convention, was virtually the only national religious leader to defend the project. Ironically, convention delegates did not share Kent's enthusiasm. Young leaders pushed through a resolution affirming that their association was "non-sectarian, being composed of persons of all shades of religious opinion," and specifically disavowing any "official connection with the so-called 'Woman's Bible,' or any theological publication." Susan B. Anthony was too devoted to free speech to vote yes, but the resolution's proponents were women she had recruited, and they would shape the future of the suffrage movement.[30]

The resolution also passed because it had the support of the AWSA constituency, which had merged with the NWSA in 1890, forming the National American Woman Suffrage Association (NAWSA). Though Stanton held the nominal post of president, Anthony guided the merged organization until a new generation was ready to take the reins. NAWSA was then dominated by the thoroughly pragmatic Carrie Chapman Catt, who steered clear of theological speculation and radical alliances and focused on grassroots organizing at the state level. Pushed to the margins, the most zealous Freethinkers and New Thought proponents organized a series of splinter groups.

Women's radicalism flowered again in the 1910s, the decade in which some radicals began calling themselves "feminists" to signify their desire for a "complete social revolution" in gender roles. Alice Paul, shaped by a Quaker tradition of women's activism and by her participation in the civil disobedience and hunger strikes of the British suffrage movement, reinvigorated work for the Susan B. Anthony amendment, first through NAWSA's Congressional Union and then through the autonomous Woman's Party. Paul gained notoriety by bringing five thousand women demonstrators to Woodrow Wilson's inauguration, and she sustained her agitation through World War I, while other suffragists observed a patriotic silence. Unitarian Marie Jenney Howe, who had first experienced intense women's community as part of the Iowa sisterhood of ministers, re-created it by organizing the Heterodoxy Club after a move to New York. Heterodoxy aspired to help women be "not just our little female selves, but our whole big human selves." Just as Heterodoxy functioned as a feminist church, so Charlotte Perkins Gilman articulated a feminist theology by calling for a woman's religion oriented not to heavenly salvation but to a better life on earth for future generations. For all the richness of this agitation, though, it was Carrie Chapman Catt who counted the votes needed to push the Nineteenth Amendment through Congress. It was ratified in 1920.[31]

———————

Just one of the founding mothers of the suffrage movement lived to see it triumph at the ballot box. Antoinette Brown Blackwell cast her first vote for Warren G. Harding. The choice of a corrupt womanizer who promised to restore American "normalcy" may seem strange for a radical who had pushed the boundaries of theology and politics for nearly a century. Perhaps Blackwell was reluctant to waste her hard-won ballot on a minor-party candidate; perhaps Harding's support for Prohibition tipped the balance in his favor. Whatever the reason, most women voters made the same choice. Though feminist radicals did not disappear, most suffragists refused to support the National Woman's Party's new campaign for an Equal Rights Amendment to the constitution. The movement entered a period of abeyance, all but forgotten even by its allies in the labor movement, who were becoming the center of American radicalism.[32]

CHAPTER 9

The Jesus of Labor

For American workers, the second half of the nineteenth century was a time of struggle. As corporations prospered and expanded, independent artisans became proletarians. Inequality increased during times of economic growth; thousands lost their jobs when the economy contracted. Workers fought back by organizing unions and labor federations, by staging dramatic strikes, and by occasional forays into electoral politics. They also relied on a surprising new ally. Though mainstream religious leaders decried the violence of strikes, labor radicals insisted that the most important religious leader of all was on their side. Had not Jesus himself been a working-class carpenter and a consistent champion of the poor?

This emphasis on Jesus marked a new departure in the theology of labor. Early artisan radicals, whether Freethinking or Protestant, were united by their hostility to established churches. The emperor Constantine, who had merged the Christian church and the Roman state, was to blame for subsequent social evils. That view had little appeal to Roman Catholics or heirs of the Puritan establishment. The new image of Jesus was more congenial to Catholic immigrants and mainline Protestants, yet still accessible to anti-Constantinians and adherents of post-Christian spiritualities. It became a bulwark of a nationwide Populist movement that nearly overturned the conservative rule of the two major parties.

Much credit for the new image of Jesus belongs to George Lippard, a young Philadelphia novelist who introduced the theme in an 1847 book, *Washington and His Generals*. Tracing the roots of the Declaration of Independence, Lippard led his reader to "the rude hut of a Carpenter," where a youth with the "laborer's sweat upon his brow" reflected on "his brothers—the Brotherhood of Toil!" In four thousand years of world history, the boy mused, "never had that Great Army of Mechanics . . . felt the free blood dance in their veins." At that moment, wrote Lippard, Jesus became divine. "The Godhead fill[ed] his veins" and the "Carpenter of Nazareth resolved to redress the wrongs of the poor." In dozens of publications in the final years of his short life, Lippard fleshed out a vision of Jesus as a class-conscious laborer who proclaimed liberty to the captives and judgment to their oppressors.[1]

Lippard was more than a visionary interpreter of Jesus. He was also a muckraking novelist who produced enduring images of urban inequality and a labor organizer whose Brotherhood of the Union provided the template for the Knights of Labor, the century's most important union. Lippard's religious influence can be traced through the rhetoric of labor leaders from Knights leader Terence Powderly, who called Jesus "the world's greatest, most sublime agitator," to Socialist Eugene Debs, who once adorned his prison cell with a portrait of the man he called "the world's supreme revolutionary leader."[2]

The idea that Jesus and his disciples were class-conscious workers was repeated until it came to seem self-evident—an idea that conservative and moderate preachers worked hard to refute. But prior to Lippard, few preachers described Jesus as a workingman, and the religious idea that galvanized worker activism was opposition to the concentrated power of established churches. Lippard himself was a product of this older theological tradition: influenced by Philadelphia Universalism, he described ministers as a "congregation of reptiles" with "microscopic souls." But it was his vivid portrayal of Jesus rather than his anticlericalism that spoke to American workers who loved Jesus more than they feared the church.[3]

By dwelling on the person of Jesus, Lippard participated in a broad cultural transition. Prior to the nineteenth century, American thinking about Jesus was dominated by Christological doctrine. Puritan churches excluded visual images of Jesus, and Protestant preaching downplayed the gospel narratives. But once revivalists began urging Christians to make an emotional connection with the savior, Jesus was on the lips of Transcendentalists and Freethinkers as well as evangelicals. The Jesus figure as a literary motif appeared almost simultaneously in the two antebellum novels that outsold Lippard's *Quaker City*—Harriet Beecher Stowe's *Uncle Tom's Cabin* and T.S. Arthur's *Ten Nights in a Barroom*. And it was at this time that Garrison added Jesus to the *Liberator* masthead.[4]

Lippard's image of Jesus was both patriotic and theologically supple. He cast Jesus as the consummate American radical and insisted that Jefferson's faith that "all men in the sight of God are equal" could be traced to the "Judean mount" where Jesus was crucified. Though Lippard's image of Jesus the worker could fit with either a literalist or a historical critical understanding of biblical authority, it had no direct scriptural basis. The notion that Joseph was a carpenter rested on a single passage (appearing in both Matthew and Mark), in which Jesus' enemies respond to his first sermon by asking derisively, "Is he not the carpenter's son?" Lippard loved that story because it was here also (in Luke's telling) that Jesus quoted the prophet Isaiah as the basis of his own vocation: "The spirit of the Lord is upon me, because he has anointed me to bring glad tidings to the poor . . . to proclaim liberty to captives . . . and to proclaim a year acceptable to the Lord." Just as Garrison had taken this passage as motto for the *Liberator,* so Lippard, at the 1848 Industrial Congress, put Jesus' words on his own lips and declared that "we look for a year, acceptable to God and Man, when the regeneration of the workers . . . shall prepare the way for the spiritual redemption of all mankind."[5]

Lippard's other writings on Jesus relied on a visionary esotericism. In one story Jesus appears as a prematurely aged worker who is given the cold shoulder in a "fashionable church." Transfigured into a "Face shrined in a halo of light," Jesus bestows blessings on the widow, the orphan, the "Black Man" and the "Felon," while the preacher hides behind a "barricade of sound Theological Works." The same "Face" appears in a later work in which George Washington is joined by the "spiritual bodies" of Swedenborg, Fourier, and others who taught "*that Heaven shall begin upon this earth, so that it may go on in the Other World.*" Lippard's invocation of "spiritual bodies" was akin to the teaching of Andrew Jackson Davis, and, for all its animus to traditional Christianity, Davis's journal echoed Lippard's theology in a "discourse by an ex-parson" that described Jesus as "the son of a carpenter" who "worked for a living" and "sought the companionship of humble men."[6]

Lippard borrowed from several esoteric traditions in organizing the Brotherhood of the Union. At one level, the brotherhood was a practically minded mutual-aid society, devoted to "protect[ing] the Man who Toils from the exactions of the Man who is too indolent or too criminal to Work." But Lippard also described it as "combin[ing] all that is beautiful in the ritual of the Rosicrucians with all that is good in Masonry," and crafted for it an elaborate array of symbols and rituals. Like both American and French revolutionaries, Lippard explained, American workers needed a secret society that would allow them to combine resources, avoid reprisals, and clothe their radical vision in "shades of mystery" that would be acceptable to an age that was "not prepared for the full force of the truth."[7]

Lippard's position was not purely pragmatic. He seems genuinely to have believed that his work on behalf of the oppressed expressed a hidden wisdom traceable not only to Jesus, but behind him to the mystery teachers of Egypt. Recalling the perhaps fictional seventeenth-century society devoted to anonymous work for human betterment, Lippard said that the Brotherhood of the Rosy Cross was "the great Fountain Head of all the Secret Societies which now exist." This esoteric genealogy gave Lippard a sense of tradition independent of the ecclesial history he saw as a betrayal of the Carpenter's Son—and he in turn would be incorporated into subsequent Rosicrucian genealogies.[8]

Lippard was not the only radical who sought to organize workers into a secret society venerating the memory of Jesus. In the middle of the 1840s, a Scottish immigrant named Robert MacFarlane created the Mechanics Mutual Protection in Buffalo, which spread to fifty other cities. His practical program was more moderate than Lippard's: he declared that "we do not war against wealth" and preferred worker-education programs to strikes. (Fittingly, he would later edit *Scientific American*.) But like Lippard, he believed that "a Secret Society above all other is the most powerful for good or evil," and used Masonic terms such as "our sacred Edifice" and "our Cornerstone" to describe his "Order." MacFarlane claimed the Ten Commandments as the "working man's *charter of rights*," and held that mechanics were "elevated" by the Incarnation. "The Son of God," he explained, "labored as a common mechanic, and selected his disciples from among the fishermen of Galilee, who . . . earned their livelihood by their own industry."[9]

Other labor radicals harnessed additional forms of religious enthusiasm. In the mid-1850s in Philadelphia, John Sidney Jones and Fannie Lee Townsend, Progressive Friends who owned a carpet factory, gathered the Jubilee Association of the Daughters and Sons of Toil at a grove where they preached about a Jesus whose millennial return would help them enact the biblical jubilee. Hundreds of textile workers joined their cooperative enterprises, reading room, and militia, and they cited biblical texts in favor of everything from land reform and women's rights to bathing and long beards. When Thomas Paine's birthday came around, they offered prayer to "the same God that sent Moses into the world, that sent Jesus Christ the Savior of mankind into the world, that sent Thomas Paine into the world."[10]

Changes in American labor accelerated after the Civil War. The expansive logic of manifest destiny planted stockyards in Chicago, mines in the Rockies, and railroads everywhere. By 1900, 40 million Americans were wageworkers or members of working-class families, and two-thirds of those workers were immigrants or children of immigrants, mostly from southern and eastern Europe. As the religious mix of American workers shifted from revivalism and Freethought to Roman Catholicism and Judaism, Lippard's Jesus-centered faith remained alive.

The heritage of the abolitionists was also alive in a new agitation for an eight-hour day that emanated from New England during the Civil War. Leaders who had absorbed abolitionist fervor in childhood insisted that eight hours was not "a panacea" but a "first measure" toward broader change. William Lloyd Garrison signed on to the cause, explaining that his abolitionism made him sympathetic with "all overtasked working classes," while Wendell Phillips declared that "the next question for our country" was "the rights of the laboring class." Local trade unions came together in the National Labor Union (NLU), a coalition that also included unskilled workers and farmers, though it relegated African Americans to a separate organization. The NLU successfully persuaded Congress to establish an eight-hour day for government workers, then collapsed after its members rejected a turn toward third-party politics.[11]

Out of the eight-hour agitation emerged a specifically religious labor organization. The Christian Labor Union brought together Congregationalist minister Jesse Jones and shipbuilder Edward Rogers, who as a young man had been denied membership in a Congregationalist church because of his opposition to Calvinism. Elected to the state legislature in the wake of the shipyard strike, Rogers was a lay preacher in Methodist churches who eventually joined an explicitly Christian socialist congregation. Another leader was Roman Catholic T. Wharton Collens, a judge in New Orleans who blended the Thomistic philosophy of the common good with Fourierist and Owenite ideas. His influence helps explain the breadth of ideas represented by the union: in 1878 its newspaper published a papal letter alongside the platform of the Marxist Socialist Labor Party (SLP), with laudatory editorial comments about both. The paper also popularized "Eight Hours," perhaps the most popular labor hymn prior to "Solidarity Forever." This anthem featured a stirring chorus that summed up the immediate demand—"Eight hours for work, eight hours for rest, eight hours for what we will"—and verses that explained, "We mean to make things over," because "we are sure that God has willed it."[12]

Even as New Englanders were rooting labor radicalism in the abolitionist heritage, German refugees from the 1848 revolution organized a succession of small parties influenced by Marxism and anarchism, among them the Workingmen's Party of 1876 and its more enduring successor, the Socialist Labor Party. Apart from Victoria Woodhull's idiosyncratic section 12 of the Workingmen, explicit religious appeals rarely entered these parties' vocabulary. But the California Workingmen, who were not formally affiliated with the national party, found a surprising champion in Baptist minister Isaac S. Kalloch, who had served Boston's Tremont Temple until a sensational adultery trial sent him west. His Metropolitan Temple in San Francisco claimed to be the largest Baptist congregation in the country. Kalloch charged a dime for admission rather than taking a collection and made the hall available for public speeches by local radicals. Recruited by the Workingmen as a mayoral candidate, Kalloch was shot and injured by a rival, and the resulting sympathy vote propelled him into office. Further scandal ensued when Kalloch's son shot and killed the assailant. Incidents like this help explain why the Workingmen struggled to build an effective national movement.[13]

The National Labor Union and Workingmen's Party did less to attract Catholic immigrants than the Noble and Holy Order of the Knights of Labor. Organized by Philadelphia garment cutters in 1869, the Knights had several leaders who had been part of Lippard's brotherhood, and it was initially organized as a secret society. Some "local assemblies" resembled traditional craft unions while others united workers in a particular industry or of a particular ethnicity—creating space for new encounters among machinists, blacksmiths, and common laborers, all of whom might speak or sing or even dance at the local assemblies. The Knights began to grow after the Panic of 1873, when hard economic times broke local craft unions and forced workers to turn to the Knights as an alternative.[14]

In 1877 the Great Railway Strike swept across the nation. Responding to a deflationary economy, the major railroads tried to safeguard their profits by coordinating a reduction in wages. Soon more than one hundred thousand workers from coast to coast joined the first nationwide labor action. The Knights, who were ambivalent about strikes, had not initiated this, but they avidly recruited strikers hungry for a long-term social change strategy. They also ventured tentatively into politics, following the lead of Terence Powderly, a Catholic machinist who was elected mayor of Scranton, Pennsylvania.

Even before his election as "Grand Master Workman," Powderly had helped purge anti-Catholics from the Knights and persuaded his predecessor to soften practices of secrecy that provoked the opposition of local priests. Much as he despised prejudice, though, Powderly shared the worldview of his liberal Protestant allies. He had been a Republican before embracing third-party radicalism, was a lifelong temperance man (a fact that made it easier for Frances Willard to cast her lot with the Knights), and eventually joined the Freemasons. Most importantly, his spirituality centered on Jesus rather than the institutional church. Contrasting Jesus with respectable ministers and priests, Powderly wrote that "Christ taught humility. . . . He walked among the poor. He denounced the unjust rich. He took the side of the laborer in the unequal struggle of life." This devotion to Jesus united the old radical constituency and the new immigrant working class.[15]

Powderly's bridging spirituality was shared by his friend Mother Jones, a Knights' organizer in the 1870s who remained at the forefront of the labor movement for nearly a half century. Like Powderly, Jones was an Irish Catholic; her family had fled to North America as a result of her grandfather's role in the Irish freedom struggle. She poured her soul into the labor movement after losing her union-member husband and children to yellow fever. Sent by the Knights to Pittsburgh during the railway strike, she made the mine workers of western Pennsylvania her surrogate children. On one occasion, she persuaded miners' wives to chase strikebreakers out with mops and brooms; on another, she led a march of working children to the vacation home of the president. Her model for agitation, she said, was the man who "agitated against the powers of Rome, against the lickspittle Jews of the local pie counter; he agitated for the Kingdom of God!"[16]

The Knights' influence peaked in March 1886, when Powderly committed the national organization to a massive strike against rail baron Jay Gould. The strike fanned out from Marshall, Texas, where a local Knight had been fired for attending a union meeting, to encompass two hundred thousand workers nationwide. Facing Gould's unscrupulous use of strikebreakers and Texas Rangers, some strikers resorted to retaliatory violence, which alienated segments of the broader public.

Weeks later, a bomb was thrown during a rally organized by anarchists at Chicago's Haymarket Square. The mostly foreign-born organizers were condemned and executed on scanty evidence, and the mainstream press fanned the flames of antilabor sentiment. By the end of the year, the Knights' vision of a broad labor alliance was widely discredited, particularly among skilled workers, who preferred more narrowly focused organizing. Samuel Gompers's American Federation of Labor (AFL) recruited those workers and embraced a cautious secularism that shunned both anticlericalism and fervent appeals to Jesus.

The Knights had, in the meantime, gained the support of some mainstream religious leaders. Powderly reached out to Roman Catholic bishops who wanted to support their parishioners' material needs, but could not ignore church teaching against secret societies. Official Catholicism saw these as rivals to its own authority, and was bitterly hostile to free love and to the liberal revolutionary movements that had deprived the popes of political authority in central Italy. But Catholicism had little stake in laissez-faire capitalism, which violated Saint Thomas's teaching that private property rights were subordinate to the common good. Powderly worked with James Cardinal Gibbons to persuade Pope Leo XIII that the Knights were neither antifamily nor a true secret society, but a reform organization devoted to the common good. Soon thereafter Leo articulated Catholicism's critique of both capitalism and socialism in the 1891 encyclical that inaugurated the modern tradition of Catholic social teaching. Drawing on nostalgia for medieval guilds and a view of the family as the basic building block of society, *Rerum Novarum* endorsed labor unions and insisted that workers be paid enough to sustain their own lives and the lives of their families.[17]

Protestant leaders were slower to embrace this position. Henry Ward Beecher, once an antislavery radical, took a mostly negative stance during the railway strike of 1877. In a sermon that was widely quoted and (from Beecher's perspective) widely misunderstood, he claimed that the rail unions had been infected by a "foreign" and "poisonous" "virus," and described one dollar a day as a family wage. "Is not a dollar a day enough to buy bread with? Water costs nothing, and a man who cannot live on bread is not fit to live." Inundated with complaints, Beecher protested that he had meant only that a dollar a day was an acceptable wage in a time of economic emergency. But the contrast between his comments and his lavish lifestyle solidified a perception that the churches were hostile to the working-class struggle.[18]

By 1886 another heir of the abolitionists was preaching a different message. During his early pastorates, Congregationalist Washington Gladden noticed the wariness workers felt toward the church. From testimony collected from potential congregants, he learned that they stayed away both because they could not measure up to the churches' "fashionable" standards and because they resented the capitalists who dominated urban congregations. "It is because the workingman is not receiving a fair compensation for his labor, that he cannot dress his wife and children well enough to go to church." Such testimony persuaded Gladden that since the capitalists had started the class war, "we must grant to labor belligerent rights." He put himself forward as a strike mediator, though he saw profit sharing, cooperatives, and eight-hour legislation as better strategies for social change. Steering clear of socialism, Gladden taught emphatically that "the wage-system, when it rests on competition as its sole basis, is anti-social and anti-Christian."[19]

Gladden's views were shaped by another middle-class reformer. Journalist Henry George first observed urban poverty when he visited New York City in the 1860s, and he spent the next decade pondering how increasing deprivation could coexist with rapid industrial growth. George saw this as a matter of theodicy: a good God would not want the world's riches to be inequitably distributed. On this basis, George rejected the prevailing economic orthodoxy that a fixed "wage fund" kept employers from raising wages. Preaching at Isaac Kalloch's Metropolitan Temple, he made the point in prophetic cadences: "Shall the millstones of greed forever grind the faces of the poor? Ladies and gentlemen, it is not in the order of the universe!" George's best-selling *Progress and Poverty* proposed that a "single tax" on land would eliminate the problem of concentrated wealth. Relatively few radicals accepted this panacea, but the clarity with which George expressed the underlying problem propelled him to national prominence and nearly earned him the office of New York mayor. It attracted the support of such eclectic radicals as Father Edward McGlynn, who explained to his parishioners that Jesus was "an evicted peasant" who "came to preach a gospel of liberty to the slave, of justice to the poor, of paying the full hire to the workman."[20]

Jesus' endorsement helped men like George, Gladden, and Powderly bridge the divides separating radicals from liberals, workers from middle-class reformers, and immigrants from native-born Protestants. To transform national politics, they needed the support of yet another constituency. Farmers in the South and Midwest also suffered during times of depression, and they blamed federal efforts to restore the gold standard and eliminate the paper currency, or "greenbacks," that had been issued during the Civil War. The resulting tight credit hurt farmers, and they organized several small parties in response. One was part of the coalition that elected Powderly as mayor of Scranton, and it gradually coalesced with others in a National Alliance of two and a half million members.

The National Alliance became the most important constituent of the new People's, or Populist, Party organized in 1892. At the founding convention, rebellious farmers joined with single-taxers and socialists, Knights of Labor and AFLers, Terence Powderly and Frances Willard to endorse the "Declaration of Union and Industrial Independence," which struck a defiant tone. "We meet in the midst of a nation brought to the verge of moral, political, and material ruin." A "vast conspiracy against mankind" threatened farmers and workers, while the two major parties were engrossed in a "sham battle" over tariffs. Only a third party could help the "plain people" regain control of the government. This declaration's author, Ignatius Donnelly, embodied the eclectic religiosity of the movement. A Catholic novelist, he was also a student of esoteric wisdom whose first book had traced the descent of all civilizations from Atlantis. Most importantly, Donnelly was a disciple of Jesus the radical. "Jesus," he insisted, "was only possible in a barefoot world, and he was crucified by the few who wore shoes."[21]

The Populists gained a million votes and carried four western states in 1892, then sent thirteen candidates to Congress in 1894. They inspired such radical mobilizations as "Coxey's Army," a great march of unemployed Ohioans to Washington, D.C., where they called for government jobs for those without work. Leader Jacob Coxey, who would soon run for the governorship of Ohio, predicted that the march would "either mark the second coming of Christ or be a total failure." But not all Populists were radicals in the full sense. Many of their successful candidates were elected through fusion, or joint nomination, with the Republicans or Democrats. Grassroots Populists responded to an immediate threat to their well-being but did not seek an ideologically consistent reordering of society. The hostility that white farmers directed toward eastern bankers could as easily be channeled against their black neighbors. The Populists' strongest religious constituency, moreover, was not with eclectics like Donnelly but among rural revivalists who preferred the authority of the Bible to that of formal creeds. Appeals to Jesus the worker spoke to these Christians—but so might reactionary forms of piety.[22]

The revivalists' champion was William Jennings Bryan, the "Great Commoner" who was nominated for the presidency in 1896 through fusion with the Democrats. Bryan crisscrossed the country making speeches that reflected his revivalist upbringing. His riveting speech at the Democratic Convention linked workers and farmers to Jesus. "You shall not press down upon the brow of labor this crown of thorns, you shall not crucify mankind upon a cross of gold," he warned, and then personally assumed the posture of Jesus on the Cross. As these words hinted, Bryan was less interested in a radical critique of capitalism than in the panacea of "free silver": by abolishing the gold standard and producing silver coinage, he hoped to induce inflation and relieve rural debtors. Bryan's narrow defeat soured most radicals on the fusion principle and caused the party to collapse.[23]

From the shattering of Populism emerged two great currents of grassroots politics in the twentieth century. Those who were dismayed by Bryan's betrayal of a broad radical agenda came together four years later to build the Socialist Party into one of the most comprehensively radical mass movements in U.S. history. Those loyal to Bryan's piety coalesced more gradually in response to what they saw as elite attacks on true Christianity. Mobilized against historical criticism in the churches and Darwinism in the schools, these populists embraced fundamentalism, broke with the mainline churches, and withdrew from political engagement—until, two generations later, some of their grandchildren forged an alliance with the pro-business, anti-Communist Republicanism of Ronald Reagan. This surprising outcome was due in no small part to the fact that Bryan's admirers eventually rejected not only eastern bankers but also educated Social Gospelers, who taught that Christian salvation was as much social as individual. Less distrustful of centralized authority and more willing to harness state and denominational power to the cause of justice than the revivalists, Social Gospelers would gradually bring the mainline churches into dialogue with socialism, and thus write a new chapter in the history of religious radicalism.

CHAPTER 10

Encountering the City

Between 1870 and 1890, mainstream Americans discovered the city. "The city," declared Rev. Josiah Strong, was both the "nerve center" and the "storm center" of civilization. Its rise, he felt, gave the nineteenth century a historical significance second only to the era of Christ's birth. As more than half a million immigrants arrived each year, causing Chicago and other cities to double their populations, Strong argued that the world's fate hinged on Americans' capacity to face the perils of immigration, "Romanism," Mormonism, intemperance, socialism, and wealth, most of them "focalized" in urban areas. In the city, Strong observed, "Dives and Lazarus are brought face to face. . . . The rich are richer, and the poor are poorer, in the city."[1]

The meeting of Dives and Lazarus made possible a new sort of transformative encounter. For nearly a century members of oppressed communities had forged new identities by encountering one another. For almost as long persons of relative privilege had been inspired by personal encounters with the oppressed. Now, middle-class reformers were more likely to be converted by meeting a whole neighborhood than by a direct connection with a Frederick Douglass or Sojourner Truth. As agricultural villages and small cities faded, so did a religious culture centered on conversions that took place one at a time. The new "collective encounters" generated a new theology of social rather than individual salvation. They inspired settlement houses, institutional churches, denominational social justice agencies, and a new ecumenical movement. Collective encounters prepared the way for a more positive relationship between major American denominations and American radicalism.

This was not inevitable, for Strong's account of the urban threat was ambiguous. Was it the social structure of the city that challenged American ideals, or its residents? Was poverty the problem, or poor people? Could middle-class Protestants recognize the new urban working class as sisters and brothers who were being excluded, unfairly, from the American dream? Strong's rehearsal of statistics about urban growth could not answer such questions. But when a few intrepid souls set out to meet their neighbors, the nascent Social Gospel began to turn to the left.

Charles Sheldon was one of the first. In 1889, three years out of Andover Seminary, he was called to launch a new congregation in a growing neighborhood of Topeka. The son and nephew of frontier ministers, Sheldon brought a familiarity with the Great Plains, a reforming sensibility, and an extroverted pastoral style. Central Congregational Church was an offshoot of a congregation founded by abolitionists, and it was close to Topeka's largest African American neighborhood. Social idealism was sufficiently strong that Sheldon felt safe to preach "a Christ for the common people . . . whose religion does not consist alone in cushioned seats, and comfortable surroundings . . . but a Christ who bids us all recognize the Brotherhood of the race, who bids throw open this room to all."[2]

Sheldon was radicalized by his first winter in Topeka, when a weak agricultural economy threw hundreds out of work during unusually cold weather. Unable to secure employment for a man who had knocked on his door, Sheldon felt compelled to experience the man's plight for himself. Walking "from coal yards to flouring mills and elevators and shoe shops" in his oldest clothes, Sheldon found no work and plenty of other disappointed job seekers. As he entered imaginatively into his experiment, Sheldon felt such a "hunger for work" that he volunteered to shovel railroad tracks for free. "Just to be in the company of human beings who were working," he mused, "added to my self-respect which I had been losing for four days and a half because no one in the wide world needed me."[3]

Sheldon's next step was to spend one week with each of several occupational or demographic groups. After encountering streetcar operators and college students, he turned to the black community of Tennesseetown. This encounter swelled to three weeks as he met job seekers, students, and community leaders. He was pleased to learn that a local restaurant did not segregate, but chagrined that a new black friend could not join the Young Men's Christian Association (YMCA). Time with other groups solidified Sheldon's sense of "the horrible blunder and stupidity of our whole industrial system that does not work according to any well-established plan of a Brotherhood of men." Soon Sheldon incorporated his congregation into participant observation, asking the youth to research social problems and then incorporating their findings into his sermons. He founded one kindergarten at his church building and another in Tennesseetown and attracted a growing, somewhat racially integrated congregation. But all of Sheldon's ministries were overshadowed by the success of his first novel.[4]

First preached, then serialized, then published as a book in 1897, *In His Steps* fictionalized Sheldon's experience in Topeka. In an opening scene that echoed one of George Lippard's stories, an unemployed man interrupts a church service with a hard-luck story. After his wife and daughter had died in an airless tenement, he had come west looking for work, but found nothing but tepid sympathy from the church. "What is meant," he asks plaintively, "by following Jesus? . . . Somehow I get puzzled when I see so many Christians living in luxury. . . . I don't expect you people can prevent everyone from dying of starvation, lack of proper nourishment and tenement air, but what does following Jesus mean?" The man then collapses and dies, inspiring the minister to organize a club for all those who are willing to use the question "What would Jesus do?" as a guide for personal decisions. A newspaper editor stops publishing tobacco ads; a young woman forgoes an operatic career to minister among alcoholics. By the book's end, the congregants have transformed their small city and made a fair start at achieving the millennial renewal of metropolitan Chicago.[5]

In His Steps sold 8 million copies and inspired both moderate and radical imitators, most notably Upton Sinclair's vehemently anticlerical *They Call Me Carpenter*. But it obscured the extent of Sheldon's own radicalism. Sheldon was a prohibitionist and socialist who believed that the government should provide jobs directly for the unemployed. But a casual reader of his book might conclude that a hymn sung by a beautiful young woman—or else the sacrificial death of a Christlike worker—is all that is needed to cure poverty. Sheldon lacked the sensitivity to see how sentimental rhetoric undermined his message of structural change; and his language could be paternalistic, as when he praised his church's white youth for "the perfect abandon with which they invaded that black territory [of Tennesseetown] and reclaimed it." For all his moral earnestness, Sheldon's work was marked by a complacency rooted in personal privilege. His life story lacked the dramatic upheavals and abrupt conversions that might seem to be the mark of true radicalism.[6]

Yet activists with very different biographies also experienced collective encounters with urban poverty in the 1890s. Born in Northern Ireland to an alcoholic mother and a father who had lost his job as shoemaker, Alexander Irvine recalled that "the world in which I first found myself was a world of hungry people." His evangelical conversion—at least as he remembered the story—had less to do with Jesus than with a budding sense of class consciousness: immediately after accepting Jesus, he "realized for the first time in my life that I had never slept in a bed, but on a pallet of straw." Eager to share his new consciousness, Irvine converted a "drunken stone mason" whose "family, relatives, and friends had all given him up." Their experience of organizing a temperance society convinced Irvine to pursue a "religious life." This aspiration propelled him to the British Navy, where he excelled as both a boxer and an evangelist, to the Plymouth Brethren, and eventually to a ministry among single men in New York's Bowery.[7]

Despite Irvine's background, he learned the meaning of urban poverty the same way Sheldon had. Preaching in a bunkhouse, he challenged the men who lived there: "I cannot help telling you of my conviction: that most of you are here because you are lazy. Now, if any man in the house is willing to test the case, I will change clothes with him to-morrow morning and show him how to find work." An Irish immigrant, Tim, accepted the challenge, and soon they made the rounds of piano and soap factories on the West Side and stevedores on the East, all to no avail. Like Sheldon, Irvine was soon overcome by a desire to work at any price. He sweet-talked store owners into giving him rags and oxalic acid on credit, and then cleaned business signs for ten cents each—"thirty cents below the regular price." A day's labor gained a dollar and a half for the two men, which satisfied Irvine until his companion protested that most unemployed men lacked the "brains" to come up with such an ingenious scheme. As he continued to listen to men like Tim, Irvine grasped that drinking was more often a symptom than a cause of poverty, and that chronic unemployment was psychologically devastating. With each job loss, he noted, a worker "loses just a little of the routine, the continuity, the habit of work," and the experience of receiving charity was equally "disorganizing."[8]

The insight propelled Irvine from one innovative ministry to the next. In every place, he engaged directly with the poorest of the poor. He traveled to Boston dressed as a homeless person to test the exaggerated claims made for a new boardinghouse there. Called to a church in the Mississippi River valley, he settled in a shantytown occupied by fifteen hundred people along the riverbank. In New Haven, he attended union meetings to invite "you craftsmen of New Haven to stand and with all the power of your lungs give three cheers for the Master Craftsman of Galilee." He even arranged to spend time as a convict laborer.[9]

Irvine's encounters radicalized him and led him to the Socialist Party. But they also traumatized him. Perhaps because he lacked Sheldon's self-regard, he was never quite sure his pastoral work measured up to his ideals. After many years in mission churches, he concluded that if he were himself a workingman he would resent such churches "for . . . the assumption that people are poor and degraded through laxity in morals." He lost several pastorates for his outspoken radicalism, and on one occasion withdrew his candidacy at a congregation as penance for having tried too hard to impress the parishioners. Chronic depression nearly drove him to suicide. His quixotic idealism also led him, despite his personal pacifism, to serve as a chaplain during World War I in order to identify fully with the suffering of the soldiers.[10]

Collective encounters also brought Northern black ministers into deeper contact with the Southern migrants who fled segregation and violence during the early decades of the twentieth century. A leader among these ministers, Reverdy Ransom was raised in a small black community in a Quaker area of Ohio. As a child, Ransom was pushed by his loving mother to emulate the white people for whom she worked. Sometimes derided as a "white folks' nigger," young Reverdy "was ever trying to explain and reconcile [the white] world to the one in which I lived." Ransom studied at historically black Wilberforce College, transferred to Oberlin for its rigorous curriculum, then returned to Wilberforce after losing his scholarship because he had protested Oberlin's racially segregated dining for female students. After experiencing a call to ministry in the African Methodist Episcopal (AME) Church, he was sent to the waterfront district of Allegheny City, Pennsylvania, near Pittsburgh.[11]

Here Ransom met a new sort of poverty. His five-member congregation worshipped "in a reeking, alley-like street, in a small room containing three benches and some chairs." As far as Ransom could see, "there was nothing there," and he asked his bishop and mentor, the highly cultivated Daniel Payne, to reassign him. "He stamped his foot," recalled Ransom later, "and shaking his trembling fingers at me said, 'Begone! Leave my presence! There are people there.'" And so, accompanied by his second wife, Ransom walked daily through the neighborhood, ascending dark stairways to reach the tenements and treading on flimsy planks in order to reach the shanty boats where hundreds lived. He moved his new family into a "dilapidated old house," converted a paint shop into a chapel, and watched as his congregation swelled with the influx of Southern blacks. Ransom's holistic approach to ministry occasionally led to conflict with lay leaders. When the unmarried organist became pregnant, Ransom had to stand against those who wished to expel her. He insisted, "Now that she is in this trouble and disgrace, she needs us. We must not cast her out."[12]

The Methodist discipline calls for a frequent rotation of pastorates, and when Ransom was sent to Chicago he launched a new model of congregation. Choosing a neighborhood of Southern migrants, he and his wife tried to meet the whole community's "religious, moral, and social" needs. The Men's Sunday Club introduced stockyard workers to the city's black leaders, while his wife's boys' club incorporated neighborhood children into her parenting. "For an hour each evening I always read to my younger son," she told a reporter, "and the first night I did so in our new home a number of little fellows in the neighborhood came in to see what the 'new boy' was like. I was reading 'Little Men' to my son, and he asked the other little chaps to remain. . . . From that night the boys' club was not only an established fact, but a successful one." Ransom also launched a political campaign to unseat an alderman who had failed to get the street in front of the church paved.[13]

The Ransoms expanded these practices at their Institutional Church, an early example of a congregational type that was proliferating across the nation. Offering space for classes, activities, and forums, institutional churches aspired to serve entire neighborhoods without regard to church membership. From this post, Ransom intervened in a 1902 stockyard strike, during which striking white workers had assaulted African American strikebreakers. Ransom confronted strike leaders, pointing out that the African Americans also "had families to support" but would be happy to join the union if permitted. This intervention soon settled the strike. Ransom's subsequent campaign to end police collusion with the "policy swindle" resulted in the dynamiting of his church, but also in a memorable encounter with a black racketeer who told Ransom that he was "proud to see the day when one of my race is standing up like some of these big white preachers do."[14]

Ransom took his vision of holistic, socially engaged ministry to subsequent pastorates in Boston and New York, to his service as the editor of the *AME Church Review,* and to his tenure as an AME bishop. An early ally of W. E. B. Du Bois's in the quest for full civil rights for African Americans, Ransom and his fiery preaching helped inspire the founding of the National Association for the Advancement of Colored People (NAACP). But as black denominations tilted away from social activism, Ransom never managed to sway the AME to an unequivocal embrace of the NAACP, much less of a more wide-ranging radicalism.

Sheldon, Irvine, and Ransom all began encountering urban poverty between 1888 and 1890. These were fruitful years for collective encounters. The new discipline of sociology, which relied heavily on participant observation in urban contexts, was founded in these years, as the University of Kansas offered the first collegiate course and Harvard, Andover, and Hartford seminaries all pioneered courses on "Christian sociology." The depression that began in 1893 made urban encounters even more important, and led countless people of faith into "settlement houses" of the sort pioneered by Jane Addams's Hull House in 1889.

Like Sheldon, Addams came from a comfortable family with a reforming heritage, and she venerated her Quaker father for his quiet devotion to principle. Since there was no Quaker meeting in their Illinois village, she attended a Presbyterian Sunday school; when she asked her father about the doctrines taught there, he replied that "he feared that he and I did not have the kind of mind that would ever understand foreordination very well." Though she did eventually join the Presbyterians, her most abiding religious convictions reflected her father's admiration for Lincoln and Mazzini. The great Roman revolutionary died in 1872, when Addams was twelve, and observing her father's sorrow instilled in her "a sense of the genuine relationship which may exist between men who share large hopes and like desires." Lincoln was for her likewise a symbol of democracy, "the most valuable contribution America has made to the moral life of the world."[15]

As a young adult, Addams gradually overcame the "snare of preparation" that led her to study and travel without putting her ideals into action. In London's East End, the sight of the "empty, pathetic, nerveless, and workworn" hands of hungry slum dwellers instilled in her a hunger for collective encounter. She resolved to create a cooperative household where city dwellers and "young women who had been given over too exclusively to study" might "learn of life from life itself." After a visit to London's Toynbee Hall, created on similar principles, she and her travel companion, Ellen Gates Starr, launched Hull House.[16]

Though Hull House was the most influential settlement house in the United States, it was not quite the first. Ethical Culture leader Stanton Coit led the way with New York's Neighborhood Guild in 1886. A year later Vida Scudder, an English professor at Wellesley who had been influenced by British Christian Socialism, organized the College Settlement Association among students and faculty at elite women's colleges; they established their first house not far from Neighborhood Guild. A hundred additional settlements followed by the end of the century, and three hundred more in the next decade. Local congregations, such as Calvary Episcopal in Pittsburgh, organized settlements, as did Andover and Chicago seminaries. Taken as a whole, the movement had an intense, and interfaith, religiosity. About half of settlement workers were Presbyterian or Congregationalist. Episcopalians and Unitarians were also overrepresented in the movement, and twenty-four settlements were explicitly Jewish. The tiny Ethical Culture movement sponsored its own settlements, and was closely associated with both Hull House and the most notable settlement in New York City, Henry Street. Like many Ethical Culturists, Henry Street founder Lillian Wald was a German Jew who cherished the prophetic, but not the ritual or doctrinal, aspects of her inherited faith. The settlement house movement was a springboard for interfaith cooperation on such issues as public health, racial justice, and clean city government.[17]

It was also a springboard for radicalism. Though the movement's commitment to "scientific charity" spawned the new professions of social work and public health nursing, movement leaders always recognized that charity was hollow without justice. This was so because of the transformative dynamism of collective encounter. Before volunteers could minister to their neighbors' needs, they had to meet those neighbors and receive *their* hospitality. "Constantly impressed with the kindness and courtesy we received" from the poor, Jane Addams insisted that settlement houses would not succeed unless their staff truly enjoyed city life and were convinced "that the things which make men alike are finer and better than the things that keep them apart." Similar revelations were available to the hundreds of idealistic college graduates who passed through settlement houses in the decades that followed. Many were persuaded by Vida Scudder to express their solidarity with the poor by joining the Socialist Party; others followed the example of Jane Addams and Lillian Wald, who were instrumental in forging pragmatic alliances between the socialists and "new liberals" who were open to government action on behalf of the poor. For the next century, the settlement impulse would be revived by deaconess communities, Catholic Worker houses, urban ashrams, and volunteer corps— all recruiting grounds for radicals.[18]

Just as settlement houses drew individuals into a revelatory experience of encounter, so institutional churches made encounter possible for whole congregations. The movement in which Reverdy Ransom's church participated had a handful of antebellum precedents, but it took its name from Andover Seminary professor William Jewett Tucker, who publicized a club for workingmen he had created at New York's Madison Avenue Presbyterian Church. Episcopalian William Stephen Rainsford transformed Saint George's, a declining parish in New York City, into an institutional church by abolishing pew rents and persuading financier J. P. Morgan to fund clubs for boys and girls, a gymnasium, a trade school, and even a cadet battalion. Not to be outdone, Cornelius Vanderbilt helped Saint Bartholomew's build an even more expansive facility. The Baptist Temple in Philadelphia spawned a university. By 1894 a national network of congregations had organized themselves as the Open and Institutional Church League, which aspired to save "all men and all of the man by all means, abolishing so far as possible the distinction between the religious and secular, and sanctifying all days and all means to the great end of saving the world for Christ." Even the nation's wealthiest men were funding experiments that could not help but radicalize some of their participants.[19]

But even as white reformers embraced radical approaches to urban poverty, many lost interest in the cause of racial justice that had motivated their abolitionist forebears. During the 1890s African Americans confronted a level of repression not seen since before the Civil War. Voting rights were stripped away with literacy tests, poll taxes, and intimidation, and as many as 150 African Americans were lynched each year. Often taking "Anglo-Saxon" supremacy for granted, many whites shared Booker T. Washington's sense that radical change was not needed: training for manual labor would gradually equip African Americans for full citizenship without requiring any changes in the white power structure. Some reformers tried to work *for* African Americans without actually encountering them—as was the case at a conference on "the Negro question" that included no Negroes. Few agreed with the participant who insisted that the "race problem" was really about "the hate, the oppression, the injustice . . . on our side."[20]

Encounter failed when antilynching agitator Ida B. Wells-Barnett attempted to draw Frances Willard into her cause. Beginning in 1890, Wells-Barnett faulted Willard for tolerating segregation in some units of the WCTU and for her persistent assumption that lynching victims really had committed "unspeakable outrages" against white women. Many lynchings had nothing to do with sex, argued Wells-Barnett, while others occurred after a white woman had initiated a consensual liaison. Offended, Willard complained of Wells-Barnett's "percussive" personality to other activists. Wells-Barnett's attack on Willard was a classic case of agitation, comparable to Garrison's critique of colonization, and it had the positive effect of shaming Willard into speaking out more clearly against lynching. But the alienation between women's rights advocates and anti-racists, which dated back to the Fourteenth and Fifteenth amendments, was reinforced.[21]

A more constructive series of encounters was initiated by Mary White Ovington, an heir of the abolitionists whose grandmother had attended the same Connecticut Unitarian congregation as William Lloyd Garrison's in-laws. As head resident of the Greenpoint Settlement in New York City, she learned to see the poor as full human beings. "When I heard the whistle blow at seven in the morning, as I lay in bed, it was not an indefinite person but Mary or Amanda or Celia, who was going to do rough work for ten and a half hours." Such experiences made her a socialist. Though she was "more revolutionary than the workers with whom I came in contact," the socialism of the time taught that professionals could play only a peripheral role in the workers' struggle, and so she turned to the abolitionists' unfinished work of racial reconciliation.[22]

Ovington's new goal was to launch a settlement for African Americans that "would not only help the poor but . . . be an excellent meeting-place for the well-to-do of each race." The grandchildren of abolitionists, she realized, no longer knew their black brothers and sisters. So she apprenticed herself to her African American neighbors, including businessmen and slum dwellers, as well as partisans of the conservative Booker T. Washington and the radical W. E. B. Du Bois. These teachers were "unendingly kind," enriching Ovington's life as they empowered her for her work. A local pastor even broke down Ovington's prejudice against the evangelical style by welcoming suffragists to his church and making "the best speech of any."[23]

Settlement work among African Americans led Ovington to help organize the National Association for the Advancement of Colored People in 1910. The mostly white activists who signed the initial call for the organization were drawn largely from settlement house networks in New York and Chicago. They included radical Unitarian ministers, Ethical Culture leaders and Reform rabbis in both cities, Protestant ministers with ties to Union Theological Seminary, and both Jane Addams and Lillian Wald. William Lloyd Garrison's grandson and Elizabeth Cady Stanton's daughter were also among the founders. But the vision came from those African American leaders who had stepped beyond Booker T. Washington's gradualism to insist on immediate and complete equality. Above all, it came from W. E. B. Du Bois.

Du Bois's work on behalf of his people was the fruit of collective encounters. Raised among white neighbors in western Massachusetts, Du Bois had chafed at his schoolmates' racism but possessed little insight into the Southern black community until he commenced undergraduate studies at Fisk University in Nashville. Visiting nearby congregations, Du Bois came to understand the black church both as the social center of the black community, functioning as school and club and employment bureau, and as a place of "awful" spiritual power, where "the tragic soul life of the slave" was transmuted into faith and hope. Though he abandoned orthodox Christianity, Du Bois retained a lifelong sense of accountability to what he called "the deep religious feeling of the real Negro heart," which he believed had "lost the guiding star of the past and [was] seeking in the great night a new religious ideal."[24]

Activists who were more closely aligned with the churches also broke new theological ground in the first decades of the twentieth century. Responding to the revelations inherent in collective encounter, ministers and professors articulated what came to be known as the Social Gospel. For Baptist minister and theologian Walter Rauschenbusch, it was a "new revelation" to realize that the phrase "Kingdom of God" applied not to an otherworldly heaven but to the social order. "Here was the idea and purpose that had dominated the mind of the Master himself," he wrote. "The saving of the lost, the teaching of the young . . . church union, political reform, the reorganization of the industrial system, international peace,—it was all covered by the one aim of the Reign of God on earth." From this flowed an understanding of both sin and salvation as social in character, an insistence on justice as well as charity, and—most troubling from the perspective of subsequent critics—a tendency to treat adherence to the "law of love," rather than acceptance of divine grace, as the defining act of the Christian.[25]

Notions of social salvation were not entirely new. Orestes Brownson, Fourierists, Spiritualists, and the church reform movement had all hoped to build God's Kingdom on earth. But it was dramatically new for large Protestant denominations to embrace this theology. This was possible in part because Rauschenbusch and his peers refused to posit a stark choice between social and individual theologies. "There are two great entities in human life,—the human soul and the human race," he explained, "and religion is to save both."[26]

The other factor that contributed to the emergence of Social Gospel theology within denominational Protestantism was the dialogue instigated by participants in the settlement house and institutional church movements. Pastors looked across denominational lines for models of good practice, and they rarely found that differing theologies prevented them from working with others to reform city government or pass legislation banning child labor. Some of this dialogue reflected the interfaith character of the settlement movement itself: the New York State Conference of Religion taught that "[r]eligion unites many whom Theology divides," and included Jews, Ethical Culturists, and New Thought leaders in its conferences promoting "cooperation for social salvation." Other dialogues were more restrictively Christian: the Federal Council of Churches, organized in 1908, sought to "promote the application of the law of Christ to every relation of human life" and to "express the fellowship and catholic unity" of those who professed "Jesus Christ as their Divine Lord and Saviour."[27]

Many of the Federal Council's founders had previously organized "social service" groups within their own denominations. The most radical of these, the Methodist Federation for Social Service, also contributed a document that would anchor ecumenical work for social justice throughout the twentieth century. The Methodist Social Creed, largely authored by Harry Ward—soon a faculty member at Union Seminary in New York and eventually a fellow traveler of the Communist Party—was adapted and endorsed at the Federal Council's founding convention. Its message was straightforward, dispensing with any elaborate theological rationale. The council was "for equal rights and complete justice for all men in all stations of life." It opposed child labor and favored protective legislation for women workers, a living wage in all industries, ongoing reduction of the hours of labor, safe workplaces, arbitration of industrial disputes, old-age insurance, "abatement of poverty," and "the most equitable division of the products of industry that can ultimately be devised."[28]

By the end of World War I, the Federal Council had broadened its social vision to encompass cooperative management of industries, comprehensive social insurance and public jobs programs, progressive income taxes, political and economic equality for women and African Americans, and an end to "the barbarism of lynching." But it opposed any attempt "to suddenly overturn the social order according to untried theories of industrial and political organization," and regarded "the doctrine of the class conscious struggle" as "a reversion to earlier forms of competitive struggle." This decidedly nonradical approach to progressive social change was mirrored by the Catholic bishops' interpretations of Catholic social teaching and by the "Program for Social Reconstruction" authored in 1919 by John Ryan, already notable as the most thorough theological defender of the idea of a living wage. Reflecting views widely shared among traditions too liberal for the Federal Council, the Universalists took the more radical ground of calling for collective ownership of industries producing "the necessaries of life" and world federation as the most promising path to peace.[29]

Whatever their personal theologies, activists who wanted to go further than the Federal Council could turn to another unifying institution in the first decades of the twentieth century. Founded eight years before the Federal Council, the Socialist Party of America converged with Social Gospel Protestantism as ministers and theologians accepted that socialism might be the best way to achieve the goals of the Social Creed, then diverged when the council embraced the "war to end war" and the party opposed it as an imperialist adventure. They came together again when global capitalism fell into the crisis of the Great Depression. As a result, it ceased to be true that American religion was most radical at the local level. Though neither denominations nor ecumenical bodies were wholly radical, they provided one of the most reliable institutional foundations for radicalism.

CHAPTER 11

The Religion of Socialism

Few radical organizations have encompassed as broad a spectrum of activists as the Socialist Party of America. Created in 1901 and enjoying significant support through the Great Depression, the Socialists integrated union members and intellectuals, Marxists and populists, heirs of the Puritans and immigrants from Russia and Finland. Some members were workers who had empowered themselves through identity encounters; others were professionals who had been radicalized by collective encounters at settlement houses or institutional churches. All agreed that the capitalist economy needed to be replaced, not reformed, though they did not agree on the precise balance of electoral campaigning and labor militancy needed to usher in the "cooperative commonwealth." In addition to its work for economic transformation, the party led the opposition to the First World War, and its members played central roles in creating the American Civil Liberties Union (ACLU), the NAACP, and the predecessor to Planned Parenthood. For a time, the party included the semianarchist members of the Industrial Workers of the World and devoted admirers of Lenin and Trotsky, though these groups ultimately left in explosive schisms. At the height of its influence, in 1912, the party polled 6 percent of the presidential vote and was synonymous with the "Left."[1]

The party's religious spectrum was broad. Though it was often perceived as irreligious, it is better categorized as radically pluralist. Socialism absorbed many heirs of Spiritualism, Theosophy, New Thought, and Free Religion, some of whom retained those traditions. In the party they encountered comrades, most of them immigrants but others native-born Freethinkers, who bitterly opposed religion in general and Christianity in particular. Most Jewish socialists fell into that category, though some favored biblical rhetoric and a few were active in Reform synagogues. Still other comrades were Christian Social Gospelers; these folks were distrusted by some party leaders but embraced by others, in the hope that they would convert churchgoing Christians to socialism.

Twentieth-century socialism was more "secular" than nineteenth-century radicalism in one sense. Nineteenth-century artisans and abolitionists had drawn organizational support from the churches partly because they had no alternative: no other institutions enjoyed such a broad constituency coupled with autonomy from political and economic power. The growth of the labor movement gave unions similar breadth and autonomy by the twentieth century. But the change was one of addition rather than substitution: while the unions provided socialism's most important base of support, congregations were a significant second.

Like the nineteenth-century movements, socialism got more support from local congregations than from national denominations, though that was changing. The most partisan ministers usually experienced tension with their denominations, and even the national organizations of Spiritualism and Theosophy were wary. Enormous support came from free-standing People's Churches and networks of individuals. Paradoxically, this unified radical movement relied on a dispersed web of religious communities. Ultimately, those communities would outlast the party itself, continuing to anchor activist work in the 1950s and 1960s.

One type of religious community that helped to sustain socialism was well described in 1923 by Paul Jones, an Episcopalian bishop who had lost his diocese because of his socialist and pacifist commitments. During World War I, Jones recalled, war resisters came together seeking the "integration of lives fused by a common impulse and experience." When some of them went to prison, they sparked a conversation that gradually transformed the churches that had at first rejected them. These small fellowships, Jones concluded, were "the divine process for saving the world."[2]

A "fellowship," in this sense, was an intimate group of individuals with a shared commitment to building God's Kingdom on earth. Though fellowships usually included laypeople, they appealed especially to idealistic young ministers who chafed at the restrictions imposed on them by conventional churchgoers. Gathering for conferences and retreats, fellowship members "searched the scriptures" and asked Charles Sheldon's question: "What would Jesus do?" Since—unlike settlement houses and institutional churches—they were not dependent on external funding, fellowships were free to find ever more radical answers.

Some fellowships were denominationally specific, such as the group of Baptist ministers who met at the family estate of Walter Rauschenbusch's socialist friend Leighton Williams. Others were interreligious, as was the "Nationalist" movement inspired by Edward Bellamy's 1888 novel, *Looking Backward*. Telling the story of a wealthy man from the nineteenth century who wakes into an egalitarian twenty-first century, *Looking Backward* suggested that collective ownership of land and capital could be achieved through an evolutionary consolidation of existing monopolies. This was a form of socialism, though Bellamy cleverly labeled it "Nationalism" to avoid Marxist stigma. A circle of Boston Theosophists soon concluded that the novel might be the basis for an organized movement. They procured the endorsement of Madame Blavatsky, who agreed that Bellamy had identified the "first great step" to the "Universal Brotherhood of Humanity" that was Theosophy's primary objective. Protestant ministers quickly joined the Nationalist clubs that sprang up across the nation. But Blavatsky got cold feet when the movement turned toward electoral politics, and urged her followers to keep Theosophy, not Nationalism, "first in your sight." Nevertheless, Theosophical ideas remained embedded in many socialist journals.[3]

New Thought adherents created energetic fellowships, among them the Unions for Concerted Moral Effort, which declared confidently that "this world is large enough and rich enough . . . to become the happy home of perfected humanity." The Union for Practical Progress spawned dozens of local unions on the principle that problems like unemployment or child labor could be solved if opinion leaders all spoke out on the same subject on the same day. And the Social Reform League, whose members include Eugene Debs and other leading Socialists, was launched by a New Thought editor and then handed over to an energetic Episcopalian, W. D. P. Bliss.[4]

A child of Congregationalist missionaries, Bliss admired the Christian Socialists of England and saw their sacramental liturgy as a model for social solidarity. But he also encouraged young ministers to risk expulsion from their churches by preaching socialism, rather than "demean themselves to become as hired men of a parish." His Church of the Carpenter followed the Episcopalian liturgy (because "we . . . start no new sect in the already divided body of the church") but welcomed persons "of any church or of no church." His brand of socialism was also quirkily catholic. He supported ameliorative social policies but also insisted that "we only go to the root of the matter when we overthrow this system." He joined the Socialist Labor Party, which insisted on proletarian revolution, and affiliated with the middle-class Fabians. His real preference was for a "new party" encompassing all radicals, and for this reason he supported the Populist ticket in 1892 and 1896, then cast his lot with the Socialist Party of America in the new century.[5]

In 1891, Bliss published an article by a fiery Minnesota Congregationalist with an oversized Messiah complex. George Herron soon launched his "Kingdom" movement in conjunction with President George Gates of Grinnell College. After a successful retreat, Gates persuaded Herron's wealthiest parishioner to endow a professorship for the preacher. Though Herron's views were in keeping with the college's abolitionist roots, his colleagues resented his frequent travels and donors balked at his radicalism. When his affair with the daughter of his patroness was discovered, Herron was sent packing.[6]

Out of the wreckage emerged a cluster of overlapping fellowships. A Chicago admirer named J. Stitt Wilson left the Methodist ministry to organize the Social Crusade, a network of Methodists and Congregationalists who devoted themselves to outdoor preaching on behalf of Herron's theology and the Socialist Labor Party. Its members included future Socialist congressman Carl D. Thompson. Wilson's move to California sparked a similar fellowship on the West Coast that included economist Lawrence Gronlund, whose work had inspired Edward Bellamy and made the phrase "cooperative commonwealth" synonymous with "Kingdom of God." Another circle relocated to a rural commune in Georgia called the Christian Commonwealth, where they launched the journal that gave the *Social Gospel* its name. A later Chicago group, which called itself simply the Fellowship, included Socialist Party stalwart John Spargo as well as Herron himself. The groups diverged theologically, as the Christian Commonwealth embraced Tolstoy, Wilson leaned toward New Thought, and Herron and Spargo became increasingly anticlerical. But all found a home in the Socialist Party.[7]

Many of the clergymen active in fellowships served People's Churches rather than denominational congregations, and several of these became hotbeds of socialism. In Eugene Debs's hometown of Terre Haute, Social Crusader James H. Hollingsworth launched a People's Church after, in Debs's words, giving "up his church and the brightest worldly prospects on account of Socialism." In Cincinnati, former settlement house worker Herbert Seeley Bigelow transformed Vine Street Congregational Church into a People's Church after lay leaders defected in protest of his "unitarian principles," single-tax preaching, and attempt to admit an African American member. (Significantly, Vine Street's roots were in the abolitionist church reform movement.) Decorating its sanctuary with quotations from Jefferson, Garrison, and Henry George—as well as the biblical promise, "Ye shall know the truth and the truth shall make ye free"—the reorganized church insisted that its only "article of faith" was the "establishment of the brotherhood of man" and attracted a multiracial congregation. Bigelow gained national notoriety in 1917, when he was abducted and horsewhipped by Klansmen just before giving a Socialist speech in Kentucky. He would later serve in Congress as a New Deal Democrat.[8]

The most sensational People's Church pastor was Benjamin Fay Mills, a Presbyterian evangelist converted to socialism by George Herron. Mills served a Unitarian church in Oakland for five years before launching the Los Angeles Fellowship in 1904. The fellowship's blend of revivalist style, socialist politics, and New Thought theology attracted a thousand members, who committed themselves to "trustful and unselfish living." Once in, they studied Whitman, Emerson, and the Bhagavad Gita, joined the fellowship's orchestra, or worked to establish daughter congregations. One writer described it as "perhaps the most significant and remarkable religious movement in the world today," yet within a decade Mills had renounced his radical views and left his congregation to a rapid collapse.[9]

This instability reflected the multiple motives that led people to People's Churches. In New Haven, Alexander Irvine discovered this when his People's Church attracted "an educated woman," who "saw in our simple creed an open door," then left when she learned of Irvine's friendship with an impoverished coal heaver. The coal heaver left when he discovered Irvine didn't believe in hell. Irvine's membership in the Socialist Party drove out the single-taxers and attracted a new crop of Socialists who, in turn, left when they discovered that his sermons featured not "economic determinism" but a search "for the hidden springs of the heart." Ultimately, Irvine retreated to a rural farm before launching his career as a socialist propagandist.[10]

Several cities also had explicitly socialist congregations. The prototype was Bliss's Church of the Carpenter, which combined an Episcopalian liturgy, a noon meal with "an informal conference as to practical work," and a Sunday evening lecture. The goal was to meld working people and idealistic Christians into a single "brotherhood" strong enough to resist the "Common Foe, the growing power of Mammon, and Wrong, and Injustice and every sin." Several years later, Bouck White's Church of the Socialist Revolution in New York City sponsored "Mud-Gutter Meetings," in which participants marched through the city carrying a red flag and signing socialist hymns, preached against capitalism on a street corner, then brought their new recruits back to the church. Perhaps channeling the agitating abolitionists Abby Kelley and Stephen Foster, church members disrupted services at the church attended by John D. Rockefeller. They also "melted" the American flag, along with those of the European powers, at a service designed to protest nationalism. That bit of theatricality not only got White arrested for flag burning but led to his expulsion from the Socialist Party itself.[11]

Fellowships and People's Churches, like institutional churches and settlement houses, flourished in the tumultuous 1890s, and then helped consolidate the Socialist Party in 1901. The party was defined by its ambivalent response to a persistent dilemma of the Left. Is it better to create an ideologically pure vanguard or to work with moderate reformers to create a mass movement? The debate pitted orthodox Marxists and anarchists against Fabians, "social democrats," and "progressives" on both sides of the Atlantic. In the 1890s the alternatives were personified by Daniel DeLeon of the Socialist Labor Party, who preached an uncompromising Marxism, and the Populists' William Jennings Bryan, who traded in the movement's radical agenda for "free silver" and Democratic fusion—only to lose the presidency anyhow. The Socialist Party's founders, drawn from the radical wing of the Populist movement and the anti-DeLeon wing of the SLP, agreed that neither DeLeon nor Bryan offered a way forward. What they wanted was a thoroughly American socialism, rooted in indigenous reform traditions, willing to make use of electoral democracy, but committed to overthrowing capitalism.[12]

The desire for an American socialism gave ministers a special role in the party. The party's immigrant, atheist strategists knew that men like themselves could not win elections beyond their own neighborhoods. The ideal candidate was Eugene Debs—an eloquent workingman with a Jesus-centered spirituality who had been heroically imprisoned in a strike. But few nonimmigrant trade unionists were socialists. So strategists turned to popular preachers who could rally voters with the radical message of Jesus. Though some preachers had belonged to earlier socialist parties, the perception that they were Christians first and partisans second gave them an aura of neutrality that allowed them to mediate between socialist factions. George Herron chaired the Unity Convention on its opening day and persuaded the delegates to approve a manifesto that specified some "immediate demands" but disavowed reforms that would merely prop up capitalism.[13]

With the formation of the party, local fellowships coalesced into the Christian Socialist Fellowship (CSF). The catalyst was a newspaper called the *Christian Socialist,* edited by Rev. E. E. Carr in tiny Danville, Illinois. Carr's goal was twofold: to urge ministers and church members "to advocate the Real Gospel of Christ" while persuading Socialists "not to ignore nor belittle the tremendous importance of religion." Carr was unequivocal in his support for the Socialist Party, to which he hoped to recruit millions of Christian voters. The CSF similarly blended a broad theology and fervent support for "the International Socialist Movement as the means of hastening that good time of God and Man, which we believe to be near at hand."[14]

The CSF functioned nationally, regionally, and locally. National conferences featured tumultuous business sessions, speeches by party leaders, visits to settlement houses, and extensive outreach. Socialist ministers preached at any local church that would receive them: the *Christian Socialist* reported thirteen such sermons after the 1908 conference. Regional conferences attracted hundreds of participants, among them advocates of "personal salvation, regeneration, premillenarianism, divine healing and adventism" who were eager for debate. The most vigorous local centers were in Chicago and New York. Chicago's was launched with a splash when founder J. O. Bentall resigned from the Anti-Saloon League to devote himself full-time to Socialism. Promising to provide a church home for Socialists disgruntled with conventional churches, Bentall recruited music director Harvey Moyer, whose *Songs of Socialism* would soon be sung by Socialists of many theological stripes. The New York center's founding gathering featured Union Seminary professor Charles Fagnani, who declared that "Socialism *is* Christianity; and Christianity *is* Socialism."[15]

CSF leaders faced the double challenge of persuading mainline Christians that Socialism was not irreligious and persuading party leaders that Marx had been wrong to dismiss Christian Socialism as "the holy water with which the priests consecrate the heartburn of the aristocrats." They differentiated themselves from European Christian Socialists, whom they judged as "vague thinkers" or reactionaries scheming to "hamper" true socialism. The CSF's Christian Socialism was not a variant form of socialism, but Marxist socialism as practiced by Christians. Though they rejected Marx's atheism, they insisted that his teachings on class struggle and economic determinism were compatible with Christianity. Indeed, noted one writer, Jesus himself had taught economic determinism "in the parable of the sower—the seed which was choked by the cares of the world and the deceitfulness of riches stood no chance." Eugene Debs praised the fellowship's ministers for softening his anticlerical prejudices: "I am glad I can call you ministers of the Man of Galilee, my comrades, for it isn't long ago that I felt a great prejudice against you as a class."[16]

Fellowship members worked strategically on behalf of the party's 1908 declaration: "The Socialist party is primarily an economic organization. It is not concerned with religious belief." During the debate, ministers allowed atheist party leaders to make the case for a broad-based party. Once the neutrality plank had passed, Carr explained its significance. The single-vote margin of victory, he claimed, was misleading because many "no" voters preferred to say that religion was "a private matter, a question of individual conscience." (Carr considered this phrasing anti-Catholic insofar as it presumed a Protestant view of conscience.) As had been the case for the Working Men and women's suffrage movements, the declaration of secularism was intended to protect mainstream Christian supporters from offensively anticlerical propaganda.[17]

After the 1908 election, Carr attacked a Socialist lecturer named Arthur Morrow Lewis, claiming that the low Socialist vote in Chicago was a consequence of Lewis's Sunday morning lectures "ridiculing the idea of God." Carr warned that unless Socialists left religion alone, "some other Party will be raised up to accomplish the glorious work we might have done." Lewis eventually backed down, prompting Carr to praise him for a "valuable Christmas Gift to the Socialist movement." But Carr's former friend J. O. Bentall, still a member of the *Christian Socialist*'s editorial board, pressed Lewis's side of the argument, insisting, "While it may not seem so at first sight, the scientific method is best, and it will win out in the end."[18]

As Bentall's evolution suggests, the Christian Socialist Fellowship's most challenging battles had less to do with atheist party leaders than with the way the shifting religious identities of its own constituency called its "Christian" identity into question. Judging from one published list of "preacher comrades," most members came from the large

Protestant denominations. But a disproportionate share were Unitarians, Universalists, Swedenborgians, or People's Church pastors on a trajectory toward New Thought or Freethought. The boundaries were fuzzy enough to include "any Jew, Hindoo, or other religious socialist who is broad enough to work with us under the name of Jesus." Much as the fellowship wanted to bring socialism to the mainstream churches, its local centers evolved into places of refuge for institutionally homeless souls who could accept neither the doctrines of the denominations nor the materialism of Marx.[19]

The tension came to a head when New York's center admitted "agnostic" John Spargo and Jewish Sol Fieldman, both party leaders, as members and placed them on a committee that recommended an end to rules restricting membership to those who affirmed "the social message of Jesus." Carr fought back by accusing the CSF's general secretary, a New Yorker, of plotting a hostile takeover. A new constitution that relegated non-Christians to "associate" membership caused the loss of centers in New York and Milwaukee, the party's two strongest cities. But it didn't make the tension go away: when an ally organized a People's Church, Carr conceded that while it was best for Socialists to remain in denominational churches, freestanding congregations could provide a "helpful, comforting home [for] the Socialist Jews, Freethinkers, and Liberals who have been moved by the Spirit of God, yet can not endure the conventional church theology or ritual."[20]

The fellowship never stopped trying to win over mainline Protestants. One strategy was the publication of denominational "special issues," published in mass numbers and featuring articles by Social Gospelers, such as Rauschenbusch, deemed sympathetic to Socialism. The conservative Lutherans, the standoffish Catholics, and the miniscule Swedenborgians all got their own issues, as did mainline Protestants. The fellowship sent delegates to denominational conventions and exulted when they persuaded the Reformed Church to launch a three-year study of socialism. It also arranged for its members to serve as guest preachers in as many pulpits as possible. In one tour through Iowa and Illinois, for example, Ella Carr spoke at Methodist, Congregational, Evangelical, and Christian Science churches as well as at a YMCA, a socialist local, and four opera halls.[21]

The prospect of gaining Christian votes caused the party to recruit ministers as candidates for public office. Job Harriman, Eugene Debs's first running mate, had previously worked as a Disciples minister. Socialist ministers were elected as mayors of Berkeley, California; Butte, Montana; and Schenectady, New York. Carl Thompson represented Milwaukee in Congress, while Bouck White and—later—Reinhold Niebuhr ran unsuccessfully in New York. Most significantly, the former Presbyterian minister Norman Thomas served as the party's presidential standard-bearer in every election from 1928 to 1948.

Clerics also worked as propagandists and educators. The party's first "national organizer," Universalist Charles Vail, was one of four ministers from different denominations who published manuals of Socialism during the party's first five years. In Chicago, Charles Kerr, formerly publisher of Jenkin Lloyd Jones's *Unity* magazine, launched the most influential socialist publishing house, churning out Marxist classics and "Why I Became a Socialist" tracts that gave credit to Jesus. John Spargo worked with George Herron and his wealthy mother-in-law to establish the Rand School of Social Science in New York City, where workers learned socialist theory and organizing techniques from such teachers as the Unitarian minister George Willis Cooke. Girard, Kansas, was home to Rev. Walter Mills's International School of Socialist Economy, as well as to the *Appeal to Reason*, a widely circulated newspaper that regularly couched its socialist arguments in millenarian terms.[22]

These clerical propagandists developed a distinctive version of Social Gospel theology. Like moderate Social Gospelers, Socialist Party theologians insisted that salvation had a social dimension and that Christians were called to build God's Kingdom on earth. But most took the further step of identifying that kingdom with socialism. "The brotherhood and comradeship which Jesus loved and labored to bring about," explained a Christian Socialist Fellowship chapter, "can only be fully realized . . . when . . . the Cooperative Commonwealth of Humanity, is established in the world."[23]

This understanding of the Kingdom of God was indebted both to George Lippard's image of Jesus and to the new religions of the nineteenth century. Jesus, socialists claimed, was not only a "Great Proletarian" but an outright socialist. "Socialism," explained one, "is only another name for the golden rule." Eugene Debs agreed that the "carpenter's son . . . taught . . . what socialism teaches." The *Christian Socialist* published detailed exegeses demonstrating that Jesus' Kingdom of God was a specific system of "external government" rather than a vague ideal.[24]

Though these exegeses were couched in terms that might have

appealed to biblical literalists as well as liberals, they were often linked to the seemingly antithetical claim that socialism was a religion unto itself, destined to supersede church-based Christianity. Everett Dean Martin explained, "Socialism is religion: not *a* religion, just religion. There is only one religion, and that is man's expression of his humanity." Indeed, socialism was the "modern expression" of the "same something" voiced by the prophets of all the world's religions.[25]

Admiration for Jesus coexisted with a desire for a new religion even among party members who were perceived as excessively irreligious by the CSF. John Spargo lifted up the "spirit" of socialism and insisted that comrades who called themselves materialists were really idealists questing after the "Holy Grail." Novelist Upton Sinclair, perhaps the nation's best-known socialist after Eugene Debs, rehearsed standard Freethought criticisms of "the church of the conquerors" and the "church of the quacks" in *The Profits of Religion*. But his final chapter on "the church of the social revolution" compared "Comrade Jesus" and his "bitterly class-conscious proletarian" brother James to Emma Goldman and Eugene Debs, before calling for a "Church of the future . . . which we Socialists will join."[26]

Among ethnically Jewish socialists, orthodox Marxism was stronger than among Gentiles, but even in this group there was a lively appreciation for the religious spirit of socialism. Those who spurned ethnic particularism worked within the Reform movement, Ethical Culture, or in some cases Unitarian congregations or Christian Socialist Fellowship centers. Others believed that successful socialist agitation required the use of the Yiddish language or even the cultivation of an autonomous *yidishe kultur*. This approach was endorsed by the Socialist Party itself, which allowed immigrant groups to establish "federations" within the party.

Though most of these activists saw their movement as "purely secular" as well as "thoroughly Jewish," they did not hesitate to identify parallels between Talmudic principles and socialist ideals. Some leaders were former rabbinical students; others positioned themselves as *rebbes* for the masses. Abraham Cahan, editor of *Forverts,* the leading Yiddish newspaper, employed biblical and Talmudic imagery in order to speak "to 'Moyshe' like a 'Moyshe,'" called himself a *proletarishker magid,* or "proletarian preacher," and promised new immigrants that socialism would give them "a spiritual pleasure which is higher than all." When one early leader of the Arbeter Ring, a mutual-aid society, insisted that anyone who believed in God was "either a fool or a swindler," the organization as a whole refused to exclude members who attended synagogue on the high holidays or more frequently. Such a policy, most believed, would doom socialism to electoral insignificance.[27]

Jewish radicals were also prominent within the anarchist movement, which shared socialism's critique of capitalism but repudiated political action on the grounds that any government would be an instrument of oppression. The anarchist critique of hierarchy extended to churches and synagogues, and so the movement functioned as a faith unto itself rather than as an expression of Jewish or Christian commitment. New York's anarchist Pioneers of Liberty held their annual ball on Yom Kippur as a direct rebuff of their neighbors' piety. Anarchism's most iconic exponent was Emma Goldman, a Russian Jew whose childhood was shaped by her father's Orthodoxy, her mother's liberal Judaism, and the drama of Russia's movement of "nihilist" revolutionaries. Goldman arrived in the United States just months before the Haymarket bombing, and she identified intensely with the anarchists who were implicated in that event. Their execution sparked a conversion experience that sealed Goldman's political identity: "I had a distinct sensation that something new and wonderful had been born in my soul. A great ideal, a burning faith, a determination to dedicate myself to the memory of my martyred comrades." In the 1890s, she promoted the anarchist strategy of "propaganda of the deed," encouraging her lover Alexander Berkman's assassination attempt on a strikebreaking capitalist; by the 1910s she was also notorious as a promoter of birth control. In the pages of Goldman's *Mother Earth,* fidelity to anarchist principle coexisted with promotion of a broad radical tradition that included Thoreau and John Brown, Victoria Woodhull and the free-love movement. Goldman's vision was in turn celebrated by the feminists of the Heterodoxy Club and the socialist editors of the *Masses.*[28]

Socialist and anarchist currents coexisted in the Industrial Workers of the World (IWW), an all-inclusive union that favored "direct action" against capitalism. The union's founders tapped former priest Thomas Hagerty to write their inaugural manifesto, and many IWW members, or "Wobblies," saw their movement as a new form of religion. Insisting that they deserved the same First Amendment privileges as the Salvation Army, one Wobblie explained, "Industrial Unionism is our religion, as through it we will have peace on earth." Like the Christian Socialist Fellowship, the Wobblies had their own hymnbook of gospel parodies that sometimes rose to the level of constructive theology. Joe Hill, who coined the term "pie in the sky" in one parody, offered a profound theology of identity encounter in his parody of "There Is Power in the Blood of the Lamb":

> There is pow'r, there is pow'r
> In a band of workingmen,
> When they stand hand in hand.

For all their disdain for Christian preachers, the Wobblies never lost faith that "Comrade Jesus" was on their side.[29]

The vision of radicalism as a new religion that would preserve the best insights of Christianity and Judaism was shared by early twentieth-century activists who were connected to the Socialist Party but labored primarily on behalf of other causes. Feminist Charlotte Perkins Gilman and racial justice advocate W. E. B. Du Bois abandoned Christianity in favor of humanistic faith, but refused to abandon religious rhetoric altogether. Gilman proposed that "his" religion, focused on heaven, be replaced by "her" religion, focused on a better "earthly future . . . for children to be born into," and promised that "seeing God as within us, to be expressed, instead of above us, to be worshipped" would empower activists "to bring heaven on earth." Du Bois affirmed a "Credo" of faith in the God who had "made of one blood all nations" but also "in the Negro Race: in the beauty of its genius, the sweetness of its soul, and its strength in that meekness which shall yet inherit this turbulent earth."[30]

The fact that both Du Bois and Gilman were involved with socialism suggests the breadth of the movement: though socialists often assumed that the demise of racism and patriarchy would be mere by-products of capitalism's fall, they were committed to the suffragist cause and, on the streets of Harlem, offered a radical alternative to the separatist preaching of Marcus Garvey. The party was also linked to antiwar and anti-imperialist agitation during World War I, though this commitment exacerbated its ideological divisions. In 1912 party leaders forced out IWW leader "Big Bill" Haywood for his insistence that "direct action" rather than electioneering was the way to build socialism. Eight years later, the party's refusal to take direction from Russian Bolshevists led many of its most energetic activists to organize the rival Communist Party. Midway between those two schisms, the party's opposition to World War I alienated pragmatists, including E. E. Carr. Carr initially sympathized with Eugene Debs's view that socialists had no place on either side of a capitalist war, but once the United States was involved he argued that a "useless agitation against the war" would reinforce native-born Americans' perception of socialism as essentially foreign.[31]

As the war forced one group of Christians out of the party, it brought others in. Debs's stance against the war was heroic: arrested for his outspokenness, he conducted his 1920 presidential campaign from a prison cell. Those ministers who dared to declare their own opposition naturally felt kinship with the martyred Debs. Facing opposition from denominational authorities, they joined Quaker activists in the U.S. branch of the international Fellowship of Reconciliation (FOR). The FOR committed itself not only to pacifism but to "a quest after an order of society in accordance with the mind of Christ." On this basis, most leaders came around to socialist principles as they reflected together on the social injustices that had led to the war.[32]

The most brilliant of the young ministers who came to the Socialist Party through the FOR was Norman Thomas. Educated at Princeton University and Union Seminary, he had served a Presbyterian mission in East Harlem until his antiwar views alienated donors. Moved by the experience of his brother Evan, who was sentenced to military prison after launching a hunger strike at a camp for conscientious objectors, Thomas signed on as editor of the fellowship's semi-independent journal, the *World Tomorrow*, which sought to help Christians prepare for the postwar world. For Thomas, this initially meant a nonpartisan, Christocentric socialism. But once the party, shorn of Communists, opened itself to non-Marxists, he became leader of the Intercollegiate Socialist Society (ISS), which recruited students and professionals for the Socialists. Thomas inspired most subsequent *World Tomorrow* editors to follow him into the party.

Throughout the 1920s, the Fellowship of Reconciliation stood as the most radical wing of the Social Gospel, promoting racial and sexual equality as well as socialism and pacifism. Members organized Brookwood Labor College outside New York City, which took the place of the Rand School as a leading center for worker education. As often happens in conservative times, the *World Tomorrow* celebrated the historical tradition in which it stood, publishing articles on William Lloyd Garrison and other radical antecedents. It continued the theological tradition of the Christian Socialist Fellowship by celebrating Jesus' radicalism and the spirituality inherent in socialism. Editors Anna Rochester and Grace

Hutchins, missionaries and settlement house workers who would eventually join the Communists, set out in *Jesus Christ and the World Today* to find "a solution of our present problems" in "the mind and experience of Jesus Christ." "Born into the home of a workingman," Jesus had a class consciousness that protected him from both the prejudices of the "wealthy Pharisees" and the "stunting" of the "outcast beggars." Norman Thomas, for his part, echoed John Spargo when he argued that even the most materialistic radicals possessed an "implicit religion."[33]

Initially, few had ears to hear. But by keeping the Social Gospel and the Socialist Party alive during a difficult decade, Norman Thomas and his comrades prepared the way for a transformation of American radicalism. When the Great Depression hit, many of America's leading seminaries were socialist hotbeds, and the nation's preeminent theologian was willing to stand for election to Congress on the Socialist Party ticket. By 1934 the Socialist Party attracted the loyalty—either as members or voters—of somewhere between 5 and 25 percent of all mainline Protestant clergy. The stage was set for a great expansion of the religious constituency of American radicalism.[34]

CHAPTER 12

The Radical Depression

Radicalism thrives in times of crisis. This was so before the Civil War; it became so again with the crash of the stock market on October 29, 1929. With millions out of work and breadlines filling the streets, a broad segment of the U.S. population entertained the idea that capitalism was itself the problem. Protestant, Catholic, and Jewish leaders joined the call for "industrial democracy" and repented of the militarism that had led them to support World War I. The labor movement turned radical, as coal miners, autoworkers, railroad porters, and tenant farmers embraced "industrial unions" that sought workplace democracy as well as better wages. These new unions drew their strength from identity encounters among ordinary workers, and they created new opportunities for religious radicals to experience collective encounters with the masses. Yet, ultimately, the nation became neither socialist nor pacifist. Instead, the Depression and the subsequent "good war" enabled thousands of radicals to enter the new political establishment created by Franklin Delano Roosevelt's New Deal.

The Depression also diversified radical religion. Diversity as such was nothing new. From the beginning, American radicalism included liberal, revivalist, and primitivist Protestants as well as adherents of new religions that were culturally Protestant in their distrust of centralized authority. It had come to include Jews who saw the ethics of the prophets as the heart of their tradition, and a smattering of liturgically inclined Episcopalians. But early twentieth-century radicalism virtually excluded Calvinists and Lutherans who took Reformation doctrines seriously, Roman Catholics unwilling to defy the magisterial authority of their church, and Jews who treasured ritual as well as ethics. Millions in these groups had economic interests that might have led them to the left, and the Depression made it possible for them to follow that path. Reinhold Niebuhr, Dorothy Day, and Saul Alinsky—talented leaders with different understandings of radicalism—led the way.

Even before the Depression began, the radicals of the Fellowship of Reconciliation and Socialist Party were drawing closer to the establishment liberals who dominated the major Protestant denominations, and to socially engaged members of the Roman Catholic hierarchy. Confronted with the collapse of Woodrow Wilson's plans for a League of Nations, previously bellicose ministers turned to pacifism. In 1918 Harry Emerson Fosdick had urged young men to enlist in the army because "the Kingdom of God needs *you*"; by 1925 he described his earlier attitude as worship of Caesar rather than God. The *Christian Century* galvanized Protestant support for the 1928 Kellogg-Briand Pact, which attempted to "outlaw" war. From the standpoint of the FOR, this was not truly radical, since "the outlawry program [made] no provision for the removal of the causes of war." But it was a vast departure from the martial mood of 1917.[1]

Mainline Social Gospelers inched toward socialism by joining the Fellowship for a Christian Social Order (FCSO). Organized by YMCA leader Sherwood Eddy and his more pacifistic protégé Kirby Page, the FCSO sponsored conferences on a variety of issues, with economic and industrial policy in the forefront. Its rising star was Reinhold Niebuhr, a Detroit pastor who had gained fame for his work on race relations and his outspoken criticism of industrialist Henry Ford. In 1928 the FCSO's twenty-four hundred members folded into the FOR. The merged organization's statement of purpose stopped short of endorsing socialism, but it placed economic justice on a par with pacifism, describing both "the method of war" and "the existing organization of society" as contrary to the "principles" of Jesus. In that year the *World Tomorrow* and Union Seminary enticed Niebuhr to join the journal's editorial staff and the seminary's teaching faculty. For the next forty years, Niebuhr would maintain his stature as the most influential theologian in the country.[2]

Throughout the Depression, Niebuhr and his comrades pushed Protestant leaders toward radicalism. By 1934 a *World Tomorrow* poll completed by one-fifth of mainline Protestant clergy found that most respondents favored the "drastic limitation" of wealth through estate and income taxes. Twenty-eight percent endorsed socialism "as represented by the Socialist Party," while only 5 percent preferred capitalism. Two-thirds hoped that the churches would "go on record as refusing to sanction or support any future war." Half of responding seminarians were socialist and three-quarters were pacifist, with even more radicalism at such elite schools as Union and Yale. Though respondents were doubtless more radical than American clergy as a whole, the results made clear that mainline ministers were at least twice as likely to be socialist as the rest of the electorate. The rabbis who responded were more radical still.[3]

These convictions often translated into partisan activism. In 1929 Niebuhr (who had voted for Democrat Al Smith in 1928) joined the Socialist Party and launched a campaign for state senate. FOR staffer Howard Kester ran for Congress in 1932, while Devere Allen helped develop the 1934 party platform. Others, perhaps troubled by the rigidity of party discipline, worked for the party indirectly through the League for Independent Political Action, which hoped to unite liberals and socialists in a British-style labor party. These activists drew inspiration from their former ministerial colleague Norman Thomas, whose 1932 campaign for the presidency earned more votes than any since the Debs era.[4]

Religious radicals were inspired in the 1930s by a revitalization of labor organizing. Ever since the American Federation of Labor had superseded the Knights of Labor, the mainstream labor movement had frustrated radicals. The AFL's craft unions represented only the most skilled segment of white male workers, often excluding women and people of color. Though Socialists and Communists worked long hours as union organizers, union members did not often reciprocate with votes. With the exception of western mine workers, unionists were even less enthusiastic about the IWW's anarchistic direct action. Federal laws were stacked against unions until 1933, when the National Industrial Recovery Act prohibited company unions and guaranteed workers the right to bargain collectively. These new rules enabled rank-and-file workers to create a new breed of "industrial unions" through which they empowered themselves and inspired their allies.

A series of strikes began in April 1934, when Toledo autoworkers confronted the Auto-Lite Company. The strike drew the enthusiastic support of the American Workers Party, which had been active in organizing unemployed workers to ensure they would not be recruited as strikebreakers. The party was the brainchild of A.J. Muste, an early FOR member who had lost his pulpit for his opposition to World War I and then entered the labor movement during the Lawrence textile strike of 1919. After years at the helm of the Brookwood Labor College, Muste had decided that America needed a Marxist party as militant as the Communists but independent of Moscow. Muste's vision was shared by his associate Louis Budenz, a former Catholic who had helped align German Catholics with the labor movement before gravitating to the editorship of the socialist *Labor Age*. Budenz organized thousands of picketers when Auto-Lite began hiring strikebreakers.

On May 23, the arrest of Budenz and four picketers sparked the two-day "Battle of Toledo," during which National Guardsmen confronted six thousand strikers and sympathizers, resulting in two deaths and multiple injuries. As a general strike loomed, representatives of the AFL, the Roosevelt administration, and the ACLU rushed to Toledo to negotiate a settlement. Ultimately, the union won recognition and a 5 percent pay increase—concessions that most workers welcomed, though they were not enough to satisfy Muste and Budenz. The events in Toledo inspired a longshoremen's strike in San Francisco and teamsters' strike in Minneapolis, and drew thousands of workers to join industrial unions. Soon John Lewis of the United Mine Workers brought them together in the Congress of Industrial Organizations (CIO), which rivaled the AFL.

The year 1934 also witnessed a new vitality within the predominantly African American Brotherhood of Sleeping Car Porters. Founded in 1925 with the motto "Fight or Be Slaves," the brotherhood was led by Socialist A. Philip Randolph, an African Methodist Episcopal preacher's kid who had first made his mark as editor of Harlem's *Messenger*. When he began organizing his union, Randolph downplayed his youthful anticlericalism as he reached out to such black ministers as New York's Adam Clayton Powell Sr., and Chicago's W. D. Cook, who had left the AME a few years earlier to launch a People's Church called Metropolitan Community Church. One of the brotherhood's organizing tactics was the mass meeting, which gave both preachers and the union access to a broader audience.[5]

Religion was at the heart of the interracial Southern Tenant Farmers' Union (STFU), based in Arkansas and the Mississippi Delta. About half of its leaders were ministers, and they fell into two groups. On the one hand were local lay preachers—white and black, Baptist and Holiness—who were themselves sharecroppers as well as ministers. Often serving congregations that met just once a month because of the sparse rural population, these men were said to "work for a living and preach because they can't help it." Many faced horsewhippings and other violence as soon as they joined the union, but they persisted, explained one admirer, "for they are religious men and when a religious man has put his hand to the plow and stuck it in God's earth he doesn't turn back."[6]

That admirer, Howard Kester, represented the other sort of STFU minister. Inspired by the interracial work of the YMCA while a college student, Kester studied at Princeton and Vanderbilt, then signed on as FOR's Southern secretary. From a base in Nashville, Kester supported striking coal miners in West Virginia and sharecroppers in Mississsippi. Yearning to connect more deeply with the "millions who liken themselves to the slaves in Pharaoh's land," he hoped to help them see Jesus not as a "worker of miracles" but as a "workman struggling with the problems of his people." Kester helped launch the Delta Cooperative Farm, organized by thirty-three sharecropping families who had lost their farms due to their involvement in the STFU. He worked closely with former fundamentalist Claude Williams, who transformed his Presbyterian congregation into the Proletarian Church and Labor Temple and never tired of calling for the "Galilean Carpenter" to be liberated from "the tomb of capitalist theology."[7]

The same spirit was present at the Labor Church of Quincy, Massachusetts, which invited Norman Thomas to speak at its founding service, and at Seattle's Church of the People, which required its members "to subscribe to the dogma that the capitalistic system is inimical to the religion of Jesus." The church welcomed individual Communists as members, and the minister praised them for "a sense of discipline that others lack." "One thing is certain," he observed, "the Communists have learned a good deal about the religion of Jesus and the religionists have learned even more about Communism." Such congregations were not calculated to attract benefactors, and Reinhold Niebuhr noted that pastoring them was best suited for "those completely unencumbered by family responsibilities." Most had dissolved by the Depression's end.[8]

The rising tide of labor radicalism created tensions within socialism. Though most industrial unionists were neither anarchists nor Communists, their militancy raised a question that the Socialist Party had tried to lay to rest a generation before. Might "direct action" by workers, rather than democratic victories at the polls, be the way to build socialism in a time of crisis? This argument was pressed vigorously by Trotskyists and members of Muste's American Workers Party, and by the youthful "Militants" within the Socialist Party, who clashed with an "Old Guard" of party leaders who were cozy with the old unions and devoted to electoral politics.

Social Gospelers held the balance of power, and they sympathized with the revolutionary idealism of the Militants, if not their willingness to use violence on behalf of revolution. Those who were open to revolutionary violence included FOR staffers J. B. Matthews and Howard Kester, both of whom signed the Militants' "Appeal." Most others— including Niebuhr and Thomas—stopped short of endorsing the Militants, but allied with them against the Old Guard. Devere Allen sealed the alliance by drafting a party declaration, endorsed in 1934, that urged workers to "assert their united power" and promised to replace "the bogus democracy of capitalist parliamentarianism by a genuine workers' democracy." Though the document rejected "capitalist war," it finessed the distinction between violent and nonviolent revolution. Should the "crumbling" of capitalism lead to fascism, it promised to "crush by our labor solidarity the reckless forces of reaction." Soon enough, the Old Guard and most trade unionists left the party, the Militant constituency drifted to the Trotskyists or Communists, and moderate Social Gospelers gravitated to the New Deal, which was evolving into a left-liberal coalition not unlike the labor and social democratic parties of Europe. But the Socialists retained the loyalties of A. Philip Randolph and Devere Allen, who would revitalize the peace and racial justice movements of the next generation.[9]

The Socialist conflict occurred just months after the FOR had experienced its own schism. The conflict centered on the most unabashed Militant within the FOR ranks, J. B. Matthews. Struggling to reconcile Matthews's brand of socialism with the FOR's founding pacifism, the organization issued a complicated survey that revealed a strong core of members who were *both* socialist and pacifist, as well as a wing of exclusive pacifists and a smaller wing of nonpacifist revolutionaries. Reaffirming the FOR's founding identity, the leadership chose to exclude the nonpacifists but not the nonsocialists. After Matthews was forced out, Niebuhr and Kester surprised their comrades by choosing to resign: though they were by no means Militants, they had come to believe that absolute pacifism refused to admit what both Marxism and orthodox Christianity freely acknowledged: without some coercion there can be no progress toward greater justice. The FOR split frayed, but did not destroy, the bonds holding radical Social Gospelers together. Though J. B. Matthews migrated to the right wing, Niebuhr worked with FOR loyalists in the Fellowship of Socialist Christians, which he had organized in 1931.[10]

Nevertheless, the final years of the 1930s were a time of Communist, not Socialist, ascendancy. As Militants pressed the Socialists to more confrontational engagement with Rooseveltian liberalism, the Communists—following the lead of Moscow—adopted a new policy known as the Popular Front. Recognizing the Depression and the rise of European fascism as organizing opportunities, the Popular Front urged Communists to join forces with any organization willing to take a strong stance against fascism. Operating openly and incognito, Communists volunteered for industrial unions, civil rights organizations, and even some Democratic campaigns. They reached out to religious groups especially through the American League against War and Fascism, which briefly gained the support of Reinhold Niebuhr and Norman Thomas. They also recruited idealistic young people to the Abraham Lincoln Brigade, which joined the struggle against fascism in Spain. A generation of American radicals came of age within the Popular Front.

The party's official atheism notwithstanding, American Communism in the 1930s was marked by a fervor that mirrored religious devotion and occasionally used explicitly Christian rhetoric. In New York City, Anna Rochester and Grace Hutchins eschewed the faith of their former comrades in the FOR, but drew inspiration from such texts as Samuel Putnam's "I Saw a Communist," which described the Communist as "tread[ing] a path of thorns, as if to meet Some Vision far ahead" and preaching "Peace on Earth as the money-changers fretted and dealt in death." The party's fervor for racial justice persuaded W.E.B. Du Bois to join, while black Young Women's Christian Association (YWCA) leaders Anna Arnold Hedgeman and Dorothy Height cooperated without joining. In Alabama, where most Communists were African American, leaders opened meetings with prayer and promised to build "a new heaven and a new earth, coming down from God to dwell forever."[11]

The Popular Front made it possible for activists to work alongside the party without renouncing religious affiliations, and no religious leader did so more devotedly than Harry Ward. Niebuhr's colleague, ally, and eventual rival at Union Seminary, Ward had written for Socialist publications but never joined the Socialist Party; indeed, he did not register to vote until 1940. The Popular Front allowed him to exercise public leadership without fully identifying with any socialist faction. He served both the American Civil Liberties Union and the American League against War and Fascism ably as chair. But it became increasingly clear that Ward's allegiance was to the Communist Party and the Soviet

Union. By 1936 the Methodist Church had repudiated Ward's Methodist Federation for Social Service, and Niebuhr spoke derisively of his views on Russia as "pathetic."[12]

Religious support for the Popular Front collapsed in 1939, when the Soviet Union entered into a pragmatic alliance with Nazi Germany. By this time, many radicals were gravitating toward the New Deal, and the old Social Gospel coalition—which had united liberal Protestants, post-Christians, and Reform Jews in the pursuit of the Kingdom of God—was giving way to a more diverse set of radical theologies. For the past decade, Reinhold Niebuhr had been turning toward the Calvinist orthodoxy that other radicals despised, along with the Lutheran and Augustinian traditions that stood behind it. Echoing (though never fully endorsing) the work of Karl Barth, Niebuhr argued that liberal and radical Christians erred in identifying the "law of love," rather than God's free grace, as the heart of Christianity. This was linked to a "sentimental" refusal to acknowledge the depths of original sin.

In his turn toward orthodoxy, Niebuhr defined himself successively against three groups of erstwhile allies. When he became a Socialist, he repudiated the "sentimentalism" of other Social Gospelers and joined in the FOR's critique of the churches—but with a subtle difference. While his comrades criticized the church for its Constantinian compromises and imagined that a socialist community might become the true church, Niebuhr believed that even the most idealistic of institutions were "inevitably tempted to compromise the very ideals justifying [their] existence." The first implication he drew from this was that social change depended on "the pure loyalty of a few prophets who fully understand and speak with courage," a view that meshed with FOR attitudes. By the 1930s the lesson was different: those who valued justice would cooperate with flawed institutions, while vesting ultimate faith only in a "religion which looks at history from the perspective of the absolute."[13]

Having rejected nonsocialist sentimentalism, Niebuhr then accused pacifist socialists of sentimentalism, insofar as they failed to recognize that even Gandhian tactics involved coercion. Embracing the possible necessity of class warfare or war against fascism, Niebuhr argued that because "the whole of human history [is] involved in guilt," idealistic attempts to avoid violence at all costs only led to a "morally perverse preference" for "tyranny over anarchy."[14]

Niebuhr's final break was with socialism as such, and this pushed him into the heart of the New Deal coalition. This shift was influenced by his discomfort with Harry Ward's blend of Stalinist fellow traveling and humanistic theology. Niebuhr was also troubled by a movement in Britain known as the "Christian Left," which for a time cooperated closely with his own Fellowship of Socialist Christians. Niebuhr complained that in their propaganda "essential Christian insights have been completely subordinated to Marxism." Niebuhr changed the name of the Fellowship of Socialist Christians to the Frontier Fellowship, and shifted his political efforts to Americans for Democratic Action, a "liberal" group that kept the New Deal faith alive within the Democratic Party. Worried that Social Gospel pacifism would leave Hitler a free hand in Europe, Niebuhr launched *Christianity & Crisis* in 1941 in order to make "Christian realist" insights available to policy makers charged with defending democracy against fascism and Communism. It would later be embraced by the architects of the Cold War.[15]

Niebuhr's apostasy from the Left was less complete than that of some others who had espoused more militant positions in the early 1930s. J. B. Matthews, whose alignment with the Militants sparked the FOR schism, was director of research for the House Un-American Activities Committee by the end of the decade. When Matthews questioned Harry Ward, Ward responded to his fellow Methodist's interrogation by reminding him that Methodists "believe in repentance, and also in the possibility of backsliding." Louis Budenz, the liaison between the American Workers Party and the Auto-Lite strikers of 1934, joined the Communists a year later, rose to the editorship of the *Daily Worker,* then in 1945 abruptly reconverted to the Catholicism of his youth and embarked on a lucrative career as an anti-Communist.[16]

The coupling of Catholic reconversion and political reaction made sense to Budenz's contemporaries. Despite the vast numbers of Catholics who belonged to trade and industrial unions, despite the New Deal advocacy of such priests as John Ryan, radicals assumed that Catholic power was on the Right. This was not wholly unjustified. Prior to the Second Vatican Council, official teaching dictated a preference for governments that would establish the church, and in Franco's Spain that translated into support for pious capitalism in its battle with socialist and anarchist atheism. Elsewhere, the expanding tradition of Catholic social teaching lent itself to centrist rather than leftist politics. Just-war principles protected Catholics from excessive war fervor during World War I but kept them out of pacifist organizations. The encyclicals that challenged capitalism also made it clear that Catholics could not join socialist organizations without violating church teaching.

Still, there was more to Roman Catholicism than hierarchical pronouncements. It retained a rich theology and a vast repertoire of liturgical practices that appealed to activists who found little sustenance in the austere ethics of liberal Protestantism. It retained a nostalgic memory of the centuries before capitalism. And, because of the accidents of immigration, it was the spiritual home of most industrial workers. These features made possible a deeper connection between Catholicism and the Left than either Louis Budenz or his detractors imagined.

That connection was realized most fully by a bit player in the movements of the 1910s and 1920s. As a college student, Dorothy Day was converted to socialism by Upton Sinclair's muckraking novels, then came of age within the "lyrical Left" of New York's Greenwich Village, writing for the *Call* and the *Masses,* drinking with playwright Eugene O'Neill, and participating intermittently in Socialist, Communist, anarchist, and women's suffrage agitation. Always inclined to intense devotion, she invested her faith in the community of workers and sought to encounter poverty by experimenting with life on "welfare rations." Jailed for her agitation, she identified so strongly with other prisoners that she felt "I would never be free again . . . when I knew that behind bars all over the world there were women and men . . . suffering . . . for crimes of which all of us were guilty." At the same time, she knew that the poor in her neighborhood poured their own devotion into Catholic liturgies and festivals.[17]

This consciousness, coupled with the "natural happiness" she experienced after her daughter's birth, led Day to join the church. The early Depression years were a time of vocational restlessness for Day: though she wrote for Catholic journals, she was poorly versed in Catholic social thought and struggled to integrate her radical commitments with her new faith. All of this changed when she encountered the man she regarded as a modern Saint Francis, Peter Maurin. A former seminarian from a French peasant family, Maurin initiated Day into a distinctive understanding of Catholic social teaching. While John Ryan and other moderates integrated Thomistic morality with the modern state and industrial economy, Maurin believed that the principle of "subsidiarity"—the idea that authority should be vested in the smallest social unit possible—called Catholics to abandon the city and the state for village communities of agriculture and hand crafts. Maurin's medievalism and his dismissive attitude toward everything from labor strikes to American democracy placed him outside of the American radical tradition as I have defined it. But Day saw the affinities between Maurin's vision and American anarchism, and for half a century she worked doggedly to bring Catholicism into dialogue with American radicalism.

Day and Maurin launched their *Catholic Worker* newspaper on May Day 1933, naming it in ironic rebuff to the Communists' *Daily Worker*. Blending Day's labor journalism with Maurin's "three point program" of round-table discussions, houses of hospitality, and "agronomic universities," the *Catholic Worker* was notable just for its existence. Suddenly Catholics had joined the rough-and-tumble of radical agitation! Catholic college graduates, with few job prospects in the 1930s, flocked to Day and Maurin, as did the hungry and homeless masses. The latter group inspired them to create the houses of hospitality they were writing about. In New York, Day organized Saint Joseph's House for men and Maryhouse for women, and admirers created daughter houses in dozens of cities.

Relatively few of the *Catholic Worker*'s one hundred thousand readers signed on to its full program of agrarianism, pacifism, and life shared with the "undeserving poor." At its heart, Day observed, the Catholic Worker organization was an "Unpopular Front," and this helped it preserve the flame of radicalism through the most conservative days of the Cold War. But the Catholic Worker had another aspect that connected it to the process by which Depression-era radicals entered the New Deal political establishment. Day combined a rigorous personal discipline with an openhearted affirmation of the diverse vocations of the individuals who passed through her movement, including those uninterested in maintaining radical purity. Her grateful but wayward disciples would eventually include Michael Harrington, architect of the War on Poverty, and antiwar presidential candidate Eugene McCarthy. Perhaps the first in this line was John Cort, a Harvard graduate who arrived at the Worker in the 1930s.

Inspired by Dorothy Day's firsthand accounts of sit-down strikes, Cort thrilled at the opportunity to spend time with striking seamen who "baptized" him "into the proletarian world." Cort considered these encounters to have more potential for social transformation than hospitality for Bowery alcoholics, and he soon gained Day's blessing for the launch of a separate organization. The Association of Catholic Trade Unionists (ACTU) was born in the kitchen of the Catholic Worker house and grew to include one hundred small labor schools training Catholic unionists. The ACTU rivaled the Communist Party in its capacity to bring dedicated activists to CIO unions, and ultimately it helped force the Communists out of the CIO.[18]

Cort's efforts were timely, for in 1931 Pope Pius XI had given a new impetus to Catholic labor activism by issuing *Quadragesimo Anno,* an encyclical marking the fortieth anniversary of *Rerum Novarum.* Addressing the crisis of the Depression, *Quadragesimo* envisioned an economy in which councils of workers and employers would set prices, wages, and policies in each industry, as the medieval guilds had done many centuries earlier. ACTU leaders urged the CIO to embrace this vision, and they were joined in this project by the National Catholic Welfare Conference, which had expanded its role under the leadership of John Ryan. They received an especially warm welcome from Philip Murray, the Catholic coal miner's son who succeeded John Lewis as president of the CIO in 1940. "What the C.I.O. is trying to do," declared Murray in the pages of *Time* magazine, "is basically in the encyclicals of the Church." The alliance between the Catholic hierarchy and the labor movement persisted for decades thereafter.[19]

A child of Chicago's Jewish neighborhoods built another enduring movement on the foundation of the Catholic-labor alliance. Educated in an Orthodox yeshiva, Saul Alinsky learned early on to cherish Rabbi Hillel's admonition, "Where there are no men, be thou a man." But he was largely alienated from religious observance when he enrolled in the University of Chicago's sociology program. Initiated into a practice of close neighborhood observation that was itself indebted to the settlement house movement, Alinsky met organizers sent by the CIO to build a union of Chicago's meatpackers. He wondered if the method of organizing workers by industry rather than trade could be taken a step further. Instead of focusing on the workplace, why not treat "the worker as a living man who votes, rents, consumes, breeds, and participates in every avenue of what we call life?" This insight led Alinsky to invent "community organizing": an approach to social change at the local level that drew on existing organizations, especially churches, and that invited ordinary people to gain power by organizing around their own self-interest.[20]

In Chicago's Back of the Yards neighborhood, Alinsky built a neighborhood council representing bowling clubs, union locals, the American Legion and, above all, Catholic parishes. Auxiliary Bishop Bernard J. Sheil introduced him to the neighborhood's priests. Days after the founding of the Back of the Yards Council in July 1939, Alinsky arranged a joint appearance of Bishop Sheil and John Lewis at a rally for the Packinghouse Workers Union. Convinced that they could not stand up against both unions and churches, the packing companies acceded to the union's demands and avoided what might have been a violent strike.[21]

Catapulted into national prominence, and funded by bishops, unions, and the heir to Chicago's Marshall Field department store, Alinsky exported the Back of the Yards model to other cities. In South Saint Paul, Minnesota, and Kansas City, Missouri, his Industrial Areas Foundation organized meatpacking neighborhoods much like Back of the Yards. Then, in 1945, he tried bringing together the black, white, and Chicano communities of Los Angeles. Bishop Sheil persuaded his Los Angeles counterpart to recommend Alinsky to the local pastors, and Alinsky hired another sociological researcher, Fred Ross, as lead organizer. Among Ross's trainees was César Chávez, a visionary who would use Alinskyite tactics to organize migrant farmworkers, demonstrating along the way that Chicano popular devotions had as much capacity to enliven radicalism as the sacramental piety of Catholic Chicago.

As his movement spread, Alinsky published an organizing manual that encapsulated the activist spirit that was replacing partisan socialism. In *Reveille for Radicals,* Alinsky declared himself a "radical" in a pragmatic, American key, indebted to Tom Paine, Tom Jefferson, the abolitionists, and the unionists. Not exactly socialist but certainly not "liberal," Alinsky's "radical" gained strength by encountering others, identifying "so completely . . . with mankind that he personally shares the pain, the injustices, and the sufferings of all his fellow men." The radical believed in people, and sought to give them power by organizing churches and other organizations around attainable goals. Alinsky's vision suited the needs of Catholic bishops and priests who wanted to implement a "common good" economics without embracing socialism. It appealed, too, to antiracism activists who wanted to keep the abolitionist legacy alive, and to all who, horrified by Stalinist excesses, wanted to keep their radicalism tied to the democratic heritage of America. It would soon appeal to migrant farmworkers, urban pastors in the black church tradition, and ecumenists yearning to blend interfaith dialogue with social action.[22]

That was still in the future as the Great Depression gave way to the good war. In 1940, Alinsky, Day, and Niebuhr were near the beginning of activist careers that would stretch into the 1960s or 1970s. Their paths diverged during the war, with Niebuhr embracing the Cold War establishment, Day espousing a consistent radicalism that eschewed effectiveness, and Alinsky following a middle path grounded in urban neighborhoods. Most Socialists and Popular Fronters followed one of these three paths to a postsocialist politics. But they were not alone: new constituencies, with little background in early radical movements, were drawn to the distinctive religious visions represented by Niebuhr, Day, and Alinsky. In the 1960s, the three groups would converge again, inspired by the courage of bus boycotters and sitting-in students in the South. From that convergence emerged a radicalism that mirrored America's religious pluralism more fully than any heretofore.

CHAPTER 13

The Gandhian Moment

World War II abruptly changed the ecology for left activism in the United States, pushing most radicals into the mainstream and a significant minority into a creative wilderness. For many activists, World War II was, in Studs Terkel's evocative phrase, "the good war" —an epic struggle that pitted the combined forces of democracy and socialism against dictatorial, genocidal, and ultracapitalist fascism. When Hitler's tanks rolled into Poland on September 1, 1939, six months after the invasion of Czechoslovakia and ten months after the wave of anti-Semitic violence known as *Kristallnacht,* it was natural that radicals would want to join the fight. The Communist Party's Popular Front policy meant that Communists and liberals were already cooperating in antifascist organizing. Many were veterans of the Spanish struggle against fascism. Jewish socialists in the United States needed little prompting to support a vigorous defense of their sisters and brothers in central Europe. And for the new unions of the CIO, U.S. industrial support for the war held out the promise of full employment and a seat at the table of power.

This might have strengthened the hand of the Left had international Communism maintained a consistent policy. But in 1939 Popular Fronters were reeling over Stalin's pact with the Nazis and revelations about his anti-Semitic policies in Russia, and Socialist Party loyalists, with their own grudge against the Communists, lashed out against those who would not renounce the Popular Front. "I feel genuinely sorry," mused Niebuhr, "for my friends who seem to be under a spiritual necessity to deny obvious facts about Russian tyranny." After twenty years of devoted service, Harry Ward was forced out of the chairmanship of the ACLU. Claude Williams was likewise forced out of the Southern Tenant Farmers' Union in 1939, when it chose to disaffiliate itself from a Communist-led union that Williams supported.[1]

Though the Popular Front partly rebounded after Hitler invaded the Soviet Union, similar conflicts weakened the Left throughout the 1940s. Popular Fronters and Catholic unionists battled for the soul of the CIO over the course of the decade, and the victory of the latter led to reunification with the AFL. Organized labor lost its radical voice and became a stalwart of establishment liberalism throughout the 1950s and 1960s. In 1947 Stephen Fritchman lost his job as editor of the Unitarian *Christian Register* because of his unremitting sympathy for the Soviet Union; his opponents were not McCarthy supporters but liberals and socialists who had hesitated to take such a drastic step. Reinhold Niebuhr and others created Americans for Democratic Action with the twofold goal of upholding the New Deal and keeping Popular Fronters out of the Democratic Party. Perhaps the last battle in this war was the 1948 presidential campaign of Henry Wallace, a former vice president who raised the old banner of a "Progressive Party" as an alternative to Truman's Cold War policies. When what remained of the Popular Front rallied to Wallace's cause, other radicals kept aloof. Wallace's erstwhile devotion to an obscure Russian Theosophist whom he addressed as "guru" demonstrated the Left's enduring connection to alternative religion but did little to help his faltering campaign.

Conflict over the Popular Front meshed with the popularity of World War II to draw most of the 1930s left-liberal coalition into the political mainstream by the middle of the 1940s. Yet one segment of the Left held fast to its earlier vision: those whose opposition to capitalism or racism was rooted in a fundamental commitment to nonviolence. Anchored by the Fellowship of Reconciliation, War Resisters League, American Friends Service Committee, and Catholic Worker, radical pacifists spent the World War II years forging a culture of "abeyance"—marked by the practice of Gandhian nonviolence, life in intentional community, and a spirituality informed by Quakerism—that sustained them through the prosperous, conservative 1950s and anticipated 1960s radicalism. The spirit of this new culture was captured in a 1936 proposal submitted to Niebuhr's *Radical Religion* for a "Kingdom of God Fellowship" that "would be composed only of those who are completely committed to a world of brotherhood and cooperation, and who are willing not only to sacrifice, but to suffer—to live as though that world were already come." It would "tear down every barrier to love" by welcoming Jews and Buddhists along with Catholics and Protestants, illiterate laborers along with college professors.[2]

The greatest influence on the emerging culture of radical nonviolence was Mohandas Gandhi. Born in Gujarat and educated in England, Gandhi developed a practice of nonviolence that was inherently interreligious, informed by his own Hindu faith, the Jainism of his native region, the Theosophy of his British friends, and the Christian writings of Leo Tolstoy. During his early career as a lawyer in South Africa, Gandhi confronted widespread anti-Indian prejudice, and encouraged his compatriots to blend assertive resistance with a consistent refusal to employ violence. He refined this method of *satyagraha,* or holding fast to the truth, during seven years of opposition to a law that imposed a special form of registration on Indians in South Africa. In 1915 he brought satyagraha home to India, where he led a decades-long struggle for independence from Britain.

Advocates of racial justice in the United States had long recognized parallels between their own cause and that of the Indian people, and activists as diverse as W. E. B. Du Bois and Marcus Garvey were quick to forge friendships with Gandhian emissaries to the United States. Their enthusiasm was shared by the interracial network that connected the NAACP to other causes. Both the NAACP's *Crisis* and the FOR's *World Tomorrow* publicized a 1921 sermon describing Gandhi as "the greatest man in the world" by John Haynes Holmes, a radical Unitarian who was among the founders of the NAACP, FOR, and ACLU. Reverdy Ransom chimed in for readers of the *AME Church Review,* explaining that while the "Western nations" had "rejected the doctrine of non-resistance as taught by Christ," Gandhi possessed a "spiritual weapon" that was "intensely practical." And a columnist in the *Chicago Defender* prayed, "Heaven send us prophets equal to the task" of applying Gandhian methods to the freedom struggle at home.[3]

The prospects for Gandhian activism in the United States seemed even more promising after the dramatic Salt March of 1930. Gandhi's ally C. F. Andrews, a radicalized Christian missionary, spread the word during tours of the United States. Black educational leaders began visiting Gandhi in India in the mid-1930s, with FOR member Howard Thurman's "pilgrimage of friendship" setting the pace. Gandhi's admirers also published manuals for satyagraha at home. Richard Gregg's *The Power of Nonviolence,* based on four years in India, sought to rebut Niebuhr's critique of liberal pacifism. "The faith of the non-violent resister," he explained, was not a "blind" belief that every person is "inherently or predominantly good," but a conviction that the "tiny spark or potentiality of goodness" in each person could be developed. Far from being utopian or perfectionist, nonviolence was the only method of social change that was "in harmony with the laws of growth." The corpus of Gandhian interpretations was rounded out by Krishnalal Shridharani's 1939 *War without Violence*. An Indian activist who participated in the Salt March before enrolling in graduate school in Columbia, Shridharani emphasized the practical effectiveness of Gandhian tactics, downplaying ascetic spirituality while highlighting the importance of Gandhi's charisma and flair for the dramatic gesture. More outgoing than Gregg, Shridharani mentored the activists who began experimenting with Gandhian methods in the 1940s.[4]

Throughout the late 1930s, radical pacifists invoked Gandhi as evidence that their method of social change was as "revolutionary" as the Communists' Popular Front. In the very first issue of the postschism *Fellowship* magazine, Kirby Page declared his opposition to the Popular Front on the grounds that "pacifist revolutionaries" needed to preserve the distinctive qualities of their "non-warlike strategy." A year later, he conceded—with echoes of William Lloyd Garrison—that "if a man for various reasons is unable to rise above hatred and violence, it is obviously better for society that he should use these unethical means in behalf of the suffering masses rather than in support of vested interests." But for "followers of Jesus," voluntary suffering and self-sacrificial love were the methods needed to achieve "the drastic transformation of the existing competitive, profit system."[5]

If Gandhi provided the method for radical nonviolence in the United States, its constituency was clarified by the Spanish Civil War. The clash between Franco's Fascist army and an elected center-left government provided an appealing test case for the Communists' Popular Front strategy. Party members played a leading role in organizing the Abraham Lincoln Brigade, which brought hundreds of Americans into the fight. Not to be outdone by its rivals, the Socialist Party of America created its own Eugene Debs Column. To participate in either organization was to take a position of heroic leadership in the still-ascendant Left coalition of the 1930s. But the Fellowship of Reconciliation broke publicly with that coalition, issuing a public statement that "We Will Not Fight in Spain." Given the overlapping membership of the FOR and the Socialist Party, this statement was directed specifically against the Eugene Debs Column, and it provoked a friendly rebuttal from Norman Thomas. On the one hand, he tried to push the FOR into a sectarian corner, suggesting that "a certain religious philosophy" could not be the "basis" of socialist unity. But he also exposed his own doubts about the best path to revolution, concluding, "No one can regret more bitterly than I a world which forces a choice between courses of action, none of which is without peril to the peace and wellbeing of mankind."[6]

Dorothy Day was even more emphatic about her opposition to participation in the Spanish Civil War, at a time when Catholics were supporting Franco and radicals were supporting the Republicans. "Fascist and Communist alike believe that only by the shedding of blood can they achieve victory," Day noted, but true Christians "must be willing to shed every drop of their own blood, and not take the blood of their brothers." Day's neutrality led partisans on both sides to suspect that the Catholic Worker was not "really" radical or "really" Catholic, while others admired its clarity of principle. For the Catholic Workers themselves, the war provoked deepening reflection on the exact contours of their pacifism. Day's position evolved from a strict interpretation of Catholic just-war principles to an emphatic declaration that "the Sermon on the Mount is our Christian manifesto."[7]

And so it was that when the attack on Pearl Harbor led the United States into the war, Day insisted that "we are still pacifists." By that point, her movement was deeply divided. Communities in Chicago, Seattle, and Los Angeles repudiated Day's pacifism prior to Pearl Harbor, and Day responded with a circular letter that was widely interpreted as an "encyclical" excluding nonpacifists from the movement. Pearl Harbor prompted several critics to close their houses of hospitality and enlist in the army. Within a few years what had been a vibrant national network with forty local centers was reduced to about half a dozen, mostly anchored by individuals or couples loyal to Dorothy Day.[8]

Since the FOR had already forced out its nonpacifists, it did not experience a comparable exodus when it declared that the attack on "our beloved country" would not "alter our opposition to all war. . . . The 'better way' of non-violence and reconciliation is to us a religion and a gospel." The FOR grew slightly as the field of peace organizations was winnowed of just-war and isolationist groups. Soon the FOR, Catholic Worker, and War Resisters League were almost alone in their absolutism.[9]

For younger radicals, the crystallizing moment for World War II pacifism was the passage of the Selective Training and Service Act on September 16, 1940. The first peacetime draft in U.S. history, the act reflected the Roosevelt administration's increasing commitment to the struggle against European fascism and Japanese imperialism. The act's implications for pacifists were benign, reflecting a widespread sympathy that had developed in American culture between the world wars. Those who could not fight because of "religious training and belief" were given the choice of noncombatant service on the battlefield or, if conscience forbade even that, "work of national importance under civilian direction." Under the oversight of the National Council for Religious Conscientious Objection, the peace churches and other pacifist organizations administered, and funded, "camps" for civilian service. The government's hope was that this mild policy would prevent the widespread mistreatment of conscientious objectors that had taken place during World War I.[10]

An unintended effect was the creation of a laboratory for Gandhian nonviolence. Young pacifist men faced a gauntlet of conscientious choices. Was their opposition to violence so absolute as to prohibit participation even in a war against Hitler? If so, was it most appropriate to serve nonviolently on the battlefield, enter a Civilian Public Service (CPS) camp, or go to prison for refusing all cooperation with militarism? If they were clergy or seminarians, should they accept draft exemption or insist on being treated like everyone else? If they found themselves in prison or a CPS camp, should they use Gandhian methods to resist the regimen imposed on them? For the lucky few whose CPS placements included meaningful work—in psychiatric hospitals, for example—to what extent could they use Gandhian principles to enhance that work?

Thousands ultimately worked through these dilemmas, but the trail was blazed by twenty-two students at Union Seminary who began meeting to discern their response on the day the Selective Service Act was passed. These young men had already taken classes with Reinhold Niebuhr and Harry Ward and visited Union alumni at the Highlander Center, Southern Tenant Farmers' Union, and Delta Cooperative Farm. Some had been active in the Young People's Socialist League and the Fellowship of Reconciliation. Dave Dellinger made his personal commitment to pacifism during an air raid in Madrid during the Spanish Civil War, and he had inspired a cluster of his classmates to leave the comfort of their dormitories to create a "Harlem Ashram" among their African American neighbors.[11]

The twenty-two reflected together on the willingness of other Americans to accept peacetime conscription without complaint, and

wondered if "the only thing that might awaken people to their prejudices is for someone to refuse to comply with the act." Perhaps because
of Niebuhr's influence, they acknowledged that all decisions are "made
in relative situations," and they listened when Norman Thomas joined
seminary officials in remonstrating that refusal to register would be quixotic. Eventually they made diverse choices. Several registered as conscientious objectors, expecting to do civilian service if drafted. Roger
Shinn concluded that the war was just but the exemption for ministers
was not; he left school to enlist. And on October 16, Meredith Dallas,
David Dellinger, Don Benedict, Howard Spragg, George Houser, Bill
Lovell, Joe Bevilacqua, and Dick Wichli appeared before the draft board
with a signed letter explaining their refusal to comply with the draft law.
They were indicted, pled guilty, and spent the next ten months at the
Danbury Federal Correctional Institution.[12]

For the Union Eight, this process of encounter with one another, as
well as with the system of war making, was profoundly religious. "We
have been on our knees for long hours," wrote George Houser in his
diary. "We have been more conscious of the reality of God and of the
Christian fellowship than ever before." He mused that "for anyone who
tries to recognize the sovereignty of God, a time may arrive when he
has to choose between the law of the state and what to him is the will
of God."[13]

The process was public. The students' discernment was written up
on the front page of the *New York Times*—something that gave Houser
a "mighty shaky hand while I shaved." His diary entries were published
in the *Union Review* and in *motive,* a new magazine for Methodist college students. After their indictment, the students were overwhelmed
with letters from around the country. With publicity came imitators.
Another seventeen resisters joined the Union Eight at Danbury prison,
even before Pearl Harbor. Ultimately, nearly five thousand people were
sentenced to prison for draft resistance during World War II, far more
than in World War I, while more than ten thousand spent time serving in CPS camps. Not all were radical pacifists: most of those in prison
were Jehovah's Witnesses and most of those in CPS were Anabaptists,
and in the 1940s neither group expected that nonviolent action could be
used to build a socialist, racially egalitarian society. But for a significant
minority, time spent in prison or CPS was time to begin building the
new social order.[14]

Many began with the racial segregation that was routine in federal prisons. At lunch one day, Don Benedict "tried falling into the food line for blacks only." He "was promptly jerked away by a guard and placed with my 'own people.'" When the Union pacifists decided to fast and refuse to work on International Student Peace Day, the warden tried to divide them from other inmates by depriving everyone of privileges. But prison solidarity won out: another inmate interrupted the warden's speech to shout, "Warden, we've heard your side of the story, now let's hear theirs!" Benedict's role as star pitcher for the prison softball team facilitated relationships across boundaries of class and ideology; he would reflect later, "The men in my dormitory were great teachers." Writing for *motive,* George Houser explained that prison time persuaded him of the importance of integrating pacifism with other radical causes. Houser was also convinced that religious discipline was needed to speak truth to power without losing sight of the humanity of those occupying power positions.[15]

By the end of the war, Gandhian practice in prison had evolved into a high art, and the acknowledged master was Bayard Rustin. Rustin had been raised in a tiny African American enclave in Pennsylvania, where he was influenced by both the African Methodist Episcopal Church and the Quaker tradition that he personally embraced. After a stint with the Communists, he aligned with the FOR in the 1940s, and early in 1944 he was sentenced to federal prison for refusing to appear for his preinduction physical. By this time, prisoners known as the "shock troops of pacifism" had staged long-standing fasts and strikes at Lewisburg and Danbury prisons, and Rustin himself had experimented with refusing to submit to segregated seating while riding buses in the South.

Once in the federal prison system, Rustin earned a classification as a "notorious offender" by refusing to accept segregation and by repeatedly subjecting authorities to concrete demands mixed with pacifist philosophizing. At Ashland prison in Kentucky, Rustin was almost immediately placed in quarantine, but still managed to organize a campaign against an abusive guard and regale black inmates with a rendition of Billie Holiday's "Strange Fruit" sung through the ventilation system. Amazingly, he persuaded the warden to let him teach a class on U.S. history to mostly Appalachian whites and to travel freely between white and black sections of the prison. He modeled calm nonviolence while a white racist prisoner (and former judge!) beat him with a mop handle. The solidarity expressed by white conscientious objectors on that occasion had a revelatory effect on black inmates: "The fact of a white man actually taking the side of a Negro in a crisis was a fact they could not believe until it happened." Six months after Rustin's arrival at Ashland he had achieved the desegregation of its dining facilities—only to see much of his work undone when he was disciplined for repeated sexual encounters with other prisoners. Both homophobia and Rustin's moral compromises in lying about his sexual behavior undermined his hopes for revolutionary action throughout the prison system.[16]

Meanwhile, the men who spent the war in CPS camps were engaged in their own Gandhian experiments. Many who became disgusted at "make-work" projects simply walked away, prompting a long-standing debate in the FOR about whether to cease cooperating with the program. Evan Thomas, then serving as national chair of the War Resisters League, resigned from the FOR over this issue, and a poll of the membership revealed deep division. Most of those who lost the vote stayed in FOR out of respect for the "honest, humble seeking for truth" of those who disagreed. And many in the camps spent the war thinking about how to transform the institutions in which they served. Carleton Mabee reflected at the end of the war that "mental patients . . . will continue to be on the conscience of pacifists long after the CPS has ended." Others dreamed of alternative colleges or intentional communities that would extend their experience of "a fellowship in which men of various temperaments, vocations, and races may be accepted without effort."[17]

Whether they spent the war in prison or CPS, radical pacifists had a transformation that was the mirror image of the broader experience of the "greatest generation" coming of age during the war. For the Catholic, Jewish, socialist, or African American youth who served in Europe or the Pacific, the war was a time of Americanization: they came into the service with identities that set them apart from the mainstream and returned home emphatically American. Once home, the GI Bill and the strong unions of the CIO helped them into the middle class. A vigorous NAACP helped African American servicemen and their families demand treatment at home commensurate with their service to the nation. By contrast, many of those who refused to serve—again, apart from the Jehovah's Witnesses and Anabaptists—were highly privileged college graduates. Their acts of resistance prepared them for a process that could almost be described as de-Americanization. By going "from Yale to jail," in the word's of Dave Dellinger's autobiography, they entered into a lifetime of refusing easy compromises with nuclear war, 1950s consumerism, and racial segregation.[18]

CHAPTER 14

Mentors of a New Left

Between World War II and the Montgomery bus boycott, a vibrant community of American radicals prepared the way for the ferment of the 1960s. Though most had come of age during World War II, a few veteran activists had experienced World War I, the 1920s, and the 1930s. They knew what it meant to sustain a radical tradition in both conservative and radical times. Such mentors as A.J. Muste, Dorothy Day, Howard Thurman, and A. Philip Randolph would eventually link 1960s activists to the radical heritage. In the 1940s and 1950s they urged the rising generation to apply Gandhian methods to the problems of nuclear weapons and racial segregation, and created space for transformative encounters in a thriving network of intentional communities. These encounters generated a "personalist" vision that made human dignity the criterion of social justice, and challenged Marxian socialism's place as the leading ideology on the left.

At the time A.J. Muste was known as "the Number One U.S. Pacifist" for his role in fostering pacifist action from the early days of the Cold War through the height of the Vietnam War. One of the pacifist ministers who lost their pulpits after the United States entered World War I, Muste had abandoned both pacifism and Christianity as he evolved into the militant leader of the American Workers Party in the 1930s. But Muste was disillusioned when his Trotskyist allies insisted on entering the Socialist Party en masse in hopes of radicalizing it—a strategy Muste regarded as dishonest. During a European vacation that included a congenial meeting with Leon Trotsky, Muste experienced a conversion. Visiting the church of Saint Sulpice in Paris, he gazed at the cross and suddenly felt, "This is where you belong, in the church, not outside it." Authentic social change, Muste now believed, required religious fellowship and a refusal to separate means from ends.[1]

Muste immediately rejoined the Fellowship of Reconciliation, and assumed the directorship of New York's Labor Temple. In an article re-introducing himself to the FOR, he laid out a vision that would inspire activists for three decades. This vision placed militant pacifism, rather than socialism, at the center of the Left. Pacifism, he argued, "must stand on its own feet" with "a clear program and an unassailable moral position." Refusing "Popular Front" alliances with Trotskyists or Stalinists, radical pacifists would promote "brotherhood or love" rather than "power or domination as the bond which holds society . . . together." Muste's vision was still socialist, but assumed that socialism would follow from the dismantling of the war machine and the transformation of personal lifestyles. And the vision was emphatically "religious," resting on affirmations that personality was sacred, that "the universe is a moral universe," and that happiness is only possible in fellowship. Muste couched his vision in terms that honored what he saw as the religious devotion of Trotskyists and Communists as well as his fellow Christians. His "credo" affirmed that "the center of all is Creative Spirit" and that "my fellows are . . . my 'other self.'" Such rhetoric, coupled with his devotion to Gandhian practice, helped Muste transform the FOR into an organization that was explicitly as well as implicitly interfaith.[2]

Muste's emphasis on personal action dovetailed with that of the Catholic Worker, which began collaborating with the FOR during Muste's tenure as executive secretary. Though Day's movement was greatly reduced in size during the 1940s, it was increasingly respected for the consistency with which it put religious ideals into practice. Such talented young Catholics as Michael Harrington, who would later lead the Democratic Socialists of America and inspire the War on Poverty, found meaningful work and a vital intellectual life at the Worker, and Day's writings contributed to a renaissance of American Catholic culture that prepared the way for Vatican II.

The most colorful of Day's disciples during this period had also come of age before World War I. Ammon Hennacy grew up in a family that so venerated John Brown that he "was ten years old before I knew the difference among God, Moses, and John Brown," and as a young man he identified with both the Socialist Party and the Industrial Workers of the World. Imprisoned for draft resistance, he read the New Testament over and over, embracing what he later identified as "Tolstoian Christianity." When he first met Dorothy Day, he demanded to know, "What jails have *you* been in and how long did *you* serve?" Soon he converted to Roman Catholicism and joined the Worker's New York staff, where he deepened the links between Maurin's Catholic vision and indigenous American radicalism. Hennacy then founded the Joe Hill House of Hospitality in Salt Lake City, honoring the legendary IWW activist and songwriter. Calling himself a "one man revolution," Hennacy exemplified individual action as a path to spiritual integrity and social change.[3]

During the years Hennacy was practicing his "life at hard labor," Howard Thurman was stirring up enthusiasm for a Gandhian assault on Jim Crow among his fellow African American ministers and educators. Raised in rural poverty, Thurman joined the Fellowship of Reconciliation as a Morehouse College student in the 1920s, hoping for "a sense of immunity to the assaults of the white world of Atlanta, Georgia." After earning a seminary degree and being ordained in the Baptist tradition, he studied independently with Rufus Jones, who helped him link the African American experience to a mystical and activist Quakerism. As dean of the chapel at Morehouse and then Howard University, he shared his enthusiasm for Gandhi with other African American leaders. Thurman also linked the Jesus of labor to the African American tradition, arguing that Jesus taught "a technique of survival" for all "cast-down people."[4]

Many of the African American activists who revered Thurman also admired A. Philip Randolph. As the United States entered World War II, Randolph launched a new movement to demand an end to segregation in the armed forces. Though concessions from the administration led Randolph to call off his planned March on Washington, he used massive urban rallies—eighteen thousand people in New York, twelve thousand in Chicago—to build a constituency known as the March on Washington Movement. Randolph's religious allies were remarkably diverse. The Chicago rally was organized by both an AME minister and Ross Brown of the Truth Seekers Temple Liberal Church, which called itself "the Church that tries to make you Think." Randolph's white allies included Ethical Culture leader Algernon Black and Jesuit John LaForge, who affirmed Randolph's strategic decision to keep the March on Washington Movement all black—in part because this would minimize the risk of Communist interference.

These alliances reflected the ongoing evolution in Randolph's religious identity. During his editorship of the Harlem *Messenger,* that journal had evolved from a mouthpiece for Freethought into a forum for diverse religious opinions. In one debate, Howard professor Kelly Miller praised the black church for empowering African Americans to demonstrate their "effective concerted will," while white ex-seminarian V. F. Calverton lambasted the "contradiction" of "a black man worshiping a white man's God in a black man's church." As Randolph became more comfortable with religious rhetoric, he traced his movement to "the religion of Jesus, planted and nurtured by a manual laborer," and declared that "the dignity of the individual personality" was "the heart of the Judeo-Christian ethic." By 1957 Randolph was sufficiently reconciled to the church of his youth to join the AME congregation in Harlem that had once been served by Reverdy Ransom.[5]

The themes of direct action against war, resistance to racial segregation, and life in intentional community were woven together in the work of these mentors. One strand of activism focused on the new threat of nuclear annihilation. When American bombs destroyed the cities of Hiroshima and Nagasaki, Dorothy Day declared, "Our Lord himself has already pronounced judgment on the atomic bomb." For Muste, the bomb clarified the course of postwar pacifism. On the one hand, the threat required energetic cooperation with nonpacifists who were opposed to the arms race; on the other, the very excess of violent power represented by the bomb created an opening for "the conversion of thousands upon thousands to . . . the pacifist way of life."[6]

Because Muste believed the bomb had created a situation in which "man no longer believes in himself," he urged activists to restore that belief through concrete acts of resistance. Some proposed "refusal to pay federal income taxes" as a way to defy "the decrees of Caesar," and in 1947 Muste joined George Houser, Bayard Rustin, and David Dellinger in the nation's first draft-card burning. Since the FOR as an organization was not wholeheartedly committed to such tactics, activists created such short-lived groups as the Committee for Non-violent Revolution and Peacemakers to orchestrate "guerrilla" Gandhianism.[7]

One organization that bridged the divide between moderate antinuclear activists and radical pacifists was the American Friends Service Committee (AFSC). Founded in 1917 to provide service opportunities for conscientious objectors (and reconcile Quaker factions), the AFSC earned the Nobel Peace Prize in 1947 for its international relief work. Its leadership overlapped with that of the FOR, and both groups defined pacifism broadly to include active promotion of justice as well as the refusal to participate in war. This commitment increasingly drew the organization into radical politics. At the invitation of Norman Thomas and the Federal Council of Churches, the AFSC got involved in relief work with striking coal miners during the Great Depression. It administered CPS camps during World War II and expanded its domestic activities to include issues of racial justice. The AFSC inspired many religiously disenfranchised radicals to join the Wider Quaker Fellowship (formed for those reluctant to join Quaker meetings), or Friends General Conference, the most liberal branch of Quakerism. For Quakers who were "pacifists first and Christians second," the AFSC provided a focal point for activism on a range of issues. Its radical vision was epitomized in the 1955 *Speak Truth to Power,* which argued for unilateral disarmament not only on pacifist grounds but also because militarism threatened American democracy. The pamphlet's authors, Muste among them, insisted that nonviolence had more to do with active love than passive suffering. Still new and controversial among Quakers, these ideas were embraced by pacifists who wished to uphold a broader radical tradition.[8]

The militant antinuclear movement flowered in 1955, when activists from the Catholic Worker, FOR, and War Resisters League gathered in a New York City park to defy the city's annual civil defense drill. The spectacle reflected the organizers' belief that "the deed is always mightier than the word" and attracted an ever-broader circle of participants in each successive year. Five hundred people risked arrest in New York in 1960, making enough of a stir that the city quietly discontinued the drills. By that time radical pacifists had moved on to more dramatic actions.[9]

The "Nevada Project" of 1957 was initiated by Lawrence Scott, an evangelical-turned-Quaker who had worked for AFSC before his impatience with "effete middle-class Friends" led him to embark on an "itinerant ministry" against nuclear testing. Scott brought three dozen pacifists to a Nevada desert that was the site of nuclear tests on the twelfth anniversary of the Hiroshima bombing, where they tried to enter the site and halt the test. A year later, a boat called the *Golden Rule* attempted to sail into the atomic testing zone of the Pacific, though it was intercepted before leaving port. Building on the excitement of African decolonization, Muste and Rustin joined an international team that traveled from newly independent Ghana to still colonized Upper Volta to protest French nuclear testing in the Sahara. Though the Ghanaian government embraced the protesters, Muste was most pleased when one young Ghanaian said that he now understood that true nonviolence meant "that if Ghana should decide to test an atomic bomb, I'd have to oppose that most of all." A similar cosmopolitanism informed the Walk for Peace, which began in San Francisco in December 1960 and arrived in Moscow ten months later. Like its predecessors, the walk garnered media coverage but little change in policy.[10]

These spectacles of pacifism sparked a debate on the relationship between religion and politics. One sympathetic observer of the Nevada action noted that the use of the religious idiom of "witness" simultaneously made the event "more successful than any recent pacifist action in reaching millions through the mass media" and prevented it from "focus[ing] attention on an intelligible policy alternative." More pointedly, Norman Thomas wrote to his former colleagues in FOR that while he hoped for unilateral disarmament, he was not willing to renounce the compromises of politics. "To my sorrow [I] lack the full assurance of religious faith which some of you have."[11]

The organizational vehicle for moderate opposition to nuclear weapons was the Committee for a Sane Nuclear Policy (or SANE), which eschewed direct action in favor of large rallies featuring the likes of Eleanor Roosevelt and Walter Reuther. On the eve of one rally, SANE infuriated militant pacifists by firing the rally's organizer on suspicion of Communist ties. Muste lashed out at the SANE leadership, arguing that the antidote to Communist infiltration was a "vigorous, militant peace movement." Though Muste claimed to have "no appetite for a campaign against SANE," he kept up the criticism for years, arguing in the wake of the Birmingham civil rights demonstrations that peace activists should "aspire to be equal to the Negro children of Birmingham" by engaging in massive civil disobedience.[12]

The link between Birmingham and antinuclear work was logical for Gandhian pacifists, who developed nonviolent strategies against segregation decades before the Montgomery bus boycott. In this area, Thurman and Randolph joined Day and Muste as mentors, and their leading disciples were Bayard Rustin and James Farmer. Son of a black Methodist theology professor, Farmer embraced interracial activism through the Christian student movements of the 1930s. Farmer experimented with integration by driving across the Deep South with a white sociology student en route to the National Negro Congress. Farmer initiated his companion into drinking at "colored fountains" and parrying the casual insults of policemen.

Once there, Farmer was impressed by Randolph's public break with Communists in the Congress, and he soon joined the Socialist Party. He found additional mentors as a graduate student at the Howard University School of Religion. In class, he was inspired by Howard Thurman; on weekends spent in New York City he absorbed a different teaching from the socialist literary critic V. F. Calverton, a hedonistic ex-seminarian who guided Farmer on the path to humanism. The two men, one black and one white, initiated Farmer into the wide spectrum of radicalism: "Thurman, who introduced me to the study of Gandhi, believed the Mahatma to be a great soul, a saint. Calverton, who led me through Marxist revisionism to Fourier and Gene Debs and Democratic Socialism, thought Gandhi a superb politician." On Thurman's recommendation, Farmer took a position, just months before the attack on Pearl Harbor, as FOR race relations secretary, with an office in Chicago.[13]

In Chicago, Farmer joined a lively circle of activists, both white and black, in Gandhian experiments. With funding from an AME pastor and alderman, graduate students and seminarians (including George Houser of the Union Eight) launched their first desegregation effort at a roller-skating rink, where they appealed to an Illinois desegregation law to force a change in policy. Troubled by the tensions between the court system and pacifist principle, they then chose the more direct method of filling all seats in a segregated coffeehouse with integrated groups. The activists gained the support of both the other diners in the restaurant and the police officers who were called in to remove them. Building on such successes, Farmer urged the FOR board to support a "Brotherhood Mobilization" involving five or ten years of "relentless noncooperation" directed against American racism. When board members objected that the Chicago activists had violated pacifist principle by using the courts, Muste suggested that they simply allow Farmer to develop his own organization, and thus was born the Congress of Racial Equality (CORE).[14]

Describing the CORE founding conference, Farmer wrote that "every posture taken shamed the Statue of Liberty; every word rang the Liberty Bell itself. . . . [The participants] could not have been more consumed with fire had they been a band of abolitionists convening in the mid-nineteenth century." The analogy was apt, for CORE revived the one-on-one practices of interracial encounter that had defined the abolitionist era. For the interracial teams that took CORE's message on the road, integration was an end in itself and not merely a means to African American empowerment. Because they insisted on a harmony between means and ends, they proudly called themselves the Congress *of*—not merely *on*—Racial Equality.[15]

Yet Farmer was personally of two minds about the balance between integration and empowerment. He was entering his sexual adulthood at the time he launched CORE, and his first romance was with a working-class, divorced woman rooted in Chicago's black community and utterly outside Farmer's circle of pacifists. Farmer's tumultuous marriage to Winnie was a "a fierce tug-of-war between two loves that were hostile and antagonistic: our love for each other and my love for an unborn movement." Her failure to comprehend his devotion to CORE alerted Farmer to the possibility that the masses of black people might not rally to a Gandhian movement with articulate white leaders. Though Farmer would later marry a white woman, this suspicion prodded him to open CORE to nonpacifists; years later, it would influence his acquiescence to Black Power activists' demand that white people be removed from CORE's leadership.[16]

Farmer's mixed feelings were not shared by CORE's other early leader. In the 1940s, Farmer and Bayard Rustin were a study in contrasts. Farmer was embarking on his first sexual relationship, with a black woman; Rustin had had a string of mostly white male lovers. Farmer was torn between the influences of Thurman and Calverton; Rustin was committed to Quaker nonviolence. Farmer had evaded prison time by accepting conscientious objector status during the war; Rustin was the most notorious pacifist prisoner of his generation. Above all, Rustin was more than willing to meet white activists' desire for transformative encounter. He fascinated comrades who saw him as "a four-way outsider"—black, Quaker, openly gay, and an artist worthy of Broadway. Rustin moved to the forefront after Farmer was forced out of the FOR staff in 1945.[17]

Before that happened, Farmer and Rustin joined A. Philip Randolph in exploring how to mobilize Randolph's black constituency for CORE-style action against segregation. Together they crystallized a vision for postwar activism. "Think," Farmer wrote, "what it would mean if, as the war draws to a close, the people of this land were to take their stand squarely on the Declaration of Independence, the Constitution of the United States, the findings of all reputable modern science, and the teachings of the Jewish and Christian scriptures, and were to launch a crusade for racial democracy and the practice of complete brotherhood in relations between the races." Having "hurled" bullets "at the master-race monster abroad," veterans were primed to fight Jim Crow, and their "veritable volcano of revolt" might be channeled by a Gandhian discipline as exacting as that of war.[18]

Soon after writing these words, Farmer resigned from FOR and did not resume CORE leadership until 1960. George Houser carried the work forward with a series of desegregation actions in midwestern and West Coast cities, then joined Rustin in organizing a national campaign in response to the 1946 Supreme Court decision banning segregation in interstate transportation. What better way to ensure enforcement of this decision than by sponsoring an interracial tour from Baltimore to New Orleans? CORE's extended network of activists made recruitment of travelers relatively easy: they included black Episcopal priest Nathan Wright, later one of the founders of Black Theology; Homer Jack, a Unitarian minister and child of Jewish socialists; African American law-yer Conrad Lynn; and white activist James Peck. Their journey was marked by friendly conversations with fellow passengers, a dozen arrests, and a mob attack on the home of their host in Chapel Hill. Its most im-portant legacy came more than a decade later, when it served as a model for the Freedom Rides that swept through the South in 1961.

During the same years, Howard Thurman shifted his own energies from the African American context of Howard University to explicitly integrationist work. In 1944, with the support of the FOR, he and a white colleague organized San Francisco's Church for the Fellowship of All Peoples. Making explicit what was implicit in Gandhian circles, this congregation aspired to be interfaith as well as interracial, with represen-tatives of the local rabbis' group, the Unitarian Church, and the Chinese YMCA participating in the inaugural service. Its members committed to "seek after a vital experience of God as revealed through Jesus of Nazareth and other great religious spirits." A few years later, Thurman published *Jesus and the Disinherited,* applying the image of Jesus as a radi-cal specifically to the cause of racial justice, and in 1953 he was chosen as dean of Marsh Chapel at Boston University—a potent symbol of the new integrationist sentiment among white institutions in the North.[19]

Just as efforts inspired by Thurman and Randolph paved the way for the Southern civil rights movement of the 1960s, and radical paci-fists inspired by Muste pioneered the tactics of the anti–Vietnam War movement, so the World War II generation's participation in inten-tional communities set the tone for the countercultural communalism that followed. In FOR publications of the 1940s, community was almost as important as antinuclear and antiracist activism. Urging members to form "cell groups," Muste promised "that it is upon such groups that the Holy Spirit descends." Most of these cells were nonresidential variants on the Methodist class meeting or Quaker meeting. Full-time residential community was a logical extension, and in 1945 two activists proposed that the fellowship's office be moved to an intentional community, both to save money and to enhance the spirit of fellowship.[20]

Such communities were soon ubiquitous in pacifist and antisegregationist culture. Several of the Union Eight had lived in community in Harlem before the war, and after their release they organized a Newark Ashram, Dave Dellinger's communal farm at Glen Gardner, and a Detroit community where Don Benedict shared his life with an FOR staffer, "a young orthodox Jew, a Chinese chemistry student, and some who were having their first run-in with the draft law." They organized an interracial milk delivery cooperative that kept food coming into black neighborhoods during a summer of race riots, and conducted a CORE-style desegregation action at a local restaurant. Benedict later launched the East Harlem Protestant Parish, a "group ministry" that he and his new wife shared with three other couples.[21]

Similarly, Farmer's antisegregation work was anchored by residential communities in Chicago and in New York, where he lived in the Harlem Ashram organized by Methodist missionaries. Though Farmer found the "credo of voluntary poverty" off-putting and the meals "an inducement to fasting," the ashram was a convivial setting for meetings of CORE's local chapter. Other ashrams cropped up in such places as Antioch College. One of the white ministers who participated in the Journey of Reconciliation, Ernest Bromley, created an interracial household with his wife, Marion, and a black pacifist couple, Juanita Morrow and Wally Nelson.[22]

While urban ashrams housed full-time activists, another set of communities traced their origins to Depression-era efforts to redress unemployment by reinvigorating rural communities. This was the original logic of the Catholic Worker farms, and farming communities were established by both Catholic and Protestant organizations, among them the Delta Cooperative Farm in Bolivar County, Mississippi, whose members had lost their homes because of their activism with the Southern Tenant Farmers' Union. Delta Farm's promoters took special delight when they learned that a radical preacher had established a similar enterprise in New Mexico. Other rural communities were formed under the auspices of the Tennessee Valley Authority (TVA), which promoted planned towns and cooperative enterprises in conjunction with its program of dam building and rural electrification.[23]

Several communities blended the pacifist and socialist vision of the ashrams with the TVA's community development agenda. The Macedonia Cooperative Community in Georgia was originally envisioned as an economic cooperative for rural people. When "war wages lured away the mountain families," they were replaced by pacifist veterans of prison and CPS camps. They embraced complete communism, and in 1949 became a local cell of Peacemakers. Further south in Georgia, Koinonia Farm was launched in 1942 by Southern Baptists who hoped to establish "a demonstration plot for the Kingdom of God," characterized by interracial cooperation and complete sharing of wealth. Though its communalism appealed mostly to white pacifists, Koinonia offered training in both agriculture and biblical scholarship to its black neighbors and sponsored an interracial summer camp that was shut down by Klansmen in 1956.[24]

The camp was revived at the Highlander Folk School in eastern Tennessee. Established by Union Seminary graduates Myles Horton and James Dombrowski, Highlander was a labor school in the tradition of Rand and Brookwood. Here both blacks and whites came to learn about union organizing and citizenship rights. Highlander was a frequent stop for folk singer Pete Seeger, who with Zilphia Horton adapted "We Shall Overcome" into a civil rights anthem. In the wake of the Montgomery bus boycott, Rosa Parks, Martin Luther King Jr., Fannie Lou Hamer, John Lewis, Andrew Young, and Stokely Carmichael all passed through the "citizenship school" anchored by Septima Clark. "I was forty-two years old," recalled Parks, "and it was one of the first times in my life up to that point when I did not feel any hostility from white people."[25]

The diverse forms of intentional community were knit together by Arthur Morgan. As president of Antioch College in the 1920s, he recruited pacifist bishop Paul Jones and Gandhian sociologist M. N. Chatterjee to his faculty, and developed with them a vision of small fellowships as the engine of social transformation. Morgan introduced a system of cooperative education in which students rotated between on-campus study and extended internships, many of them based in intentional communities or social change organizations. He then brought his community vision to the TVA, which he chaired from 1933 to 1938. After being fired by FDR for insubordination, Morgan organized Community Service, Inc., to put his communal vision into practice.

Community Service's offshoot, the Fellowship of Intentional Communities, began organizing annual gatherings for intentional communities in the late 1940s. At one gathering, a presentation by the Bruderhof—German pacifists who were more sectarian than radical —sparked a division within Georgia's Macedonia community, half of whose members ultimately joined the Bruderhof. There were also friendly debates about the purpose of intentional community. Staughton Lynd, a member of the Macedonia faction that declined to join the Bruderhof, nevertheless argued in 1957 that, in order to succeed, a community needed to break with liberal individualism. Preferring the "vision of the ancient Greeks and medieval Catholics," the Macedonians insisted that individuals would bring "the seeds of all the evils in the larger society" into community unless they sacrificed themselves entirely. Taken seriously, this position would have pushed intentional community outside the liberatory tradition of the Left, and so Dave Dellinger urged communitarians to "distinguish between the progressive act of abolishing wages, rent, and private food bills and the regressive act of turning over to the 'group mind' . . . decisions on such questions as whom one is to marry [or] whether to attend community worship." Admitting the fragility of libertarian communities, Dellinger insisted that their "pioneering work" would transform the larger society. Soon enough, Lynd himself relocated from Macedonia to Glen Gardner (and then a career in academia), drawing a distinction between the healthy "dedication of the individual to a vision transcending personal interests" and the unhealthy practice of asking the individual to "put his life into the hands of other human beings."[26]

The distinction was clear at the community that housed much of the FOR's New York leadership, Skyview Acres. This cluster of freestanding suburban households was home to an interracial group who hoped to change local attitudes through simple involvement. Jean Houser, married to CORE leader George Houser, served as president of the local PTA. Charles Lawrence, an African American sociologist and national vice chair of the FOR, was on an advisory committee for the local schools and organized a local chapter of the NAACP. The community spawned the Council of Community Brotherhood, which made it possible for local African Americans to get a haircut in town. Conceding the value of more rigid communities, the Skyviewers found "greater appeal in the community of diverse interests and attachments."[27]

Skyview illustrates the reasons that intentional community made sense to the radicals of the 1940s and 1950s. As the World War II generation began to raise children, community allowed them to keep their radical edge while shielding their children from the "serious dilemma" of being the only pacifists in their Brownie or Cub Scout troops. Intentional community was also an antidote to the culture of consumerism spawned by postwar prosperity. Building on the work of Peter Maurin or modern "homesteaders" Scott and Helen Nearing, postwar radicals stressed the spiritual benefits of planting one's own garden and making one's own bread. Intentional community was an ideal "abeyance structure"—a social form that preserves the memories and practices of a tradition during hard times, preparing it for a future resurgence. Like the Fourierist communities of the 1840s, postwar intentional communities gave radicals space to develop a distinct culture and preserve faith in a new social order.[28]

As a new era of large-scale activism dawned, diverse strands of religious and spiritual radicalism came together in a magazine whose editors included Dellinger, Muste, and Rustin. Founded in 1956, *Liberation* aspired to renew the inclusive vision of the Populist and Farm Labor movements (as well as of the early Socialist Party) by creating a broad but decidedly non-Stalinist radical coalition. Much like the *World Tomorrow* in the 1920s, *Liberation* brought radical Christians into conversation with equal numbers of post-Christian humanists. Its readers were active in pacifist and antiracist organizations, and were extremely well educated. This demographic anticipated the flowering of student radicalism in the next decade.[29]

Liberation's readers were less certain than those of the *World Tomorrow* that socialism could be the basis for a broad-based radical movement. In one survey, a third identified as socialists and a quarter as anarchists, while nearly half endorsed "cooperative communities." Most of the editors were anarchists who were open to dialogue with Communists and gushingly enthusiastic about the Cuban revolution. Dorothy Day, who shared these perspectives, was often featured in the magazine, prompting one letter writer to observe that Christian leftists were willing to consort with Communists because they wanted to "bring the gospel to pagans and sinners." In the presidential election of 1956, the editors urged "a deliberate refusal to vote," while a slight majority of readers opted for Adlai Stevenson as a personally appealing individual and lesser evil.[30]

If socialism divided *Liberation*'s constituency, the new radical glue was the practice of nonviolent direct action: its readers were veterans of Walks for Peace, the *Golden Rule* voyage, Civilian Public Service, or imprisonment during World War II. For them, civil rights, antinuclear, and communitarian activism were embodiments of a unifying Gandhian vision. *Liberation* articles delved into the theory and tactics of civil disobedience, testing the boundaries of nonviolence and even wondering if reliance on federal coercion might undermine the Southern freedom struggle. These questions reflected a profound commitment to harmonize ends with means, but they also contributed to a lack of clarity—endemic through the 1960s and beyond—about the shape of radicalism's ultimate ends.[31]

Liberation placed itself within a "radical" tradition that was broader than socialism. An emphasis on tradition is a characteristic feature of abeyance periods, and in a founding statement called "Tract for the Times" the editors sketched out a comprehensive version of the radical tradition. Since the "great dominant traditions" of liberalism and Marxism had run out of ideas, they argued, it was time to return "to root traditions from which we derive our values and standards." These included the "ancient Judeo-Christian prophetic tradition which gave men a vision of human dignity and a reign of righteousness, equality and brotherhood on earth"; the unrealized and "all but lost" American tradition of liberty and equal rights embodied by Jefferson, Paine, Thoreau, Debs, and the abolitionists; the late nineteenth-century movements that inspired "the impoverished and distressed" to dream of a "class-less and war-less world"; and finally the perennial tradition of nonviolence, currently embodied by Gandhi. The editors advocated "a creative synthesis of the individual ethical insights of the great religious leaders and the collective social concern of the great revolutionists" and concluded with a call for "*action now.*"[32]

One label for the sort of thinking found in the "Tract" was "personalism," a term that evoked both the European antecedents of the Catholic Worker and one strand of Social Gospel Protestantism. It signified devotion to the inborn dignity of each person and a refusal to accept any ideology that treated persons as means rather than ends. Dellinger suggested that in a "Here-and-Now Revolution [that] begins with one self," the boundaries between politics and religion would dissolve. Since "the Kingdom of God is now," "Francis of Assisi has more meaning than Thomas Aquinas, Dorothy Day than Billy Graham, the conscientious objector than the anti-war orator." This vision, he went on, was becoming reality in Montgomery, where "men are growing spiritually . . . [by] attacking the seeds of evil in their own lives, while participating in one aspect of the struggle for a new society."[33]

———

Dellinger's judgment that Montgomery was the heart of a personalist revolution reflected lessons he had learned from his mentors. Their experience in preserving the radical tradition during the 1920s had taught them the importance of persistent, small-scale action; their experience during the 1930s had taught them to keep their eyes open for new centers of radical power. Back then, new energy came from the industrial unions; now it came from the black preachers, students, and sharecroppers of the South. Once again, people who had been excluded from the American dream were coming together to claim a powerful new identity and a full stake in America's revolutionary heritage. What was new this time was that others would embrace and emulate the style of encounter on display in Montgomery. Within a decade, the resulting alliance made the encounter of identity the defining practice of a new multicultural radicalism. The mentors had prepared the way well.

CHAPTER 15

New Encounters in the South

A few months after the African American citizens of Montgomery, Alabama, began boycotting a bus system that denied their human dignity, Rev. Martin Luther King Jr. published an article in *Liberation* that explained the meaning of this action. The article, ghostwritten by Bayard Rustin, explained that over centuries of slavery and segregation, many African Americans had "lost faith in themselves," believing "that perhaps they really were what they had been told they were—something less than men." Many wondered if "we Negroes had the nerve" to fight segregation. But the boycott *did* succeed: from the very first day, virtually no blacks rode the city's buses, and they kept up their discipline for more than a year, until the authorities (prompted by the Supreme Court) accepted their demand for a fully integrated seating policy. Even before this result was achieved, King's article concluded, "*We Negroes have replaced self-pity with self-respect and self-depreciation with dignity.* . . . Montgomery has broken the spell."[1]

These words expressed the founding revelation of the 1960s Left. Ordinary African Americans—maids and sharecroppers, schoolteachers and professors—had unleashed power by encountering one another in a new way. On dusty sidewalks they discovered the power to bring the white system to a standstill; gathered in their churches they found new energy in old hymns. Veteran activists were surprised by their neighbors' new enthusiasm—had not Rosa Parks heard others "mumbling and grumbling" about the waste of time when she stood up to aggressive drivers previously? Suddenly the whole community was meeting violence with courage, as when King's home was bombed and his neighbors defied the police to stand vigil until King personally assured them he was safe. Shared protest, wrote one activist, created "a new person in the Negro. The new spirit, the new feeling did something to blacks individually and collectively. . . . There was no turning back!"[2]

Montgomery pushed the encounter of identity to the center of American radicalism. Over the next decade, one movement after another—student sit-ins, campus free speech, feminist consciousness-raising, Chicano farmworker organizing, gay and lesbian liberation—sought the power that had kept black Montgomerians on their feet through the chilly winter and hot summer of 1956. Earlier movements had begun with empowering encounters among African Americans or workers or women, but they had achieved national scope only after other encounters, crossing the boundaries of class or race, brought privileged allies into the struggle. Many activists, notably the founders of CORE, had come to believe that boundary-crossing encounters were the source of radical power. Once Montgomery had revealed the power of identity encounters, activists rethought their vision. Soon even persons of relative privilege were organizing around particular identities.

Montgomery is not always remembered as the birthplace of identity politics. White Americans especially recall the early civil rights movement as a time of "black and white together," epitomized by the famous photographs (taken in Selma in 1965, not Montgomery in 1956) that show equal numbers of blacks and whites, among them nuns and rabbis, marching for freedom. But white people scarcely figured in the experiences that led Montgomerians to declare that a new Negro was being born. For a handful of local white allies, the boycott was a time of transformative interracial encounter. But there just weren't enough radical whites to encounter all the blacks drawn into the movement. For blacks in Montgomery, the significant meetings were with one another.

These meetings were not unlike the founding gatherings of the African Methodist Episcopal Church, or Margaret Fuller's "Conversations" for women, or the encounters among wageworkers during the strikes of 1934. Yet they evoked a different response. Earlier encounters of identity generated either terror or condescension among outsiders, a pattern that held true for white Southern responses to Montgomery. But perhaps because the Southern freedom struggle was the first encounter of identity to be televised, it stimulated a different response from more distant observers. These people saw a new form of power, and many reacted with wonder, admiration, or envy. Such responses enabled a rapid transition from protest to structural change, as Congress passed legislation banning formal segregation and disenfranchisement less than a decade after Montgomery. In contrast to the changes of the Civil War, Progressive Era, and New Deal, all of which were orchestrated by the privileged allies of slaves and workers, these changes were the direct work of the rising wave of newly empowered African Americans. While Abraham Lincoln gave credit for emancipation to Garrison, Lyndon Johnson honored Martin Luther King Jr. by declaring, "We shall overcome!" in calling for a Voting Rights Act. Visible success inspired emulation.

In addition to television, nonviolence was crucial to the positive response to Montgomery. Past identity encounters had evoked fear among privileged people, who sensed that social institutions might be transformed in ways beyond their own power. Sometimes the encounters were accompanied by threats of violence, but the empowerment alone was frightening. Martin Luther King's repeated profession of love for his adversaries mitigated that fear. But nonviolence was generally possible only for those who had already experienced some degree of empowerment, as activist Jo Ann Robinson discovered when she was arrested. After being pushed and harassed by a police officer, she realized that he was more frightened by her defiance than she was by his violence. Inundated by "sorrow and pity," she prayed that he would find peace.[3]

Seen from the perspective of practices of encounter, the contrast between Montgomery and CORE activism in the 1940s was sharper than that between Montgomery and late 1960s Black Power. In principle, King and his lieutenants embraced the integrationist goals and nonviolent strategies pioneered by CORE. But in practice, Montgomery was worlds away from CORE's scripted actions undertaken by disciplined, racially balanced teams. The Northern acolytes of nonviolence saw Montgomery not as a culmination of their own efforts but as a stunning new fact in radical history. "As I watched the people walk away," Bayard Rustin mused during his first visit to Montgomery, "I had a feeling that no force on earth can stop this movement. It has all the elements to touch the hearts of men." Eight years later, Dave Dellinger was still marveling at the way Southern blacks had rewritten the Gandhian script. "There is no doubt in my mind," he wrote, "that the Negro nonviolent movement is sounder because its direct knowledge of Gandhi is so slight."[4]

Montgomery was also transformative because black congregations managed to wed the religious practice of mutual empowerment to traditional black church practices of singing, preaching, and testifying. This achievement was a testament to the creative humility of boycott organizers Jo Ann Robinson, E. D. Nixon, and Rosa Parks. Previously, these leaders had worked primarily through the NAACP and the Women's Political Council, which in turn relied upon labor unions and Alabama State College for support. "Secular" in the sense that they were not inclined to public expressions of their religiosity, the three recognized that "black ministers could do more to mobilize support in the community than anyone else," and they propelled Martin Luther King into the leadership of the nascent Montgomery Improvement Association. King drew on his upbringing in the church and his education among Social Gospel liberals to craft a message that would appeal to the full spectrum of African Americans. In Montgomery, he reported, the pious masses were becoming "militant" in their faith, "while upper-class Negroes who reject the 'come to Jesus' gospel" were embracing gospel nonviolence. Even Robinson experienced a spiritual presence during the mass meetings and was able to "put myself in the hands of the unseen power from above."[5]

The new black religiosity took institutional form in January 1957, when the Southern Christian Leadership Conference (SCLC) began taking the Montgomery experience to other cities. The SCLC was largely an organization of black ministers, who shunted aside its talented founding staffer, Ella Baker. Even Baker's admirers at *Liberation* conceded that a movement truly owned by Southern blacks "must be essentially church-centered and preacher-led." By deferring to the ministers' need for the limelight, the SCLC preserved its access to African Americans whose lives revolved around the church. Young John Lewis, for example, was dreaming of a future as a preacher when he heard King "taking the teachings of the Bible and applying them to . . . earthbound problems." "On fire," Lewis launched a campaign to desegregate his local library.[6]

The SCLC empowered its preacher-leaders to stand up against National Baptist Convention president Joseph H. Jackson, a patriotic conservative who repeatedly scolded activists for "spurn[ing] the achievement of their fathers." The SCLC's radical vision never captured the *entire* black church, which has in recent decades seen a trend away from liberation and empowerment toward soul saving and prosperity preaching. But just as Social Gospelers had made space within mainline Protestantism for a vision of social salvation that had previously existed on the margins, so the SCLC opened black Protestantism to a freedom theology that honored the revelation of identity encounters.[7]

What happened in Montgomery was rooted in the history of the black church, but it was not merely a continuation of what the black church had been doing all along. This point is sometimes missed by commentators who divorce the Christian roots of the early civil rights movement from what they see as the secularity of subsequent identity politics. When we see Montgomery as the unleashing of new forms of power, it is easier to understand late 1960s activism as a collection of competing attempts—some militant and nationalist, some nonviolent and integrationist—to capture the same spark.[8]

Montgomery alone would not have changed the direction of American radicalism. By the late 1950s the nation's attention shifted to Little Rock, where Arkansas's governor tried to block the implementation of school desegregation and President Eisenhower responded by sending soldiers and National Guardsmen to safeguard the nine African American children chosen to desegregate Central High. Northern radicals saw this as a time of "doldrums," and worried that the movement's excessive reliance on "legislative and judicial machinery" would generate "massive resistance" among racist opponents of integration. But then the practice of identity encounter was renewed, simultaneously in many places, by hundreds of students who launched sit-ins and came together to form the Student Nonviolent Coordinating Committee.[9]

In his autobiography, John Lewis eloquently describes the cluster of students that gathered in Nashville, Tennessee, around the tutelage of FOR field secretary James Lawson, a black United Methodist fresh from several years in India. Lawson's class on nonviolence, sponsored by the SCLC, attracted students from both Fisk College and the American Baptist Theological Seminary, a school that catered to budding preachers who could not afford a liberal arts baccalaureate. Already an admirer of King, Lewis persuaded his seminary classmates to join in learning about Niebuhr, Thoreau, Lao-tzu, and above all Gandhi's principles of ahimsa (nonviolence) and satyagraha. The students readily linked these exotic ideas to the traditional values of their sharecropping families. When Lawson talked about "redemptive suffering," Lewis thought about his mother's repeated comment that "the seeds of the righteous must never be forsaken." She had always suffered, he knew, and now he understood that there was "something in the very essence of anguish that is liberating, cleansing, redemptive." Similarly, when Lawson told them about the Beloved Community or "kingdom of God on earth," Lewis realized that he was already experiencing this promise among his classmates and friends. "We all became brothers and sisters. . . . We really were our own Beloved Community."[10]

That Beloved Community was solidified by a visit to Highlander, where Lewis was impressed by Septima Clark, whose emphasis on work with sharecroppers helped him envision a movement made up of "men like my father, women like my mother, children like the boy I had been." Soon he and his friends were mapping out plans to sit in at department store lunch counters. Morehouse and Spelman students were doing the same in Atlanta, but the spark was lit at North Carolina A&T, among students whose only connection to the earlier Gandhian movement was a comic-book version of the Montgomery story published by FOR. On February 1, 1960, Joe McNeill, Ezell Blair, Frank McCain, and David Richmond sat in at a Woolworth's lunch counter. Within days, the number of protesters had swelled to three hundred, inspiring similar protests among students across the South.[11]

The Nashville group jumped in with their whole hearts. "We had nothing to lose," recalled Lewis. "We were young, free and burning with belief—the perfect foot soldiers for an assault like this." The bonds of the Beloved Community were deepened by the shared experience of facing arrest and insisting, together, on "jail without bail." Though Lewis described this as "an act of baptism," the movement was changing his religious identity, to the point that he soon abandoned his ordination plans. "I had crossed over. . . . But this was not Jesus I had come home to. It was the purity and utter certainty of the nonviolent path." For Lewis's Beloved Community, nonviolent action was not only a means of softening the hearts of the oppressors and liberating one's individual heart from fear. It was also a powerful practice of identity encounter, binding participants together through shared struggle and shared victory. And in Nashville the victories came surprisingly fast. By May, the movement had weathered a bombing, brought thousands of marchers to city hall, and gained the mayor's support for desegregation.[12]

Suddenly the nation's attention was focused again on the mutual empowerment of African Americans. One writer observed that the "Negro community" had displayed "more mature and authentic unity than ever before in history," bringing together "laborers and maids, merchants and office workers, professors and doctors, students and the retired. . . . Some Negroes are surprised at their power, as are many whites, but it is evident." The same author also noticed, presciently, that the practice of identity encounter was beginning to spread from the community of African Americans to that of students. "The so-called 'silent generation' has just been waiting for the right time to speak."[13]

Empowered in their identity as African Americans and as students, sit-in leaders converged on Easter 1960 to coordinate their efforts. Key mentors advised them to honor what they had experienced together by forging an independent path. Ella Baker—then working for the SCLC—urged them, "Don't let anyone else, especially the older folks, tell you what to do. Think and act for yourselves." And so they organized the Student Nonviolent Coordinating Committee (SNCC), affirming that "the philosophical or religious ideal of non-violence [is] the foundation of our purpose, the presupposition of our faith, and the manner of our action." The students persuaded Martin Luther King to join them in a sit-in, resulting in his being sentenced to four months of hard labor. This set the stage for an intervention by the Kennedy brothers that got King released and propelled a shift of black voters to the Democratic Party.[14]

As these events unfolded, Gandhians watched with excitement. "Mass action by the Negro people," predicted *Liberation,* would bring about a revolution building on "the moral power that is generated when people who have been fragmented individuals because they accepted inferior status, are transformed, because together they demand freedom." Hoping for a movement that would "fill the jails," the editors urged leaders to steer the movement toward greater use of nonviolence. Reflecting their socialist roots, they also called for the creation of "integrated mass Southern unions" that would expand the revolution. In line with the best traditions of militant nonviolence, they argued that black empowerment would ultimately benefit all races, for "in carrying on their relentless nonviolent struggle for their own liberation, *Negroes are liberating white Southerners.*"[15]

CORE leaped into the Southern struggle when Greensboro activists requested a nonviolence trainer. Convinced that a white-led organization could not be a major player in the South, CORE's board persuaded James Farmer to resume his old position, and soon Farmer was planning a new Journey of Reconciliation to challenge segregated bus facilities throughout the Deep South. Though Farmer changed the name to "Freedom Ride" to reflect the "scrappy nonviolent movement" in the South, the plan initially reflected CORE's old style. Participants were chosen through an extensive application process and brought to Washington for thorough training. The racially balanced team was mostly Northern and included only two students, one of them John Lewis. It included James Peck, a veteran of the 1947 journey, and his comrade Albert Bigelow from the *Golden Rule* antinuclear action. One staffer nixed a plan for a kickoff rally in Harlem by arguing, "We are not interested in the black community. We are interested only in the *activists* in the black community."[16]

In the tumultuous ride that followed, Jim Peck was arrested (for illegally transporting a bottle of brandy!) and John Lewis was knocked down and bloodied. The riders spoke at packed mass meetings at every stop, then confronted massive violence in Alabama. Peck was hospitalized, requiring fifty-six stitches; sixty-year-old Walter Bergman suffered a cerebral hemorrhage and permanent paralysis; and other riders narrowly escaped death when their bus was firebombed. With most of the original riders too injured to continue, Farmer decided to call off the ride, and Southern students seized the initiative from CORE's leadership. Convinced that "surrender in the face of brute force" violated Gandhian principle, they recruited a group of seven blacks and two whites to continue with Lewis into Mississippi. Mobbed again in Montgomery, the riders urged Jim Farmer and Martin Luther King Jr. to join them. Though King demurred that "I think I should choose the time and place of my Golgotha," Farmer—who had previously called the plan "suicide"—succumbed to the students' moral pressure. By this point, Southern authorities were determined to avoid the spectacle of mob violence, and the bus rolled without incident into Jackson, Mississippi, where the Riders were arrested and packed away to prison. They were joined by waves of spontaneous Freedom Riders who followed their path to Mississippi.[17]

Because Mississippi prisons were strictly and violently segregated, imprisonment provided the black Freedom Riders with a new opportunity for intense encounters. Steeled to fearlessness by the violence they had survived, the Riders responded to taunts with dignified politeness, then burst into defiant song:

Paul and Silas, bound in jail
Had nobody to go their bail
Keep your eyes on the prize
Hold on.

Some had a gift for song, others for enduring violence with smiles on their faces, others for interpreting Gandhi's principles. When one contemplated a fast to protest the bad food, another argued that "we didn't come here to improve the food or reform the prison system. We came to fill up the jails." When guards confiscated clothing, James Bevel urged, "What's this hang-up about clothes? Gandhi wrapped a rag around his *balls* and brought down the whole British *Empire!*" inspiring the others to wear their ill-fitting shorts as a badge of honor. When the guards threatened to take away their mattresses if they didn't stop singing, they stopped momentarily, then burst out louder than before, shouting, "Come get my mattress—I'll keep my soul!" as they piled their mattresses against the cell walls. By the end of their (symbolically chosen) forty days in prison, reflected Farmer, "not one of the men and women who shared the Freedom Ride could ever be the same. . . . A Promethean spark somehow had been infused into the soul of each of us." Coming from a committed humanist, the allusion to Greek mythology acknowledged the spirituality of encounter.[18]

While several SNCC leaders were still in prison, Robert Kennedy urged the organization to change direction: by focusing on voter registration rather than civil disobedience, they might gain financial support from Northern philanthropists. Coming from Kennedy, who obviously hoped the votes would benefit his brother, the proposal offended devoted Gandhians, who argued that SNCC should continue "dramatizing the issue of segregation, by putting it onstage and *keeping* it onstage." But it was endorsed by pragmatists who hoped to enter the political mainstream and nonpacifist militants who resented the "pain and suffering school." Soon enough, the Gandhians discovered that voter registration projects generated as many dramatic confrontations as sit-ins. After initial forays in a variety of locations, SNCC launched a collaborative voter education project in rural Mississippi, led by the charismatic and enigmatic black existentialist Robert Moses.[19]

Moses challenged students to build "a leaderless movement . . . a truly indigenous, nonviolent revolution." This opened up a new sort of identity encounter. While sit-ins had empowered black students through deep identification with one another, the Mississippi project helped them identify with "everyday people" who were much like their mothers and fathers. The students were a new sort of missionary, recalled Lewis, "because we were meeting the people on *their* terms, not ours. If they were out in the field picking cotton, we would go out in that field and pick with them." Donning "blue denim bib overalls with a white T-shirt underneath," the students gained strength from the local matriarchs who held rural communities together. These "incredibly resilient women . . . had been through so much unspeakable hell that there was nothing left on this earth for them to be afraid of."[20]

Fannie Lou Hamer was the most famous of these matriarchs. Leading her companions in song on the day she registered to vote, Hamer got the attention of Bob Moses; soon she led the Mississippi Freedom delegation that demanded a seat at the 1964 Democratic convention. Hamer inspired others with the depth of her faith and the power of her singing. "I have never met or read about anyone else who so lived the doctrine of her Christianity," recalled a later coworker. "Her talks at community meetings were always peppered with biblical parables to emphasize her points. . . . Her singing, which gave momentum to the whole civil rights movement, was 90 per cent old spirituals."[21]

Across the South, identity encounter was inseparable from the power of song. John Lewis, describing the Montgomery mass meeting during the Freedom Ride, wrote that after the sermon "the people took their fear and mixed it with faith and put it into their singing." And Bernice Johnson Reagon, who translated her civil rights experiences into an acclaimed musical career, recalled that the tradition of black church singing in which she'd grown up was transformed by the movement because "black people were doing some stuff around being black people. . . . If you have a people who are transformed and they create the sound that lets you know they are new people, then certainly you've never heard it before." While some people objected to the theological arrogance of the line "God is on our side" in "We Shall Overcome," Reagon found it apt. "God was lucky to have us . . . doing what we were doing. I mean, what better case would he have?"[22]

Reagon's words convey the distinctive spirituality of the movement. What happened at each mass meeting was a profound release of spiritual power that could be described in specifically Christian terms. But it was never exclusively Christian, and it cannot be understood solely as an outgrowth of earlier prophetic traditions. New spiritual power was being created as people came together, and it was accessible to pious Christians, to the existentialist Bob Moses, and to John Lewis, who was coming to identify "my work, my commitment to community" as "my church." Alongside his activism, Lewis was writing a college thesis proving that the movement was "essentially . . . religious" and that "church . . . was the major gateway for the movement." Even as he affirmed all this, Lewis placed his faith in the "Spirit of History" and insisted with equal fervor that spirituality was of value only when it "flowed through the church and out into the streets." Soon an identity-based spiritual radicalism would flow in streets across the nation.[23]

CHAPTER 16

Expanding Circles of Encounter

The work of mutual empowerment pioneered in the Southern freedom struggle has been at the heart of radical activism for the past half century. It is evident in energetic movements for Native American, Latino, Asian American, and African American rights; in "womanist" and "*mujerista*" movements that exist alongside white feminism; in gay, lesbian, bisexual, transgender, and queer activism; and among self-consciously evangelical, Buddhist, and Jewish radicals. Much of this diversity did not flower until the 1970s. In the 1960s themselves, the circle of encounter was expanded first by the mostly Northern pioneers of the "Black Power" movement, the women who raised their own consciousness while working in the South, the Chicano farmworkers organized by César Chávez, and—most prominently—the army of radical students who saw themselves as the vanguard of a new American revolution.

The transition began during the "Freedom Summer" program of 1964. A year earlier, Americans had been shocked by televised images of Birmingham police officers attacking protesters with fire hoses, inspired by the witness of Birmingham's children, and motivated by Martin Luther King's resonant call to "let freedom ring" at the March on Washington. Voting rights activists capitalized on the interest by inviting eight hundred students to join them in Mississippi for the summer. A diverse group of "Young Democrats, SDS types, Christian Fellowship types, all types of eager, earnest, dying-to-get involved college students," joined by hundreds of ministers, converged in Ohio. Even before the final cohort finished their training, their sense of urgency was deepened by the murder of three volunteers: black Mississippian James Chaney and Jewish New Yorkers Mickey Schwerner and Andy Goodman. Meanwhile, Bob Moses admonished the volunteers: "Don't come

to Mississippi to save the Mississippi Negro. Only come if you understand, really understand, that his freedom and yours are one." Moses's
message reinforced the volunteers' hope that they might gain access to
the power that had been unleashed by the marchers of Montgomery.
And that is what happened.[1]

One of the first groups to achieve its own encounter of identity
consisted of (mostly) Northern blacks who rallied around a militant rejection of Gandhian nonviolence. Among those who participated in
spontaneous Freedom Rides in 1961 was Stokely Carmichael, a Howard
University student raised in the Bronx. In Parchman prison, Nashville's
Gandhians were bemused by Carmichael's contrasting view of activism.
When they decided to relinquish their mattresses, he and a friend clung
tightly to their own, forcing the guards to pull them away. Carmichael's
arguments were echoed by James Forman, an Air Force veteran and
journalist from the black-owned *Chicago Defender* who began making
trips south in 1957. During the Freedom Rides Forman spent time in
Monroe, North Carolina, where he got to know Robert Williams Jr.,
another veteran who had been fired from the presidency of his NAACP
chapter for urging blacks to stop "lynchings with lynchings." While
radical pacifists admired Williams in the way Garrisonians had once admired Nat Turner—as a symbol of the justifiable violence that might be
wreaked upon white society if it did not embrace nonviolent revolution—Forman accepted him as a mentor and brought his way of thinking into SNCC through his service as executive secretary, a position he
held until 1966.[2]

Freedom Summer reinforced Forman's perspective by alerting activists to the difficulty of fostering authentic interracial encounters without
first attending to black empowerment. As the staff expanded, privileged
and articulate whites began squeezing rural blacks out of leadership positions. Observing this devastated Northern blacks who had never known
the communal solidarity enjoyed by Southern blacks. When activists
who had grown up in mostly white contexts encountered the violence
of Southern segregation alongside the solidarity enkindled by the Southern movement, they felt "compelled to throw off their past." For them,
identity encounter meant "purging themselves of all that self-hate, asserting a human validity that did not derive from whites," while for
Lewis—who had scarcely known white people as a child—the same sort
of encounter involved a deeper affirmation of his past.[4]

The tension between nonviolence and militancy came to a head as

SNCC's young leaders were struggling to make sense of their prominence on the national stage. At one tense meeting, Bob Moses, who was never comfortable with his own charisma, announced his departure from the organization and urged other leaders to follow suit lest they become "creatures of the media." But a sharp break was delayed by the dramatic events that unfolded in Selma, Alabama, in the spring of 1965. In February a black activist named Jimmie Lee Jackson was killed, and at his funeral SCLC organizer James Bevel proposed a march to the state courthouse in Montgomery. In a dramatic confrontation that became known as Bloody Sunday, state troopers turned the march back at the Edmund Pettis Bridge. This inspired hundreds of out-of-town ministers to come to Selma, and the southward flow of clergy became a flood after one of them was murdered. Jewish theologian Abraham Joshua Heschel, Catholic sisters in full habit, and the nation's most prominent ecumenists joined Martin Luther King in a massive march that traveled triumphantly to Montgomery, galvanizing national support for the Voting Rights Act that passed Congress a few months later. The martyrdom of a second white ally in Selma kept the faith in a single interracial movement alive.[4]

But the Selma movement coincided with Malcolm X's climactic last days: he spoke in Selma in February and was assassinated in New York City while Jimmie Lee Jackson lay on his deathbed. Malcolm was a powerful symbol for all people of African descent who doubted that nonviolence could give them the freedom for which they yearned. Son of a Baptist preacher who was devoted to Marcus Garvey's brand of black nationalism, Malcolm's resentment of white power had led him to a criminal career, and in 1948 he heard Elijah Muhammad's message in prison. He soon became the most charismatic exponent of Muhammad's teaching that American blacks were the "Lost Sheep" of Islam, held captive by a devilish white race, and destined to rebuild heaven on earth by separating from white society.

At the time of Malcolm's conversion, the Nation of Islam stood outside the American radical tradition. Not only did Elijah Muhammad preach that the "so-called Negro" had no stake in the American experiment, he was more interested in building autonomous institutions than in confronting white power. Malcolm changed that by directly criticizing the Christian nonviolence of Martin Luther King, whose emphasis on integration would do nothing for the black masses. This nudged some Black Muslims from a sectarian identity toward a radical one, but it did not sit well with Elijah Muhammad, who disciplined Malcolm for saying that the "chickens had come home to roost" when President Kennedy was assassinated. That incident only propelled Malcolm toward greater left identity. Traveling in Africa and the Middle East, Malcolm encountered the multiracial reality of mainstream Islam, the left-wing flavors of anticolonialism, and the leaders of SNCC, who noticed that the young Africans they met "wanted to know all about Malcolm X."[5]

After his return to the United States, Malcolm broke with Elijah Muhammad and created the Organization of Afro-American Unity, hoping to link the Southern struggle to the global movement for freedom. His death crystallized a power shift within civil rights organizations, as Stokely Carmichael took John Lewis's place as national chair of SNCC and Floyd McKissick succeeded James Farmer at CORE. Both believed that black empowerment, rather than integration, was the movement's goal. Then James Meredith—the activist who had desegregated the University of Mississippi—launched a quixotic one-man "March against Fear" through Mississippi. After Meredith was shot and injured, a protest march put tensions among civil rights leaders in public view. SNCC marchers provoked Martin Luther King Jr. by chanting "Black Power" instead of "Freedom Now!" When King repudiated the phrase, Carmichael countered that Black Power was "a call for black people in this country to unite, to recognize their own heritage, to build a sense of community." That explanation encapsulated the continuity that lay beneath his differences with King.[6]

The Black Power impulse was picked up by such militant, urban organizations as the Black Panthers, as well as by Harlem's prominent minister-turned-congressman Adam Clayton Powell Jr. It also appealed to black ministers in predominantly white denominations. Though most served black congregations, they had been educated in white seminaries and, like Carmichael, yearned for intimate encounters with their own people. Organized in denominational caucuses and an umbrella group called the National Committee of Negro Churchmen (later the National Conference of Black Christians, or NCBC), these ministers articulated a theological rationale for Black Power that aptly conveyed the power of identity encounter. "Getting power necessarily involves reconciliation," they wrote, in a rebuff of those who saw power and reconciliation as antithetical. "We must first be reconciled to ourselves . . . as persons and . . . as an historical group. . . . As long as we are filled with hatred for ourselves we will be unable to respect others." Black Power was thus couched as a means to an integrationist goal, for "we and all other

Americans *are* one." The NCBC organized radical responses to the "urban crisis" following Martin Luther King's assassination, and in 1970 it issued "The Black Declaration of Independence," which denounced "Despotic White Power" but did not quite renounce America. Instead, the authors warned that they would "renounce all Allegiance to this Nation" if past injustices were not redressed. This warning placed the document in the tradition of the radical jeremiad.[7]

Black Power evolved in parallel—and often in conflict—with the self-empowerment of women, many of whom were radicalized as SNCC activists in Mississippi. SNCC's first manifestation of feminism was an anonymous "position paper" prepared in 1964. It began with a list of grievances: the Freedom Summer leadership was all male even though many experienced activists were women; women were referred to as "girls"; women were routinely expected to take minutes and type. Such incidents demonstrated that SNCC women were exposed to the same "paternalism" that "token Negroes" faced in corporate America.[8]

Two of the paper's authors, Casey Hayden and Mary King, were white Southerners who had come to SNCC through the Student Christian Movement. King was a Methodist minister's daughter who saw her work at SNCC as an expression of John Wesley's theology of grace; Hayden (then Casey Cason) had chaired the campus Y's race relations committee at the University of Texas as well as participating in an intense residential community called Christian Faith-and-Life. At the 1960 gathering of the National Student Association, she praised the sit-ins as the "only way to maintain [one's] humanity" in the face of segregation and challenged her audience with Thoreau's famous words from jail: "What are *you* doing out *there?*" In a sense, their feminist challenge to SNCC was simply a call to restore the culture of the campus Y— a shared project of the YMCA and YWCA whose parallel authority structure virtually guaranteed women and men equal power.[9]

Women also led a network of ecumenical and denominational missionary and women's organizations—almost the only places in 1950s America where women chaired their own meetings and managed their own budgets. As SNCC members wrestled with Hayden and King's paper, these organizations were discussing Betty Friedan's *The Feminine Mystique,* which highlighted the frustrating experiences of college-educated women who were expected to compress their diverse gifts within the narrow frame of the household. It was required reading for the national leaders of United Methodist Women as well as dozens of local women's groups. When Friedan proposed creating a national organization to ensure enforcement of the 1964 Civil Rights Act's prohibition of sex discrimination, church-based activists stepped forward. Friedan's closest collaborator in organizing the National Organization for Women (NOW) was Pauli Murray, a civil rights lawyer who later became the first African American woman ordained as an Episcopal priest. The YWCA and National Council of Churches (NCC) were represented by another black woman, Anna Arnold Hedgeman. Friedan was especially impressed by the participation of Franciscan sister Joel Read, whose long experience of building women's community equipped her to resolve the "quibbling over details that could have kept the organization from getting born."[10]

Read represented a group that was uniquely situated to embrace feminism. Roman Catholic sisters, like their Protestant counterparts, had long exercised their talents within female-controlled organizations; the difference was that they lived their whole lives under the umbrella of those organizations. The upheaval of the 1960s coincided with other factors propelling them toward deeper conversations with one another. Part of an upwardly mobile generation of Catholics, 1960s sisters were three times as numerous as male priests. The Sister Formation Conference promoted cooperation among the orders and encouraged young sisters to pursue education and "apostolic" careers of service to the world. These sisters were the Catholics best prepared to embrace the Second Vatican Council's vision of a church fully engaged with the larger society.[11]

Vatican II urged religious orders to return to their founding vocations; for many sisters, this meant reviving their founders' devotion to direct work with the poor. It required each order to prepare a new constitution, and as result "things came to the surface that were never dreamed of" in Rome. When the Los Angeles archbishop rejected the constitution of one local community, these "new nuns" threatened a walkout from their teaching jobs and reorganized themselves as a lay community. Sisters were literally on the front lines of the 1965 march in Selma, and they have remained in the forefront of radical movements ever since. Such experiences equipped them to reflect on their own exclusion, as women, from ecclesial and political power.[12]

In SNCC, NOW, religious orders, and local congregations, 1960s women found power by talking to one another. In 1968 the New York Radical Feminists began identifying this practice as "consciousness-raising." Its inherent religiosity was explicated in a 1970 article, "Growing Up a Woman," *Christianity & Crisis*'s first serious engagement with feminist thought. Authors Kathy Mulherin and Jennifer Gardner explained that "there is nothing one woman by herself can find out about women's liberation—all discoveries are elicited from her or taught to her by other women." Consciousness-raising was "a revelation" because through it they discovered that experiences they had thought unique—discomfort with gender roles, fights with husbands over dirty dishes, faked orgasms—were widely shared. This discovery called them to radical action.[13]

What Mulherin and Gardner did not do—two years after the emergence of Black Theology—was to translate their "revelation" into a formal theology or program for ecclesial change. The delay was partly because second-wave feminism had begun almost a decade after the Southern freedom struggle, and partly because church-based feminists lacked the formal theological education enjoyed by black ministers. Feminists also had to confront the fact that feminist consciousness-raising pushed the boundaries of mainstream Christianity (and Judaism) more radically than earlier radical movements. It was easy to find biblical evidence of God's solidarity with the poor and enslaved, more difficult to find feminist inspiration amid a host of sexist texts. This meant that the religious consequences of "1960s feminism" were especially far-reaching, but would not unfold until the 1970s.

A movement for Chicano liberation was also beginning in the 1960s. Among the activists who had been drawn into Alinskyite organizing in the 1950s were César Chávez and Dolores Huerta. After helping to build the Community Service Organization in southern California, Chávez and Huerta took Alinsky's eclectic religious style back into the labor movement, using Gandhian nonviolence and devotion to Our Lady of Guadalupe to organize the United Farm Workers (UFW). Chávez evolved into a "living saint" in the tradition of Mexican folk Catholicism. When he fasted, visitors approached him on their knees and conducted masses with vestments cut from his flag. But Chávez was also eclectic enough to carry banners depicting the Star of David alongside Guadalupe, "because we ask the help and prayers of all religions." He inspired newly assertive Latino priests and sisters as well as "Chicano cultural nationalists" who directed their religious fervor to the ancestral heritage of Aztlán.[14]

Before the Chicano movement had fully emerged, another group used encounters of identity to take the national stage. The students of the 1960s, part of the largest generation in U.S. history, came together to resist the soulless technology of the university and claim a vanguard status akin to that of the Marxist proletariat. Once again, SNCC was an important starting point. Sit-in leaders defined themselves not only against Southern racists but against an older generation of black leaders, including the thirty-something Martin Luther King. Radical observers greeted SNCC as the leading edge of a student movement, noting that going to jail meshed well with the developmental tasks of college: it was "a step toward manhood and towards freedom." SNCC advisor James Lawson, himself a graduate student at Vanderbilt Divinity School, argued that the sit-ins belied the widespread image of 1950s students as "'silent,' 'uncommitted,' or 'beatnik.'" It was now clear, he wrote, that students had been "waiting in suspension" for something to "catapult their right to speak powerfully to their nation and world." "In his own time," Lawson concluded in millennial tones, "God has brought this to pass."[15]

Students quickly graduated to forms of activism that challenged the university. At the University of California, students protested against ROTC and launched a political party that aspired to link student government to the broader issues of the day. Accompanied by activist Episcopal bishop James Pike, they demonstrated against a meeting of the House Un-American Activities Committee, singing "We Shall Not Be Moved" when police turned fire hoses on them. The Gandhians of *Liberation* magazine were delighted that a "raw generation" whose ideology was "a strange hash of *Mad* magazine, civil libertarianism, and anarchistic good spirits" had spontaneously "accepted the militant but nonviolent measures advocated by CORE and many American pacifists." It appeared that the broad-based national movement for which socialists had yearned since the days of Debs would finally be created by students.[16]

A new radical organization, Students for a Democratic Society (SDS), sometimes acted as if it had given birth to itself, but its true parents were the Student Christian Movement and the old Intercollegiate Socialist Society (ISS), with SNCC playing midwife. The ISS, renamed the League for Industrial Democracy in 1921, tried to revive its founding mission by bringing students together, but participants in its first national gathering—at Port Huron, Michigan, in 1962—distanced themselves from the league's strident anti-Communism and its view of the labor movement as the engine of social change. Eager to show that they were as revolutionary as the unions, Tom Hayden and the other SDS students never quite remembered that both the ISS and the Socialist Party had also once resisted the mystique of the proletariat, striving to build a grand coalition of intellectuals, artists, religious leaders, and workers.

"We are people of this generation," began "The Port Huron Statement," "bred in at least modest comfort, housed now in universities, looking uncomfortably to the world we inherit." It highlighted the paradoxes of the postwar world in which the authors had grown up: American ideals of freedom and equality were belied by black suffering; the Bomb promised security but endangered all life. Setting themselves against the "liberal and socialist preachments of the past"—by which they meant the antiutopian liberalism epitomized by Reinhold Niebuhr on the one hand and the Communist Popular Front on the other—they called for a prophetic and utopian politics. The university was the "overlooked seat of influence" from which such a politics might emerge. Universities possessed the tradition of dialogue that a "new left" would need and were situated at society's tension points. In prosperous times, the students urged, "a new left cannot rely on only aching stomachs to be the engine force of social reform."[17]

The idea that the moral dilemmas of students could be as revolutionary as the "aching stomachs" of workers echoed C. Wright Mills's argument that "the young intelligentsia" had displaced the industrial working class as the most promising "radical agency of change." But it also reflected the worldview of the denominational and ecumenical organizations collectively known as the Student Christian Movement. At state universities as well as private colleges, these organizations offered not only worship services but discussion groups, volunteer opportunities, cooperative living arrangements, and massive national gatherings with speeches by the likes of Martin Luther King Jr. The movement responded to the increase in college enrollments caused by the GI Bill and postwar prosperity: by 1965 half of all high school graduates were enrolling in college, a fourfold increase over twenty years that meant that as many young Americans were participating in higher education as in local religious congregations. This shift would eventually contribute to the "secularization" of the Left, as radicals drew institutional support from universities instead of churches. In the early 1960s, though, the Student Christian Movement was one of the few places where academic complicity in the emerging military–industrial complex was regularly questioned.[18]

Among the denominational groups, the Methodist Student Movement (MSM) led the way. By far the largest component of mainline Protestantism, the Methodist Church (United Methodist after 1968) mirrored the national population. Formed in 1939 with the reunification of churches that had divided during the Civil War, it was both Northern and Southern, white and black. It had black congregations in Northern cities and the rural South, many of them affiliated with colleges planted during the post–Civil War missionary movement. Though these congregations were administratively segregated—a practice that helped propel James Farmer out of the denomination—they participated fully in the MSM, making it one place where Southern whites encountered blacks on a basis of equality. And though Methodism did not grant women full ordination rights until 1956, its handful of women ministers were prominent within campus ministry.[19]

The MSM's vision was illustrated in *motive,* the journal launched in 1941 to support campus ministries. Based in Nashville, *motive* was situated to keep students abreast of the struggle for racial justice, and its founding editor, Harold Ehrensperger, also participated in the Gandhianism of the Fellowship of Reconciliation. *motive*'s editorial departments mirrored FOR preoccupations: one focused on "cooperatives" and another promoted spiritual disciplines for small fellowship groups that would "put new life in the church" by working with "the 'left-wing' in society at home." Ehrensperger blended a personalist philosophy with a wariness toward institutional religion, promising that the magazine would "base its belief, as [Jesus] did his, upon the value of human personality. . . . If creeds and institutions have clouded rather than clarified your vision, then *motive* still may probe behind the face of things to seek the broader, deeper meanings that are valuable in life." As this quote might suggest, the Student Christian Movement blended Social Gospel idealism with the challenging new philosophy of existentialism. A similar vision appeared in the personalist rhetoric of Port Huron, which described all people as "infinitely precious and possessed of unfulfilled capacities for reason, freedom, and love" and called for a "participatory democracy" in which politics would "bring people out of isolation and into community." Such language broke with Niebuhrian realism and helped bring Gandhianism closer to the surface of 1960s activism.[20]

A symbolic marriage between SDS and SNCC was consummated with the actual marriage of Casey Cason and Tom Hayden, and for the next few years the two organizations worked together for a nationwide revolution. SDS was a major conduit for student participants in Free-dom Summer; it also took to heart the argument of SNCC activists who urged that white people and Northerners should organize in their "own" communities. This vision led to the Economic Research and Action Project (ERAP), an SDS initiative funded by the United Auto Workers that placed one hundred volunteers as community organizers in the summer of 1964, preparing the way for a renewal of the Alinskyite tradition in the 1960s and 1970s. As was the case with SNCC's work in Mississippi, ERAP had an antileadership ideology encapsulated in the slogan "Let the People Decide." Their work revived the "collective en-counters" of the settlement house movement, and at least some ERAP participants claimed that they had learned, in Casey Hayden's words, "to see the world from [the] perspective [of the poor]: from the bottom."[21]

As SDS students encountered one another in new and explosive ways, they sharpened their sense of vanguard status. The tension be-tween identification with the slums and with one another was evident in one observer's comment that the "worker priests" of ERAP were "more proletarian than the proletariat," subsisting on "powdered milk and large quantities of peanut butter and jelly." Both Freedom Sum-mer and ERAP took place immediately after the first cohort of baby boomers—those born in 1946—graduated from high school. These students' fall semester was marked by the Free Speech protests against University of California policies limiting political activism by students. After the arrest of a CORE organizer, students occupied the university's Sproul Hall and forced the school to make space for open discussion.[22]

At Berkeley and elsewhere, that space was filled by opponents of the war in Vietnam, who turned the burning of draft cards into the defin-ing sacrament of the student Left. Though the United States had had a military presence in Vietnam since the 1950s, the issue was not a priority even for pacifists until 1963, when the spectacle of Buddhist monks im-molating themselves to protest the war grabbed the attention of radicals. President Johnson began expanding the war in that year, but what gal-vanized student interest was his deployment of ground troops in 1965. In April of that year, twenty-five thousand people rallied around the Washington Monument to hear SDS president Paul Potter observe that the war was opposed not only by pacifists but by all "participants . . . in a movement to build a more decent society," among them blacks, poor people, and students opposed to "bureaucratized, depersonalized institu-tions called universities." Robert Moses, now using the name Robert

Parris, made his last public appearance at this event, just before fleeing to Canada (and eventually Tanzania) to avoid conscription.[23]

Soon enough, fear of the draft led students to ally with the pacifist movement that centered on FOR and the Catholic Worker. Reviving a practice pioneered by the Peacemakers in the 1940s, Catholic Workers began burning draft cards in the summer of 1965, and the government responded by criminalizing the practice. The first to defy the new law was Catholic Worker David Miller (a former student of Daniel Berrigan) who took the step in part because he was too nervous to give a speech. Miller's action was emulated en masse, until the self-immolation of two American pacifists—one a Quaker and one a Catholic Worker—tempered the militancy of antiwar activism. But the war continued to escalate, and in 1967 a new organization called the Resistance, identifying itself as "young Americans who still believe in the ideals our country once stood for," urged men of draft age to turn in their draft cards on October 16, 1967.[24]

The call was endorsed by prominent religious leaders, and many October 16 events had a religious flavor. At Boston's Arlington Street Church, thousands gathered for a service at which 260 men turned in their cards at the altar, or burned them in the flame of altar candles, after hearing Rev. William Sloan Coffin call upon all churches to provide sanctuary to draft resisters. One young resister, Michael Ferber, spoke powerfully of the way ritual could enhance the experience of identity encounter: "Each of our acts of returning our draft cards is our personal No; when we put them in a single container or set fire to them from a single candle we express . . . our unity." Five days later, Daniel Berrigan and Phil Berrigan led a raid at the Baltimore Customs House, where they poured blood over draft records in a liturgy of destruction that inspired dozens of similar events, including their use of napalm to destroy draft files at Catonsville, Maryland, in May 1968.[25]

Though the Catonsville action incorporated Catholic liturgy, its protest was directed not only against the government but also against "the Roman Catholic Church, other Christian bodies, and the synagogues of America," all of which were "racist," "hostile to the poor," and guilty of "cowardice in the face of our country's crimes." Ferber voiced a similar critique at Arlington Street, noting the paradox that "here we are receiving the help of many clergymen, and yet some of us feel nothing but contempt for the organized religions that they represent." Ferber added, aptly, that many of the clergy shared the anger about religious hypocrisy but had remained loyal to their faiths' "radical tradition . . . of love and compassion . . . [and] facing other people as human beings."[26]

On October 21, 1967, religious and antireligious perspectives converged when Abbie Hoffman brought together practitioners of Eastern and esoteric religion with parodic pranksters in an attempt to levitate the Pentagon. Coming at the end of a one-hundred-thousand-person march on Washington, the ritual featured Allen Ginsberg leading Tibetan chants and an exorcism conducted by Ed Sanders, who invoked "the demons of the Pentagon to rid themselves of the cancerous tumors of the war generals." Though neither Hoffman nor Sanders was Catholic, both had ties to the Catholic Worker. A Jewish atheist, Hoffman had cut his activist teeth running an informal campus ministry with Catholic Worker priest Bernie Gilgun, and Sanders had once used the New York Catholic Worker press to publish an avant-garde literary magazine called *Fuck You*. The event Hoffman and Sanders created together opened up a new epoch in activism, as Catholic liturgy, pagan ritual, and avant-garde theater flowed together, inviting demonstrators to use their whole embodied selves to call for a new society.[27]

This was possible because the identity encounters experienced by students, women, and African Americans were reinventing American spirituality. Most who experienced such encounters sensed that they were touching the sources of power that had inspired prophets Moses and Muhammad, Jesus and Buddha. But they also knew that traditional religious congregations would not easily absorb such intense energies. Over the next decade, 1960s radicalism transformed American denominations and generated new religious movements on a scale not seen since the 1840s.

CHAPTER 17

From Encounter to Confrontation

Like the abolitionists' personal encounters and the urban encounters of the Social Gospel, the 1960s encounter of identity opened a new door for adherents of mainstream religion to enter the Left. In this case, people who had been deradicalized during World War II were reradicalized by the Southern freedom struggle and the students' revolt. Ecumenical Christianity—now expanded into a tripartite dialogue of Protestants, Catholics, and Jews—reversed the path it had followed since World War II, when Reinhold Niebuhr's *Christianity & Crisis* led previously socialist and pacifist clergy into a more "realistic" engagement with Cold War power politics. Throughout the 1950s, heirs of the Protestant Social Gospel and Catholic social teaching traditions, with their Jewish counterparts, had been divided between a "liberal" majority loyal to the New Deal and Cold War and a "radical" minority aligned with Gandhian groups. The postwar organization of a World Council of Churches (WCC), with the National Council of Churches as its domestic counterpart, coupled with the Catholic reforms of Vatican II, gave liberals confidence to take seriously the claims of blacks, women, and students.

The distinction between radicals and liberals soon broke down, and by the end of the 1960s denominational and ecumenical leaders had moved far to the left of the lay benefactors who controlled church finances, yet not far enough to satisfy those who believed the United States had entered a revolutionary crisis. The tensions exploded in a series of public confrontations: between Black Power activists demanding reparations and the Protestant establishment in New York City; between Chicano activists and a Catholic archbishop in Los Angeles; between feminists and academia at Harvard University. Some doubted that denominational Christianity could survive. What happened instead was that the Protestant establishment lost its hegemony, depriving radicalism of what had briefly been a valuable ally.

The trail to churchly radicalism was blazed by several clusters of white people who allied themselves with the Southern freedom struggle. The Gandhian pacifists constituted the first cluster; a second included white professors at historically black colleges and white ministers of black congregations. Standing in a tradition dating back to the American Missionary Association, Lutheran pastor Robert Graetz participated fully in the Montgomery bus boycott, while Fisk and Spelman professors bolstered SNCC. A third cluster included members of the lay-led Unitarian fellowships that had been planted across the South (and elsewhere) beginning in the 1940s. Defining themselves in opposition to conservative local culture, these fellowships attracted veterans of the Socialist Party and the Popular Front, and counted as members most of the white lawyers who worked with King in Montgomery.[1]

The most advantageously situated white allies were campus ministers. Influenced by the interracial and anti-imperialist culture of the World Student Christian Movement, and eager to liberate students from the shallowness of campus culture, they affirmed that "segregation has become incompatible . . . with the Christian ideal." Among the most colorful to take this stance was Rev. Will Campbell, a University of Mississippi chaplain whose support for integration earned him appointment as director of the National Council's "Southern Project," which gave him latitude to offer support to emerging grassroots movements. Whether he was interacting with white segregationists or black activists, Campbell was unafraid to speak his mind: on one occasion, he told John Lewis that his desire to continue sit-ins in the face of increasing violence was "just a matter of pride." Such sentiments ultimately alienated Campbell from the ecumenical establishment: convinced that his Northern colleagues were both insufficiently radical and insufficiently concerned for poor whites, he launched a quixotic ministry among "rednecks" and KKK supporters.[2]

Campbell paved the way for Northern campus ministers and professors to follow the nation's "sons and daughters" southward beginning in 1961. Unwilling to let his students' radicalism outstrip his own, Yale chaplain William Sloane Coffin gained national headlines when he was arrested on a Freedom Ride. Another professorial Freedom Rider, Robert McAfee Brown, described a coffee break with black ministers in a newly integrated airport terminal as being "as close to a sacramental experience as I ever expect to have away from the communion table." Brown urged Northerners to join the "world-wide revolution" and insisted, "Segregation is not a Southern problem. It is not a Northern problem. It is a human problem."[3]

For those who joined the struggle in the early 1960s, intimate encounters with their black counterparts were life changing. Men who had identified with Reinhold Niebuhr's Cold War liberalism now saw themselves as radicals, and they pushed *Christianity & Crisis* to a stance of revolutionary commitment reminiscent of Niebuhr's own politics in the 1930s. In the wake of the Birmingham campaign of 1963, Roger Shinn—who had left the Union Eight in order to enlist in World War II—offered ten "axioms for white liberals." These were intended to guide new activists through the process of identification with African Americans he had already experienced. Shinn warned whites not to "set the strategy or timetable" or try to speak for blacks, and urged them to accept humbly the "exaggerated racial consciousness" of some black activists. But his keynote was hopeful invitation: "In so far as the white liberal actually shares in the life and cause of the Negro, he stands to gain an immensely more profound understanding of his colored brothers and of himself." In offering such counsel, Shinn sought to take on the same mentoring role that Reinhold Niebuhr had played in his own life.[4]

In January 1963, the most vocal Freedom Riders joined top ecumenists from the NCC, National Catholic Welfare Council, and Synagogue Council of America in sponsoring the Conference on Religion and Race. The resulting "Appeal to the Conscience of the American People" prepared the way for an NCC statement that echoed the anti-Nazi Barmen Declaration of the German Confessing Church, identifying a historical "crisis" in which "the integrity of the Church as the agent of God's reconciling purpose in his world" was at stake. Repenting of the white church's past gradualism, it declared that "words and declarations are no longer useful in this struggle unless accompanied by sacrifice and commitment" and promised that board members would join in direct action. In a notable departure from Social Gospel rhetoric, which had hoped to save the mainline churches by identifying with labor, the board openly (and accurately) acknowledged that the action it was calling for would likely "jeopardize the organizational goals and institutional structures of the Church." Within a month, Eugene Carson Blake—past president of the NCC and a future general secretary of the WCC—was arrested trying to desegregate a Maryland amusement park.

An iconic photo of Blake in a paddy wagon sealed the alliance among Protestant officialdom, the black freedom movement, and Gandhian activism.[5]

The new mood of ideological and racial unity extended from the 1963 March on Washington to the 1965 march in Selma. The scent of freedom in the air, wrote one participant, made white allies "feel two inches taller than the day before." But fissures were present even in 1963. William Stringfellow blasted the Conference on Religion and Race as "too little, too late and too lily white." Will Campbell resigned from the Southern Project, arguing that Northern Protestants were scapegoating white Southerners. Noting the decline in nonviolent commitment among black activists, Stephen Rose of *Christianity & Crisis* issued a Garrisonian jeremiad about the need for immediate action to forestall violent revolution: "From a theological standpoint, the judgment—that the Negro *will* attain equality—has been delivered upon America."[6]

Clergy who participated in the Selma movement of 1965 experienced even more transformative moments of encounter and wrenching struggles over Black Power. One first-time activist stayed with a black family and felt that something "incredibly beautiful" had happened when he gained the trust of the nine-year-old daughter, while the more seasoned Malcolm Boyd reflected that any white activist who was not "a paternal do-gooder or dilettante" was destined to become "something of a Black Nationalist." Confronted with "vulgarly pietistic paintings of the white Jesus," Boyd felt antiwhite; when he saw committed white volunteers "being shunned on all social occasions by the Negroes," he felt antiblack.[7]

By 1965 the South was not the only arena for encounters across the racial divide. As ERAP's student activists wrestled with urban poverty, white ministers debated whether Saul Alinsky's organizing methods could uproot the entrenched racism of Northern cities. Though the *Christian Century* alternately described Alinsky as an agent of racist Catholics and suggested that he hoped to spark a Peasant's Revolt in American cities, his confrontational tactics appealed to the Niebuhrians of *Christianity & Crisis,* who charged that the *Century* had not outgrown its sentimental aversion to power. From his base at Chicago's City Missionary Society, Stephen Rose praised Alinsky for reminding Christians that "the perils of power . . . do not justify the avoidance of power when the end is just." Concerns about the racial implications of community organizing were allayed when Presbyterians and Catholics funded a project in the Woodlawn neighborhood with a black Pentecostal leader. Protestants then invited Alinsky to promote racial reconciliation after urban riots in Rochester, New York—a job that the SCLC had declined. Alinsky's success in Rochester established community organizing as a viable middle path between Black Power and white backlash.[8]

Church leaders also joined the global struggle against imperialism, with campus ministers leading the way. Quadrennial gatherings of the Student Volunteer Movement in the late 1950s focused intensively on Third World revolutionary movements and linked them to the Southern struggle. These links were possible because event organizer Ruth Harris had been inspired by revolutionary students when she volunteered in China during Mao Tse-tung's rise to power. Before the Korean War pushed the regime in a more militarist direction, Harris saw the Chinese church "come remarkably alive" as awareness "of the people and their suffering" helped Christians "see the gospel in a new light." Back in the United States, she gravitated to such international students as Eduardo Mondlane, future leader of Mozambique's liberation struggle and a regular presenter at student gatherings.[9]

The study guide for Harris's conferences was Richard Shaull's *Encounter with Revolution,* a slim volume prepared by a former missionary, Princeton professor, and leader of the World Student Christian Federation. Shaull's message was simple: God was at work in the global "revolt of the disinherited" and Christians had a duty to respond. Though Shaull's position was well to the left of 1950s Niebuhrianism, he framed his theological message in Niebuhrian terms and this helped him emerge as *Christianity & Crisis*'s interpreter of Latin American events. Countering Cold War prejudices, Shaull insisted that not Communists but Christians were at the forefront of change in Latin America. "When the preaching of the Gospel produces a generation of revolutionaries," he asked, "is the Church able to accept and support them?"[10]

By the time Shaull posed this question, American attention was on Southeast Asia. Student opponents of the war in Vietnam found allies in ministers, priests, and rabbis who hoped for a dual encounter with the rising generation and with the people of Vietnam. In 1963 the Ministers' Vietnam Committee published a *New York Times* advertisement that raised questions about the undemocratic character of the South Vietnamese regime, the use of defoliants, and the treatment of Buddhists in Vietnam. Strongly supported by pacifists and Freedom Riders, the advertisement was notable for the participation of Reinhold Niebuhr and John Bennett, the most prominent representatives of nonpacifist Protestant sentiment. It coincided with a more militant demonstration organized by Catholic Workers and *Liberation* magazine in cooperation with such groups as the Iranian Students of New York and the India Youth League. Continuing expansion of the war prompted three thousand ministers to sign another advertisement two years later. By that time, John Bennett spoke for most Niebuhrians when he editorialized for an immediate end to the bombing campaign and a negotiated settlement. *Christianity & Crisis* was sometimes late in speaking out, he acknowledged, but now the time had come.[11]

In July 1965 *Christianity & Crisis* and the *Christian Century* jointly called on the NCC to give as much priority to Vietnam as to civil rights. The NCC responded by acknowledging "the profound and widespread suffering of the Vietnamese people both North and South" and joining the call for an end to the bombing. This fell short of radical demands for immediate withdrawal, but it placed ecumenical Christianity squarely on the left side of a national debate. Within a few years Niebuhr was saying publicly, "I am ashamed of our beloved nation," prompting his disciple Paul Ramsey—one of the few who had not moved left of Niebuhr—to bemoan that even Niebuhr had begun signing petitions "as if Reinhold Niebuhr never existed." The Vietnam debate cut short rapprochement between the NCC and moderate evangelicals, as Billy Graham, *Christianity Today,* and the National Association of Evangelicals all repudiated opposition to the war.[12]

The first draft-card burnings provided an opening for respectable and nonpacifist ministers to question the war and speak out for the right of dissent. Following the "Protestant-Catholic-Jew" model of ecumenism, a young Missouri Lutheran minister named Richard John Neuhaus recruited Abraham Joshua Heschel and Daniel Berrigan to join him as cochairs of Clergy Concerned about Vietnam (eventually renamed Clergy and Laity Concerned about Vietnam, or CALCAV). Enlisting William Sloane Coffin as director, CALCAV positioned itself as the "moderate" opposition to the war, informally coordinating its work with that of more radical groups.[13]

The distinction between moderates and radicals was breaking down by the time CALCAV hosted Martin Luther King Jr. in his first antiwar speech, at Riverside Church in April 1967. Days later, King joined Daniel Berrigan and Dorothy Day at a demonstration that featured not only draft-card burning but also the participation of Viet Cong supporters—prompting one SCLC staffer to explain that "we're going to get left of Karl Marx and left of Lenin. We're going to get way out there, up on that cross with Jesus." One by one, CALCAV leaders came out in support of draft resistance, and they were joined by such luminaries as Thomas Merton. By year's end, William Sloane Coffin was among the "Boston Five" indicted for conspiracy to encourage violation of the draft law.[14]

As religious leaders deepened their solidarity with draft-defying students, they also encountered the Vietnamese victims of war. A ministers' trip to South Vietnam in July 1965 prepared the way for Thich Nhat Hanh's national tour of 1966. Nhat Hanh, who had previously urged Martin Luther King to take a public stance against the war, captured the imagination of Thomas Merton, whose essay "Nhat Hanh Is My Brother" noted that he and the Vietnamese leader were both monks, poets, and existentialists. Predicting a "new solidarity and a new brotherhood," Merton urged his admirers to "do for Nhat Hanh whatever you would do for me if I were in his position. In many ways I wish I were." Events sponsored by FOR and CALCAV deepened the bonds between pacifist and nonpacifist opponents of the war.[15]

By 1967 the newly empowered communities of African Americans and students had the support of most of the religious constituency that had backed the New Deal. Professors and editors who had written glowingly of "revolution" in the 1930s were doing so again. A new generation of scholars that included Catholics and even women joined the chorus. Michael Novak explained that Freedom Summer had marked the revelatory beginning of a new theology, for young radicals had "discovered a pride, a courage, and a beauty in the lives of the poor that put the lives of their parents and their friends to shame." Rosemary Radford Ruether, a white Catholic launching her career at Howard University, announced the "profound collapse" of the traditional church and insisted that only a "theology of radical social change" could point the way forward. Those who agreed gathered in "underground churches" to do the work of creative destruction.[16]

But all was not well for the Left. Protests had not prevented President Johnson from intensifying the war in Vietnam. Riots in the Watts neighborhood of Los Angeles in 1965 and in Newark and Detroit in July 1967 symbolized the despair of urban blacks, whose lives had been little affected by Southern marches or civil rights laws. Intense ideological disputes were emerging in the radical community, pitting black nationalists against nonviolent integrationists and SDS personalists against Maoist revolutionaries. As hope turned to rage, encounters between empowered communities and their allies became angry confrontations.

The moment when hope turned to rage depended on one's perspective. Many who entered the movement early on were disillusioned or sorrowful by the middle of the decade, when others were flush with the enthusiasm of new activism. John Lewis's "season of darkness" began days after the March on Washington, when four girls in Birmingham were murdered. But the ecumenical establishment largely shared the optimism of the baby boomers, who first tasted the power of encounter at Selma in 1965. Riding a tide of activist energy, ecumenical leaders interpreted rioting as a divine judgment on white racism and an opportunity for expanded partnership with the Black Power movement. The process was tumultuous and energizing. Benjamin Payton, the first black director of NCC's Commission on Race and Religion, lost his job for trying to direct ecumenical funds to racially separate programs, but the NCC board subsequently pledged a tenth of its capital to projects led by inner-city activists. The Episcopalians committed a million dollars a year to similar causes, and Unitarian Universalists pledged a quarter of that amount. By 1967 racial caucuses were prominent in denominational and ecumenical gatherings, on the grounds that "honest and intensive confrontation" with racism necessitated "strategic withdrawal into our own separate staging-areas." The mood extended to such evangelical organizations as InterVarsity, which rewarded black dissidents with a place on the steering committee for its 1968 gathering.[17]

Few organizations seized the revolutionary moment as fully as the University Christian Movement (UCM), led by recent Duke graduate Charlotte Bunch. Organized in 1966, the UCM aspired to build on the radical energies flowing from campus ministry offices. In what Bunch would later call a "radical three-year utopian experiment," it reached out simultaneously to denominational bureaucracies and to activist groups rooted in the student uprising. Its caucuses reflected openness to Black Power and ties to anti-imperialist students from abroad; one caucus helped spark the North American Congress on Latin America, which outlived UCM itself by decades. Then the UCM dissolved its national office in 1969, on the grounds that the times demanded "creative risk" and "experimentation" that "must happen locally or not at all."[18]

The students who embraced the "creative risk" of revolution were living in a different world from many of their parents. While radicals mourned the martyrdom of Martin Luther King Jr. and campaigned for antiwar candidates Eugene McCarthy and Robert Kennedy, other Americans yearned for the return to law and order promised by Rich ard Nixon. Nixon's voters included a disproportionate share of main-line Protestant laypeople, while most Catholics remained loyal to the Democratic establishment represented by Lyndon Johnson and Hubert Humphrey. These divisions did not dampen revolutionary ardor on the left, but they lent credence to the argument that ordinary democratic processes could not bring about radical change. And so the confron-tational tactics of the 1968 Democratic convention—Abbie Hoffman's Yippies threatened to put LSD in the delegates' food and the authorities responded with conspiracy indictments—were replayed in churches and ecclesiastical gatherings around the nation.

On May 4, 1969, former SNCC executive secretary James Forman brought a message of prophetic confrontation to New York's Riverside Church. His long beard and Afro reminiscent of the biblical prophets, Forman declared that black Americans were the "vanguard" of a world-wide revolution because they were the "most oppressed" and "most humane" people within the United States. Forman demanded half a billion dollars in reparations from white churches and synagogues that were "part and parcel of the system of capitalism." "This total comes to 15 dollars per nigger," he explained, "only a beginning of the repara-tions due us as people." The fund would be invested in a Southern land bank, organizing efforts among welfare recipients and low-wage work-ers, regional media centers and universities, and other building blocks of an Afrocentric socialism.[19]

For some Riverside parishioners, Forman doubtless appeared as a hostile outsider to the churches. He had never enjoyed the same con-nection to organized religion as his early SNCC comrades. But the text of his "Black Manifesto" was the work of a church conference orga-nized in response to the 1967 riots. Both black caucuses and their white allies held that, in order to avoid old patterns of missionary control, urban programs should be created through no-strings-attached grants to black activists. But voluntarily renouncing their institutional power was a tough step for denominational executives to take because it ran against the wishes of their wealthy white donors. When Forman brought his re-quest to the NCC days before the confrontation, the board failed either to reach a decision or to complete its other business.[20]

The "Manifesto" set off a debate among Protestant leaders, with

Christianity & Crisis editors and Union Seminary professors joining the National Committee of Black Churchmen in speaking up for reparations. The "demand is just," insisted Stephen Rose, and acknowledging it could bring about "something new in America." Rose warned against the "colonialist" implications of channeling funds through existing missionary agencies. Gayraud Wilmore made the point more theologically, insisting that the churches needed to support race-specific endeavors because "the achievement of authentic personhood" through deep encounter with members of one's own group "is a prerequisite of discipleship." But this advice went mostly unheeded. Some money passed out of white hands into creative black endeavors, including the development of the Afrocentric holiday Kwanzaa, and more was directed to programs under denominational control and Alinskyite organizing. But the total fell far short of the manifesto's demand, in part because the churches bypassed the logic of reparations, which called for the transfer of accumulated wealth rather than the reallocation of annual budgets. Grants that were frustratingly small from the radical perspective still infuriated conservative parishioners, and many denominations scaled back their initial pledges of support.[21]

Though Forman designated "black" people alone as the revolutionary vanguard, other groups were equally ready for confrontation with the ecclesiastical representatives of American power. The events at Riverside were echoed when Chicano activists disrupted the 1969 Christmas Eve service at Saint Basil's Cathedral, the newly constructed seat of Los Angeles's powerful Catholic archdiocese. Just as Forman was an urban African American who had been drawn south by SNCC's rural organizing, so Católicos por la Raza was a group of urban Latinos who hoped to share the empowering rituals of César Chávez's United Farm Workers. They brought diverse spiritual influences: some had attended Catholic high schools and knew the social encyclicals well; others were influenced by the emerging cultural nationalism of Rodolfo "Corky" Gonzales. Most admired the militancy of Colombian priest-guerrilla Camilo Torres, and knew that Latin American bishops had endorsed the cause of the poor at Medellin in 1968. They were frustrated with their church's lack of support for the Chicano movement and hoped the movement could become more powerful with Catholic support.[22]

Católicos balanced affirmations of loyalty to the church with criticism of its practices. "We have gone to Catholic schools and understand the Catholic tradition," they affirmed, and they knew that Christ, "a genuinely poor man," would have condemned the hypocrisy of soliciting donations from Mexican Americans for church programs that did not address their poverty. They resented the fact that the archdiocese owned a billion dollars of tax-exempt property in Los Angeles County but had not built any low-cost housing, and they decried the exclusion of Latinos from the ranks of Catholic bishops. "Is there any wonder why the Hispanic people across this land see the Church as an entity outside and away from themselves?" They even cited Thomas Aquinas's defense of revolution against tyranny as justification for their own "fight against the mismanagement of our Church." The Catholic Church, they argued, could demonstrate its conversion to the Chicanos by funding housing, health, and educational projects, embracing shared governance and seminary training for Chicanos, and assigning some priests as chaplains to the movement, so that activists would have direct access to spiritual guidance. Católicos also demanded "freedom of speech for all priests and nuns" and church support for antiwar activists.[23]

In December, Católicos began picketing the cathedral. When the cardinal passed them off to a subordinate, they burst into his office, then began planning a Christmas Eve demonstration. Hoping to gain the sympathy of worshippers, they planned a liturgical sequence of events: a procession, a "people's mass" at the doorway of the cathedral, held simultaneously with the cardinal's Mass inside, and a candlelight procession to the altar, where they would read their demands. When the time came, they found the main doors locked and encountered physical resistance from the ushers. The congregation sang, "O Come, All Ye Faithful" to drown out the activists' chants of "Let the poor people in!" Eventually, the demonstrators were maced by police as the cardinal explained to the assembly that "their conduct was symbolic of the conduct of the rabble as they stood at the foot of the cross, shouting 'Crucify Him!'" Though a new cardinal would meet with Católicos and embrace the UFW within a year, the hoped-for alliance between the church and the Chicano movement as a whole spilled with the Communion wine on Christmas Day.[24]

Another hoped-for alliance was symbolically dismantled at Harvard in the fall of 1971. Harvard had invited feminist theologian Mary Daly to be the first woman to preach at Memorial Church. A classically trained Catholic theologian and philosopher, Daly earned the sympathy of Harvard's liberal Protestants and Unitarian Universalists with her call for the redistribution of power within Catholicism. But her views were radicalizing, and she used the Harvard occasion to stage a walkout, calling the women's movement an "exodus community" with no home in patriarchal religion. She urged her sisters to join her in leaving the church for "a future that will be our *own* future." Though the walkout did not diminish the admiration that many Christian feminists felt for Daly, it made clear that henceforward the institutional church would be an arena for feminist struggle rather than an ally in the feminist effort to transform society. Like the whites who supported the "Black Manifesto" or the Anglo allies of the Católicos, the men who invited Daly to Harvard had not changed their institutions fast enough to meet the demands of the time.[25]

The confrontations at Riverside Church, Saint Basil's Cathedral, and Memorial Church marked the beginning of one of the most creative decades in American religion. In the 1970s the seeds of feminist, Latina/o, black, and other theologies of liberation would flower and take root in dozens of communities. But the confrontations dashed hopes that the religious establishment might translate radical energies into systemic change. In 1965 the ecumenical establishment enjoyed unprecedented social prestige, built on two decades of steady membership growth. By the end of the decade mainline churches were experiencing membership declines—in part, no doubt, because the baby boomers had moved into a life stage that correlates with low church attendance, but also because the church's social witness was too radical for some members and insufficiently revolutionary for others. Perhaps no American institution has ever spent so much social capital, to such disappointing effect, as the mainline churches in the last years of the 1960s.

And so it was that the NCC's 1969 gathering featured a funeral. Styling the event Jonathan's Wake in reference to Jonathan Edwards, radical ministers created a free-speech zone and carried a coffin into a meeting to symbolize the death of organized religion. Calling for a new "disestablishment" through the disbursal of church wealth, Jonathan's Wake and the National Committee of Black Churchmen tried to elect two African Americans, Albert Cleage and Leon Watts, as president and general secretary. A majority of delegates voted to hold a war resister's draft card "in trust" as an expression of solidarity, though they fell short of the requisite two-thirds. Many participants were thrilled at the range of voices that spoke the "naked truth." But the election turned acrimonious, and the election of the NCC's first female president, Cynthia Wedel, was overshadowed by the defeated Cleage's promise to "be a plague on your house." Though some radicals correctly sensed that women like Wedel might transform the churches, most concluded that ecumenical leaders had rejected "almost any form of new life." The stage was set for four decades in which the most visible face of American religion would be on the far right.[26]

CHAPTER 18

Rebuilding the Left

The confrontations of the late 1960s redrew the organizational map of American radicalism and American religion. Such radical institutions as the Student Nonviolent Coordinating Committee and Students for a Democratic Society collapsed in a spectacular burst of factional infighting, and almost took the liberal establishment with them. As Southern and working-class whites walked away from the Democratic Party, many Protestants took their money and their memberships away from churches that they perceived as in bed with black nationalists and Third World revolutionaries. The revolutionaries and their allies also broke with the churches when early promises of support were withdrawn. Coupled with declining birthrates among middle-class Americans, these defections pushed mainline Protestantism to the sideline, as membership began a decades-long slide.

For activists on the left, the confrontations at Riverside Church, Saint Basil's Cathedral, Memorial Church, and elsewhere constituted a rebuff and an invitation. Activists were rebuffed to the extent that they imagined they could build a grand coalition of radicals akin to the early twentieth-century Socialist Party. Just years after ecumenists had dreamed of organic unity among the mainline traditions, the loudest voices on the left were now shouting, "Organize in your own community!" But this rebuff invited more people to experience the identity encounters that African Americans and college students had practiced to such transformative effect in the 1960s. Over the course of the 1970s, groups ranging from Latinas/os and Native Americans to evangelicals and LGBT people used encounters of identity to build enduring new institutions.[1]

Most of these were abeyance structures, albeit with large constituencies. Like the pacifist communities of World War II, radical organizations of the 1970s did not hope to transform national politics in the short term. Richard Nixon's victory in 1968 signaled that voters were unwilling to move further to the left. But unlike World War II pacifists, 1970s radicals were far from an insignificant share of the population. Fed by each year's graduating class of baby boomers, the radical community was larger in the early 1970s than ever before. Some had followed Bobby Kennedy or George McGovern back into the Democratic Party, but there was no unifying cause comparable to the Civil War or World War II to soften the divide between radicals and conservatives. Instead, the nation was moving into four decades of ideological stalemate, with a large community of activists faithful to the vision of the 1960s squaring off against resurgent conservatism.

The religiosity of the 1970s Left was marked by tension between those who hoped to revitalize mainstream Christianity and those who sought explicitly identity-based forms of religious community. The tension was paradoxical. Those who repudiated Christianity usually believed that they were more radical than those who did not, but their embrace of culturally specific traditions sometimes separated them from the tradition of American radicalism. This was so because of an ambiguity within the practice of identity encounter. When women met one another as women, when Chicanos met one another as Chicanos, were they oriented primarily to their community's struggle for liberation and empowerment or to a broader range of common experiences? The question arose because each of these groups had an identity that was not entirely a product of oppression. To the extent that identity-based groups focused on the internal dynamics of their community rather than on confrontation with the American power structure, they ceased to see themselves as part of a broader Left. On balance, the transition was enriching, but it contributed to the apparent disappearance of the Left in the post-1960s decades.

On the other side of the divide, those who worked within Christian institutions faced indifference or hostility from denominational authorities and fellow congregants, and this resistance kept their radical fervor alive. Many spent more time on "church reform" than on changing social, political, and economic structures. This reflected the centrifugal logic of the age and the fact that some new causes, particularly feminism and LGBT liberation, responded to injustices rooted in authoritative religious texts. A new cadre of organizations made changing the churches their primary goal.

The 1970s were also a time of theological ferment. The past decade's experience of revelatory encounter begged for theological interpretation, and seminary students and professors participated in the ongoing radicalization of higher education. Building on the explicitly "radical" theologies of the late 1960s, new "theologies of liberation" emerged from the liberatory struggles of particular identity groups beginning in 1969. The new theologies, each in its own way, passed through parallel stages of theological development during the 1970s.

The works that put theologies of liberation on the map typically placed the experience of one identity group at the center of the theological project. Echoing Marxist vanguardism, they presented their group as the primary vehicle of divine activity in the world. Subsequent critics who faulted them for neglecting all forms of oppression save their own sometimes assumed this vanguardism reflected a long history of separation among radical causes, but this was not so. The early SNCC and SDS, the Student Christian Movement, the Popular Front, and the Socialist Party had all noted the intersections of race, class, and gender. But late 1960s liberationism emerged from uniquely intense encounters of identity, and its first move was to testify to the special revelation of those encounters.

Ironically, the vanguardist texts proclaimed their new revelation using the old words of white, male, academic theology. By the middle of the 1970s liberationists shifted to what might be called resourcement—rooting their theologies in the particular cultures and histories of their various identity groups, and thus expanding the pool of images available to inspire activists. Then, at the end of the decade, a third phase emerged as scholars found ways to combine identity-based practices with a more generous acknowledgment of intersections. This shift was driven both by theologians whose careers had begun in the less centrifugal days of the mid-1960s and by those who had experienced multiple forms of oppression. Womanists, mujeristas, lesbian feminists, and other emerging identity groups insisted on the particularity of their experience but did not claim vanguard status. By 1980, the stress on intersectionality dominated most radical seminaries and such journals as *Sojourners* and *Christianity & Crisis*. It served radicalism well as it became more and more oriented to resisting a resurgent conservative movement.

Not surprisingly, the organizational and theological changes of the 1970s were first visible within the African American liberation movement. The Southern Christian Leadership Conference managed to survive under the leadership of Ralph Abernathy, who continued King's socialist and pacifist radicalism. But Abernathy lacked sufficient charisma to hold King's talented and ambitious lieutenants in a single organization. Several pursued political careers within the Democratic Party, while Jesse Jackson transformed Operation Breadbasket—SCLC's program to develop black businesses in Chicago—into Operation PUSH. Jackson would eventually make this the base of the most broad-based radical movement of the 1980s, but in the 1970s it was just one local expression of a fragmented movement.

Meanwhile, the Black Power impulse propelled many adherents toward non-Christian spiritualities or forms of political activism tinged with millennial fervor. Key leaders signified their sense of new identity by taking on new names. Poet and cultural critic LeRoi Jones was among the first, choosing the name Imamu Amear Baraka, later Amiri Baraka, in 1967. Stokely Carmichael became Kwame Ture as a way of honoring the African leaders Kwame Nkrumah and Ahmed Sékou Touré, who mentored him after he exiled himself from the United States. H. Rap Brown, Carmichael's successor as chairman of SNCC, converted to Islam and became Jamil Abdullah al-Amin while serving a prison term in the early 1970s. Ronald McKinley Everett, who became Maulana Karenga, is best known for developing Kwanzaa as a unifying annual festival for persons of African descent.

Karenga's US Organization has survived to the present as a base of black nationalist activism and as the guardian of the Kwanzaa tradition. Another enduring institution of black nationalist religion is Detroit's Shrine of the Black Madonna, organized by Jaramogi Abebe Agyeman (formerly Albert Cleage) as the center of a movement known as Black Christian Nationalism. Originally a Congregationalist who led an activist-oriented institutional church in Detroit, Cleage was the unsuccessful radical candidate for the NCC presidency in 1969 and a Black Power proponent who had once offered to ordain SNCC activists for their work in Mississippi. He now sought to build an Afrocentric denomination on the basis of his belief that "Jesus was the non-white leader of a non-white people struggling for national liberation." But his movement set itself apart from ecumenical Christianity by refusing to recognize the full canon of the New Testament, on the grounds that Paul had betrayed Jesus' radicalism.[2]

The early 1970s saw a dramatic reorganization of African American Islam. Malcolm X's Organization of Afro-American Unity, intended to link the black movement in the United States to revolutionary struggles in Africa, survived his death by only a few years. Malcolm's case for reconciliation with mainstream Sunni Islam persuaded Wallace D. Muhammad, Elijah Muhammad's son and successor, to forge ties to international Islam and the interfaith movement, but he stepped back from Malcolm's radicalism. Louis Farrakhan then revived Elijah Muhammad's separatist vision, claiming the name Nation of Islam for the minority of African American Muslims who preferred that approach. Like Black Christian Nationalism, Farrakhan's movement stood outside the American radical tradition insofar as its principled separatism assumed that African culture was the only tradition in which militant blacks should stand.

Those who wanted to take Black Power seriously without cutting ties to ecumenical Christianity gravitated to the National Black Evangelical Association or the National Conference of Black Christians, groups that functioned as caucuses within the National Association of Evangelicals and National Council of Churches. The latter was the primary midwife for Black Theology. "*All* theologies," it declared in 1969, "arise out of communal experience with God," including "a theology of black liberation . . . [that] seeks to plumb the black condition in the light of God's revelation in Jesus Christ."[3]

The most influential individual exponent of this tradition, James Cone, had just finished his doctorate when the NCBC was organized. His early books *Black Theology and Black Power* and *A Black Theology of Liberation,* coupled with his appointment to the faculty of Union Seminary, propelled him to national prominence. Cone identified Black Power as "the spirit of Christ himself in the black-white dialogue which makes possible the emancipation of blacks from self-hatred and frees whites from their racism." Through such acts as "voting for black people" or "building stores for black people," Black Power enabled the "slave" to "know that he is a man" and forced "the enslaver [to] recognize him." Trained in the neoorthodox tradition of Karl Barth, Cone presupposed a Barthian understanding of revelation as something that breaks into human culture but went beyond Barth in describing the black experience of empowerment as itself a form of revelation. The spirit of Black Power was "not merely compatible with Christianity; in America in the latter twentieth century it is Christianity."[4]

In keeping with this claim, Cone affirmed that "God is black" and that the movement for black liberation was the church. Yet Cone never embraced an absolute separatism. He identified "forming a coalition

with poor whites against middle-class whites" as a valid political path
and interpreted "blackness" in terms of oppression rather than biology.
"Black is holy," he explained, because "it is a symbol of God's presence in history on behalf of the oppressed man." Cone's early theology
is thus best understood as a form of vanguardism. At a moment when
self-empowered American blacks seemed to be at the heart of a global
revolution, Cone claimed for blacks the same role in history that orthodox Marxists claimed for the proletariat.[5]

Mentoring new scholars for forty years, Cone helped Black Theology move beyond its original vanguardism toward greater emphasis on
resourcement and intersectionality. When his brother Cecil argued that
an authentically Black Theology should not depend on the methodolo-
gies of white scholars, James replied with *The Spirituals and the Blues,* an
exploration of theological resources within black culture. His dialogue
with Latin American theologians equipped him to nuance his assertion
that "God is black," adding that "'God is mother,' 'rice,' 'red,' and a
host of other things that give life to those whom society condemns to
death." The point was to locate God not everywhere, but in a variety of
particular justice struggles.[6]

Black Theology's influence has always been greatest in the seminaries. Few ministers or laypeople within the historically black denominations have embraced the movement, in part because of its roots in the
black caucuses of white denominations. It is no accident, therefore, that
the best-known pastoral exponent of Black Theology served a United
Church of Christ (UCC) congregation. Beginning in 1972, Jeremiah
Wright transformed Trinity UCC on Chicago's Southside into a radical
megachurch by incorporating African drums and rhythms into the worship experience and declaring solidarity with the South African freedom
struggle. The principles of Black Theology are evident in "The Black
Value System," the vision statement endorsed by the congregation in
1981. Linking "commitment to God" with "commitment to the Black
Church," the statement disavowed "the pursuit of 'middleclassness'" in
favor of building up "Black institutions."[7]

Other activist congregations of the 1970s found other sources for
radicalism. A new Progressive National Baptist Convention was organized by disciples of King who resented the conservatism of the black
Baptist leadership. At Saint Paul's AME in Cambridge, Massachusetts,
and Bethel AME in Baltimore, Pastor John Bryant promoted a "black
awareness" rooted both in Pentecostal tradition and in his Peace Corps

experience in Liberia. And beginning at the end of the decade, black churches from across the theological spectrum participated in congregation-based community organizations.[8]

Much like the African American community, the Native American community of the 1970s was divided between an activist minority that sought to root itself exclusively in indigenous traditions and a larger constituency that incorporated culturally specific elements into its practice of Christianity. The former approach was championed by the American Indian Movement (AIM), organized in the late 1960s by tribal activists inspired by black liberation. In 1972, AIM followed a "Trail of Broken Treaties" to the Bureau of Indian Affairs' office in Washington, D.C., where activists delivered a manifesto calling for the return of stolen land and protection for "Indian religious freedom and cultural integrity." A year later, AIM activists at Wounded Knee, South Dakota, endured a deadly standoff with the FBI. AIM revived Native spiritual traditions at its Heart of the Earth Survival School in Minneapolis and subsequent educational initiatives.

AIM's religious viewpoint was systematized by Vine Deloria Jr., a son and grandson of Episcopal ministers who published *God Is Red* in 1973. The title was intended to spark a dialogue with Black Theology, yet Deloria faulted liberation theologies for helping to "control the minds of minorities" because they did not reject Western epistemologies. Native American traditions, he argued, were oriented to space while Western traditions focused on time. Seen in this light, both American radicalism in general and Black theology in particular are unabashedly "Western," for both invite adherents to orient their present life to the just society that will be created in the future.[9]

Despite the sharp antithesis Deloria drew between Native American and Western Christian ways of thinking, much of his critique was absorbed by those Native American Christian theologians who pursued doctoral study in the late 1970s and began teaching in the following decade. At Iliff Seminary in Denver, George "Tink" Tinker wrote on Christian complicity in genocide and articulated a systematic theology that refused to choose between Native and Christian identities. Similarly, Episcopal bishop Steven Charleston insisted that Native America had its own "Old Testament," an original covenant between God and Native peoples that was in no way superseded by the ministry of Jesus. These integrative theologies were not fully articulated until long after the 1970s.[10]

The Latina/o movement, like its African American and Native American counterparts, had both a nationalist wing aloof from organized Christianity and a wing that hoped to radicalize the churches. Both drew inspiration from the United Farm Workers, one of the few radical movements that remained faithful to its nonviolent roots in 1970. The union won its defining victory in that year, achieving a contract with the grape growers in part because of widespread religious participation in the grape boycott—though subsequent events forced a second boycott in the middle of the decade. Chicano nationalism was galvanized at the 1969 Denver Chicano Youth Liberation Conference, sponsored by Rodolfo "Corky" Gonzales's Crusade for Justice. This gathering endorsed "El Plan Espirituel de Aztlán," a manifesto that has been described by one scholar "as a Chicano version of the Ten Commandments." It identified the American Southwest as the mythical homeland of Aztlán. Activists expressed their spirituality by calling themselves "people of the sun" and insisting that "brotherhood unites us, and love for our brothers makes us a people whose time has come." But they named "writers, poets, musicians, and artists," rather than priests or ministers, as the carriers of renewal.[11]

Meanwhile, Chicano priests organized PADRES, a national network seeking to increase leadership opportunities for Latinos within Catholicism. The founders were UFW supporters who had been inspired by the Latin American bishops' 1968 gathering in Medellin, Colombia, which endorsed the emerging liberationist ideal of a "preferential option for the poor." Drawing on the Latin American "base community" model, PADRES sponsored a traveling ministry that engaged Chicanos across the Southwest. Soon its members moved into important positions in diocesan offices, especially in San Antonio, where Archbishop Robert Lucey was attentive to the needs of both migrant laborers and the young Chicano priests in his care.[12]

One of the young priests who accompanied Lucey to the Medellin gathering was Virgilio Elizondo, who found his faith transformed by the concept that sin can be structural as well as individual. PADRES tapped Elizondo as the founding director of the Mexican American Cultural Center (MACC), a permanent center for the training of pastoral and community leaders. The insight that defined Elizondo's work was that the suffering of Latinos in the United States—in contrast to that of their Latin American brothers and sisters—involved the denial of their culture by Anglo-dominated institutions. MACC addressed not just "economic poverty" but "the poverty of non-being," developing liturgical resources for celebrations of Our Lady of Guadalupe and Día de los Muertos, as well as the legitimation of popular devotions as important expressions of Catholic faith. [13]

PADRES in turn inspired Las Hermanas, a network of Chicano sisters who came together in 1971. The founders had been active in both community organizing and Catholic education; one had lost her position at a Catholic school after supporting a Chicano student walkout. They expanded to include laywomen and women of all Latina heritages, and had both supportive and tense relationships with the hierarchy and the leadership of their orders. Like other women's organizations, Las Hermanas stressed consciousness-raising. Members told one another how they had been expected "to leave behind your past" upon joining the order, or of how "my community was teaching more children for less pay than the Irish sisters." The mutual empowerment that resulted prepared them for radical ministries and provided the rich soil for the emergence of mujerista theology. Yolanda Taranga and Ada María Isasi-Díaz based their *Hispanic Women: Prophetic Voice in the Church* on conversations held at Las Hermanas retreats.[14]

While the Catholic hierarchy sometimes embraced Latina/o calls for greater power within the church, the chronologically parallel movements of gay men and lesbians (eventually to be joined by bisexuals, transgender persons, and self-identified "queers") faced more challenges in gaining a foothold within religious institutions. Prior to the late 1960s, gays and lesbians found community in "homophile" advocacy organizations and a clandestine bar culture. Neither can be described as radical, for neither sought to revolutionize the institutions that oppressed them. That changed on June 28, 1969, when patrons of Greenwich Village's Stonewall Inn chose to resist a police raid. They crystallized a militant national movement, with a Gay Liberation Front emerging in alliance with the Black Panthers, and Gay Pride parades spreading to a dozen cities within a few years.

A few religious organizations responded positively to the wave of LGBT empowerment. Much of the pre-Stonewall religious conversation about homosexuality had centered on a British Quaker report endorsing homosexual relationships (as well as premarital sex and some forms of extramarital sex), and Friends General Conference promoted similar views in the United States. The Unitarian Universalist Association declared its solidarity with gay liberation in 1970, a few months after

Rev. James Stoll had declared his homosexuality in a series of sermons that explicitly linked the gay cause to racial and gender justice. The Unitarian Universalists also adapted their pathbreaking sexual education curriculum, *About Your Sexuality,* to affirm the naturalness of gay sex. The United Church of Christ ordained its first openly gay man in 1972 and its first open lesbian in 1977. Reconstructionist Judaism embraced a similar policy in the mid-1980s with minimal debate. And the convert Buddhist community, long linked to the gay community through the beat movement, was quietly supportive of gays and lesbians.[15]

The vast majority of LGBT people were brought up in much less affirming religious contexts. Evangelical churches promoted "ex-gay" ministries and therapies, while Catholics, mainliners, and most Jewish groups settled into a posture of affirming LGBT civil rights, while teaching that the physical expression of sexuality should be reserved for heterosexual marriage. Yearning for a more authentic embrace, LGBT folks created such new communities as Dignity USA. Dignity's story began in early 1969, even before Stonewall, when priest psychologist Patrick Nidorf hosted gatherings for gay and lesbian Catholics who were neglected by the church. Dignity's "Statement of Position and Purpose" described homosexuality as "natural" and encouraged gays and lesbians to use "their power of sex" responsibly and "with a sense of pride." When Nidorf dropped out of the organization in response to hierarchical pressure, it continued under lay leadership, sponsoring chapter gatherings that often functioned like small gay parishes. By 1975 parallel organizations appeared in most Protestant denominations, and even among Mormons and Christian Scientists.[16]

Gay and lesbian Christians also built a religious institution that was solidly Christian but independent of the mainstream denominations. The Metropolitan Community Churches (MCC) originated from a 1968 gathering of twelve people in the home of Rev. Troy Perry, a Pentecostal minister who had been defrocked because of his homosexuality. Attracting adherents and ministers from a spectrum of Christian traditions, the MCC developed an eclectic worship style within a network that would grow to three hundred local congregations in the United States and beyond. Its success would eventually be replicated on a smaller scale by such groups as the Unity Fellowship Church, a network of congregations for LGBT people of color that describes itself as "rooted in spirituality, not in religion."[17]

For other LGBT persons, even the most supportive Christian (or

Jewish) community was suspect because of its connection to homo-phobic scriptures. Some forged new forms of religious identity rooted entirely in the LGBT experience, such as the communally oriented Rad-ical Faeries. Believing that the urban gay ghetto was not a good place to heal from homophobia, these gay men blended pagan and Native American spiritualities with drag culture, embraced nonmonogamous forms of intimacy, and chose new names—Eden, Granite, Owl—that expressed spiritual and ecological values. Similar practices blended with militant feminism at a network of lesbian communes.[18]

Though many of the institutional expressions of identity politics fo-cused on identities that faced significant oppression in the United States, the centrifugal logic of the era also generated organizations that linked leftist causes to self-conscious Jewish, Buddhist, and evangelical identi-ties. Jews, both observant and nonobservant, had been overrepresented on the left for at least a century. But most had downplayed the specific connections between Judaism and radicalism prior to the 1960s. This began to change with the high-profile civil rights and antiwar activism of Abraham Joshua Heschel, whose position on the faculty of the Con-servative movement's Jewish Theological Seminary of America put him in dialogue with Christian radicals at Union Seminary. Looking like a prophet himself, Heschel helped activists see their work as an extension of that of Amos and Isaiah.

Heschel's faculty rival, Mordecai Kaplan, built another bridge by or-ganizing the Reconstructionist movement. Like others rooted in Con-servative Judaism, Kaplan saw Judaism as a holistic identity and opposed the Reform tendency to portray Judaism as a religion separate from cul-ture. But he sought to preserve Jewish communal identity without a classically theistic understanding of God or a traditional understanding of Jewish chosenness. Kaplan's vision of a nonhierarchical community that would use human action to usher in the messianic age took organi-zational form by 1968. Though Reconstructionism never achieved great numbers, it led the way in bringing women into the rabbinate: by 1974 half of its rabbinical students were female.[19]

Heschel's influence was at its peak and the Reconstructionists were launching their seminary when the Six Days' War of 1967 gave all Jews a new source of pride. Radicals who had previously spurned religious ob-servance were now drawn to such movements as Chavurat, which en-couraged individual exploration of Jewish mysticism. Socialist-Zionists created the Jewish Liberation Project to ensure a link between their values and their practice. One fruit of their labors was the Jewish Liberation Seder, which incorporated reflection on modern "struggle[s] against oppression" into traditional liturgy. A similar rewriting was produced in 1968 by Arthur Waskow, a founder of the Institute for Policy Studies (IPS). His "Freedom Seder" added non-Jewish liberation struggles, citing Nat Turner and John Brown to show that "the winning of freedom has not always been bloodless." Waskow incorporated A. J. Muste's folksy rewriting of the Exodus story and admonished participants "to struggle, work, share, give, think, plan, feel, organize, sit-in, speak out, hope and be on behalf of Mankind!" Waskow eventually left IPS to pursue ordination as a Reconstructionist rabbi and found his own Shalom Center for "religious renewal." [20]

American Buddhists were at the forefront of an international movement of "engaged Buddhism" that was also championed by Thich Nhat Hanh, the Dalai Lama, and activists in Thailand, Sri Lanka, and India. The leading organization was the Buddhist Peace Fellowship (BPF). An affiliate of the Fellowship of Reconciliation, the BPF was created in 1977 by Robert Aitken Roshi (who had first encountered Zen as a prisoner of war during World War II) and his students. Aitken's approach was inclusive, and he was joined by immigrant Japanese Buddhists from the Pure Land school and teachers of the Vipassana meditative practice of Theravada Buddhism, as well as Zen roshis. The BPF sponsored Thich Nhat Hanh's return tour of the United States in the 1980s, prompting some members to organize a separate organization devoted to his vision known as the Order of Interbeing. [21]

Another strand of Buddhist activism stemmed from the U.S. attacks on Hiroshima and Nagasaki. The Japanese Nipponzan Myohoji order was founded to rid the world of nuclear weapons, and its emissaries to the United States built "peace pagodas" and engaged in cross-country peace walks to raise awareness of the nuclear threat. They joined both the War Resisters League's 1976 walk for disarmament and the American Indian Movement's 1978 "Longest Walk" from Alcatraz Island to Washington, D.C. Their visible presence brought them American converts and an especially close relationship with Haley House Catholic Worker, whose founder was embracing Tibetan Buddhist practice at the time. Firmly planted in the 1970s, engaged Buddhism has since become an integral part of American radicalism as a whole. [22]

Self-described "evangelicals" also became integral to the Left in the 1970s. This was a major shift, for Protestants who rejected historical criticism had maintained a low political profile ever since the Scopes trial. Some saw personal virtue as the basis of a good society; some espoused a premillennial eschatology that made social change irrelevant; some gravitated to the patriotic anti-Communism of Billy Graham. Though these trends persisted, especially in the South, during the 1970s, a dramatic alternative emerged within the sector of Northern evangelicalism associated with the National Association of Evangelicals (a rival to the National Council of Churches), the journal *Christianity Today,* InterVarsity Christian Fellowship, and such schools as Wheaton in Illinois and Fuller in California. Having achieved middle-class status, these evangelicals were eager for great social engagement, and their champion, Carl F. H. Henry, taught that it was possible to confront social evils without sacrificing biblical fidelity. Because Henry was not specific about policies, his admirers fleshed out his vision with a range of competing ideologies.[23]

Among Henry's admirers were baby boomers who identified with the radical movements of the 1960s. The trail was blazed by John Alexander, son of an activist Southern Baptist minister from Ohio. Troubled by the apoliticism of the evangelicals he met in college, Alexander used his 1965 term as president of InterVarsity to push for solidarity with African Americans. During a stint on the faculty of Wheaton College, he preached that students should stop "thinking white" and administrators should recruit a student body at least 20 percent black. He then launched a Philadelphia intentional community that hosted local offices of CAL-CAV and published a radical journal called *The Other Side.* Alexander's influence persisted at InterVarsity, whose 1970 national gathering welcomed an expanded contingent of black delegates with an opening worship featuring soul music, and a keynote by former gang member Tom Skinner. Groups like the Black Panthers had correctly diagnosed the depth of racism, Skinner argued, but like the biblical Barabbas they erred in thinking they could replace a corrupt system without addressing their "own corrupt nature." The only path forward, according to Skinner, was racial reconciliation centered on the cross.[24]

InterVarsity's more conservative rival, Campus Crusade for Christ, made its own contribution to the Left by sponsoring a group devoted to parodic confrontation with Berkeley radicals. The Christian World Liberation Front tried to add a discussion of Jesus as "the ultimate solution to the problems facing the world" to an SDS meeting agenda and reserved the campus's most popular rally site for its own event on May Day 1971. But over time, its members saw an underlying harmony between evangelical faith and radicalism, and they participated wholeheartedly in antiwar demonstrations. Though they never gained the trust of Berkeley radicals, they participated in the forging of subsequent evangelical Left organizations, though their own group faded after a leader embraced a splinter of Eastern Orthodoxy.[25]

The most influential leader of the evangelical Left was the one who identified most fully with student radicalism during his own college career. As a high school student in white suburban Detroit, Jim Wallis was more devoted to the black community than to his own Plymouth Brethren heritage, and as an SDS organizer at Michigan State he helped organize a national student strike in spring 1970. Disillusioned by his comrades' violence, Wallis started reading the Bible again, enrolled at Trinity Evangelical Divinity School, and introduced the style and tactics of the student Left to Trinity's campus. Wallis and his friends issued one manifesto entitled "At Trinity—Students Are Niggers" and another that insisted that "the Christian response to our revolutionary age must be to stand and identify with the exploited and oppressed." Facing expulsion, they left school to organize intentional households and publish a magazine called the *Post-American,* signaling their "rejection of the permeating American ethos."[26]

Initially, the *Post-American* used evangelical rhetoric to promote a New Left agenda. Early articles highlighted the Black Power and anti–Vietnam War movements as the two great causes of the day. Echoing the "Port Huron Statement," Wallis's inaugural essay condemned the "power elite" and "technocratic society," noting that "suffering is not confined to the exploited classes, but exists throughout the society as people experience the meaninglessness and oppression of their own lives." This vision caught the attention of Mark Hatfield, an idiosyncratic Baptist and Republican who was one of the first senators to oppose the Vietnam War. Hatfield called Wallis to ask, "Is it true that there are actually other evangelical Christians against the war?" and encourage him to move the entire operation to the nation's capital. Hatfield was joined on the journal's editorial board by the leading Latino and African American evangelicals, as well as Mennonite John Howard Yoder and Episcopalian lay theologian William Stringfellow.[27]

Stung by explosive community conflicts, Wallis and his friends accepted Hatfield's invitation to move to the capital, renamed themselves the Sojourners Community, and shifted from New Left confrontation to the creation of "a new community . . . intended to be . . . the first fruits of a new creation." In addition to publishing a magazine, the community sent members up and down the East Coast to protest nuclear weapons and agitated for tenants' rights through the Columbia Heights Community Ownership Project. It forged ties with more than a hundred sister communities around the nation. Some of these were part of the charismatic renewal within Catholicism and Protestantism; others were rooted in the Concern movement, which brought the peace witness of the Anabaptist churches into greater dialogue with mainstream society, much as Quaker activists had reached out a generation earlier. In D.C. itself, Sojourners connected with the Church of the Savior, an ecumenical congregation whose leaders included Richard Barnet of the radical Institute for Policy Studies. It found a kindred spirit at the Community for Creative Non-Violence (CCNV), established in 1971 by a Catholic priest who chose life with the poor over a parish assignment. CCNV evolved into a live-in community of twenty-five Catholics, Protestants, and humanists, along with hundreds of "extended community" members who added their efforts to the cause.[28]

Sojourners and CCNV joined a national network of pacifist communities akin to those of the 1940s and 1950s. Just as A.J. Muste had been the "Number One U.S. Pacifist" of the previous generation, so now the Berrigan family used symbolic confrontations with the war machine to inspire others. Brothers Philip and Daniel began the new decade on a dramatic note, going underground rather than face imprisonment for the Catonsville draft-file burning. Philip was apprehended a few weeks later, but Daniel evaded federal authorities throughout the summer of 1970. This made them heroes to some, while others felt they had betrayed Gandhian principles by refusing to accept the legal consequences of their action. The controversy was heightened by revelations that they had contemplated nonlethal forms of violence and that Philip, then still a priest, had secretly married activist nun Liz McAlister. These revelations deepened divisions within the Catholic Left just as it found its place in the national spotlight.

By the time the Berrigans had completed their sentence, they were convinced that "resistance" could not be a lifelong vocation without communal support. Daniel remained in the Jesuits, while Phil and Liz created the Jonah House community in Baltimore to promote the values of "community, nonviolence, and resistance." Sustaining themselves with a painting business and by caring for a local cemetery, Jonah House members shared household responsibilities, allowing Phil, Liz, and other parents to engage in civil disobedience without risking the loss of their children. Jonah House organized the Atlantic Life Community as an enduring network of resistance activists, prompting West Coast pacifists to sponsor their own Pacific Life Community. And Jonah House functioned as a sort of Mother House to resistance-oriented Catholic Worker communities. About twice as many Catholic Worker communities were organized between 1965 and 1980 as during the Great Depression, most by baby boomer activists who yearned for a more grounded activism.[29]

The many communities described in this chapter, both radical congregations and live-in communes, renewed the spirit of the People's Churches and Fourierist phalanxes of the nineteenth century. American religion remained most radical in local contexts, where activists fleshed out their particular visions without constraints imposed by donors or bureaucracies. Yet in the 1970s the tension between national denominations and local radicals was more muted. Protestant denominations continued the Social Gospel legacy of issuing left-liberal social statements on economic and military policy. The spirit of Vatican II allowed such Catholic parishes as Saint Joan of Arc in Minneapolis to embrace preaching by lay activists and other People's Church practices. Unitarian Universalist fellowships made a similar activist orientation accessible to residents of small and conservative cities from Alabama to Utah. Denominationally affiliated seminaries joined university divinity schools and Union Seminary as among the most radical segments of academia. Such schools as Iliff (Methodist) in Denver, United (United Church of Christ) in the Twin Cities, Starr King (Unitarian Universalist) in Berkeley, and the Episcopal Divinity School in Cambridge built faculty and curricula around the principles of liberation theology.

Denominations also supported local radicalism by funding a new generation of Alinskyite community-organizing projects. In the wake of the "Black Manifesto," Protestant denominations directed funds to community-organizing projects that had grassroots support but were not aligned with black nationalist ideology. The Catholic bishops, hoping to avoid similar confrontations, pledged 50 million dollars to the new Catholic Campaign for Human Development (CCHD), and placed responsibility for distributing the money in the hands of activist priests with ties to Alinsky. The most influential project to receive CCHD funding was San Antonio's Communities Organized for Public Service (COPS), created in 1974 with support from PADRES. COPS incorporated intensive theological reflection into its training and built on people's concrete commitment to their parishes rather than on their abstract commitment to social change. This style of "relational organizing" resulted in a movement that rapidly changed the racial power structure in San Antonio, culminating in the 1981 mayoral election of Henry Cisneros.[30]

Though the Industrial Areas Foundation splintered into several rival federations during the 1970s, all embraced COPS's congregational emphasis. Eventually they organized more than 150 affiliates in metropolitan areas. These affiliates have worked for "living-wage" legislation, for fair housing, and for neighborhood revitalization; they have pioneered new organizing techniques including "one-on-one" encounters between activists and the "asset mapping" of a neighborhood's strengths rather than liabilities. They have raised up prominent Hispanic and African American leaders, and in many places they bring together Catholic, mainline Protestant, and black church congregations in roughly equal numbers. They have also formed some of America's mainstream leaders: Hillary Clinton wrote her undergraduate thesis on Saul Alinsky, and Barack Obama became a Christian while working for an Alinskyite project in Chicago.[31]

To the extent that the radical vision of the 1960s has remained alive over the past generation, it is because of organizational work done in the 1970s, by activists who claimed powerful new identities and then turned their power to the task of coalition building. Each group made a vital contribution, yet one particular constituency, more numerous than the others, did the most to translate empowered identity into effective activism. The heart of 1970s radicalism was the women's movement, and its story deserves its own chapter.

CHAPTER 19

A Women's Decade

Just as student activism was at the heart of 1960s radicalism, so the 1970s proved to be the decade of women. Even without the protection of the proposed Equal Rights Amendment, women of the baby boom generation streamed into professional life, transforming economic and political institutions as well as the household. Radical women created a network of women's studies programs, rape crisis centers, and feminist communes, and built the National Organization for Women into a bridge between liberalism and radicalism. By the end of the decade, they had fought for and gained ministerial recognition in all mainline Protestant denominations, as well as in Reform and Reconstructionist Judaism. (Conservative Judaism followed a few years later.) Women constituted one-quarter of mainline seminarians. Women also served as president and general secretary of the National Council of Churches, preparing the way for their entry into denominational hierarchies. And women had founded new religious traditions to connect spirituality to activism.[1]

As they gained authority, women knit the radical traditions that had unraveled at the end of the 1960s back together. This took time, for each constituency had to integrate the revelatory impact of identity encounters before forging coalitions. The feminist constituency itself divided at the beginning of the decade, over the question of whether it was possible to bring a feminist consciousness into Christianity and other inherited religions. Those who yearned for a tradition centered on women's experience were inspired by new historical and archaeological evidence about goddess worship in ancient cultures. As feminists began identifying with the witches and goddesses of the past, they found themselves in creative partnership with a previously underground network of neo-pagan communities.

Neopaganism is an umbrella term for traditions that identify with the polytheistic, earth-centered religious traditions of pre-Christian Europe. Some groups claim to be in a direct lineage from ancient communities; others acknowledge that their rituals are as much invented as remembered. Most have decentralized leadership structures, privilege ritual practice over binding doctrine, and use magical ritual to generate ecstatic energies for personal or social transformation. Neopagan communities exhibit enormous diversity of sociopolitical views, though there are more anarchists and libertarians than in the general public. Prior to the late 1960s, however, very few neopagans were politically active *as neopagans*.

The most influential strand of neopagan tradition in the United States prior to the 1970s, and the one that converged most fully with feminist spirituality, was so-called Gardnerian Wicca. Centered on the Triple Goddess (Maiden, Mother, Crone) and her consort, the Horned God, this system was not explicitly feminist, and in some ways promoted normative heterosexuality and essentializing notions of gender. But its emphasis on the goddess as the fundamental aspect of divinity (she both gives birth to her son-lover and revives him after his death) legitimated women's leadership. By 1970 Gardnerian covens were present in many communities in the United States, and other groups had a modest presence within the counterculture. Popular books were also publicizing the widespread practice of goddess worship in ancient cultures and suggesting that this was evidence of an ancient matriarchy.[2]

Feminists who identified as witches and goddess worshippers did not always realize that they were moving onto the terrain of an existing movement with ambivalent attitudes toward feminism. In 1968 the Women's International Terrorist Conspiracy from Hell (WITCH) issued a manifesto declaring, "Witches and gypsies were the original guerrillas and resistance fighters against oppression." WITCH and its imitators (many of which adapted the acronym to specific causes) staged a series of mock-magical rituals: placing a hex on the United Fruit Company for its mistreatment of agricultural workers abroad and secretaries at home, showering "hair cuttings and nail clippings" on the University of Chicago sociology department after a feminist professor's contract was not renewed. Like Gardnerian Wicca, WITCH encouraged women to form small covens, but did not require formal initiation. One became a witch "by saying aloud, 'I am a Witch' three times, and *thinking about that*. You are a Witch by being female, untamed, angry, joyous, and immortal."[3]

The two Witchcrafts converged on the winter solstice of 1971, when Zsuzsanna Budapest gathered the Susan B. Anthony Coven No. 1 in California. A "hereditary" witch who had learned the craft from her Hungarian ancestors, Budapest was a feminist who valued autonomous relationships among women. Disavowing sexual complementarity, her coven modeled its structure on "the Amazon nations," with a "Mother" "in charge of the political direction of the Coven," a "Maiden" "responsible for the protection of the Coveners," and a "Nymph" who "insures that the Coven plays." They pledged to seek "revolutionary or personal" favors from the Goddess and to have "a fine time shared with the life force." Like radical evangelicals, these witches used a New Left rhetoric of revolution but insisted that no revolution could succeed without spirituality: "We believe that just as it is time to fight for the right to control our bodies, it is also time to fight for our sweet womon souls." Budapest's coven grew into a network known as Dianic Wicca. While Dianic witches observed the same annual cycle of "sabbats" as Gardnerians, Budapest wrote disparagingly of the hostility she had experienced from "the male-dominated multi-million dollar business" of neopaganism and encouraged new covens to form without traditional initiation. She also offended publicity-shy neopagans by capitalizing on her 1975 arrest for fortune-telling to raise publicity and funds for the Woman Soul Defense Fund.[4]

Witchcraft was soon an integral part of radical feminist culture. A team that traveled the country in search of women's "survival institutions," such as rape crisis centers and health collectives, reported that these were typically intertwined with "surging interest in . . . the spiritual aspects of life," including astrology, Tarot, and homeopathy. (They did not notice the rise of Christian feminism or surging female enrollment at seminaries.) Feminist journals, including one edited by former University Christian Movement leader Charlotte Bunch (along with a radical lesbian collective known as the Furies), published special issues on spirituality that insisted that the "intimate relationship between spirituality and politics" was the most innovative aspect of feminism. One author confessed that she had once disparaged spirituality but now recognized that spiritual power was created whenever women encountered one another deeply: "We all know the joy and power of our collective woman energy. . . . Our revolution is about . . . finally understanding that [our love and our power] are the same."[5]

Women's spirituality relied on a dispersed network of lesbian communes, many in rural settings. Oregon's Wolf Creek community sponsored festivals, produced a hymnal called *The Turned-On Woman Songbook,* and published *WomanSpirit,* a journal that linked traditional neopagans to feminists. Hoping to build a "new culture" that was "so deep, profound, and all-inclusive we are calling it spiritual," *WomanSpirit* emphasized rituals that would "put women in touch—in communion—with each other and ourselves." One article described a ritual in which women told stories about recent accomplishments and used symbolic objects to visualize "change from seed to plant to flower to seed." In a more ecstatic ritual, women painted one another with menstrual blood, saying, "This is the blood that promises life," and wove themselves together with red yarn, saying, "We are all woven together . . . nurtured by the same umbilical cord."[6]

Feminist festivals offered "the experience of a total woman-environment" for those who could not live communally. Like the Student Christian Movement gatherings of the 1950s, these helped forge radical commitments for conservative times. One 1976 conference at Boston's Arlington Street Church—site of the most famous draft-card burning liturgy of the 1960s—drew hundreds of participants who were challenged by Sally Gearhart's call for feminist revolutionaries to separate themselves from the patriarchal system in order to access the "womanpower" or "re-sourced energy that is collectively shared among women." Chanting "The Goddess is Alive—Magic is Afoot," participants "stood on pews and danced bare-breasted on the pulpit and amid the hymnbooks."[7]

To the extent that feminist spirituality focused on sustaining an autonomous women's culture, it was outside the American radical tradition. But most feminist witches stopped short of disavowing concern for the rest of the world. Sally Gearhart's "resourcement" was just one phase of feminist activism, and the Susan B. Anthony Coven promised to offer "'Pan' workshops" and otherwise "work together with men who have changed themselves into brothers." Still, many socialist and Christian feminists denounced any form of separatism on the plausible, but not entirely accurate, grounds that it excluded women who were also struggling against racial or class oppression.[8]

Christian and Jewish feminism evolved parallel to the Goddess tradition, beginning with local networks that became nationally visible at mid-decade. The most influential were at seminaries, where women who were newly eligible for ordination sought educational qualifications. At Harvard Divinity School, the Women's Caucus and another

WITCH (Women's Inspirational Theological Coalition from Harvard) pressed a sympathetic dean and somewhat more resistant faculty to appoint two women to the full-time faculty. A similar caucus at Yale, organized by doctoral students Carol Christ and Judith Plaskow, paved the way for the Women and Religion section at the American Academy of Religion. Roman Catholic sisters transformed the schools and colleges they already controlled. NOW cofounder Joel Read was perhaps the most important leader in this process. When she became president of Alverno College, the college reorganized its curriculum around the theme of women's studies and established a national Research Center on Women.[9]

Seminary women realized that extensive theological work was needed to align Christian and Jewish scriptures with their cause. While activists for racial and economic justice could appeal to dozens of liberatory passages, the majority of biblical texts addressing gender did so in ways that—at least on the surface—reinforced patriarchal power. The national community of feminist theologians came together at Alverno's 1971 conference on women's studies and then at Grailville, the U.S. center for an international Catholic laywomen's movement. In the wake of Vatican II, Grailville was becoming more ecumenical and explicitly feminist, and in 1972 it collaborated with NCC general secretary Clare Randall to bring together women ministers and theologians from the Jewish, Catholic, and Protestant traditions. For participants, some of whom had been doing feminist work in isolation for years, the conference was a first chance to meet a community of women who "claimed the 'doing of theology' as their birthright."[10]

At Grailville, Jewish feminist Judith Plaskow recognized the inherent religiosity of consciousness-raising. In one session, participants used words like "grace" or "illumination" to describe the "double recognition" that occurred when one woman saw herself in an experience described by another: women discovered both their individual identities and their communal solidarity. Calling this the "yeah, yeah" experience, the participants concluded that it was a form of conversion, in which "the pieces of my life fall together in a new way." But they were uneasy about seeing feminism as a form of religion, out of respect for antireligious feminists and because they couldn't quite say "what we added to the 'root' experiences by calling them *religious*." The relationship between feminism and religion was more one of sisterhood than of full identity.[11]

The most dramatic early interpreter of Plaskow's "yeah, yeah" experience was Mary Daly. A Catholic who had received her theological and philosophical education in Europe, Daly had not been deeply involved in civil rights activism or the student movement of the 1960s. But she captured the mood of the early 1970s in a *Commonweal* article (later expanded into *Beyond God the Father*) that sought to think theologically from the standpoint of the women's movement. That movement, she wrote provocatively, "will present a growing threat to patriarchal religion less by attacking it than by simply leaving it behind." Daly urged feminists to reject the official church and its defining symbols of a father God and a male Christ, though at this point she still spoke of Jesus as "a free person who challenged ossified beliefs and laws." God's "Second Coming," she promised, would be realized when women empowered themselves for full partnership with men.[12]

Like James Cone's early works, *Beyond God the Father* was not so much separatist as vanguardist. Spurning the work of other liberationists on the ground that "a black or white, Marxist or capitalist, counter-cultural or bourgeois male chauvinist deity (human or divine) will not differ essentially from his opposite," Daly promised that women would "initiate a real leap in human evolution." Yet even as she insisted that it was "more important to listen to women's experiences" than to explore past theologies, she leaned as much on Paul Tillich as Cone did on Karl Barth, a fact that was evident to theologically informed readers and painfully distracting to the uninitiated.[13]

The next step for feminist theology was resourcement, or finding the basis within women's experience for a theology that would not rely on men's words. Daly embarked on this task in her third book, *Gyn/Ecology,* and subsequent publications that sought to reinvent the English language itself from a feminist perspective. Others delved into women's dreams, women's storytelling, or "the spiritual dimension of the life crises associated with having a female body." Newly minted as professors of women's studies in religion, Yale classmates Carol Christ and Judith Plaskow asked their students to compose their own "myths" on the basis of personal experience and devoted much of their pioneering anthology, *Womanspirit Rising,* to experience-based essays. All who yearned for new sources found an inspiring older sister in Nelle Morton, a longtime activist who had participated in the 1947 Journey of Reconciliation and who taught that any authentic feminist theology would be grounded in autobiographical narrative—a point that both Christians and Goddess worshippers readily embraced.[14]

Feminists whose pursuit of resourcement did not take them out of traditional religion pointed to their own life stories as evidence that Christian and Jewish communities could be more empowering than a suspicious reading of sacred texts might lead one to expect. It was her "commitment to Christian faith and love," recalled Catholic biblical scholar Elisabeth Schüssler Fiorenza, that initially led her "to question the feminine cultural role" imposed on her by the larger society. Schüssler Fiorenza devoted her scholarly career to a reconstruction of Christian origins that would make historically apparent what she already knew by experience: that Christian women had always been active creators of their tradition. Judith Plaskow, in turn, was inspired by Schüssler Fiorenza's work to harness the power she had within the Jewish community—by, for example, creating a ritual for girls that would parallel the Brit Milah, or covenant of circumcision. Other Jewish feminists of the 1970s were similarly focused on liturgy. Letty Cottin Pogebrin, a founder of *Ms.* magazine, began saying the prayers for an informal Rosh Hashanah service at her summer community even before there were female rabbis. Feminists who rewrote the Sabbath prayers or Passover Haggadah stressed the importance of claiming Jewish as well as female particularity, noting, "Our prayers . . . are . . . an affirmation of our choice to remain within the tradition and to sanctify our everyday lives as women."[15]

Some Protestant feminists continued the work of resourcement in the congregations they served as ministers, pressing for the incorporation of "inclusive" language for God and humanity in liturgies and lectionaries. Others fought just to have their leadership recognized. One great drama of the decade was the 1974 ordination of eleven women into the Episcopal priesthood, a year after the denomination's General Convention had voted down the bishops' proposal for women's ordination. The 1974 ordinations, performed by retired bishops, were "irregular" and unrecognized by the rest of the church until 1977. The ceremony, conducted at a predominantly black parish in Philadelphia, reflected a continuing alliance between feminist and black liberation. An African American layman preached the sermon and Barbara Harris, then a lay leader of the host parish and later the first Anglican woman bishop, led the procession. Four of the white ordinands were sponsored by black parishes. The event's drama meant that Episcopal priests were more visible as representatives of feminism than ordained women whose denominations had recognized women's ministry for decades.[16]

Much the same can be said for Roman Catholic feminists, whose struggle against a celibate male hierarchy made them the face of feminist agitation within the churches. Mary Daly had started as a Catholic, and the Christian feminist who was most widely read in Protestant seminaries, Rosemary Radford Ruether, was also Catholic. In 1971 Mary Lynch entered a Catholic seminary to prepare herself for ordination. Inspired by the Episcopalian ordinations, Lynch worked with Priests for Equality to organize what they thought would be a small conference. Instead, two thousand people spent Thanksgiving of 1975 at the founding meeting of the Women's Ordination Conference. Among them was Ada María Isasi-Diaz, a former nun who had left her community shortly before immigrating to the United States. When participants were asked to stand if they felt called to ordination, Isasi-Diaz hesitated because she was "tired of battles," but was soon thrilled to realize that she was "surrounded by a 'cloud of witnesses.'" As she sat down she mused, "I have been born, baptized, and confirmed in this new life all at once!"[17]

A second "Call to Action" brought radical Catholics back to Detroit a year later. The bishops who organized this conference were inspired by Pope Paul VI's teaching that the laity had a "call to action" to translate Christian ideals into public policy. Building on a consultation process that included nearly a million Catholics, 1,340 delegates agreed on the church's role in society—but they also insisted that the credibility of Catholic social teaching was compromised by policies that relegated women to second-class status. The resulting organization pushed for the ordination of women and married men, for overturning the church's ban on birth control, and for democratizing church governance, eventually prompting some bishops to excommunicate its members.[18]

A specifically evangelical movement grew up alongside Catholic feminism. During the same Thanksgiving weekend that the Women's Ordination Conference was established in Detroit, evangelical women in Washington, D.C., formed the Evangelical Women's Caucus. These women had already launched a journal called *Daughters of Sarah,* which announced, "We are Christians; we are also feminists. Some say we cannot be both, but Christianity and feminism for us are inseparable." In Washington, they voted to endorse the Equal Rights Amendment and the campaign for women's ordination in the Catholic Church, and they listened to presentations on egalitarian marriage and the feminist commitments of nineteenth-century evangelicals.[19]

Virginia Mollenkott's keynote address, "Women and the Bible," prefigured the issues that would split the caucus in half a decade later. A literature professor with a B.A. from Bob Jones University and a doctorate from Temple, Mollenkott articulated the common ground that "when properly understood, the Bible supports the central tenets of feminism." But she fleshed this out in terms that reflected mainline rather than evangelical principles of exegesis, distinguishing the saving message of the gospel from culturally conditioned aspects of scripture. "Because patriarchy is the cultural background of the scriptures," she explained, "we must make careful distinctions between what is 'for an age' and what is 'for all time.'" Mollenkott even suggested that "we ought to re-think our doctrine of the Trinity, which traditionally has been pictured as totally masculine."[20]

There was little here to distinguish Mollenkott's position from that of the many feminists who remained within mainline Protestant and Catholic churches, and soon these women joined the caucus. Their influence troubled those evangelicals who believed that it was possible to affirm women's equality without repudiating a characteristically evangelical emphasis on biblical authority. Significantly, though, the organization did not split in two until 1986, when members voted narrowly to support gay and lesbian rights. Opponents of that decision organized Christians for Biblical Equality, which affirmed the "totality of Scripture" as "the authoritative Word of God." Both groups remain active to the present.[21]

Just as Catholic and evangelical women were articulating their own feminist theologies, so too did African American, Latina, and Asian women experience encounters of identity that transformed their Christian faith. The most influential circle of African American female theologians was drawn to Union Theological Seminary by James Cone's presence on the faculty, but chafed at his reluctance to take seriously the "oppressive realities in the Black community" that were not directly the result of racism. In 1979 Jacquelyn Grant warned that Black Theologians "have yet to realize that if Jesus is liberator of the oppressed, all of the oppressed must be liberated." Grant's classmates Delores Williams and Katie Cannon agreed and introduced Alice Walker's concept of "womanism" into theological discourse. By focusing on the lived experience of black women, and the distinctive ways in which they had fostered their community's survival when full liberation was not imaginable, womanists refuted the vanguardism of Cone and Daly's early work.

No single group could transform society, but each could access its own wellspring of power by telling its own story.[22]

In the decades that followed, Latina, Asian, and Native American women, as well as advocates of queer and disability-based theologies, expanded the list of oppressions whose intersections liberation theologians felt obliged to trace. Both Asian feminist Chung Hyun Kyung and mujerista theology founder Ada María Isasi-Diaz arrived at Union in the wake of the founding womanists. Their sisterhood was strong enough to bridge cultural differences without effacing them. "We cannot struggle for justice for women thinking only of our own communities," reflected Isasi-Diaz, reflecting on the inspiration she received from womanists. Isasi-Diaz and Kyung made extensive use of the voices of ordinary women in their inaugural publications, underscoring the power available to all who came together around shared experiences of oppression.[23]

James Cone eventually embraced this expanded vision of liberation, as did most black men inspired by his work. White feminists also embraced the imperative of intersectionality. Seeking a framework for her feminism that did not reduce all oppressions to those of sex, Elisabeth Schüssler Fiorenza eventually renamed patriarchy as "kyriarchy" to signal that the "pyramidal system of structured oppressions" was the root problem. Cannon and Isasi-Diaz joined white allies in the Mudflower Collective, which published a pioneering text of collaborative theology called *God's Fierce Whimsy.* But no one spoke more vehemently for intersectionality than Rosemary Radford Ruether. No theological newcomer in the late 1970s, she had come in into her own theologically not during the explosions of the late 1960s but in the more cooperative years that preceded them. As a young mother and graduate student, she had spent the summer of 1965 working in Mississippi's Delta Ministry during the most dangerous phase of the civil rights movement. On the faculty of Howard University, Ruether had produced significant works on black liberation theology, radical peace activism, and Christian-Jewish relations before penning her feminist magnum opus, *Sexism and God-Talk,* in the late 1970s. By displacing Mary Daly—who retained a narrow focus throughout her career—Ruether ensured that a multi-issue focus would dominate Christian feminism.[24]

Ruether's inclusivity did not, however, fully embrace witches. Implicitly and at times explicitly, Ruether suggested that a feminism attentive to interlocking oppressions would stop short of a categorical break with Christianity or other inherited religious traditions, since such a break implied that women's religion was wholly good and Christianity wholly bad. She faulted Goddess feminists for unwarranted faith in a prehistoric matriarchy and bigoted hostility to Judaism and Christianity. Zsuzsanna Budapest replied bitterly that "the 'inheritance' of Christianity for women is pain," while Carol Christ observed that Ruether's picture of the movement resorted to the same "hostile caricature" that she accused others of. A more nuanced pagan vision, she promised, would soon appear in the new work of coven leader Starhawk.[25]

Indeed, Starhawk proved that Goddess spirituality was as capable as Christian feminism of acknowledging intersecting oppressions. A college student when Budapest organized the Susan B. Anthony Coven, by the end of the decade she was displacing Budapest as the public face of feminist Wicca. After forming a coven without any connections to traditional neopaganism, she was initiated into both Dianic Wicca and the Faery tradition of Victor and Cora Anderson. An invitation to represent witchcraft at the American Academy of Religion translated into a book contract for *The Spiral Dance,* which introduced Americans to the creative work that pagans had been doing over the past decade. Equally committed to feminism and traditional neopaganism, Starhawk showed that pagan practice could be thoroughly feminist without excluding men. She was also eager to connect to other radical causes. The "Spiral Dance Ritual" she created for Halloween developed into an annual festival in San Francisco and a collective of pagan activists called Reclaiming. Reclaiming's founding vision was subsequently articulated in a statement that explained that "[o]ur feminism includes a radical analysis of power, seeing all systems of oppression as interrelated, rooted in structures of domination and control."[26]

The group's first visible participation in activism was in the Abalone Alliance's campaign against a nuclear power plant at El Diablo, California. Modeled on an East Coast campaign known as the Clamshell Alliance, Abalone organized participants into "affinity groups," many of which shared a religious affiliation or particular experience of oppression. Empowering themselves through small-scale consciousness-raising, affinity groups used consensus to decide exactly how to participate in any given action, and delegated representatives to a broader decision-making council that also used consensus. This structure allowed environmentalists and pacifists, Christians and pagans, to come together without losing their distinct identities. Pagan affinity groups opened their rituals to other participants who were attracted to what they were doing. As a leader in this process, Starhawk joined Dan Berrigan, Jim Wallis, and Jesse Jackson in the circle of nationally prominent religious leaders who were regularly arrested for civil disobedience in radical causes. Soon, a visible pagan presence was expected in radical coalitions.[27]

For at least one participant observer, pagans set an inspiring new tone for radicalism. Where earlier groups had divided bitterly over minor ideological differences, the emerging tradition of nonviolent direct action honored differences through ritual, as when a group of jailed women formed a human bridge and sang, "We will never forsake you" to those who had chosen to bail out. Along with Quakers steeped in the practice of consensus, pagans provided the spiritual grounding for such practices. This was because witches had not allowed fear of "separatism" to prevent them from embracing the full power of identity encounter. Having internalized their new identity as witches, they came to the work of coalition building from a position of strength.[28]

For Starhawk, what happened when pagans entered radical coalitions was a form of magic. In an essay that became the nucleus of her second book, she described the same problems with identity politics that troubled Rosemary Ruether: "Our efforts are too easily scattered. . . . We are taught . . . that rape is a separate issue from nuclear war, that women's struggle for equal pay is not related to a Black teenager's struggle to find a job." Such perceptions, she argued, reflected our estrangement from the underlying interconnectedness symbolized by the Goddess. Magic, "the art of changing consciousness," reenergized its practitioners by naming and ritualizing the connections.[29]

Magic, thus understood, was the ideal practice for a radical tradition beginning to reassemble its divided body. Starhawk acknowledged that magic was not able to overcome any obstacle at any moment, for its energy was inherently cyclical. Sometimes the best magic could do was to recognize the ebbing of energy, so that it would not feel like a failure. "We can use the downswing of the cycle," she explained, "for observation, education, and building support for the actions we take when energy is on the upswing." The observation was salutary, for American radicalism would soon face the most daunting challenge in its two-hundred-year history: a resurgent movement of grassroots conservatism that also drew on the powerful energies of religion.[30]

CHAPTER 20

Resisting the Right

By 1980 American radicalism was as healthy as ever. No single movement was as strong as abolitionism in 1850, socialism in 1912, or civil rights in 1963, nor were there leaders of the stature of Eugene Debs, Martin Luther King, or Dorothy Day. But a seasoned generation of activists led a vast array of radical movements. The student radicals of the 1960s had weathered personal and ideological crises, learned to integrate activism with the everyday demands of family and community, and gained positions of influence in churches, synagogues, and universities. The lines between "liberals" and "radicals" had faded to the point that such leaders as Tom Hayden, Shirley Chisholm, Andrew Young, Julian Bond, and John Lewis were all prominent Democratic Party politicians. Under the influence of former Catholic Worker Michael Harrington, a socialist remnant was also moving toward greater alliance with the Democrats. In 1983 Harrington's Democratic Socialist Organizing Committee (DSOC) merged with the New American Movement, itself a remnant of the New Left. The resulting Democratic Socialists of America (DSA) included a vigorous Religion and Socialism Coalition, founded in 1977 under the auspices of the DSOC. The DSA also provided one base of support for Jesse Jackson's "rainbow" campaigns in 1984 and 1988, during the latter of which he earned 7 million primary votes and almost gained the presidential nomination.

But the Left faced a new challenge. Less divided than before, it was outmatched by a newly energized grassroots conservatism. The anti-tax, anti-Communist ideology of Barry Goldwater flowed together with the militant fundamentalism of Jerry Falwell, who had been drawn into the political arena by his loathing for feminism and LGBT liberation. As mainline Protestantism shed members, its authority was usurped by the Southern Baptist Convention (which sponsored the aggressively conservative Christian Life Commission), the Assemblies of God, and nondenominational conservative churches. Popular perceptions of religion in politics now focused on the Moral Majority and its successors.

In the new context brought about by Reagan's election, the Left was reduced to saying no: no to an expanded Cold War, no to support for oppressive governments in Central America, South Africa, and the Middle East, no to the dismantling of social welfare programs and labor protections. Religious voices were prominent among the naysayers, both because the prophetic idiom of biblical religion was admirably suited to the work of critique and because the rise of the religious Right generated interest in all forms of religious engagement with the public sphere.

The new decade also began with martyrdoms. On March 24, 1980, Oscar Romero was murdered in El Salvador while saying mass. As archbishop of one of the most repressive countries in Latin America, Romero was a recent convert to the radical vision of the base communities. He had spoken out against the unequal distribution of land, the suppression of voting rights, and the chilling violence of "death squads" who targeted labor organizers, students, and radical priests. Romero's murder was retaliation for his prophetic witness, and its significance for U.S. Christians was underscored half a year later, when four American Catholic volunteers were murdered in El Salvador. Soon mainline and Catholic leaders—along with a sprinkling of Southern Baptist, Assemblies of God, and Missouri Synod Lutheran ministers—were demanding an end to military aid to El Salvador. On Good Friday 1981, fourteen denominational heads used a Holy Week procession in the nation's capital to call attention to this demand.[1]

The Reagan administration saw things in Central America differently. Both El Salvador's and Guatemala's governments were fighting guerrillas who were supported by Cuban and Soviet Communists, and in nearby Nicaragua the Sandinista guerrillas had seized state power in 1979. Though the Sandinista regime was friendlier to religion than the Cuban or Soviet governments, with Ernesto Cardenal and other liberationist priests occupying prominent posts, it was aligned with the Soviet bloc internationally. Convinced that Central America was a front in the cosmic battle between Christian democracy and godless Communism, Reagan and his Christian conservative supporters channeled guns and money to the Sandinistas' "Contra" adversaries. Religious radicals replied that counterinsurgency was "demonic" and that "in trying to prevent a Cuba in Nicaragua, Reagan may be creating a Vietnam in El Salvador."[2]

Reagan's opponents often commented on what they saw as his bizarre obsession with tiny countries that posed no threat. But they were equally obsessed themselves—so much so that one 1980s reader commented that *Christianity & Crisis* might be renamed *Christianity & Central America*. Thousands of religious radicals traveled to Central America to learn about liberation theology. Mark and Louise Zwick, who later launched a Catholic Worker community in Houston, testified to the transformative character of their visit to El Salvador: "The institutional Church . . . was all over the place working with the poor, celebrating the liturgy . . . fighting against slave wages and being killed for standing with the poor. . . . Our experience in El Salvador brought us to our knees." As more of their new friends were murdered, people like the Zwicks got off their knees and onto their feet, fighting for a change in policy.[3]

The religious response took several forms. The sanctuary movement combined political resistance with direct service to Central American refugees, highlighting the ancient tradition that individuals could find safety from persecution within churches. When John Fife, pastor of the activist Southside Presbyterian Church in Tucson, encountered political refugees from El Salvador among the economic refugees from Mexico, he and a Quaker rancher named Jim Corbett envisioned a revitalized Underground Railroad for asylum seekers. Southside Presbyterian and five churches in Berkeley publicly declared their intent to offer "sanctuary" in a letter to the attorney general on the second anniversary of Romero's assassination. Two hundred congregations joined a movement that, like earlier settlement houses, blurred the boundary between humanitarian direct service and leftist advocacy for policy change. At its best, the movement stressed that the two practices were inseparable, but there were also tensions. On one occasion, Chicago activists, eager to raise consciousness about the war, sent two refugees back to Tucson because they did not understand the conflict well enough to be effective public speakers. The movement also attracted negative attention from the government, spurred on by the newly founded Institute for Religion and Democracy's sweeping critique of liberation theology. One activist was classified as a prisoner of conscience by Amnesty International and sixteen others were indicted for conspiracy. But the number of sanctuary congregations doubled as a result.[4]

Other radicals took the nonviolent struggle to Central America. Working with Nicaraguan evangelicals, Sojourners urged activists to travel there to observe the human consequences of the "Contra" war. Catholics, Quakers, mainliners, and people of no religious affiliation joined Witness for Peace's work of "accompaniment"—walking alongside the peoples of Latin America in order to shield them from the violence that had killed Oscar Romero and thousands of others. One delegation was kidnapped by the Contras, an incident that the organization skillfully exploited for media attention. After the Contra war died down, Witness for Peace began accompanying Guatemalan refugees who were returning home, and it would later send long-term volunteers and short-term delegations to Haiti, Cuba, and Colombia.[5]

In addition to organizing Witness for Peace, *Sojourners* magazine invited its readers to sign a "Pledge of Resistance" promising to engage in massive civil disobedience should the United States invade Nicaragua. The "pledge" strategy had a long radical pedigree, with roots in the temperance movement and in the War Resisters League's effort to persuade Americans to refuse to participate in war. Jim Wallis began hinting at this strategy in an April 1982 letter warning Reagan that he would "have to persecute us too" if he continued the war. The FOR, Clergy and Laity Concerned (CALC), Catholic Worker, and even a few denominations endorsed a 1983 pledge promising that in the event of an invasion "We will assemble as many North American Christians as we can to join us and go immediately to Nicaragua to stand unarmed as a loving barrier in the path of any attempted invasion." A thousand pledgers were arrested in actions staged after Congress passed a bill providing aid to the Contras in 1985, perhaps forestalling invasion and certainly contributing to the backlash against Reagan's policy.[6]

Central American solidarity's influence on radical activism extended long after the United States lost interest in fighting Communism there. The 1989 murder of the Jesuits who had inspired Romero, along with their housekeeper and her daughter, sparked an ongoing resistance campaign against the School of the Americas, which had trained perpetrators of massacre in Latin America. A host of subsequent movements have created their own "Pledges of Resistance," the most recent of which was written by Starhawk and Saul Williams to oppose military responses to September 11. Witness for Peace also inspired new organizations dedicated to nonviolent intervention in situations of conflict. Ronald Sider offered a pointed theological justification for such activism in a

1984 speech to a Mennonite gathering. Melding the Anabaptist tradition of martyrdom with Gandhianism, Sider predicted that Christians could "impact the course of world history," but only if "we . . . are ready to start to die by the thousands in dramatic vigorous new exploits for peace and justice." The audience founded Christian Peacemaker Teams (CPT), which continues to "get in the way" of violence in Colombia, Israel/Palestine, and Iraq. CPTers typically die by the twos and threes rather than by the thousands, and their model is shared by such groups as Voices in the Wilderness and the Nonviolent Peace Force.[7]

The Central America solidarity movement evolved in parallel with efforts to support the antiapartheid struggle in South Africa—and to oppose U.S. involvement in the Nicaragua-style wars raging in nearby Mozambique and Angola. Ever since Mozambican Eduardo Mondlane had wowed Methodist student gatherings in the 1950s, Christian leftists had noticed the work of southern Africa's religiously rooted activists. While conservatives faulted the WCC for supporting the African National Congress's policy of limited violence, radicals were inspired by the "Kairos Document" issued by South African theologians in 1985. Modeled on the anti-Nazi Barmen Declaration, "Kairos" announced a "moment of truth not only for apartheid but also for the Church" and urged Christians to move beyond facile reconciliation to a "prophetic" stance that "sides unequivocally and consistently with the poor and oppressed." Prodded by this statement, American radicals joined sanctions campaigns and contemplated whether the United States was facing its own "kairos" moment.[8]

Reagan's support for anti-Communist governments coincided with a renewed nuclear arms race with the Soviet Union. Gandhians responded to the challenge with spectacles of "resistance" that echoed the protests of the 1940s and 1950s. Weeks before Reagan's election, Phil and Dan Berrigan led eight activists who took the biblical injunction to beat swords into plowshares literally by assailing nuclear warheads with sledgehammers. Subsequent "Plowshares" actions also drew on biblical images and the sacramental practices of Catholicism. By pouring blood, sprinkling ashes, and planting flowers, they demonstrated that their work was connected to the most elemental life forces, while nuclear weapons represented the demonic powers of death.

The Berrigans' brand of sacramental civil disobedience flowed together with Central American popular religion, Starhawk's pagan rituals, and the work of avant-garde artists to engender a full-bodied practice of activism. Radicals were no longer content to give soapbox speeches, lead marches, and sing songs, as they had been doing for decades; now they also used massive puppets to dramatize the struggle between good and evil, scheduled their actions to coincide with Good Friday or the Feast of the Holy Innocents, and styled their protests as funerals or exorcisms. The shift reflected the visual preoccupations of the television age; it also revealed that the old radical alliance between Protestants and Freethinkers had given way to a liturgical spectrum stretching from Roman Catholics to neopagans.

Throughout the 1980s most religious activists retained the preoccupation with international affairs that had crystallized during the struggle against the Vietnam War. But Reagan's domestic policies, coupled with the recession of the early 1980s, sparked a related wave of activism focused on homelessness. Ninety Catholic Worker communities were organized during the 1980s, twice as many as during the movement's first decade. Though many of these communities focused narrowly on direct service to the poor, others embraced a mix of hospitality and resistance or aligned themselves with the sanctuary movement. In Atlanta, Presbyterians involved in ministry to the homeless launched the Open Door community as a "Protestant Catholic Worker" determined to resist "that culture which crushes the prophets for profits." At Washington's Community for Creative Non-Violence, Mitch Snyder—converted to Christian radicalism by the Berrigans while serving time for auto theft— used civil disobedience to prod the federal government and the Catholic Church to put the needs of the poor first.[9]

In the middle of the decade, several high-profile statements signaled that the leadership of the Catholic and mainline churches shared the sentiments that led Snyder, Wallis, Starhawk, and the Berrigans to be arrested. The Catholic bishops made headlines with a pastoral letter, "The Challenge of Peace." The document identified the just-war and nonviolence traditions as "distinct but interdependent methods of evaluating warfare," united by their "common presumption against the use of force." Stopping short of condemning nuclear weapons outright, the bishops repudiated the targeting of civilians and any nuclear first strike, and accepted the policy of nuclear deterrence only "as a step on the way toward progressive disarmament." Three years later, "Economic Justice for All" challenged Catholics to judge each economic practice and institution "in light of whether it protects or undermines the dignity of the human person" and proposed a "new American experiment" of partnership between workers and owners, citizens and government.

The bishops also considered four drafts of a pastoral letter on women's issues before failing, in 1992, to gain the two-thirds majority needed for publication.[10]

Though the Catholics got the most press, similar sentiments appeared in social statements issued by mainline Protestants, Unitarian Universalists, Reform and Conservative Jews, and the NCC. In their own statement on nuclear war, the United Methodists went beyond the Catholics, arguing that "it is wrong for any nation to possess" nuclear weapons. Unitarian Universalists took the most radical ground on sexual issues, with consistent support for LGBT sexuality and abortion rights. By the end of the decade virtually every mainline denomination was on record in opposition to the arms race, the wars in Central America, apartheid, and environmental injustice. Such positions fell short of the radicalism proposed in late 1960s ecumenical gatherings. Statements castigated racism but did not demand the transfer of white church resources to black-controlled enterprises; they defended government's role in reducing poverty and unemployment but did not call on workers to build a postcapitalist economy. But they were newsworthy because they were dramatically out of step with the sentiments that led American voters to elect Ronald Reagan in 1980 and 1984. As the nation moved to the right, the once-dominant churches stood still, and that was enough to make radicals cheer.[11]

But radicals groaned to see the Moral Majority and Christian coalition emulate Martin Luther King's success at organizing a grassroots movement within local congregations. Frequently sought out by journalists to provide a counterpoint to Christian Right pronouncements, faith-based radicals heightened the "religiosity" of their activism and drew a sharper line between their own "prophetic" vision and that of the so-called secular Left. Such lines were not without precedent. Peter Maurin consistently contrasted the Communist Party and the Catholic Worker, tracing the latter not to eighteenth-century revolutions but to "a philosophy so old that it looks like new." But for most of the previous two centuries, radicals typically blamed the conservative churches for engendering anticlericalism. Now, in the face of the Left's failure to build socialism, end racism, or resist Reagan—and in light of left-leaning pronouncements by the churches!—it was tempting to blame secularists themselves for excluding people of faith, and to lift up Martin Luther King Jr. and Dorothy Day as exemplars of a more authentic mode of activism.[12]

This line of argument was most prominent in *Sojourners* magazine.

This was a change of tone. From its beginnings as the *Post-American,* the journal's goal was to merge the personal spirituality of evangelicalism with the social agenda of the New Left, and it contained at least three criticisms of conservative piety for every barb directed against secularists. Far from appreciating Jimmy Carter's linking of evangelical piety with Democratic Party politics, *Sojourners* accused Carter of "seducing the church" and perpetuating "the extraordinary principalities" of "technocracy." Things changed because of Reagan's alarming victory and because many editors sympathized with the antiabortion movement. (That sympathy was shared by the Berrigan family and by many Catholic Workers, but not by advocates of liberation theology or most mainline, Jewish, Buddhist, and pagan radicals.) Worried that the controversy over *Roe v. Wade* would distract attention from the struggle against poverty and war, *Sojourners* embraced Cardinal Joseph Bernardin's idea of a "seamless garment" of opposition to abortion, capital punishment, and war, and encouraged readers to use nonviolent direct action at both abortion clinics and nuclear weapons facilities.[13]

Such activism, explained Joe Holland, promised to "transcend both the Right and the Left" and usher in a new politics. Reagan voters were correct to reject the leftist assumption "that the traditional family was a problem," but they were dead wrong to imagine "authoritarianism and militarism as the solution," when in fact nuclear weapons might be used to "blow up all the families of the world." New Leftists who blamed the plight of the family on corporate power and male privilege were closer to the truth, but their refusal to grant "moral status to unborn children" betrayed a "moral shallowness." Only a "richer spiritual vision," Holland concluded, could resolve the family crisis and socioeconomic injustice simultaneously.[14]

The New Leftist whom Holland singled out for guarded praise was Michael Lerner, a rabbi and the original convenor of the New America Movement who had recently published a manifesto, "Recapturing the Family Issue," in the *Nation.* Lerner's thesis was that conservative attacks on women, people of color, and gays and lesbians were misguided responses to an authentic crisis that might better be addressed by a deeper spirituality coupled with economic policies designed to aid families. Feeling rebuffed by feminists who were hostile to the family and Democrats who were spiritually tone deaf, Lerner launched *Tikkun* magazine in 1986 as a forum for voices excluded from "secular and often overtly-hostile-to-religion magazines like *The Nation* and *Mother Jones.*" His timing was impeccable: a year later, Palestinians began the first intifada, or uprising against Israeli occupation, and *Tikkun* gained a national stage as the preeminent voice of Jewish opposition to Israeli policies.[15]

By the end of the 1980s, *Tikkun* and *Sojourners* had displaced *Christianity & Crisis*—the primary mouthpiece for theologies of liberation, fatally tied to the declining financial fortunes of the Protestant mainline—as the leading journals of radical religion. Unlike their predecessors, *Sojourners* and *Tikkun* presupposed a "secular" context in which religion needed defense. Whether or not this assessment was correct, it spoke to the spirit of the age. *Sojourners* and *Tikkun*'s religious assertiveness, and apparent distance from the fading mainline, attracted the attention of observers seeking a better understanding of religion and politics. The two journals would eventually anchor the activist organizations Call to Renewal (organized by Wallis in 1995) and Network of Spiritual Progressives (created by Lerner in 2005).

Wallis and Lerner each published multiple manifestos for their movements. Though they agreed in opposing what Lerner called "the current misguided, visionless, and often spiritually empty politics of the Left," they had somewhat different emphases. Speaking to evangelicals, mainliners, Catholics, and peace church Christians, Wallis called for an integration of the evangelical and Social Gospel heritages. He promised to "go beyond the present definitions of Left and Right" by taking "special notice of those at the bottom" and thus moving "to higher ground." Lerner, for his part, reached beyond his Jewish base toward New Age as well as Christian radicals. Retaining the rhetoric of "progressivism," he acknowledged partisan loyalties in his hope that the Network of Spiritual Progressives would "be for the Democrats and Greens what the Religious Right has been for the Republicans." Both men occasionally resorted to straw-man images of godless Marxists inclined toward totalitarianism and opportunistic Democratic politicians unwilling to take moral stands against poverty and war. Both espoused positions on war, economics, and race solidly rooted in the radical tradition, and they failed to acknowledge that radical critics of their pro-family policies were as likely to be pagan or Unitarian Universalist as "secular."[16]

Ironically, Wallis and Lerner began articulating their critique of the secular Left in the 1980s, when the most unifying political leader for American radicals and liberals was Rev. Jesse Jackson. The irony is its own explanation: Lerner and Wallis attacked secularism in the 1980s because its tide was ebbing, not rising. Confuting academic theories of secularization, Jerry Falwell and Pat Robertson proved that religion was politically important, and Jesse Jackson and the Catholic bishops proved that it was not monolithically conservative. The time was ripe to get beyond the anti-Constantinianism that had long united religious radicals with their Freethinking counterparts. What sense did it make to blame injustice on the alliance of church and state when the heirs of establishment were calling for state-sponsored social welfare? Since Reagan's conservatives had co-opted antigovernment rhetoric, radicals needed a new framework, and Lerner and Wallis hoped to provide it.

Though ideological anticlericalism was declining, from the institutional perspective Lerner and Wallis were right to suggest that American radicalism had become increasingly secular over the course of the twentieth century. This was so because denominations, seminaries, and congregations were no longer the only mass-constituency institutions independent of state and corporate power. Labor unions and universities had expanded exponentially, and Lerner and Wallis were part of the first generation for whom college education was as widespread as church membership. Because the baby boomers who experienced the identity encounter as students often pursued professorial careers, the university now provided more social capital to radicals than did the churches. University-based radicals were not necessarily antireligious, but they spoke the language of academia more readily than that of theology. As SDS leaders at two of the largest state universities in the nation, Wallis and Lerner had come up in, and then reacted against, this tradition. Much of their criticism applied more to their own college classmates than to the Left as a whole.

The most salutary aspect of their critique was its implication that a radicalism dependent only on the universities as its organizing base would never transform American society as a whole. As the Democratic Party gained votes among professionals and lost them among white workers, *Tikkun* and especially *Sojourners* insisted that rust belt workers, small farmers, and inner-city dwellers of all races were essential to a true radical movement. The best politics, explained columnist Danny Duncan Collum, would be a populism that connected directly to the "felt needs and aspirations of ordinary, 'undissident' Americans," rather than the "resistance" of late 1960s radicals who found nothing to like in America beyond the campus. Such a politics would necessarily draw on religious language because religious institutions alone had "access to a broad cross section of the American people."[17]

Wallis and Lerner's earnest appeals for more forthright moral language on the left were not enough to overcome the sibling rivalry between religion and radicalism. When Wallis claimed that the Right "gets it wrong" and the Left "doesn't get it," he reduced a complex relationship to a matter of misunderstanding or poor analysis. And when Lerner argued that the religious Right's "perversion of religious values" appealed to people because they were spiritually starving, he came ironically close to repeating Marx's argument that religion is the heart of a heartless world. Many on the right dismissed them as secularists in disguise.[18]

The radical debate over religion heated back up after the 1980s. Anti-Constantinianism made sense again as conservative Protestants achieved the quasi-established position once held by mainliners and a new cohort of bishops and popes led the Roman Catholic Church to the right, especially on sexual issues. Wallis and Lerner responded by lifting up the stories of religious radicals, both past and present, and reminding readers (as this book seeks to do) that "most of the important movements for social change in America have been fueled by religion." Though their retelling gave disproportionate attention to the most orthodox of religious radicals, it made an important contribution to the tradition building that is one of the most important activities of the Left during times of conservative ascendancy.[19]

Lerner and Wallis's feud with secularism was perhaps an unavoidable instance of the infighting that will arise in any movement that finds itself on the defensive. A parallel problem was the era's tendency to see "resistance" rather than encounter as the defining radical practice. The rhetoric of resistance expressed radicals' sense that the Reagan administration was perpetrating monstrous evils. It also reflected the hard lessons of the past: since the ideological and utopian visions of the past had generated radical schisms in both the 1930s and the 1960s, was it not better to build a broad alliance around opposition to particular policies? But simply "saying no" to Reagan proved less energizing than the old radical hope of building God's Kingdom on earth, which may be why Wallis and Lerner hoped to anchor their resistance work by recovering the authentic Christianity or Judaism of a less secular past.

All the while, people continued to encounter one another, and both secularists and people of faith were drawn to those encounters. People met one another across racial and national lines in the sanctuary and antiapartheid movements, across denominational boundaries in Alinskyite community organizing, and across class lines at homeless shelters and "tent cities." Even the resistance work of the Plowshares movement involved deeply emotional interchange among activists as they prepared to act. As had always been the case, these encounters were the true source of spiritual power for social change. Much more than a new rhetoric of faith and values, interpersonal encounters provided the antidote to the religious Right. Conservatism was rising because it gave people a more powerful sense of identity, and the Left could thrive only to the extent that it did the same.

Encounters were at the heart of the Rainbow Coalition presidential campaign of Jesse Jackson, which was the high point of 1980s radicalism. Building on his surprisingly strong showing in 1984, Jackson used the 1988 campaign to facilitate new encounters among the identity groups that had built up distinct movements during the 1970s. Drawing on his personal ties to Martin Luther King Jr., he made "the redemptive history of black America" available to people of all cultures. He spent weeks with displaced industrial workers and the new movement of (mostly white) farm families mobilized against foreclosures and declining crop prices. Ultimately, Jackson earned nearly 7 million votes, but lost the Democratic primary to Michael Dukakis, a university-identified secularist who epitomized everything that troubled Wallis and Lerner about the Democrats. Wallis rightly praised Jackson for creating "a new coalition for change which crossed boundaries of race, class, and issues." Though the Left would remain on the defensive, inclined more to "resistance" than to cultural creation for the next two decades, Jackson helped it transcend the ideological partisanship of the late 1960s. In the face of many new things to resist—new military adventures in the Middle East; a backlash against empowered women, gays, and lesbians; and the threat of environmental catastrophe—most radicals kept the faith.[20]

CHAPTER 21

The Future of Radicalism

The American radical tradition may have ended on November 9, 1989. The fall of the Berlin Wall, symbolizing the collapse of Communist regimes in the Soviet Union and Eastern Europe, ended fifty years of Cold War and an even longer period when Americans saw the world as divided between the forces of East and West, capitalist and communist. The crisis of meaning was most intense for the handful of radicals who adhered to orthodox Marxist economic theories; others insisted that their proposals for anarchism or a mixed economy or radical cultural change were unaffected by what had happened to the Soviet bureaucracy. But, insofar as the Soviet Union and China (which was abandoning communism in its own way) were the most recent fruits of the revolutionary tradition that had begun in 1776, their transformation called into question the entire tradition built on revolutionary ideals. Was the mobilization of activists to extend liberty, equality, and solidarity really the best path to human betterment?

If the radical tradition ended in 1989, many radicals chose not to notice. Resistance to the policies of Reagan and Bush continued at Catholic Worker houses, Alinskyite community-organizing projects, global solidarity organizations, and denominational social justice offices. When Saddam Hussein invaded Kuwait a year later and the United States responded with what evolved into an intermittent twenty-year war in the Muslim world, the old coalition of opposition to the war in Vietnam revived. Religious activists who had come of age in the late 1960s, among them Jim Wallis and Starhawk, offered new pledges of resistance to American imperialism, and solidarity activists brought practices of "accompaniment" honed in Central America to Iraq and Israel/Palestine. With the beginning of the second Iraq War in 2003, NCC general secretary Robert Edgar—a Methodist minister and former congressman—emerged as the leading representative of Win Without War, a broad coalition that revived CALCAV's tradition of mainstream religious opposition to war. Religious activists were equally prominent in opposing so-called globalization, or the imposition of Western capitalism on the entire global economy. Pagans were visible at the 1999 Battle in Seattle, in which activists confronted a meeting of the World Trade Organization, while Christian and Jewish activists revived the biblical tradition of "jubilee" in calling for the forgiveness of debts owed by developing nations.

Both the antiwar and antiglobalization movements continued the 1980s trend toward forms of activism that emphasized resistance more than encounter. Activists certainly had opportunities to encounter Two Thirds World allies who were empowering themselves through their own acts of resistance, notably the Zapatistas of Mexico and participants in the Palestinian intifada. But most no longer believed—as had allies of the Sandinistas and African National Congress in the 1980s—that they were tasting the first fruits of a coming millennium of justice. The fall of the Soviet Union caused economic support for grassroots socialism to dry up, and the idealistic regimes of Nicaragua, Mozambique, and even the newly liberated South Africa came to terms with global capitalism. Overseas opposition to American hegemony began to center on politicized Islam and Chinese state capitalism, traditions that had little affinity with the Left. American radicals could hardly feel the same sympathy for Osama bin Laden that many had felt for Fidel Castro and Ho Chi Minh.

The tilt toward resistance reflected the fact that many turn-of-the-millennium movements were still led by 1960s activists who had settled into habits of persistent, lonely opposition to the mainstream. In 1979 Daniel Berrigan had described a Holy Week demonstration at the Pentagon as a liturgical way of "repeating ourselves"; twenty-five years later, my own undergraduate students were making the same repetition as they spent spring break at Jonah House, then traveled to Washington to sprinkle ashes and pour their own blood on the Pentagon. At the time of this writing, the first generation of college students to have been inspired by the Berrigans are vital leaders in their early sixties, still at the forefront of organizations they created a generation ago. Some of the first generation of liberation theologians, notably James Cone and Rosemary Radford Ruether, are still teaching or publishing. At no previous point in radical history have so many leaders retained their positions for forty years.[1]

The persistence of baby boomer activists raises questions about whether the American radical tradition will be embraced by activists who came of age after the end of the Cold War. Absent a global struggle between Left and Right, these activists may gravitate to more pragmatic approaches to social change. The Barack Obama campaign of 2008, in particular, drew an enormously energetic response from the children of baby boomers—as well as from Jim Wallis and other seasoned radicals—without offering a radical critique of any aspect of contemporary society. Having experienced the trauma of September 11, the steady decline of American power, and the conservative dismantling of New Deal policies, many young idealists are more concerned with preserving American institutions than subjecting them to radical critique. Earlier American radicals all presupposed a fundamentally expansive society, even as they fought the hypocrisy of poverty amid prosperity or slavery amid freedom. Their vision will not translate easily into a time of social contraction.

Still, empowering encounters among people did not end with the millennium. In recent years, two groups of Americans have experienced significant identity encounters, creating movements that inspired outsiders in much the same way as the bus boycotts and student sit-ins of the 1950s and 1960s. Queer activists came together in response to the AIDS crisis of the 1980s, building a movement that blended direct care for the sick and dying with prophetic denunciation of social structures indifferent to the suffering of gay men. The combination mirrored the founding vision of the Catholic Worker movement, which responded by creating communities devoted to AIDS work. Some—not all—Catholic Worker houses were among the first Catholic organizations to call for complete affirmation of sexual diversity.

Catholic and evangelical churches were also at the forefront of opposition to LGBT liberation, and so AIDS activism involved a substantial measure of confrontation with, and within, the churches. Forty-five hundred people joined the AIDS Coalition to Unleash Power (ACT UP) for its 1989 demonstration at Saint Patrick's Cathedral in New York, protesting the Catholic Church's opposition to AIDS education and condom distribution. AIDS also pushed the Metropolitan Community Churches to adopt a public, activist role. Mel White, a former ghostwriter for Pat Robertson and Jerry Falwell, carved out a new role as the church's "minister of justice," traveling across the country to confront political and, especially, ecclesiastical homophobia with Gandhian satyagraha.

In the 1990s most mainline Protestant denominations began an extended debate over whether LGBT persons could be ordained or marry in the church. Gay or lesbian pastors who "came out" were often supported by their congregations but disciplined by their denominations; in a few cases, pastors were disciplined for performing marriages or commitment ceremonies for LGBT couples. These debates pulled in the friends, families, and congregations of LGBT persons, and led to the creation of a new cluster of denominational organizations. While Dignity and its imitators were primarily for LGBT persons themselves, "Reconciling" or "Open and Affirming" movements encouraged entire congregations to affirm full inclusion of sexual diversity. Typically, status as a reconciling congregation flagged a community's sympathy with left-liberal positions on other issues, marking these churches as an activist network similar to the old People's Churches.

In the first decade of the new millennium, LGBT activism focused on the cause of "marriage equality" or providing all people access to civil and religious marriage, regardless of sexual orientation. In some ways, this cause was a step back from the radicalism of early gay or lesbian activism, which often spurned marriage as a form of accommodation to heterosexual norms. But the call for equality in marriage tapped into one of the most venerable ideals of the American Revolution, and intersected with calls for universal access to health care—since the prevailing system of employment-based health insurance extended coverage to workers' spouses but not their unmarried partners. Perhaps most importantly for the broader radical movement, the marriage equality campaign linked activism to the public celebration of marriage. Weddings as a form of civil disobedience fit nicely with the trend toward theatrical and liturgical elements in activism.

Almost simultaneous with LGBT folks, Latinas/os moved to the forefront of a radical tradition that had once relegated them to the shadows. Building on decades of accelerating migration from Latin America, Latinas/os achieved status as the largest minority group at the beginning of the new millennium, and flexed their political muscle by tipping close races to Barack Obama in several states. But they also faced special challenges. Partisan gridlock prevented the federal government from enacting even moderate reforms to the immigration system, excluding millions of "undocumented" persons from political participation. Post–September 11 concerns about national security led to a dangerous militarization of the U.S.-Mexico border, and popular conservatism fanned the flames of nativist hostility. All of these threats came together in the spring of 2010, when the state of Arizona took the enforcement of immigration laws into its own hands, passing a law that required local and state police to check the immigration status of individuals whom they suspected of being in the country illegally.

Radicals and liberals saw the Arizona law as the first step toward a new Jim Crow regime in the Southwest. At the time of this writing, a broad array of religious organizations have embraced the immigrants' cause as the civil rights issue of our generation, sending thousands of idealistic activists to show their solidarity in Phoenix and Tucson. It is not yet clear whether these actions will have the same long-term significance as Mississippi Summer or the Selma marches of 1965. But the yearning for encounters on that scale is palpable.

The immigrant rights and marriage equality movements sit comfortably within the tradition of American radicalism, both in their espousal of revolutionary values of liberty and equality and in their reliance on intense encounters among people lifting themselves out of oppression. Three other strands of post–Cold War activism may also come to be seen as important parts of the radical story—but may also represent an entirely new departure. The first of these is the academic tradition of "queer theory," and with it a cluster of "theoretical" approaches that call into question the very notion of "identity" or insist that all identities (of sexuality, race, gender, even biological sex) are contingent, hybrid, and culturally constructed. Deeply indebted to the work of Michel Foucault, queer theory emerged as a distinct academic tradition in the 1990s. Its leading proponents, like Foucault himself, espoused a variety of radical causes, but they broke sharply with the logic of the politics of identity. While other identity-based activists see particular identities as a basis for solidarity and power, queer theorists understand queerness as "an identity without an essence," constituted solely by the queer person's opposition to whatever is culturally normative. This position is echoed by those who see race as a pure cultural fiction, and on that basis criticize James Cone and others for essentializing blackness.[2]

Such arguments create a basis for resistance to forms of oppression that stigmatize people on the basis of identity: if there are no essential identities, it is absurd to single out particular groups for violence or exclusion. To the extent that queer theory discourages people from organizing around their identities, it could also contribute to the shift of activist energies from encounter to resistance. But this need not be the case: to say that an identity is contingent might also invite radical activists to take the task of constructing identities into their own hands. This seems to be the approach that informs most queer activism: Michelangelo Signorile's "Queer Manifesto" of 1993 was classically radical in its use of the "queer" category to bring together people, arguing that "the gay Republicans and the black lesbian mothers and the computer nerds and the congressional staffers" might come together as "out, proud, and queer in America."[3]

Queer theory brought to the surface two long-standing tensions within the radical tradition. First was the question of the family: was it the most intimately repressive of institutions, or a permanent aspect of human nature? Were rebels against all family structures the true heroes of human liberation, or was it better to join marriage equality advocates in pressing for the full participation of LGBT people in family life? The other involved the relationship between academia and other institutional bases of activism. To the extent that queer theory was expressed in abstruse, philosophical terms, it sharpened the divide between those who had been radicalized by their education and the millions too poor to attend college.

A similar criticism might be made of another movement that departed from key elements of American radicalism. Since 1989 increasing numbers of activists have held that the antidote to racism, militarism, and capitalism is not to be found in the revolutionary heritage of 1776 and 1789, but exclusively in pre-Enlightenment religious traditions. These activists draw on several threads of tradition that emerged in the middle of the twentieth century. One was Peter Maurin's intensely romantic adherence to the Catholic Middle Ages. Another was the idiosyncratic Barthianism of William Stringfellow, a white Episcopalian lawyer whose experiences in Harlem in the 1940s and 1950s turned him into a radical critic of both American society and Niebuhrian theology. Drawing on Saint Paul's analysis of "principalities and powers," Stringfellow argued that the whole world was governed by spiritual powers that had fallen from grace, and the only path of redemption lay in a church that set itself apart from worldly ways. This theology was compatible with New Left activism, but it entailed a rhetorical break with "America." Comparing the ideals of 1776 to Barrabas's revolutionary vision, Stringfellow taught that "we who are Americans witness in this hour the exhaustion of the American revolutionary ethic."[4]

The most influential strand was the Concern movement. This was a tradition of theological renewal among Mennonites who had been involved in alternate service during World War II. Concern members opposed the sectarianism of their Mennonite ancestors and the cultural accommodation of their contemporaries; they wanted to make the Anabaptist heritage more relevant by reconnecting with its roots. The appeal of this position extended beyond the Anabaptist community. Just as Protestant pacifists and Quakers had converged during World War I, so in the wake of World War II the Concern vision appealed to those who accepted the neoorthodox critique of liberalism but not Reinhold Niebuhr's embrace of the Cold War. It also appealed to evangelical radicals who yearned for deep historical roots and a theological alternative to Calvinism.[5]

The appointment of John Howard Yoder, foremost of the Concern theologians, to the faculty of Notre Dame helped bring these ideas into dialogue with parallel trends in Catholicism and evangelicalism. Urging Christians to create a new politics by "being the Church," Yoder presented a form of pacifism that differed sharply from that promoted by the Fellowship of Reconciliation. While most FOR members grounded their activism in what Mary Evelyn Jegen called "an intuition of . . . sheer human goodness," Yoder espoused a pessimistic view of human nature and insisted that nonviolent practice could not be grounded in the universal morality of the Enlightenment, but only through particular identification with the life, death, and resurrection of Jesus. Through the 1970s his ideas, as well as those of Maurin and Stringfellow, coexisted with classical American radicalism in the Sojourners community, Catholic Worker houses, and the Plowshares movement.[6]

Eventually, Yoder found a more polemical ally in the person of Stanley Hauerwas, a Methodist with Catholic and Anabaptist sympathies who taught first at Notre Dame and then at Duke Divinity School. Attracting Catholic and evangelical students, Hauerwas encouraged them to criticize liberalism and liberationism as stridently as they battled against war and capitalism. Some shook up the academy; others turned to the more constructive task of building a network of "New Monastic" communities—so named because they anticipated a period of cultural decline akin to that which gave birth to Benedictine monasticism. Partly modeled on Catholic Worker houses, New Monastic communities planted themselves in the "abandoned places of Empire" and pledged to practice voluntary poverty, "hospitality to the stranger," and gospel peacemaking. More committed to solidarity than to liberty or equality, they identified "humble submission to Christ's body, the Church," as an essential mark of true community. It is too early to know whether this movement will prove as enduring as the Catholic Worker, but its distance from the American revolutionary vision may prove increasingly appealing as U.S. global power declines.[7]

Queer theory and self-consciously Christian radicalism are both dwarfed by the environmental movement, which poses a third set of challenges to the classical Left. Concern for the environment has been a minor note throughout the history of American radicalism. Transcendentalists, Fourierists, and other communal socialists celebrated agricultural lifestyles in harmony with nature, as did twentieth-century Gandhians. A few prominent radicals, notably Scott Nearing of the Rand School and (briefly) the Communist Party, turned to environmentalism as their most important cause.

So it was not an accident that the Earth Day celebration of 1970, the event that galvanized the contemporary environmental movement, was perceived by both proponents and critics as an integral component of 1960s radicalism. For 1970s radicals, the New Left critique of technology as a threat to human dignity easily translated into an ecological critique of it as a threat to nature. Opposition to nuclear power—at the time the most visible of the environment-threatening technologies—fit easily with opposition to nuclear weapons. But the environmental movement included many people whose views on other issues were liberal or moderate. As had been the case since the days of Theodore Roosevelt, some zealous proponents of wilderness conservation were more interested in their own recreational opportunities than in global economic justice, and on more than one occasion environmentalists concerned with population control allied themselves with anti-immigration nativists. Still, by the 1990s environmentalism was as closely associated with the Left as temperance had been in the nineteenth century: while there were many nonleftist environmentalists, few radicals failed to embrace some version of the environmentalist agenda.

In the 1970s, the religious radicals who placed the greatest emphasis on environmental issues were Native Americans, keen to preserve their sacred sites from nuclear waste and water pollution; latter-day Transcendentalists; and neopagans, for whom breaking down the boundaries between humans and nature was a form of religious practice. Most of these folks criticized classical Christianity for its anthropocentric teaching about human "dominion" over nature, and a widely read essay by historian Lynn White argued that Christian suppression of nature-based spiritualities, dating back to Constantine, was the root cause of the entire environmental crisis.[8]

Yet the Protestant denominations, beginning with the United Church of Christ's Commission for Racial Justice, led the way in challenging "environmental racism," or the tendency for environmental degradation to be the greatest in areas populated by people of color. That issue provided an important bridge between ecumenical Protestantism's long-standing concern with racial and economic justice and the emerging environmental crisis. Ecumenical concern for indigenous rights led to some expressions of solidarity with Native Americans' environmental concerns, as was the case at the 1983 assembly of the World Council of Churches, where Ojibway elder Art Solomon led a prayer confessing that "in all creation, only the family of man has strayed from the sacred way." Protestant and Catholic theologians also responded to White's indictment by lifting up ecological elements in Christian history, retranslating "dominion" as "stewardship," or constructing new theologies that broke down the barriers between humans and animals, God and nature. Catholic Thomas Berry cast the findings of ecological science as a new sacred myth; Protestant Sallie McFague suggested that Christians treat the earth as the "body of God." Jewish radicals, meanwhile, played up the ecological implications of Sabbath keeping.[9]

For the most part, environmentalism has been comfortably integrated into the roster of radical causes. As early as 1975, Rosemary Radford Ruether—always the champion of intersectionality—produced a feminist theology that blended the insights of antiracism, socialism, and environmentalism. Ecological theology exploded in the 1990s, gaining a place in seminary curricula and in most liberation-oriented anthologies. There have certainly been tensions, particularly between advocates of vigorous population control and Catholic solidarity activists who oppose abortion. But these have been no greater than those that divide other radical causes. And, as was the case for tensions between African Americans and labor activists in the nineteenth century, the differences tend to fade among the most radical advocates of both causes.[10]

Nevertheless, the core environmental value of sustainability poses a challenge to the logic of the Left. Radicals have traditionally been skeptical of all inherited institutions, while environmentalists seek to foster cultural and economic practices that can be handed down to the "seventh generation." Radicals have also taken for granted the expansive mood of the United States as a whole. They have sought to expand political and environmental rights to an ever-larger community; they have wrestled with the paradox of poverty amid prosperity but have seldom questioned the value of prosperity itself. The challenge of climate change, coupled with the limited supply of both fossil fuels and fresh water, may require humanity as a whole—and Americans in particular—to make a transition from a growth-oriented to a steady-state culture. It is far from certain what role radicalism would play in such a culture.

I would not go so far as to say that any of these three movements are outside the American radical tradition, only that it is too soon to tell. Environmentalism in particular might be compared to the Spiritualist movement: in the 1850s it was growing rapidly and its most zealous adherents anticipated that it would soon supersede the "partial" reforms of the past. Instead, it declined while radicalism continued to regenerate itself for the next century and a half.

What I do know is that no tradition lasts forever. American radicalism has endured because it has never been thoroughly defeated and because it has never completely triumphed. We are still living in the age that began in 1776, still trying to discern whether new institutions would better serve the core values that are cherished by almost all Americans. Though the Civil War, New Deal, and 1960s all brought about institutional changes that were in some ways greater than those of 1776, none created a broad enough consensus to efface earlier ideological divisions and force a new start. If the United States, in partnership with the community of peoples, is able to respond adequately to climate change—if, that is, we learn to live in harmony with the natural world, instead of monopolizing an ever-increasing share of its finite wealth—that achievement might generate enough consensus for a fresh start.

Such an outcome—and something between that and climate apocalypse may be more likely—would necessarily involve transformative encounters between humans and a variety of natural phenomena. We will not cherish the lives of elephants and oaks, of prairies and tundras, unless we come to know them as intimately as we know one another. These encounters—long a part of Native American and pagan religious practice—could add an exciting element to American radicalism.

But an adequate response to global warming will also depend on a revitalization of interpersonal practices of encounter. Already, urban Americans are meeting one another as they weed carrots at community gardens, savor strawberries at farmers' markets, or use barn-raising techniques to install solar panels. A countryside that had been depopulated by the farm crisis is filling up again with intentional communities, small organic farms, and the WWOOFers (Willing Workers on Organic Farms) who inhabit them. New Orleans, the Gulf Coast, and other front lines of climate change play host to encounters between out-of-town volunteers and local residents who are rebuilding their lives. And activists in the "350" movement (pledged to reduce carbon to 350 parts per million in the atmosphere) are getting to know the inspiring activists from island nations who have mobilized to save their ancestral homes.

These many meeting places are all sacred space. Wherever humans encounter one another deeply, they find the power that has been known variously as spirit, mana, God. For two centuries, this power has placed Americans on the path toward justice—and it is still available to us today.

ACKNOWLEDGMENTS

My own formation as a radical has largely taken place at church. The vital communities of University Lutheran Church in Cambridge, Massachusetts, the Lutheran Volunteer Corps, the Community of Saint Martin in Minneapolis, the Saint Cloud Unitarian Universalist Fellowship, and the Unitarian Universalist Church of Medford, Massachusetts, created the spaces for some of the most prophetic encounters in my life, and I thank comrades in these places, and many others, for making it obvious to me that religion and radicalism are sisters and not enemies. I am grateful to students and colleagues at Saint John's University and the College of Saint Benedict, where the idea for this book emerged from my teaching of a survey course on religion in the United States. At Harvard Divinity School, I benefited from a one-semester leave and from the ideas and passion of students who enrolled in Religion and the Left in United States History in 2008 or 2010: Jennifer Channin, John Cosgriff, Kate DeConinck, Will Dewey, Garrett FitzGerald, Miriam Lazewatsky, Liz Miller, Paul Nauert, Rob O'Rourke, Rachel Sauer, Laura Votey, Sarah Benckart, Casey Bohlen, Charles Buehler, John Coggin, Madeline Desantis, Kye Flannery, Zack Grossman, Robert Harvey, Emily Jendzejec, Jack Jenkins, Michael Knight, Heidi Morgans, Paulina Pina Garcia, Allison Redfearn, Rachel Rosenberg, David Ruffin, and Rachel Stevens, as well as teaching fellow Elizabeth Gish. My understanding of religion and socialism was deepened by feedback from Harvard's North American Religions Colloquium and from anonymous reviewers at the *Journal of the American Academy of Religion*. I am especially grateful for the insights of those who read part or all of the manuscript: Patricia Appelbaum, Ann Braude, John Buehrens, Dawn Coleman, Healan Gaston, Craig Idlebrook, Kip Kosek, John Lomperis, Jason Lydon, Tim

McCarthy, John Gibb Millspaugh, Sarah Gibb Millspaugh, Erik Resly, Kip Richardson, Leigh Schmidt, and John Stauffer, as well as my editor, Amy Caldwell. Tammy McKanan was a tireless champion of this book, as well as a faithful comrade in the work of embodying radical values in our household. Oriana McKanan displayed patient forbearance during the birth travails of this book, which seemed to last as long as her own nativity eight years earlier. I hope that when I am finishing my next book she will be ready to enrich it with her formidable knowledge of metaphor and poetry. Before that happens, though, we will have plenty of time to play.

American and Foreign Anti-Slavery Society (AFASS, 1840). Alternative abolitionist organization organized by those who opposed the Garrisonian agenda of women's rights, nonresistant pacifism, and strident criticism of the churches.

American Anti-Slavery Society (AASS, 1833). The leading organization committed to abolition of slavery and full equality for African Americans.

American Civil Liberties Union (ACLU, 1917). Organization created to provide legal aid to World War I conscientious objectors, later involved in defending a wide range of personal freedoms.

American Equal Rights Association (AERA, 1866). Short-lived organization committed to full civil equality for African Americans and women.

American Federation of Labor (AFL, 1886). Broad, generally moderate federation of craft unions.

American Friends Service Committee (AFSC, 1917). Major Quaker organization for service and social justice.

American Missionary Association (AMA, 1846). Missionary organization created by moderate abolitionists.

American Peace Society (APS, 1828). First national peace organization distinct from the historic peace churches.

American Woman Suffrage Association (AWSA, 1869). Women's rights organization led by Lucy Stone and others who wished to work simultaneously for African American and women's suffrage.

American Workers Party (AWP, 1933). Short-lived socialist party organized by A.J. Muste.

Association of Catholic Trade Unionists (ACTU, 1937). Organization that mobilized Catholic support for the labor movement in general and the CIO in particular.

Benevolent Empire (early 1800s). Loose network of voluntary societies that distributed Bibles, planted new churches, and promoted moderate social reform.

Católicos por la Raza (1969). Chicano activist organization that disrupted Christmas Eve services at the Los Angeles cathedral in 1969.

Christian Socialist Fellowship (CSF, 1906). Network of ministers and others who supported the Socialist Party of America.

Christian Union movement (1838). Network of congregations that had separated from denominations deemed insufficiently opposed to slavery.

Clergy and Laymen Concerned about Vietnam (CALCAV, 1965). Organization that worked to mobilize Protestant, Catholic, and Jewish leaders against the Vietnam War.

Committee for a Sane Nuclear Policy (SANE, 1957). Organization that sought to unite pacifists and nonpacifists in opposition to nuclear weapons.

Communist Party (CP, 1919). Offshoot of the Socialist Party that was closely aligned with the leadership of the Soviet Union.

Communities Organized for Public Service (COPS, 1974). First of a new generation of Alinskyite community organizations, initiated by Chicano Catholic activists in San Antonio.

Congress of Industrial Organizations (CIO, 1935). Federation of unions that organized workers by industry rather than by craft; merged with the American Federation of Labor in 1955.

Congress of Racial Equality (CORE, 1942). Organization created to apply Gandhian practices to the struggle against racial segregation.

Dignity USA (1969). Organization for gay and lesbian Catholics.

Economic Research and Action Projects (ERAP, 1964). Program that placed college students as community organizers in urban neighborhoods, sponsored by Students for a Democratic Society.

Ethical Culture (1876). Movement of nontheistic religion, with a deep commitment to practical social work, founded by Felix Adler.

Evangelicals for Social Action (ESA, 1973). Major organization for social justice activists connected to the National Association of Evangelicals.

Federal Council of Churches (FCC, 1908). Major Protestant ecumenical organization in the first half of the twentieth century, founded and led by Social Gospelers.

Fellowship for a Christian Social Order (FCSO, 1922). Social Gospel organization focused primarily on economic and industrial policy; merged with the Fellowship of Reconciliation in 1928.

Fellowship of Intentional Communities (FIC, 1948). Network of intentional communities, with roots in Arthur Morgan's advocacy of small-scale community during the Great Depression.

Fellowship of Reconciliation (FOR, 1915). The leading Christian (and ultimately interfaith) pacifist organization of the twentieth century.

Fellowship of Socialist Christians (FSC, 1931). Small activist network created by Reinhold Niebuhr.

Fourierist socialism. A network of communal societies in the 1840s. Also known as Associationism.

Free Religious Association (FRA, 1867). Coalition of Transcendentalists, Garrisonians, and other religious liberals that promoted post-Christian spirituality.

Free Soil Party (1848). Third party that united abolitionists from the Liberty Party with more moderate opponents of slavery.

Freethought. A loose network of individuals and organizations devoted to religious freedom and scathing criticism of traditional religious institutions.

Industrial Areas Foundation (IAF, 1940). Network of community-organizing projects founded by Saul Alinsky.

Industrial Workers of the World (IWW, 1905). Radical organization that sought to unite all workers in a single union.

Intercollegiate Socialist Society (ISS, 1905). Organization created to mobilize students and professionals on behalf of the Socialist Party of America, renamed the League for Industrial Democracy in 1921.

Knights of Labor (1869). First national labor organization with a mass constituency, prominent in the railroad strikes of 1877 and 1886.

Liberty Party (1839). The most significant abolitionist third party.

Methodist Federation for Social Service (MFSS, 1907). The most prominent of several denominational organizations promoting Social Gospel ideals.

Methodist Student Movement (MSM, 1939). Campus ministry organization that promoted interracial encounter and anticipated many of the themes of 1960s student radicalism.

Metropolitan Community Church (MCC, 1968). The most significant predominantly LGBT denomination.

Mexican American Cultural Center (MACC, 1972). Organizational base for Chicano activists within Roman Catholicism.

National American Woman Suffrage Association (NAWSA, 1890). Merged organization that united the women's rights traditions of Lucy Stone and of Elizabeth Cady Stanton and Susan B. Anthony.

National Association for the Advancement of Colored People (NAACP, 1909). Leading organization pursuing full social and civil equality for African Americans.

National Conference of Black Christians (NCBC, 1966). Network of black caucuses that provided organizational support for the emergence of Black Theology. Originally the National Committee of Negro Churchmen.

National Council of Churches (NCC, 1950). Ecumenical body that succeeded the Federal Council of Churches.

National Organization for Women (NOW, 1966). Feminist organization created to push for full enforcement of the antidiscrimination provisions of the 1964 Civil Rights Act.

National Woman's Party (NWP, 1915). Suffragist organization that split from the National American Woman Suffrage Association in order to promote more militant action for a constitutional amendment.

National Woman Suffrage Association (NWSA, 1869). Women's rights organization led by Elizabeth Cady Stanton and Susan B. Anthony.

New England Non-Resistance Society (NENRS, 1838). Radical pacifist organization that opposed war, violence, and coercive governments.

New Thought. Loosely organized religious movement that blended a liberal theology with practices of mind cure, especially in the last part of the nineteenth century.

Owenite socialism. Network of communal societies in the 1820s, the most famous of which were New Harmony and Nashoba.

Padres Asociados para Derechos Religiosos, Educativos y Sociales (PADRES, 1969). Activist organization created by priests who admired César Chávez and drew inspiration from Latin American liberation theology.

People's Churches. Network of freestanding, often radical congregations in the late nineteenth and early twentieth centuries.

People's Party (1892). Third party that united labor and farm activists, also known as the Populists.

Popular Front (1935). Network of radical organizations in which the Communist Party played a central role.

Progressive Party (1912, 1924, 1948). Name of several distinct third parties, all with a generally left-liberal orientation.

Socialist Labor Party (SLP, 1876). Oldest explicitly socialist party in the United States, it was founded as the Workingmen's Party and changed its name in 1877.

Socialist Party of America (SPA, 1901). The only American socialist party to achieve significant electoral success, under the leadership of Eugene Debs and then Norman Thomas.

Southern Christian Leadership Conference (SCLC, 1957). The organizational outgrowth of the Montgomery bus boycott.

Southern Tenant Farmers' Union (STFU, 1934). Depression-era organization of tenant farmers.

Spiritualism (1848). Loosely organized religious movement that combined the practice of contacting the spirits of the dead with a cosmology of correspondences between heaven and earth.

Student Nonviolent Coordinating Committee (SNCC, 1960). Organizational outgrowth of the student sit-ins, and later a major exponent of Black Power.

Students for a Democratic Society (SDS, 1962). The major organization of the 1960s New Left.

Theosophical Society (1875). New religious movement that combined Western esoteric traditions with an intense interest in the religions of the East.

United Farm Workers (UFW, 1962). Predominantly Chicano labor union organized by César Chávez. It came to prominence with the Delano Grape Strike of 1965–70.

Wicca. Movement that seeks to revive ancient practices of witchcraft.

Women's Christian Temperance Union (WCTU, 1874). The largest social reform organization in the postbellum period; espoused women's suffrage and socialism as well as temperance.

Working Men's Party (1828). Loose network of local parties that promoted class-consciousness and solidarity among craft workers. Not to be confused with the Workingmen's Party of 1876; see Socialist Labor Party above.

Abzug, Robert H. *Cosmos Crumbling: American Reform and the Religious Imagination.* New York: Oxford University Press, 1994.

Adler, Margot. *Drawing Down the Moon.* 3rd ed. New York: Penguin, 2006.

Alpert, Rebecca T., ed. *Voices of the Religious Left: A Contemporary Sourcebook.* Philadelphia: Temple University Press, 2000.

Appelbaum, Patricia. *Kingdom to Commune: Protestant Pacifist Culture between World War I and the Vietnam Era.* Chapel Hill: University of North Carolina Press, 2009.

Bloom, Alexander, and Wini Breines, eds. *"Takin' It to the Streets": A Sixties Reader.* 2nd ed. New York: Oxford University Press, 2003.

Branch, Taylor. *America in the King Years.* 3 vols. New York: Simon & Schuster, 1988–2006.

Braude, Ann. *Transforming the Faith of Our Fathers: Women Who Changed American Religion.* New York: Palgrave, 2004.

Buhle, Mari Jo, Paul Buhle, and Harvey J. Kaye, eds. *The American Radical.* New York: Routledge, 1994.

Buhle, Paul. *Marxism in the United States: Remapping the History of the American Left.* New York: Verso, 1987.

Christ, Carol P., and Judith Plaskow, eds. *Womanspirit Rising: A Feminist Reader in Religion.* New York: Harper & Row, 1979.

Clarkson, Frederick, ed. *Dispatches from the Religious Left.* Brooklyn: Ig, 2009.

Craig, Robert H. *Religion and Radical Politics: An Alternative Christian Tradition in the United States.* Philadelphia: Temple University Press, 1992.

Dorn, Jacob H., ed. *Socialism and Christianity in Early Twentieth-century America.* Westport, CT: Greenwood, 1998.

Dorrien, Gary. *Soul in Society: The Making and Renewal of Social Christianity.* Minneapolis: Fortress, 1995.

Espinosa, Gaston, Virgilio Elizondo, and Jesse Miranda, eds. *Latino Religions and Civic Activism in the United States.* New York: Oxford University Press, 2005.

Farrell, James J. *The Spirit of the Sixties: Making Postwar Radicalism.* New York: Routledge, 1997.

Frederick, Peter J. *Knights of the Golden Rule: The Intellectual as Christian Social Reformer in the 1890s.* Lexington: University Press of Kentucky, 1976.

Harding, Vincent. *There Is a River: The Black Struggle for Freedom in America.* New York: Harcourt Brace Jovanovich, 1981.

Kazin, Michael. *The Populist Persuasion: An American History.* New York: Basic, 1995.

Kearns, Laurel, and Catherine Keller, eds. *Ecospirit: Religions and Philosophies for the Earth.* New York: Fordham University Press, 2007.

Kosek, Joseph Kip. *Acts of Conscience: Christian Nonviolence and Modern American Democracy.* New York: Columbia University Press, 2009.

Lerner, Michael. *The Left Hand of God: Taking Back Our Country from the Religious Right.* San Francisco: Harper, 2006.

Marsh, Charles. *The Beloved Community: How Faith Shapes Social Justice, from the Civil Rights Movement to Today.* New York: Basic, 2005.

McCarthy, Timothy Patrick, and John McMillian, eds. *The Radical Reader.* New York: New Press, 2003.

McKanan, Dan. *Identifying the Image of God: Radical Christians and Nonviolent Power in the Antebellum United States.* New York: Oxford University Press, 2002.

Morone, James A. *Hellfire Nation: The Politics of Sin in American History.* New Haven, CT: Yale University Press, 2003.

Queen, Christopher S., ed. *Engaged Buddhism in the West.* Somerville, MA: Wisdom, 2000.

Rossinow, Doug. *The Politics of Authenticity: Liberalism, Christianity, and the New Left in America.* New York: Columbia University Press, 1998.

———. *Visions of Progress: The Left-Liberal Tradition in America.* Philadelphia: University of Pennsylvania Press, 2008.

Spretnak, Charlene, ed. *The Politics of Women's Spirituality: Essays on the Rise of Spiritual Power within the Feminist Movement.* Garden City, NY: Anchor, 1982.

Stansell, Christine. *The Feminist Promise: 1792 to the Present.* New York: Modern Library, 2010.

Thumma, Scott, and Edward R. Gray. *Gay Religion.* Walnut Creek, CA: AltaMira, 2005.

Wallis, Jim. *God's Politics: Why the Right Gets It Wrong and the Left Doesn't Get It.* San Francisco: Harper, 2005.

Warren, Mark R. *Dry Bones Rattling: Community Building to Revitalize American Democracy.* Princeton, NJ: Princeton University Press, 2001.

Wilmore, Gayraud S. *Black Religion and Black Radicalism.* 3rd ed. Maryknoll, NY: Orbis, 1998.

Wilmore, Gayraud S., and James H. Cone. *Black Theology: A Documentary History, 1966–1979.* Maryknoll, NY: Orbis, 1979.

Zinn, Howard. *A People's History of the United States.* New York: Harper & Row, 1980.

Introduction

1. Frederick Douglass, *Narrative of the Life of Frederick Douglass,* in Douglass, *Autobiographies,* ed. Henry Louis Gates Jr. (New York: Library of America, 1994), 96; William Lloyd Garrison, preface to *Narrative,* 3–4; Frederick Douglass, "A Reform Absolutely Complete," in *The Frederick Douglass Papers,* ser. 1, ed. John W. Blassingame (New Haven, CT: Yale University Press, 1979–92), 4:264.

2. Dorothy Day, *The Long Loneliness* (New York: Harper, 1952), 46, 139, 165.

3. Starhawk, *The Spiral Dance: A Rebirth of the Ancient Religion of the Great Goddess* (San Francisco: HarperSanFrancisco, 1999), 58–59.

4. Paul Tillich, *Dynamics of Faith* (New York: Harper, 1957), 1–5; Charles Taylor, *A Secular Age* (Cambridge, MA: Harvard University Press, Belknap Press, 2007); Norman Thomas, "The Implicit Religion of Radicalism," *World Tomorrow,* August 1920, 231–33.

5. Seymour Martin Lipset and Gary Marks, *It Didn't Happen Here: Why Socialism Failed in the United States* (New York: W. W. Norton, 2000).

Chapter 1. The Faith of the Working Men

1. William Heighton, "An Address Delivered before the Mechanics and Working Classes," in *William Heighton: Pioneer Labor Leader of Jacksonian Philadelphia,* ed. Philip S. Foner (New York: International, 1991), 69–90; Working Men's Party, "Declaration of Independence," in *The Radical Reader,* ed. Timothy Patrick McCarthy and John McMillian (New York: New Press, 2003), 217–19; Philip Yale Nicholson, *Labor's Story in the United States* (Philadelphia: Temple University Press, 2004); Sean Wilentz, *Chants Democratic: New York City & the Rise of the American Working Class, 1788–1850* (New York: Oxford University Press, 1984).

2. William R. Sutton, *Journeymen for Jesus: Evangelical Artisans Confront Capitalism in Jacksonian Baltimore* (University Park: Pennsylvania State University Press, 1998), 22–25.

3. J. A. McC., "For the Mechanics' Free Press," *Mechanics' Free Press,* April 26, 1828.

4. Cornelius C. Blatchly, *Some Causes of Popular Poverty* (New York, 1817), 209; Working Men's Party, "Declaration of Independence"; "Paul," "Practical Christianity," *Mechanics' Free Press,* May 24, 1828.

5. Sutton, *Journeymen,* 52–53; Ronald Schultz, *The Republic of Labor: Philadelphia Artisans and the Politics of Class, 1720–1830* (New York: Oxford University Press, 1993), 212; Thomas Branagan, *Rights of God, Written for the Benefit of Man,* 5th ed. (Philadelphia: Enoch Johnson, 1815), 46–47.

6. Blatchly, *Some Causes,* 195–99, 206.

7. Ibid., 207–10, 219–20; Blatchly, *An Essay on Commonwealths* (New York: New York Society for Promoting Communities, 1822), 3–4, 27.

8. Blatchly, *An Essay on Commonwealths,* 38, 46, 50.

9. Robert Owen, *The Book of the New Moral World,* part 4, *Explanatory of the Rational Religion* (London: James Watson, 1852); Donald E. Pitzer, "The New Moral World of Robert Owen

and New Harmony," in *America's Communal Utopias,* ed. Donald E. Pitzer (Chapel Hill: University of North Carolina Press, 1997), 88–89; J. F. C. Harrison, *Robert Owen and the Owenites in Britain and America: The Quest for the New Moral World* (London: Routledge, 1969).

10. Celia Morris Eckhardt, *Fanny Wright: Rebel in America* (Cambridge, MA: Harvard University Press, 1984).

11. "Prospectus of the Free Enquirer," *Free Enquirer,* October 29, 1828, 5; "Sunday Lectures at Lower Julien Hall," *Boston Investigator,* April 23, 1831, 15.

12. Heighton, "Address," 70, 74–75, 84.

13. Ibid., 79–82.

14. Abel C. Thomas, *A Century of Universalism in Philadelphia and New York* (Philadelphia, 1872), 72–87; Bruce Laurie, *Working People of Philadelphia, 1800–1850* (Philadelphia: Temple University Press, 1980).

15. Jama Lazerow, *Religion and the Working Class in Antebellum America* (Washington, DC: Smithsonian Institution Scholarly Press, 1995), 93, 103–6.

16. Kyle T. Bulthuis, "Preacher Politics and People Power: Congregational Conflicts in New York City, 1810–1830," *Church History* 78 (June 2009): 270–81.

17. Sutton, *Journeymen,* 76–78.

18. Ibid., 89, 97, 121.

19. Ibid., 215–216; *Mechanics' Free Press,* 3 July 1830.

20. Henry F. May, *Protestant Churches and Industrial America* (New York: Harper, 1949), 9.

21. Cornelius C. Blatchly, "A Calumny Contradicted," *Working Man's Advocate,* November 14, 1829, 2; Cornelius C. Blatchly, "No. V," *Working Man's Advocate,* December 12, 1829, 1.

22. Lazerow, *Religion,* 46; E. K. B., "Messrs. Editors," *Mechanics' Free Press,* 27 February 1830; Editorial, *Mechanics' Free Press,* October 16, 1830.

23. Lazerow, *Religion,* 44–46.

24. David R. Roediger and Philip S. Foner, *Our Own Time: A History of American Labor and the Working Day* (New York: Greenwood, 1989), 23–25.

25. Lazerow, *Religion,* 38, 89, 159–61.

Chapter 2. African Identity and Black Radicalism

1. "A Voice from Philadelphia," in William Lloyd Garrison, *Thoughts on African Colonization* (Boston, 1832), 2:9.

2. Ibid.

3. *Confessions of Nat Turner* (Baltimore: Thomas R. Gray, 1831).

4. Richard Newman, "A Chosen Generation: Black Founders and Early America," in *Prophets of Protest: Reconsidering the History of American Abolitionism,* eds. Timothy Patrick McCarthy and John Stauffer (New York: New Press, 2006).

5. Corey D. B. Walker, *A Noble Fight: African American Freemasonry and the Struggle for Democracy in America* (Urbana: University of Illinois Press, 2008).

6. Richard S. Newman, *Freedom's Prophet: Bishop Richard Allen, the AME Church, and the Black Founding Fathers* (New York: New York University Press, 2008).

7. Timothy Patrick McCarthy, "'To Plead Our Own Cause': Black Print Culture and the Origins of American Abolitionism," in McCarthy and Stauffer, *Prophets,* 115–16.

8. Peter P. Hinks, *To Awaken My Afflicted Brethren: David Walker and the Problem of Antebellum Slave Resistance* (University Park: Pennsylvania State University Press, 1997).

9. David Walker, *Walker's Appeal, in Four Articles; Together with a Preamble, to the Coloured Citizens of the World,* 3rd ed. (Boston: David Walker, 1830), 3.

10. Ibid., 2.

11. "Walker's Boston Pamphlet," *Genius of Universal Emancipation,* April 1830, 15; Walker, *Appeal,* 18, 85.

12. Walker, *Appeal,* 69, 5, 45.

13. Ibid., 39–40, 20, 41, 21, 60, 49–57.

14. David R. Roediger, *The Wages of Whiteness: Race and the Making of the American Working Class* (New York: Verso, 1991).

Chapter 3. Encounters with William Lloyd Garrison

1. William Lloyd Garrison, "To the Public," *Liberator*, January 1, 1831, 1; Dorothy Sterling, *Ahead of Her Time: Abby Kelley and the Politics of Antislavery* (New York: W. W. Norton, 1991), 1; Henry Mayer, *All on Fire: William Lloyd Garrison and the Abolition of Slavery* (New York: St. Martin's, 1998); Aileen S. Kraditor, *Means and Ends in American Abolitionism: Garrison and His Critics on Strategy and Tactics* (New York: Pantheon, 1969); Lewis Perry, *Radical Abolitionism: Anarchy and the Government of God in Antislavery Thought* (Ithaca, NY: Cornell University Press, 1973).

2. Ralph Waldo Emerson, journal, October 17, 1840, in *The Journals and Miscellaneous Notebooks of Ralph Waldo Emerson*, eds. A. W. Plumstead and Harrison Hayford (Cambridge, MA: Harvard University Press, Belknap Press, 1969), 7:407–8.

3. Garrison, "To the Public."

4. Ellen Carol DuBois, *Feminism and Suffrage: The Emergence of an Independent Women's Movement in America, 1848–1869* (Ithaca, NY: Cornell University Press, 1978), 39; Wendell Phillips Garrison and Francis Jackson Garrison, *William Lloyd Garrison: The Story of His Life* (New York: Century, 1885), 1:178.

5. Garrison and Garrison, *Garrison*, 1:56.

6. *National Philanthropist*, March 21, 1828.

7. Paul Goodman, *Of One Blood: Abolitionism and the Origins of Racial Equality* (Berkeley: University of California Press, 1998), 31.

8. *Genius of Universal Emancipation*, February 5, 1830; Mayer, *All on Fire*, 82.

9. "Walker's Appeal," *Liberator*, January 8, 1831, 6; "The Insurrection," *Liberator*, September 3, 1831, 143.

10. Garrison and Garrison, *Garrison*, 1:214; Lydia Maria Child to Anne Whitney, May 25, 1879, in *Lydia Maria Child: Selected Letters*, eds. Milton Meltzer and Patricia G. Holland (Amherst: University of Massachusetts Press, 1982), 558.

11. Garrison and Garrison, *Garrison*, 2:51; Anna Davis Hallowell, ed., *James and Lucretia Mott: Life and Letters* (Boston: Houghton Mifflin, 1890), 296.

12. "Declaration of Sentiments," *Liberator*, October 13, 1837, 166.

13. "Declaration of the National Anti-Slavery Convention," *Abolitionist*, December 1833, 178.

14. Garrison and Garrison, *Garrison*, 3:7–9, 145–56, 386.

15. *Liberator*, May 31, 1850.

Chapter 4. Personifying Radical Abolitionism

1. Gerda Lerner, *The Grimké Sisters from South Carolina: Rebels against Slavery* (Boston: Houghton Mifflin, 1967); Sterling, *Ahead*; Waldo E. Martin, *The Mind of Frederick Douglass* (Chapel Hill: University of North Carolina Press, 1984); Nell Irvin Painter, *Sojourner Truth: A Life, a Symbol* (New York: W. W. Norton, 1996); Herbert Aptheker, *Abolitionism: A Revolutionary Movement* (Boston: Twayne, 1989); Lawrence J. Friedman, *Gregarious Saints: Self and Community in American Abolitionism, 1830–1870* (New York: Cambridge University Press, 1982).

2. Robert H. Abzug, *Passionate Liberator: Theodore Dwight Weld and the Dilemma of Reform* (New York: Oxford University Press, 1980), 129.

3. Goodman, *Of One Blood*, 184.

4. Sterling, *Ahead*, 48.

5. Catherine A. Brekus, *Strangers & Pilgrims: Female Preaching in America, 1740–1845* (Chapel Hill: University of North Carolina Press, 1998).

6. Maria W. Stewart, "An Address Delivered at the African Masonic Hall," in *Productions* (Boston: Friends of Freedom and Virtue, 1835), 63.

7. Sally G. McMillen, *Seneca Falls and the Origins of the Women's Rights Movement* (New York: Oxford University Press, 2008), 63–64.

8. Sarah Grimké, *Letters on the Equality of the Sexes* (Boston: Knapp, 1838), 16.

9. McMillen, *Seneca Falls*, 67.

10. Sterling, *Ahead*, 64–65.

11. Ibid., 117–18, 107–8.

12. Ibid., 137–42, 224.
13. Ibid., 225; Stephen S. Foster, *The Brotherhood of Thieves; or, A True Picture of the American Church and Clergy* (Boston: Anti-Slavery Office, 1844), 5.
14. Goodman, *Of One Blood*, 248–54; Kathi Kern, *Mrs. Stanton's Bible* (Ithaca, NY: Cornell University Press, 2001), 23.
15. Goodman, *Of One Blood*, 248–49; Martin B. Pasternak, *Rise Now and Fly to Arms: The Life of Henry Highland Garnet* (New York: Garland, 1995), 11–14.
16. Frederick Douglass, *My Bondage and My Freedom*, in Douglass, *Autobiographies*, 366, 233.
17. Ibid., 366; Douglass, *Narrative*, 36, 97.
18. Douglass, *My Bondage*, 367.
19. John Stauffer, *The Black Hearts of Men: Radical Abolitionists and the Transformation of Race* (Cambridge, MA: Harvard University Press, 2001), 93, 107.
20. *Narrative of Sojourner Truth* (Battle Creek, MI: self-published, 1878), 134.

Chapter 5. Radicals Fight and Unite

1. Ralph Waldo Emerson, "Man the Reformer," *Dial*, April 1841, 523–24.
2. William Lloyd Garrison to Helen E. Garrison, September 21, 1838, in *The Letters of William Lloyd Garrison*, ed. Walter M. Merrill (Cambridge, MA: Harvard University Press, Belknap Press, 1971–81), 2:391; "Declaration of Sentiments," *Liberator*, September 28, 1838, 154.
3. John R. McKivigan, *The War against Proslavery Religion: Abolitionism and the Northern Churches* (Ithaca, NY: Cornell University Press, 1984), 203–20.
4. Ibid., 65; Sterling, *Ahead*, 207, 192; Ralph Waldo Emerson, "Chardon Street and Bible Conventions," *Dial*, July 1842, 101.
5. McKivigan, *War*, 113.
6. Ralph E. Luker, *The Social Gospel in Black and White: American Racial Reform, 1885–1912* (Chapel Hill: University of North Carolina Press, 1991), 12–14.
7. Abzug, *Passionate Liberator*, 218; Stauffer, *Black Hearts*, 106.
8. *Philanthropist*, November 10, 1841; Friedman, *Gregarious Saints*, 113; Stauffer, *Black Hearts*, 26.
9. Pasternak, *Rise*, 45–47.
10. Douglas M. Strong, *Perfectionist Politics: Abolitionism and the Religious Tensions of American Democracy* (Syracuse, NY: Syracuse University Press, 1999).
11. Stauffer, *Black Hearts*, 121–22; McKivigan, *War*, 95–96.
12. Silas Hawley, "Reminiscences of Groton during the Years 1839, 1840, and 1841," in *Groton Historical Series*, ed. Samuel Abbott Green (Groton, MA, 1887–), 11:1–18, 23; "Christian Union," *Practical Christian*, August 1, 1840, 26; Debra Gold Hansen, "The Boston Female Anti-Slavery Society and the Limits of Gender Politics," in *The Abolitionist Sisterhood: Women's Political Culture in Antebellum America*, eds. Jean Fagan Yellin and John C. Van Horne (Ithaca, NY: Cornell University Press, 1994), 54.
13. *A Statement of the Principles of the Christian Union* (New York: Press of Hunt's Merchants' Magazine, 1843), 12.
14. John T. Cumbler, *From Abolition to Rights for All: The Making of a Reform Community in the Nineteenth Century* (Philadelphia: University of Pennsylvania Press, 2008), 27–28; Margaret Lamberts Bendroth, *Fundamentalists in the City: Conflict and Division in Boston's Churches, 1885–1950* (New York: Oxford University Press, 2005), 103.
15. Ralph Waldo Emerson to Thomas Carlyle, October 30, 1840, in *The Correspondence of Thomas Carlyle and Ralph Waldo Emerson*, ed. Charles E. Norton (Boston, 1883), 1:308–9; Adin Ballou, *History of the Hopedale Community: From Its Inception to Its Virtual Submergence in the Hopedale Parish*, ed. William S. Heywood (Lowell, MA: Thompson & Hill—Vox Populi, 1897), 9–14.
16. "Strange Notions Respecting Hopedale," *Practical Christian*, May 16, 1857, 5; Adin Ballou, "Hopedale," *Practical Christian*, May 16, 1857, 6; Edward K. Spann, *Hopedale: From Commune to Company Town, 1840–1920* (Columbus: Ohio State University Press, 1992).
17. Octavius Brooks Frothingham, *George Ripley* (Boston: Houghton Mifflin, 1882), 71, 310; Sterling F. Delano, *Brook Farm: The Dark Side of Utopia* (Cambridge, MA: Harvard University Press, Belknap Press, 2004).

18. "Northampton Association of Education and Industry," *Liberator*, September 9, 1842, 144.

19. Carl Guarneri, *The Utopian Alternative: Fourierism in Nineteenth-Century America* (Ithaca, NY: Cornell University Press, 1991), 153.

20. James Freeman Clarke, "The Christian Examiner on the Doctrine of Fourier," *Phalanx*, August 24, 1844, 248–49; William Henry Channing, "Heaven upon Earth," *Present*, March 15, 1844, 422; "Fundamental Doctrines on Which Association Is Based," *Phalanx*, April 1, 1844, 96.

21. "Constitution of the Brook Farm Association," *Phalanx*, March 1, 1844, 80–81; "The Harbinger," *Phalanx*, May 3, 1845, 340.

22. Andrew E. Hunt, "The Wisconsin Phalanx: A Forgotten Success Story," *Canadian Review of American Studies* 28.2 (1998): 119–43; "Provisional Prospectus of the Raritan Bay Union," *Practical Christian*, December 18, 1852, 68; Charles Sears, *The North American Phalanx: An Historical and Descriptive Sketch* (Prescott, WI: J. M. Pryse, 1886).

23. John Humphrey Noyes, *History of American Socialisms* (Philadelphia: Lippincott, 1870), 161–80; Thomas D. Hamm, *God's Government Begun: The Society for Universal Inquiry and Reform, 1842–1846* (Bloomington: Indiana University Press, 1995).

24. Orestes Brownson, *The Laboring Classes: An Article from the Boston Quarterly Review*, 3rd ed. (Boston: Benjamin H. Greene, 1840), 21, 24, 14; "Commerce," *Harbinger*, June 21, 1845, 31–32.

25. Lazerow, *Religion*, 30.

26. Goodman, *Of One Blood*, 153.

27. Cumbler, *From Abolition*, 58–60; Goodman, *Of One Blood*, 153–57, 163–67.

28. Stauffer, *Black Hearts*, 136–38, 174–75.

29. John Allen, "Introductory," *Voice of Industry*, June 19, 1846.

30. Lazerow, *Religion*, 83; *Voice of Industry*, May 29, 1845, 3; John R. Commons et al., eds., *A Documentary History of American Industrial Society* (Cleveland: A. H. Clark, 1910–11), 8:303–4; *Gleaner*, April 4, 1846, in Lazerow, *Religion*, 58, 65, 59; see *Voice of Industry*, September 4, 1846, June 19, 1846, October 9, 1846, June 8, 1847, July 9, 1847, September 3, 1847.

31. Adam Tuchinsky, *Horace Greeley's* New-York Tribune*: Civil War–Era Socialism and the Crisis of Free Labor* (Ithaca, NY: Cornell University Press, 2009), 134–39; Lazerow, *Religion*, 131–32.

32. Tuchinsky, *Greeley*, 82–107.

33. Tony Michels, *A Fire in Their Hearts: Yiddish Socialists in New York* (Cambridge, MA: Harvard University Press, 2005), 41–42.

Chapter 6. Confronting the Slave Power

1. Eric Foner, *Free Soil, Free Labor, Free Men: The Ideology of the Republican Party before the Civil War*, rev. ed. (New York: Oxford University Press, 1995).

2. Stauffer, *Black Hearts*, 20.

3. Harriet Beecher Stowe, *Uncle Tom's Cabin* (New York: Penguin, 1981), 629, 344.

4. Stauffer, *Black Hearts*, 13.

5. James Redpath, *The Public Life of Capt. John Brown* (Boston: Thayer & Eldridge, 1860), 69, 190.

6. Stephen B. Oates, *To Purge This Land with Blood: A Biography of John Brown* (New York: Harper, 1970), 351.

7. *Liberator*, December 31, 1859; Perry, *Radical Abolitionism*, 258; *Liberator*, December 16, 1859.

8. Mayer, *All on Fire*, 597–604.

Chapter 7. New Religions for Radicalism

1. Henry Clarke Wright, *Anthropology; or, The Science of Man* (Boston: Bela Marsh, 1850), 87; Stauffer, *Black Hearts*, 38.

2. Ernestine Rose, in Elizabeth Cady Stanton et al., eds., *History of Woman Suffrage* (New York: Fowler & Wells, 1881), 1:662.

3. Lawrence B. Goodheart, *Abolitionist, Actuary, Atheist: Elizur Wright and the Reform Impulse* (Kent, OH: Kent State University Press, 1990), 113, 128–29, 180.

4. Orestes Brownson, "Church Unity and Social Amelioration," *Brownson's Quarterly Review*, July 1, 1844.

5. Catherine Albanese, *A Republic of Mind and Spirit: A Cultural History of American Metaphysical Religion* (New Haven, CT: Yale University Press, 2007), 177–253.

6. "The Univercoelum and Spiritual Philosopher," *Univercoelum*, February 24, 1829, 208; Andrew Jackson Davis, *The Principles of Nature, Her Divine Relations, and a Voice to Mankind* (New York: S. S. Lyon, 1847), 1–2.

7. S. B. Brittan, "Organization," *Univercoelum*, September 2, 1848, 216.

8. Davis, *Principles*, 5–6.

9. Ann Braude, *Radical Spirits: Spiritualism and Women's Rights in Nineteenth-Century America* (Boston: Beacon, 1989), 57, 78–81, 91, 98.

10. Robert S. Cox, *Body and Soul: A Sympathetic History of American Spiritualism* (Charlottesville: University of Virginia Press, 2003), 143; Bret E. Carroll, *Spiritualism in Antebellum America* (Bloomington: Indiana University Press, 1997), 35–36.

11. John B. Buescher, *The Remarkable Life of John Murray Spear: Agitator for the Spirit Land* (Notre Dame, IN: University of Notre Dame Press, 2006); Carroll, *Spiritualism*, 162–76.

12. Adin Ballou, "Modern Spiritualism: Its Good and Evil," *Practical Christian*, August 26, 1854; Cox, *Body and Soul*, 197–235.

13. Braude, *Radical Spirits*, 69–73.

14. Helena Petrova Blavatsky, *The Key to Theosophy* (London: Theosophical, 1889), 39.

15. J. Gordon Melton, "The Theosophical Communities and Their Ideal of Universal Brotherhood," in Pitzer, *America's Communal Utopias*, 396–418.

16. Ralph Waldo Trine, *In Tune with the Infinite* (Indianapolis: Bobbs-Merrill, 1970), 19.

17. Gail M. Harley, *Emma Curtis Hopkins: Forgotten Founder of New Thought* (Syracuse: Syracuse University Press, 2002), 82.

18. Albanese, *Republic*, 323–25.

19. W. D. Wattles, *The Science of Getting Rich* (Holyoke, MA: E. Towne, 1910).

20. Leigh Erik Schmidt, *Restless Souls: The Making of American Spirituality* (San Francisco: Harper, 2005); Stow Persons, *Free Religion* (New Haven, CT: Yale University Press, 1948), 47, 132.

21. "Constitution of the National Liberty League," in *Equal Rights in Religion* (Boston: National Liberal League, 1876), 175; Goodheart, *Abolitionist*, 179–93; Persons, *Free Religion*, 118–25.

22. Persons, *Free Religion*, 71; Edward K. Kaplan, *Spiritual Radical: Abraham Joshua Heschel in America, 1940–1972* (New Haven, CT: Yale University Press, 2007), 24.

23. Doug Rossinow, *Visions of Progress: The Left-Liberal Tradition in America* (Philadelphia: University of Pennsylvania Press, 2008), 13–59; James T. Kloppenberg, *Uncertain Victory: Social Democracy and Progressivism in European and American Thought, 1870–1920* (New York: Oxford University Press, 1986), 145–95.

24. Aaron Ignatius Abell, *The Urban Impact on American Protestantism, 1865–1900* (Cambridge, MA: Harvard University Press, 1943), 152–53; Alfred Theodore Andreas, *History of Chicago* (Chicago: A. T. Andreas, 1886), 3:827; Larry Millett, *Lost Twin Cities* (St. Paul: Minnesota Historical Society, 1992), 207–9.

Chapter 8. Women's Rights, Women Ministers, and a Woman's Bible

1. Phebe Ann Coffin Hanaford, "The Question Answered," in *Standing before Us: Unitarian Universalist Women and Social Reform, 1776–1936*, ed. Dorothy May Emerson (Boston: Skinner House, 2000), 441–42.

2. Cynthia Grant Tucker, *Prophetic Sisterhood: Liberal Women Ministers of the Frontier* (Boston: Beacon, 1990).

3. Carol Lasser and Marlene Deahl Merrill, *Friends and Sisters: Letters between Lucy Stone and Antoinette Brown* (Urbana: University of Illinois Press, 1987), 54; Elizabeth Cazden, *Antoinette Brown Blackwell: A Biography* (Old Westbury, NY: Feminist Press, 1983), 45, 49.

4. Lori Ginzberg, *Elizabeth Cady Stanton: An American Life* (New York: Hill & Wang, 2009).

5. "Declaration of Sentiments and Resolutions," in McCarthy and McMillian, *Radical Reader*, 173–74.

6. Ibid., 175.

7. McMillen, *Seneca Falls*, 113.
8. Ellen Carol DuBois, *Feminism and Suffrage: The Emergence of an Independent Women's Movement in America, 1848–1869* (Ithaca, NY: Cornell University Press, 1978), 48; Cazden, *Antoinette Brown*, 58, 70.
9. Margaret Fuller, *Woman in the Nineteenth Century* (New York: Greeley & McElrath, 1845), 26.
10. McMillen, *Seneca Falls*, 143.
11. Cazden, *Antoinette Brown*, 74–78, 89, 94–95.
12. Ibid., 162, 190–92, 243, 204–5.
13. Beverly Zink-Sawyer, *From Preachers to Suffragists: Woman's Rights and Religious Conviction in the Lives of Three Nineteenth-Century American Clergywomen* (Louisville, KY: Westminster John Knox, 2003), 42–43, 110.
14. Cazden, *Antoinette Brown*, 190; Zink-Sawyer, *From Preachers*, 58–63.
15. *Report of the International Council of Women, Assembled by the National Woman Suffrage Association* (Washington, DC: Rufus H. Darby, 1888), 181.
16. DuBois, *Feminism*, 59–60; McMillen, *Seneca Falls*, 161; Sterling, *Ahead*, 347.
17. McMillen, *Seneca Falls*, 162–67; DuBois, *Feminism*, 97–98.
18. DuBois, *Feminism*, 187–89.
19. Sterling, *Ahead*, 365–68, McMillen, *Seneca Falls*, 185.
20. DuBois, *Feminism*, 126–61.
21. "Woman Suffrage," *New York Tribune*, May 12, 1871.
22. "Woman Suffrage," *New York Tribune*, May 11, 1872.
23. McMillen, *Seneca Falls*, 191–93.
24. Gaines M. Foster, *Moral Reconstruction: Christian Lobbyists and the Federal Legislation of Morality, 1865–1920* (Chapel Hill: University of North Carolina Press, 2002), 90, 50; Ruth Bordin, *Woman and Temperance: The Quest for Power and Liberty, 1873–1900* (Philadelphia: Temple University Press, 1981), 95.
25. Kern, *Mrs. Stanton*, 123; Robert H. Craig, *Religion and Radical Politics: An Alternative Christian Tradition in the United States* (Philadelphia: Temple University Press, 1992), 60.
26. McMillen, *Seneca Falls*, 113–14; Kern, *Mrs. Stanton*, 124–25.
27. Kern, *Mrs. Stanton*, 40–43, 53–62, 93–98; Garrison and Garrison, *Garrison*, 4:336; Stanton et al., *History of Woman Suffrage*, 1:787.
28. Kern, *Mrs. Stanton*, 100–102, 136–51, 256.
29. Elizabeth Cady Stanton, *The Woman's Bible* (New York: European Publishing, 1895), 1:39–44, 2:187–88, 2:213–14; Kern, *Mrs. Stanton*, 164, 215–16.
30. Kern, *Mrs. Stanton*, 174–213.
31. Katherine H. Adams and Michael L. Keene, *Alice Paul and the American Suffrage Campaign* (Urbana and Chicago: University of Illinois Press, 2008); Nancy F. Cott, *The Grounding of Modern Feminism* (New Haven, CT: Yale University Press, 1987), 15, 39; Charlotte Perkins Gilman, *His Religion and Hers* (New York: Century, 1923).
32. Verta Taylor, "Social Movement Continuity: The Women's Movement in Abeyance," *American Sociological Review* 54 (1989): 761–75.

Chapter 9. The Jesus of Labor

1. George Lippard, *Washington and His Generals; or, Legends of the Revolution* (Philadelphia: G. B. Zieber, 1847), 404–6.
2. Powderly, cited in Robert E. Weir, *Beyond Labor's Veil: The Culture of the Knights of Labor* (University Park: Pennsylvania State University Press, 1996), 74; Debs, cited in Upton Sinclair, *The Cry for Justice: An Anthology of the Literature of Social Protest* (self-published, 1921), 345; Nick Salvatore, preface to *Eugene V. Debs: Citizen and Socialist*, 2nd ed. (Urbana: University of Illinois Press, 2007), xvi.
3. Lippard, *Washington*, 414–15.
4. Stephen Prothero, *American Jesus: How the Son of God Became a National Icon* (New York: Farrar, Straus, & Giroux, 2003); Richard Wightman Fox, *Jesus in America: Personal Savior, Cultural Hero, National Obsession* (San Francisco: Harper, 2004).
5. Lippard, *Adonai*, in *George Lippard, Prophet of Protest: Writings of an American Radical, 1822–1854*,

ed. David S. Reynolds (New York, Lang, 1986), 134–40; Lippard, "Valedictory of the Industrial Congress, 1848," in Reynolds, *Lippard*, 193.

6. Lippard, "Jesus and the Poor," in Reynolds, *Lippard*, 69–79; Lippard, *Adonai*, 152; "Cowardly Courtesy: A Brief Discourse by an Ex-Parson," *Univercoelum*, September 30, 1848, 281–82.

7. *Quaker City Weekly*, June 30, 1848, in Reynolds, *Lippard*, 205; *Quaker City Weekly*, June 2, 1849, in Reynolds, *Lippard*, 210, 212.

8. *Quaker City Weekly*, August 18, 1849, in Reynolds, *Lippard*, 203–4; "The Fraternitas Rosae Crucis," at http://www.soul.org/.

9. Robert MacFarlane, *Address Delivered before the Mechanics of New-York, in the Broadway Tabernacle, June 10, 1847* (New York, 1847), in Commons et al., *Documentary History*, 8:251–56; Robert MacFarlane, "Religion—Freedom," part 2, *Mechanics' Mirror*, April 1846, 81–82; MacFarlane, "Religion—Freedom," part 3, *Mechanics' Mirror*, May 1846, 104.

10. Lazerow, *Religion*, 219–20.

11. Robert H. Craig, *Religion and Radical Politics: An Alternative Christian Tradition in the United States* (Philadelphia: Temple University Press, 1992), 25; William Lloyd Garrison to Ira Steward, March 20, 1866, in *Letters of William Lloyd Garrison*, 5:401; Roediger and Foner, *Our Own Time*, 85.

12. Craig, *Religion*, 17–28; "The New Pope on the Labor Question," *Labor Balance*, April 1878, 12–14, and "Platform of the Socialistic Labor Party," *Labor Balance*, April 1878, 14–15; I. G. Blanchard, "Eight Hours," *Labor Balance*, April 1878, 2–3.

13. M. Marion Marberry, *The Golden Voice: A Biography of Isaac Kalloch* (New York: Farrar, Straus, 1947).

14. Craig Phelan, *Grand Master Workman: Terence Powderly and the Knights of Labor* (Westport, CT: Greenwood, 2000), 23; Leon Fink, *Workingmen's Democracy: The Knights of Labor and American Politics* (Urbana: University of Illinois Press, 1983).

15. Phelan, *Grand Master*, 11–46; Rev. Robert L. Uzzel, "Freemasonry and the Knights of Labor: Brothers Uriah S. Stephens and Terence V. Powderly," http://www.srmason-sj.org/council/journal/aug99/Uzzel.html; Craig, *Religion*, 42.

16. Mother Jones, *The Autobiography of Mother Jones* (Chicago: Charles H. Kerr, 1925), 219; Elliot J. Gorn, *Mother Jones: The Most Dangerous Woman in America* (New York: Hill & Wang, 2001).

17. Leo XIII, *Rerum Novarum*, in *Catholic Social Thought: The Documentary Heritage*, eds. David J. O'Brien and Thomas A. Shannon (Maryknoll, NY: Orbis, 1996), 12–39.

18. Henry Ward Beecher, "Plymouth Pulpit," *Christian Union*, August 1, 1877, 92–94.

19. Washington Gladden, *Applied Christianity: Moral Aspects of Social Questions* (Boston: Houghton Mifflin, 1886), 155–56, 125, 33.

20. Henry George Jr., *The Life of Henry George, by His Son* (London: Heinemann, 1900), 295–96; Michael Kazin, *The Populist Persuasion: An American History* (New York: Basic, 1995), 33.

21. Kazin, *Populist Persuasion*, 27–29.

22. Ibid., 32.

23. Michael Kazin, *A Godly Hero: The Life of William Jennings Bryan* (New York: Knopf, 2006), 61.

Chapter 10. Encountering the City

1. Josiah Strong, *Our Country: Its Possible Future and Its Present Crisis* (New York: Baker & Taylor, 1885), 128, 180, 130.

2. Timothy Miller, *Following in His Steps: A Biography of Charles M. Sheldon* (Knoxville: University of Tennessee Press, 1987), 23.

3. Charles M. Sheldon, *Charles M. Sheldon: His Life Story* (New York: George H. Doran, 1925), 81–87.

4. Ibid., 82.

5. Charles Sheldon, *In His Steps: "What Would Jesus Do?"* (Chicago: Advance, 1897), 14.

6. Sheldon, *Sheldon*, 92.

7. Alexander Irvine, *From the Bottom Up: The Life Story of Alexander Irvine* (New York: Doubleday, 1910), 3, 11–12, 16–17, 21.

8. Ibid., 96–104.

9. Ibid., 215.

10. Ibid., 143, 156.

11. Reverdy Ransom, *The Pilgrimage of Harriet Ransom's Son* (Nashville, TN: Sunday School Union, n.d.), 15, 21–26, 33.

12. Ibid., 47–49.

13. Ibid., 83, 108.

14. Ibid., 114, 118, 134.

15. Jane Addams, *Twenty Years at Hull House* (New York: Macmillan, 1912) 14–15, 79, 21, 42.

16. Ibid., 68–69, 85.

17. Allen F. Davis, *Spearheads for Reform: The Social Settlements and the Progressive Movement, 1890–1914* (New York: Oxford University Press, 1967), 3–39.

18. Addams, *Twenty Years*, 111–12.

19. Abell, *Urban Impact*, 137–51; David Hein and Gardiner H. Shattuck Jr., *The Episcopalians* (Westport, CT: Praeger, 2004), 97; "Platform of the Open and Institutional Church League," in E.B. Sanford, *Origin and History of the Federal Council of Churches of Christ in America* (Hartford, CT: Scranton, 1916), 397.

20. Ronald C. White Jr., *Liberty and Justice for All: Racial Reform and the Social Gospel (1877–1925)* (New York: Harper & Row, 1990), 10–12, 3.

21. Patricia A. Schechter, *Ida B. Wells-Barnett and American Reform, 1880–1930* (Chapel Hill: University of North Carolina Press, 2001), 102–12.

22. Mary White Ovington, *Black and White Sat Down Together: The Reminiscences of an NAACP Founder,* ed. Ralph E. Luker (New York: Feminist Press at CUNY, 1996), 8–11.

23. Ibid., 13, 28.

24. W.E.B. Du Bois, *The Souls of Black Folk* (Chicago: A.C. McClurg, 1903), 190–91, 206; Edward J. Blum, *W.E.B. Du Bois: American Prophet* (Philadelphia: University of Pennsylvania Press, 2007); Jonathon S. Kahn, *Divine Discontent: The Religious Imagination of W.E.B. Du Bois* (New York: Oxford University Press, 2009).

25. Walter Rauschenbusch, *Christianizing the Social Order* (New York: Macmillan, 1914), 93; Christopher Evans, *The Kingdom Is Always but Coming: A Life of Walter Rauschenbusch* (Grand Rapids, MI: Eerdmans, 2004).

26. Walter Rauschenbusch, *Christianity and the Social Crisis* (New York: Macmillan, 1913), 367.

27. *Addresses before the New York State Conference of Religion,* 1906; "The Constitution of the Federal Council," in Elias Benjamin Sanford, *Origin and History of the Federal Council of the Churches of Christ in America* (Hartford, CT: Scranton, 1916), 464–66; Donald K. Gorrell, *The Age of Social Responsibility: The Social Gospel in the Progressive Era, 1900–1920* (Macon, GA: Mercer University Press, 1988).

28. Harry F. Ward, *The Social Creed of the Churches* (New York: Abingdon, 1914), 6.

29. "The Church and Social Reconstruction," in Samuel McCrae Cavert, *The Churches Allied for Common Tasks* (New York: Federal Council, 1921), 109–13; "Universalist Declaration of Social Principles," http://universalistchurch.net/universalist-history/a-declaration-of-social-principles-1917/.

Chapter 11. The Religion of Socialism

1. David A. Shannon, *The Socialist Party of America: A History* (New York: Macmillan, 1955).

2. Paul Jones, "The Breath within the Clay," *World Tomorrow* 6 (1923): 242–44.

3. Melton, "Theosophical Communities."

4. Beryl Satter, *Each Mind a Kingdom: American Women, Sexual Purity, and the New Thought Movement, 1875–1920* (Berkeley: University of California Press, 1999), 206–13.

5. "Church Unity," *Dawn,* December 18, 1890, 10; Bliss, "The Kingdom of Christ," *Dawn,* December 4, 1890, 9; "Our Aim," *Dawn,* December 4, 1890, 1; Editorial, *Dawn,* December 4, 1890, 2.

6. George Herron, "The Message of Jesus to Men of Wealth," *Dawn,* January 1, 1891, 8.

7. Douglas Firth Anderson, "'An Active and Unceasing Campaign of Social Education': J. Stitt

Wilson and Herronite Socialist Christianity," in Jacob H. Dorn, *Socialism and Christianity in Early Twentieth-Century America* (Westport, CT: Greenwood, 1998), 45–46.

8. Debs to Fred D. Warren, August 2, 1912, in *Letters of Eugene V. Debs,* ed. J. Robert Constantine (Urbana: University of Illinois Press, 1990), 1:525; Zane L. Miller, *Boss Cox's Cincinnati: Urban Politics in the Progressive Era* (Columbus: Ohio State University Press, 2000), 143–45; M. E. Thalheimer, "History of the Vine Street Congregational Church of Cincinnati," *Papers of the Ohio Church History Society* 9 (1898): 41–56; "Herbert S. Bigelow," *Official Journal of the Brotherhood of Painters, Decorators, and Paperhangers,* November 1904, 587–88; "Pacifist Whipped in Kuklux Style," *New York Times,* October 30, 1917, 3; "Ohio: Two & None," *Time,* January 13, 1936; Daniel R. Beaver, *A Buckeye Crusader: A Sketch of the Political Career of Herbert Seely Bigelow* (Cincinnati: People's Church, 1957).

9. W. A. Corey, "The Benjamin Fay Mills Movement in Los Angeles," *Arena,* June 1905, 593–95; "Rev. Benj. Fay Mills Dead," *New York Times,* May 2, 1916, 13; Carey McWilliams, *Southern California: An Island on the Land* (Santa Barbara, CA: Peregrine Smith, 1973), 257.

10. Irvine, *From the Bottom,* 227–33.

11. Bliss, "The Kingdom of Christ," *Dawn,* December 4, 1890, 9, and "Church Reform," *Dawn,* February 26, 1891, 8; Mary Kenton, "Christianity, Democracy, and Socialism: Bouck White's Kingdom of Self Respect," in Dorn, *Socialism,* 165–97.

12. Kloppenberg, *Uncertain Victory,* 199–415.

13. Howard H. Quint, *The Forging of American Socialism* (Indianapolis: Bobbs-Merrill, 1953), 383–84.

14. "Knights of the Cross," *Christian Socialist,* March 1, 1905, 3; E. E. Carr, "The Reason for It," *Christian Socialist,* April 15, 1905, 4; "A Christian Socialist Fellowship," *Christian Socialist,* August 15, 1905, 7.

15. "Socialist Preachers in Metropolitan Pulpits," *Christian Socialist,* June 15, 1908, 5; "Christian Socialist Fellowship Conference at Old Orchard, Maine," *Christian Socialist,* September 15, 1908, 4; J. O. Bentall, "Christian Socialist Fellowship Center," *Christian Socialist,* January 1, 1907, 5; "Christian Socialist Fellowship Center Organized in New York," *Christian Socialist,* November 15, 1907, 1.

16. Karl Marx and Friedrich Engels, "Manifesto of the Communist Party," in *The Marx-Engels Reader,* ed. Robert C. Tucker (New York: W. W. Norton, 1978), 492; Rufus W. Weeks, "What the Christian Socialists Stand For," *Christian Socialist,* June 1, 1908, 1; Mabel R. White, "A Woman's View of Socialism," *Christian Socialist,* October 15, 1908, 3; "Metropolitan Press Reports of the C. S. F. Conference," *Christian Socialist,* June 15, 1908, 3.

17. E. E. Carr, "Editorial Comment," *Christian Socialist,* March 21, 1912, 3–4; E. Guy Talbott, "Socialism, Labor Unions, and the Church," *Christian Socialist,* March 21, 1912, 1–3.

18. "Two Reasons Why the Chicago Socialist Vote Was So Small," *Christian Socialist,* November 15, 1908, 5–6; "Lewis Turns over a New Leaf," *Christian Socialist,* December 15, 1908, 4–5; "What Bentall Thinks," *Christian Socialist,* December 15, 1908, 5.

19. E. E. Carr, "The Christian Socialist Fellowship," *Christian Socialist,* October 15, 1905, 4.

20. "New Statement of Objects Proposed," *Christian Socialist,* April 1, 1909, 3; E. E. Carr, "The Real Issue," *Christian Socialist,* April 1, 1909, 4; E. E. Carr, "The Real Issue," *Christian Socialist,* April 15, 1909, 5; John Long, "Letter from Dr. Long," *Christian Socialist,* April 15, 1909, 5–6; "A General Referendum Proposed," *Christian Socialist,* July 1, 1909, 5–6; "Why Dr. Long Was Deposed," *Christian Socialist,* July 15, 1909, 4; "Minutes of the Fourth General Conference of the Christian Socialist Fellowship," *Christian Socialist,* June, 1909, 12; "Constitution of the Christian Socialist Fellowship," *Christian Socialist,* June, 1909, 14; William A. Ward, "Annual Report of the General Secretary," *Christian Socialist,* May 1, 1910, 7; E. E. Carr, "William A. Prosser and the Methodist Church," *Christian Socialist,* March 1, 1915, 8–9.

21. *Christian Socialist,* March 1, 1907, and *Christian Socialist,* November 1, 1907; "Mrs. Carr's Lectures in Iowa and Illinois," *Christian Socialist,* April 18, 1912, 4.

22. Franklin Monroe Sprague's *Socialism from Genesis to Revelation,* Charles Vail's *Principles of Scientific Socialism,* Walter Thomas Mills's *The Struggle for Existence,* and John Spargo's *Socialism* are highlighted with Walter Rauschenbusch's *Christianity and the Social Crisis* in E. E. Carr, "The

Christian Socialist Fellowship: A Brief Account of Its Origin and Progress," *Christian Socialist,*
August 15, 1907, 5.

23. "A Christian Socialist Fellowship," *Christian Socialist,* August 15, 1905, 7.
24. T. W. Woodrow, "Points of Propaganda," *Christian Socialist,* February 1, 1909, 8; George
Washington Woodbey, "What to Do and How to Do It," in *Black Socialist Preacher,* ed. Philip
S. Foner (San Francisco: Synthesis, 1983), 72–73; Eugene V. Debs, "Suffer Little Children to
Come unto Me," *Christian Socialist,* October 1, 1913, 1–2; E. E. Carr, "Words of Jesus III,"
Christian Socialist, February 15, 1905, 5; E. E. Carr, "The Social Message of Jesus," *Christian
Socialist,* June, 1909, 7–8.
25. Everett Dean Martin, "Why I Am a Socialist," *Christian Socialist,* February 1, 1909, 2.
26. John Spargo, *The Spiritual Significance of Modern Socialism* (New York: B. W. Huebsch, 1912),
20–21; Upton Sinclair, *The Profits of Religion: An Essay in Economic Interpretation* (Pasadena, CA:
Upton Sinclair, 1918), 279–300.
27. Michels, *Fire in Their Hearts,* 79–80, 132, 179, 184.
28. Ibid., 107; Marian J. Morton, *Emma Goldman and the American Left: "Nowhere at Home"* (New
York: Twayne, 1992), 23; Emma Goldman, *Living My Life* (New York: Penguin, 2006), 10.
29. Donald E. Winters Jr., *The Soul of the Wobblies: The I.W.W., Religion, and American Culture in
the Progressive Era, 1905–1917* (Westport, CT: Greenwood, 1985), 8, 78, 55, 98, 67.
30. Gilman, *His Religion,* 30, 292; W. E. B. Du Bois, "Credo," in *Darkwater* (New York: Harcourt,
Brace, & Howe, 1920), 3–4.
31. E. E. Carr, "Remove All Profit from War," *Christian Socialist,* May 2, 1917, 4.
32. John Nevin Sayre, "Twenty Years of the Fellowship of Reconciliation," *Fellowship,* September 1935, 1.
33. Grace Hutchins and Anna Rochester, *Jesus Christ and the World Today* (New York: George H.
Doran, 1922), v, 12–13, 41; Norman Thomas, "The Implicit Religion of Radicalism," *World
Tomorrow,* August 1920, 231–33.
34. "Clergymen Swinging Leftward," *World Tomorrow,* May 10, 1934, 219–36.

Chapter 12. The Radical Depression

1. Susan Curtis, *A Consuming Faith: The Social Gospel and Modern American Culture* (Baltimore:
Johns Hopkins University Press, 1991), 206, 214; Kirby Page, "War as an Institution: A Review of 'The Outlawry of War,'" *World Tomorrow,* November 1927, 447–50.
2. "A Step toward Unity," *World Tomorrow,* February 1928, 82; Donald Meyer, *The Protestant
Search for Political Realism, 1919–1941* (Berkeley: University of California Press, 1960).
3. Kirby Page, "20,870 Clergymen on War and Economic Injustice," *World Tomorrow,* May 10,
1934, 222–31.
4. Rossinow, *Visions,* 119–26.
5. Cynthia Taylor, *A. Philip Randolph: The Religious Journey of an African American Labor Leader*
(New York: New York University Press, 2006), 98–105.
6. Howard Kester, "Religion—Priestly and Prophetic—in the South," *Radical Religion,* Autumn
1936, 23–31.
7. Ibid.; Sam H. Franklin Jr., "Adventures in Applied Christianity," *Radical Religion,* Autumn
1936, 32–36; Craig, *Religion,* 144–51, 166.
8. "New Labor Church," *Radical Religion,* Autumn 1935, 48; Fred W. Shorter, "An Experiment
in Radical Religion," *Radical Religion,* Autumn 1936, 19–22; Reinhold Niebuhr, "The Radical Minister and His Church," *Radical Religion,* Winter 1936, 25–27.
9. "An Appeal to the Socialist Party from 47 Members," *World Tomorrow,* April 12, 1934, 183–
88; Devere Allen, "Why the Declaration Must Pass," *World Tomorrow,* June 28, 1934, 323–26.
10. Kirby Page, "The Future of the Fellowship," *World Tomorrow,* January 4, 1934, 9–11; Reinhold Niebuhr, "The Fellowship of Socialist Christians," *World Tomorrow,* June 14, 1934,
297–98.
11. Janet Lee, *Comrades and Partners: The Shared Lives of Grace Hutchins and Anna Rochester* (Lanham, MD: Rowman & Littlefield, 2000), 184–85; Thomas J. Sugrue, *Sweet Land of Liberty:
The Forgotten Struggle for Civil Rights in the North* (New York: Random House, 2008), 21–24;

Robin D. G. Kelley, " 'Comrades, Praise Gawd for Lenin and Them!' Ideology and Culture among Black Communists in Alabama, 1930–1935," *Science and Society* 52 (Spring 1988): 59–82.

12. David Nelson Duke, *In the Trenches with Jesus and Marx: Harry F. Ward and the Struggle for Social Justice* (Tuscaloosa: University of Alabama Press, 2003), 170–87.

13. Reinhold Niebuhr, "The Paradox of Institutions," *World Tomorrow*, August 1923, 231–32; Reinhold Niebuhr, "Optimism and Utopianism," *World Tomorrow*, February 22, 1933, 179–80.

14. Niebuhr, "Why the Christian Church Is Not Pacifist," in *The Essential Reinhold Niebuhr*, ed. Robert McAfee Brown (New Haven, CT: Yale University Press, 1986).

15. "Christian Socialism," *Radical Religion*, Fall 1938, 3–4.

16. Duke, *In the Trenches*, 179.

17. Dorothy Day, *The Long Loneliness* (New York: Harper & Row, 1952), 52, 78; William Miller, *Dorothy Day: A Biography* (San Francisco: Harper, 1982); Mel Piehl, *Breaking Bread: The Catholic Worker and the Origin of Catholic Radicalism in America* (Philadelphia: Temple University Press, 1982).

18. Rosalie Riegle Troester, *Voices from the Catholic Worker* (Philadelphia: Temple University Press, 1993), 12–14.

19. "Religion: Pro-Labor Priests," *Time*, July 22, 1946.

20. Sidney Schwarz, *Judaism and Justice: The Jewish Passion to Repair the World* (Woodstock, VT: Jewish Lights, 2006), 214; Saul Alinsky, *Reveille for Radicals* (1946; 2nd ed., New York: Vintage, 1969), 35; Sanford D. Horwitt, *Let Them Call Me Rebel: Saul Alinsky, His Life and Legacy* (New York: Knopf, 1989).

21. P. David Finks, *The Radical Vision of Saul Alinsky* (New York: Paulist, 1984), 13–18.

22. Alinsky, *Reveille*, 15.

Chapter 13. The Gandhian Moment

1. Duke, *In the Trenches*, 175; Craig, *Religion*, 163–64.

2. Patricia Appelbaum, *Kingdom to Commune: Protestant Pacifist Culture between World War I and the Vietnam Era* (Chapel Hill: University of North Carolina Press, 2009); Scott H. Bennett, *Radical Pacifism: The War Resisters League and Gandhian Nonviolence in America, 1915–1963* (Syracuse, NY: Syracuse University Press, 2003); Joseph Kip Kosek, *Acts of Conscience: Christian Nonviolence and Modern American Democracy* (New York: Columbia University Press, 2009); Marian Mollin, *Radical Pacifism in Modern America: Egalitarianism and Protest* (Philadelphia: University of Pennsylvania Press, 2006); James Tracy, *Direct Action: Radical Pacifism from the Union Eight to the Chicago Seven* (Chicago: University of Chicago Press, 1996); "From the Editor's Mail Bag," *Radical Religion*, Spring 1936, 44–45.

3. Sudarshan Kapur, *Raising Up a Prophet: The African-American Encounter with Gandhi* (Boston: Beacon, 1992), 10–30.

4. Richard B. Gregg, "Non-violent Resistance," *Fellowship*, May 1935, 5–6; C. F. Andrews, *Mahatma Gandhi's Ideas: Including Selections from His Writings* (New York: Macmillan, 1930); E. Stanley Jones, *Mahatma Gandhi: An Interpretation* (New York: Abingdon, 1948); Krishnalal Shridharani, *War without Violence: A Study of Gandhi's Method and Its Accomplishments* (New York: Harcourt, Brace, 1939).

5. Kirby Page, "The United Front," *Fellowship*, March 1935, 6–7; Kirby Page, "The Cross and Social Change," *Fellowship*, November 1936, 5–7.

6. "We Will Not Fight in Spain," *Fellowship*, January 1937, 10; "Norman Thomas Replies," *Fellowship*, February 1937, 13.

7. Dorothy Day, "The Use of Force," *Catholic Worker*, November 1936, 4; Dorothy Day, "Our Stand," *Catholic Worker*, June 1940, 1, 4.

8. Dorothy Day, "Our Country Passes from Undeclared to Declared War; We Continue Our Christian Pacifist Stance," *Catholic Worker*, January 1942, 1, 4; McKanan, *The Catholic Worker After Dorothy* (Collegeville, MN: Liturgical, 2008), 36–43.

9. Herman Will Jr., "Among the Peace Organizations," *motive*, February 1942, 39.

10. Burk-Wadsworth Act, 54 Stat. 885.

11. Don Benedict, *Born Again Radical* (New York: Pilgrim, 1982), 21–30.

12. Ibid., 30–34; George Houser, "Diary," *motive*, February 1941, 13–14, 46.

13. Houser, "Diary."

14. Ibid., 13; and Benedict, *Born Again*, 32; Ernest Lefever, "Conscientious Objectors in Prison," *Fellowship*, February 1945, 28–30.

15. Benedict, *Born Again*, 33, 36, 38; George Houser, " A Year and a Day: Thoughts of an Unrepentant Non-registrant," *motive*, November 1941, 23–24.

16. John D'Emilio, *Lost Prophet: The Life and Times of Bayard Rustin* (Chicago: University of Chicago Press, 2003), 72–120.

17. "FOR Council Votes to Continue in NSBRO," *Fellowship*, January 1944, 11, 14; Evan W. Thomas, "CPS and the Second Mile," *Fellowship*, February 1944, 28; Muste, "Fellowship in Discovering Truth," *Fellowship*, November 1944, 188–89; "Council and Staff Vote on NSBRO," *Fellowship*, November 1944, 192; "Thomas Resigns," *Fellowship*, November 1944, 193; F. Carleton Mabee, "What Can Grow out of CPS?" *Fellowship*, October 1945, 176–77.

18. David Dellinger, *From Yale to Jail: The Life Story of a Moral Dissenter* (New York: Pantheon, 1993).

Chapter 14. Mentors of a New Left

1. Nat Hentoff, *Peace Agitator: The Story of A. J. Muste* (New York: Macmillan, 1963), 98.

2. A. J. Muste, "Peace Is Indivisible," *Fellowship*, October 1936, 5–7; "A. J. Muste: A Biographical Sketch," *Fellowship*, January 1937, 5 6.

3. Ammon Hennacy, *The Book of Ammon*, 2nd ed. (Baltimore: Fortkamp, 1994), 2; Dorothy Day, *Loaves and Fishes* (Maryknoll, NY: Orbis, 1997), 109.

4. Kosek, *Acts*, 76, 108; Howard Thurman, *Jesus and the Disinherited* (New York: Abingdon, 1949), 28–29.

5. Taylor, *Randolph*, 72–77, 138, 144–45, 197, 176.

6. Dorothy Day, "We Go on Record," *Catholic Worker*, September 1945, 1; A.J. Muste, "A New Year—A New Era," *Fellowship*, January 1946, 3–4.

7. Kosek, *Acts*, 195, 197; "National Conference Draws 300 Registrants," *Fellowship*, October 1947, 160–61.

8. Clarence E. Pickett, *For More than Bread* (Boston: Little, Brown, 1953); Appelbaum, *Kingdom*, 40; Thomas D. Hamm, *The Quakers in America* (New York: Columbia University Press, 2003), 174–76; Allen Smith, "The Renewal Movement: The Peace Testimony and Modern Quakerism," *Quaker History* 85 (Fall 1996): 1–23.

9. Kosek, *Acts*, 198; David Dellinger, "They Refused to Hide," *Liberation*, July–August 1957, 5 6; Dorothy Day, "Thoughts After Prison," *Liberation*, September 1957, 5–7; A.J. Muste, "The 500 Who Didn't Hide," *Liberation*, May 1960, 3–4.

10. Mollin, *Radical Pacifism*, 77, 79; Smith, "Renewal Movement"; A.J. Muste, "Africa against the Bomb," *Liberation*, January 1960, 4–7; Muste, "Africa against the Bomb (II)," *Liberation*, February 1960, 11–14; Erich Fromm, "The Pathology of the Cold War," *Liberation*, October 1961, 9–13.

11. Robert Pickus, "The Nevada Project: An Appraisal," *Liberation*, September 1957, 3–4, 19; Norman Thomas, "An Open Letter to American Pacifists," *Liberation*, November 1959, 13.

12. A.J. Muste, "The Crisis in SANE," *Liberation*, July–August 1960, 10–13; Muste, "The Crisis in Sane: Act II," *Liberation*, November 1960, 5–8; Norman Cousins, "Letter from Norman Cousins," *Liberation*, December 1960, 3; David Dellinger, "Uncle Tom-ism in the Peace Movement," *Liberation*, June 1963, 3; C. V. Parkinson, "Levelling with the Public," *Liberation*, June 1963, 24–25; A.J. Muste, "Let's Radicalize the Peace Movement," *Liberation*, June 1963, 26–30.

13. James Farmer, *Lay Bare the Heart: An Autobiography of the Civil Rights Movement* (Fort Worth: Texas Christian University Press, 1985), 136, 137, 142.

14. Ibid., 67–108; George M. Houser, "Tackling Jim Crow Is a Dangerous Job," *Fellowship*, August 1944, 140–41; George M. Houser, "We Say No to Jim Crow," *Fellowship*, April 1945, 61–63; Farmer, *Lay Bare*, 101–14, 356–60.

15. Farmer, *Lay Bare*, 112, 105.

16. Ibid., 104.

17. D'Emilio, *Lost Prophet,* 65–66.

18. Ibid., 57–63; Jim Farmer, "The Coming Revolt against Jim Crow," *Fellowship,* May 1945, 90–91.

19. "The Commitment," Church for the Fellowship of All Peoples, http://www.fellowshipsf. org/history.html.

20. A.J. Muste, "The Direction of Growth," *Fellowship,* September 1944, 158–59; "National Conference Draws 300 Registrants"; "Thine Is the Power," *Fellowship,* May 1952, 7–8; Elisabeth Dodds and Marion Coddington, "New Methods for New Growth," *Fellowship,* October 1945, 178–79.

21. Benedict, *Born Again,* 38–57.

22. Farmer, *Lay Bare,* 149–52; Mollin, *Radical Pacifism,* 44.

23. Sherwood Eddy, "The Delta Cooperative Farm," *Fellowship,* May 1936, 9–10; John Klasson, "A Preacher Practices Brotherhood," *Fellowship,* June 1937, 7–8.

24. http://www.swarthmore.edu/library/peace/DG051–099/dg071MacedoniaCC.htm; William Edward Zeuch, "Macedonia and the Shared Life: A Critical Evaluation," *Liberation,* September 1957, 16–19; Dave Dellinger, "Crosses in Conflict in Southern Georgia," *Liberation,* December 1956, 11–13; Tracy Elaine K'Meyer, *Koinonia Farm: Building the Beloved Community in Postwar Georgia* (Chapel Hill: University of North Carolina Press, 1993).

25. Rosa Parks, *My Story* (New York: Puffin, 1992), 106; John M. Glen, *Highlander: No Ordinary School* (Knoxville: University of Tennessee Press, 1996).

26. Staughton Lynd, "The Individual Was Made for Community," *Liberation,* January 1957, 15–18; Dave Dellinger, "The Community Was Made for Man," *Liberation,* January 1957, 18–19; Staughton Lynd, "Can Men Live as Brothers? Lessons of a 19th Century Community," *Liberation,* February 1958, 12–14.

27. Alfred Hassler, "Commuters' Community," *Fellowship,* April 1953, 5–11, 17–18.

28. Mary Etter, "Families Make a Neighborhood," *Fellowship,* July 1953, 52–53; Taylor, "Social Movement"; Appelbaum, *Kingdom,* 34.

29. Roy Finch, "The Liberation Poll," *Liberation,* November 1959, 14–17; Maurice Isserman, *If I Had a Hammer: The Death of the Old Left and the Birth of the New Left* (New York: Basic, 1987).

30. Roy Finch, "A Strange Mistake," *Liberation,* June 1957, 13–14; Dave Dellinger, "United Front, No; Public Debate, Yes," *Liberation,* June 1957, 14–16; Roy C. Kepler, "Letters," *Liberation,* July–August 1957, 31; "Shall We Vote?" *Liberation,* October 1956, 3–7; "Our Readers and the Election," *Liberation,* October 1956, 15–17.

31. Finch, "Liberation Poll"; Harris Wofford, "A Lawyer's Case for Civil Disobedience," *Liberation,* January 1961, 12–14; Dave Dellinger, "Ten Days in Jail," *Liberation,* August 1961, 5–8, 19; David Wieck, "The Invention of Responsibility," *Liberation,* October 1957, 5–7; David Thoreau Wieck, "Report from Little Rock," *Liberation,* October 1958, 4–9; "Mississippi Muddle," *Liberation,* November 1962, 9–12.

32. "Tract for the Times," *Liberation,* March 1956, 3–6.

33. Dave Dellinger, "The Here-and-Now Revolution," *Liberation,* June 1956, 15–18.

Chapter 15. New Encounters in the South

1. Martin Luther King, "Our Struggle," *Liberation,* April 1956, 3–6.

2. Parks, *My Story,* 117; Jo Ann Gibson Robinson, *The Montgomery Bus Boycott and the Women Who Started It,* ed. David J. Garrow (Knoxville: University of Tennessee Press, 1987), 131–33, 76.

3. Robinson, *Montgomery,* 152–53.

4. Bayard Rustin, "Montgomery Diary," *Liberation,* April 1956, 7–10; Dave Dellinger, "The Negroes of Birmingham," *Liberation,* Summer 1963, 17–21.

5. Parks, *My Story,* 127; King, "Our Struggle"; Robinson, *Montgomery,* 157.

6. "Struggle for Integration," *Liberation,* May 1960, 5–9; John Lewis, *Walking with the Wind: A Memoir of the Movement* (New York: Simon & Schuster, 1998), 45.

7. Joseph H. Jackson, "Annual Address [of 1962]," in *Afro-American Religious History: A Documentary Witness,* ed. Milton C. Sernett (Durham, NC: Duke University Press, 1985), 425; David J.

Garrow, *Bearing the Cross: Martin Luther King, Jr., and the Southern Christian Leadership Conference* (New York: Vintage, 1986).

8. Charles Marsh, *The Beloved Community: How Faith Shapes Social Justice, from the Civil Rights Movement to Today* (New York: Basic, 2005), 127–49; David L. Chappell, *A Stone of Hope: Prophetic Religion and the Death of Jim Crow* (Chapel Hill. University of North Carolina Press, 2004).

9. "Struggle for Integration."

10. Lewis, *Walking,* 85–92.

11. Ibid., 89; Kosek, *Acts,* 218–21.

12. Lewis, *Walking,* 101–15.

13. Jameson Jones, "Issues in the Sit-ins," *motive,* May 1960, 10–15.

14. Lewis, *Walking,* 114; "SNCC Statement of Purpose," in *The Columbia Documentary History of Religion in America since 1945,* eds. Paul Harvey and Philip Goff (New York: Columbia University Press, 2005), 156; Clayton Carson, *In Struggle: SNCC and the Black Awakening of the 1960s* (Cambridge, MA: Harvard University Press, 1981).

15. "Struggle for Integration."

16. Farmer, *Lay Bare,* 191–97.

17. Ibid., 1–32, 198–207; Lewis, *Walking,* 147–66.

18. Farmer, *Lay Bare,* 25–30; Lewis, *Walking,* 172–73.

19. Lewis, *Walking,* 180.

20. Ibid., 189, 260, 187.

21. L. C. Dorsey, "A Prophet Who Believed," *Sojourners,* December 1982, 21.

22. Lewis, *Walking,* 163; Bernice Johnson Reagon, from *Eyes on the Prize* interview, in Harvey and Goff, *Columbia Documentary,* 150.

23. Lewis, *Walking,* 381–82, 73, 474.

Chapter 16. Expanding Circles of Encounter

1. Lewis, *Walking,* 246, 250.

2. Ibid., 173; Farmer, *Lay Bare,* 27; James Forman, *The Making of Black Revolutionaries* (Washington, DC: Open Hand, 1985), 158–86.

3. Lewis, *Walking,* 243, 297.

4. Ibid., 366.

5. Ibid., 295.

6. Stokely Carmichael and Charles V. Hamilton, *Black Power: The Politics of Liberation* (New York: Random House, 1967).

7. National Committee of Negro Churchmen, "Black Power," in *Black Theology: A Documentary History, 1966–1979,* eds. Gayraud S. Wilmore and James H. Cone (Maryknoll, NY: Orbis, 1979), 23–30; and National Committee of Black Churchmen, "The Black Declaration of Independence, July 4, 1970," in Wilmore and Cone, *Black Theology,* 108–11.

8. "SNCC Position Paper," in *"Takin' It to the Streets": A Sixties Reader,* eds. Alexander Bloom and Wini Breines, 2nd ed. (New York: Oxford University Press, 2003), 38–40; Casey Hayden and Mary King, "Sex and Caste: A Kind of Memo," in Bloom and Breines, *"Takin' It,"* 40–43.

9. Mary King, *Freedom Song,* in Harvey and Goff, *Columbia Documentary,* 158; Doug Rossinow, *The Politics of Authenticity: Liberalism, Christianity, and the New Left in America* (New York: Columbia University Press, 1998), 102–4.

10. Ann Braude, "A Religious Feminist—Who Can Find Her? Historiographical Challenges for the National Organization for Women," *Journal of Religion* 84 (October 2004): 555–72; Ann Braude, ed., *Transforming the Faith of Our Fathers: Women Who Changed American Religion* (New York: Palgrave, 2004).

11. Amy L. Koehlinger, *The New Nuns: Racial Justice and Religious Reform in the 1960s* (Cambridge, MA: Harvard University Press, 2007).

12. Nadine Foley, in Braude, *Transforming,* 229; Robert S. Ellwood, *The Sixties Spiritual Awakening: American Religion Moving from Modern to Postmodern* (New Brunswick, NJ: Rutgers University Press, 1994), 213.

13. Susan Brownmiller, *In Our Time: Memoir of a Revolution* (New York: Dial, 1999), 21, 78–79; Kathy Mulherin and Jennifer Gardner, "Growing Up a Woman," *Christianity & Crisis*, October 5, 1970, 202–9.

14. Stephen R. Lloyd-Moffett, "The Mysticism and Social Action of César Chávez," in *Latino Religions and Civic Activism in the United States*, eds. Gaston Espinosa, Virgilio Elizondo, and Jesse Miranda (New York: Oxford University Press, 2005), 42; Luís D. León, "César Chávez and Mexican American Civil Religion," in Espinosa, Elizondo, and Miranda, *Latino Religions,* 60–61.

15. Robert F. Stowell, "A New Spirit in the South," *Liberation,* June 1960, 14; James M. Lawson Jr., "From a Lunch-Counter Stool," *motive,* May 1960, 16–18.

16. Robert Martinson, "A Black Eye for the Un-Americans," *Liberation,* July–August 1960, 15–17.

17. "The Port Huron Statement," in Bloom and Breines, *"Takin' It,"* 50–61.

18. C. Wright Mills, "Letter to the New Left," in Bloom and Breines, *"Takin' It,"* 61–66.

19. Farmer, *Lay Bare,* 142–43, 146.

20. Harold Ehrensperger, "Walking Revolutionist," *Fellowship,* January 1953, 1–3; "Student Co-operatives as a Constructive Force," *motive,* February 1941, 37; "The Rochdale Principles," *motive,* March 1941, 39; Franklin H. Littell, "Christian Community: Fellowship in the New Order," *motive,* February 1941, 41; "motive," *motive,* February 1941, 3; "Port Huron Statement."

21. Casey Hayden, "Raising the Question of Who Decides," in Bloom and Breines, *"Takin' It,"* 67.

22. Andrew Kopkind, in Sara Evans, *Personal Politics: The Roots of Women's Liberation in the Civil Rights Movement and the New Left* (New York: Vintage, 1980), 130.

23. Paul Potter, "The Incredible War," in Bloom and Breines, *"Takin' It,"* 175.

24. David Miller, "Reclaiming Our History: Memoirs of a Draft-Card Burner," *Reclaiming Quarterly,* Spring 2001; "We Refuse to Serve," in Bloom and Breines, *"Takin' It,"* 196.

25. Ellwood, *Sixties,* 207; Michael Ferber, "A Time to Say No," in Bloom and Breines, *"Takin' It,"* 197–98; Murray Polner, *Disarmed and Dangerous: The Radical Lives and Times of Daniel and Philip Berrigan* (New York: Basic, 1997).

26. Sharon Erickson Nepstad, *Religion and War Resistance in the Plowshares Movement* (New York: Cambridge University Press, 2008), 47; Ferber, "A Time," 198.

27. Norman Mailer, *The Armies of the Night* (New York: New American Library, 1968), 122; Marty Jezer, *Abbie Hoffman: American Rebel* (New Brunswick, NJ: Rutgers University Press, 1992), 49–50; Troester, *Voices,* 34–35.

Chapter 17. From Encounter to Confrontation

1. Gordon Gibson, "Freedom Moves South" (paper presented at Collegium: An Association for Liberal Religious Studies, November 2009).

2. James Thomas, "Race Relations Dilemma—A Case Study," *motive,* February 1956; Edwin Brock, "Between Resolution and Action," *motive,* February 1956, 8–9; Herbert Hackett, "Desegregation . . . Has Many Facets," *motive,* February 1956, 14–17, 27; "Report from the South," *motive,* February 1956, 19–27; Lewis, *Walking,* 131.

3. Michael B. Friedland, *Lift Up Your Voice Like a Trumpet: White Clergy and the Civil Rights and Antiwar Movements, 1954–1973* (Chapel Hill: University of North Carolina Press, 1998), 107; Robert McAfee Brown and Gaylord B. Noyce, "Special Report: Further Reflections on Freedom Riding," *Christianity & Crisis,* August 7, 1961, 146–48; John David Maguire, "When Moderation Demands Taking Sides," *Christianity & Crisis,* June 26, 1961, 114–17; James F. Findlay, *Church People in the Struggle: The National Council of Churches and the Black Freedom Movement, 1950–1970* (New York: Oxford University Press, 1993).

4. Roger Shinn, "Axioms for White Liberals," *Christianity & Crisis,* September 30, 1963, 167.

5. "World Church: News and Notes: National Council Action on Race," *Christianity & Crisis,* July 8, 1963, 131–32; Roger Shinn, "The Testing of the Church," *Christianity & Crisis,* July 8, 1963, 122–23; John C. Bennett, "The Churches and Civil Rights," *Christianity & Crisis,*

September 16, 1963, 153–54; Mathew Ahmann, ed., *Race: Challenge to Religion* (Chicago: H. Regnery, 1963).

6. Frances S. Smith, "Special Report: The March on Washington," *Christianity & Crisis,* September 30, 1963, 171; Stephen C. Rose, "Special Report: Religion and Race," *Christianity & Crisis,* February 4, 1963, 10–11; Stephen C. Rose, "Epitaph for an Era: A Firsthand Report from Birmingham," *Christianity & Crisis,* June 10, 1963, 103–10.

7. Friedland, *Lift,* 134; Malcolm Boyd, "Maintaining Humanness in the Freedom Movement," *Christianity & Crisis,* October 4, 1965, 199–203.

8. Finks, *Radical Vision,* 127–28, 141–43; Stephen C. Rose, "Saul Alinsky and His Critics," *Christianity & Crisis,* July 20, 1964, 143–52; Stephen C. Rose, "Rochester's Racial Rubicon," *Christianity & Crisis,* March 22, 1965, 55–59.

9. Ruth Harris, in Sara M. Evans, ed., *Journeys That Opened Up the World: Women, Student Christian Movements, and Social Justice, 1955–1975* (New Brunswick, NJ: Rutgers University Press, 2003) , 22–25; Eduardo C. Mondlane, "Africa in a Revolutionary World," *motive,* November 1955, 4–7.

10. M. Richard Shaull, *Encounter with Revolution* (New York: Association Press, 1955), 4, 87, 64–65, 58; Richard Shaull, "The Second Latin American Church and Society Conference," *Christianity & Crisis,* May 2, 1966, 89–91.

11. Friedland, *Lift,* 142; "Pacifists, Socialists, Liberals Protest 'Dirty War' in Vietnam," *Liberation,* October 1963, 10; John C. Bennett, "Where Are We Headed in Vietnam?" *Christianity & Crisis,* March 8, 1965, 29–30.

12. "A Joint Appeal to the National Council of Churches," *Christianity & Crisis,* July 12, 1965, 145–46; "The National Council of Churches Speaks on Vietnam," *Christianity & Crisis,* December 27, 1965, 282–84; Gary J. Dorrien, *Social Ethics in the Making: Interpreting an American Tradition* (Malden, MA: Wiley-Blackwell, 2009), 269; David R. Swartz, "Left Behind: The Evangelical Left and the Limits of Evangelical Politics, 1965–1988" (PhD diss., Notre Dame, 2008), 192.

13. Mitchell K. Hall, *Because of Their Faith: CALCAV and Religious Opposition to the Vietnam War* (New York: Columbia University Press, 1990).

14. Ellwood, *Sixties,* 205.

15. Merton, "Nhat Hanh Is My Brother," in Robert Harlen King, *Thomas Merton and Thich Nhat Hanh: Engaged Spirituality in an Age of Globalization* (New York: Continuum, 2001), 106–7.

16. Michael Novak, *A Theology for Radical Politics* (New York: Herder & Herder, 1969), 34; Rosemary Radford Ruether, *The Church against Itself* (New York: Herder & Herder, 1967), 221–23; Malcolm Boyd, *The Underground Church* (New York: Sheed & Ward, 1968).

17. Lewis, *Walking,* 227; "The Church and the Urban Crisis," in Wilmore and Cone, *Black Theology,* 44; Swartz, "Left Behind," 171.

18. Charlotte Bunch Weeks, "The UCM Decision: Romance or Reality," *Christianity & Crisis,* June 23, 1969, 181–83.

19. "The Black Manifesto," in Wilmore and Cone, *Black Theology,* 80–89.

20. Ellwood, *Sixties,* 276.

21. Stephen C. Rose, "The Manifesto and Renewal," *Christianity & Crisis,* May 26, 1969, 142; Stephen C. Rose, "Colonial Brokerage," *Christianity & Crisis,* June 9, 1969, 159–60; Gayraud S. Wilmore, "A Black Churchman's Response to the Black Manifesto," in Wilmore and Cone, *Black Theology,* 95.

22. Mario T. García, "Religion and the Chicano Movement: Católicos Por La Raza," in *Mexican American Religions: Spirituality, Activism, and Culture,* ed. Gastón Espinosa and Mario T. García (Durham, NC: Duke University Press, 2008), 125–49.

23. Ibid.

24. Ibid.

25. Mary Daly, "The Women's Movement: An Exodus Community," *Religious Education* 67 (1972): 327–35.

26. Thelma Stevens and Robert S. Lecky, "The NCC Detroit Assembly: Two Views," *Christianity & Crisis,* January 5, 1970, 345–47.

Chapter 18. Rebuilding the Left

1. I use the now current LGBT label—lesbian, gay, bisexual, transgender—to describe a movement that has evolved over the past forty years.
2. Albert B. Cleage Jr., *The Black Messiah* (Trenton, NJ: Africa World Press, 1989), 35–47, 3; Wilmore and Cone, *Black Theology,* 251.
3. NCBC, "Black Theology," in Wilmore and Cone, *Black Theology,* 100–101.
4. James H. Cone, *Black Theology and Black Power* (New York: Seabury, 1969), 62–63.
5. Ibid., 63, 69.
6. Cone, "God Is Black," in *Lift Every Voice: Constructing Christian Theologies from the Underside,* ed. Susan Brooks Thistlethwaite and Mary Potter Engel, rev. ed. (Maryknoll, NY: Orbis, 1998), 103.
7. Anthony B. Pinn, *The Black Church in the Post–Civil Rights Era* (Maryknoll, NY: Orbis, 2002), 24; "The Black Value System," http://www.trinitychicago.org/index.php?option=com _content&task=view&id=114.
8. Lawrence H. Mamiya, "A Social History of the Bethel African Methodist Episcopal Church in Baltimore: The House of God and the Struggle for Freedom," in *American Congregations,* vol. 1, *Portraits of Twelve Religious Communities,* ed. James P. Wind and James W. Lewis (Chicago: University of Chicago Press, 1994), 221–92.
9. Andrea Smith, "Native Feminist Theology," in *Liberation Theologies in the United States: An Introduction,* ed. Stacey M. Floyd-Thomas and Anthony B. Pinn (New York: New York University Press, 2010), 149.
10. George E. Tinker, *Spirit and Resistance: Political Theology and American Indian Liberation* (Minneapolis: Fortress, 2004); Steve Charleston, "The Old Testament of Native America," in Thistlethwaite and Engel, *Lift Every Voice,* 69–81.
11. García, "Religion and the Chicano Movement," 129; "El Plan de Aztlán," in *Aztlan: An Anthology of Mexican American Literature,* ed. Luis Valdez and Stan Steiner (New York: Knopf, 1973), 402–6.
12. Mario T. García, "PADRES: Latino Community Priests and Social Action," in Espinosa, Elizondo, and Miranda, *Latino Religions,* 77–84.
13. Ibid., 92–93.
14. Lara Medina, "The Challenges and Consequences of Being Latina, Catholic, and Political," in Espinosa, Elizondo, and Miranda, *Latino Religions,* 97–110; Lara Medina, *Las Hermanas: Chicana/Latina Religious-Political Activism in the U.S. Catholic Church* (Philadelphia: Temple University Press, 2004), 127–28; Ada María Isasi-Díaz and Yolanda Tarango, *Hispanic Women: Prophetic Voice in the Church* (San Francisco: Harper & Row, 1988).
15. Mark Oppenheimer, *Knocking on Heaven's Door: American Religion in the Age of Counterculture* (New Haven, CT: Yale University Press, 2003), 29–60; Scott Thumma and Edward R. Gray, *Gay Religion* (Walnut Creek, CA: AltaMira, 2005), 395; "The United Church of Christ and Homosexuality," http://www.religioustolerance.org/hom_ucca5.htm.
16. "Highlights of Dignity's History," http://www.dignityusa.org/history/1970; Leonard Norman Primiano, "The Gay God of the City: The Emergence of the Gay and Lesbian Ethnic Parish," in Thumma and Gray, *Gay Religion,* 7–30; "LGBT Religious Support and Advocacy Group Information," in Thumma and Gray, *Gay Religion,* 377–406.
17. Aryana Bates, "Liberation in Truth: African American Lesbians Reflect on Religion, Spirituality, and Their Church," in Thumma and Gray, *Gay Religion,* 221–37.
18. Jay Hasbrouck, "Utopian Imaginaries and Faerie Practice: Mapping Routes of Relational Agency," in Thumma and Gray, *Gay Religion,* 239–58.
19. Rebecca Alpert and Goldie Milgram, "Women in the Reconstructionist Rabbinate," in Catherine Wessinger, *Religious Institutions and Women's Leadership: New Roles inside the Mainstream* (Columbia: University of South Carolina, 1996), 291–310.
20. Ellwood, *Sixties,* 244–47; Aviva Cantor, "Jewish Women's Haggadah," in *Womanspirit Rising: A Feminist Reader in Religion,* ed. Carol P. Christ and Judith Plaskow (New York: Harper & Row, 1979), 185–92; Arthur Waskow, "Original 1969 Freedom Seder," http://www .theshalomcenter.org/node/899; Arthur Waskow, "A Time to Renew," *Sojourners,* June 1982, 24–26.

21. Judith Simmer-Brown, "Speaking Truth to Power: The Buddhist Peace Fellowship," in *Engaged Buddhism in the West*, ed. Christopher S. Queen (Somerville, MA: Wisdom, 2000), 67–94; Patricia Hunt-Perry and Lyn Fine, "All Buddhism Is Engaged: Thich Nhat Hanh and the Order of Interbeing," in Queen, *Engaged Buddhism*, 35–66.

22. Paula Green, "Walking for Peace: Nipponzan Myohoji," in Queen, *Engaged Buddhism*, 128–56; McKanan, *Catholic Worker*, 80–81.

23. Carl F. H. Henry, *The Uneasy Conscience of Modern Fundamentalism* (Grand Rapids, MI: Eerdmans, 1947); Swartz, "Left Behind," 25–41.

24. Swartz, "Left Behind," 93–95, 164–65, 172–78, 335; Tom Skinner, *How Black Is the Gospel?* (Philadelphia: Lippincott, 1970).

25. Swartz, "Left Behind," 231, 273, 478–78.

26. "What Is the People's Christian Coalition?" *Post-American*, 1971, 5; Jim Wallis, "Post-American Christianity," *Post-American*, 1971, 2–3.

27. Wallis, "Post-American Christianity"; Swartz, "Left Behind," 92.

28. Wallis, "Sojourners in the Land," *Sojourners*, January 1976, 3–4.

29. "Atlantic Life Community: Toward a Statement of Purpose," http://www.jonahhouse.org/ALC/statement1976.htm; McKanan, *Catholic Worker*, 71–94.

30. Lawrence J. Engel, "The Influence of Saul Alinsky on the Campaign for Human Development," *Theological Studies* 59 (1998): 636–61; Mark R. Warren, *Dry Bones Rattling: Community Building to Revitalize American Democracy* (Princeton, NJ: Princeton University Press, 2001), 40–71.

31. Richard L. Wood and Mark R. Warren, "A Different Face of Faith-Based Politics: Social Capital and Community Organizing in the Public Arena," *International Journal of Sociology and Social Policy* 22 (Fall 2002): 6–54; Richard Wood, *Faith in Action* (Chicago: University of Chicago Press, 2002); Samuel G. Freedman, *Upon This Rock: The Miracles of a Black Church* (New York: HarperCollins, 1993).

Chapter 19. A Women's Decade

1. Wessinger, *Religious Institutions*, 370–77.

2. Elizabeth Gould Davis, *The First Sex* (New York: Putnam, 1971); Marija Gimbutas, *The Gods and Goddesses of Old Europe* (Berkeley: University of California Press, 1974); Merlin Stone, *When God Was a Woman* (New York: Dial, 1976).

3. "WITCH," in *Sisterhood Is Powerful: An Anthology of Writings from the Women's Liberation Movement*, ed. Robin Morgan (New York: Vintage, 1970), 538–40.

4. Z. Budapest, "witch is to womon as womb is to birth," *Quest*, Summer 1975, 50–56.

5. Susan Rennie and Kirsten Grimstad, "Spiritual Explorations Cross-Country," *Quest*, Spring 1975, 49–51; Judy Davis and Juanita Weaver, "Dimensions of Spirituality," *Quest*, Spring 1975, 2–6; Dorothy Riddle, "New Visions of Spiritual Power," *Quest*, Spring 1975, 7–16.

6. "Why *WomanSpirit*?" *WomanSpirit*, Fall Equinox 1974, 1; "Our Vision of *WomanSpirit*," *WomanSpirit*, Spring Equinox 1975, 2; Jean Mountaingrove, "Speaking to Ourselves," *WomanSpirit*, Autumn Equinox 1974, 27; "A Ritual Celebration," *WomanSpirit*, Autumn 1975, 25–28.

7. "Where," *WomanSpirit*, Summer Solstice 1975, 60; Jean Mountaingrove, "How To," *WomanSpirit*, Summer Solstice 1975, 61; Carol P. Christ, "Why Women Need the Goddess: Phenomenological, Psychological, and Political Reflections," in Christ and Plaskow, *Womanspirit*, 273–87; Sally Gearhart, "Womanpower: Energy Re-Sourcement," in *The Politics of Women's Spirituality: Essays on the Rise of Spiritual Power within the Feminist Movement*, ed. Charlene Spretnak (Garden City, NY: Anchor, 1982), 194–206; Naomi R. Goldenberg, *Changing of the Gods: Feminism and the End of Traditional Religions* (Boston: Beacon, 1979), 92–95.

8. Zsuzsanna Budapest, *The Holy Book of Women's Mysteries* (Berkeley, CA: Winghow, 1980), 3.

9. Alice L. Hageman, *Sexist Religion and Women in the Church: No More Silence!* (New York: Association, 1974); Judith Plaskow, in Braude, *Transforming*, 221; "Alverno College," in *The New Woman's Survival Catalog*, eds. Kirsten Grimstad and Susan Rennie (New York: Coward, McCann & Geoghegan/Berkley, 1973), 139.

10. Elisabeth Schüssler Fiorenza, in Braude, *Transforming,* 144.

11. Judith Plaskow, "The Coming of Lilith: Toward a Feminist Theology," in Christ and Plaskow, *Womanspirit,* 198–209.

12. Mary Daly, "After the Death of God the Father: Women's Liberation and the Transformation of Christian Consciousness," in Christ and Plaskow, *Womanspirit,* 53–62.

13. Mary Daly, *Beyond God the Father: Toward a Philosophy of Women's Liberation,* 2nd ed. (Boston: Beacon, 1985), 33–37.

14. Christ and Plaskow, *Womanspirit,* 193, x–xi; Nelle Morton, "The Dilemma of Celebration," in Christ and Plaskow, *Womanspirit,* 159–65.

15. Elisabeth Schüssler Fiorenza, "Feminist Spiritualtiy, Christian Identity, and Catholic Vision," in Christ and Plaskow, *Womanspirit,* 136–48; Schüssler Fiorenza, in Braude, *Transforming,* 146–47; Plaskow, in Braude, *Transforming,* 221–23; Plaskow, "Bringing a Daughter into the Covenant," in Christ and Plaskow, *Womanspirit,* 179–84; Letty Cottin Pogebrin, in Braude, *Transforming,* 38; Naomi Janowitz and Maggie Wenig, "Sabbath Prayers for Women," in Christ and Plaskow, *Womanspirit,* 174–78.

16. Suzanne Radley Hiatt, "Women's Ordination in the Anglican Communion: Can This Church Be Saved?" in Wessinger, *Religious Institutions,* 211–27.

17. Arlene and Leonard Swidler, translators' foreword to Haye van der Meer, *Women in the Catholic Church?* (Philadelphia: Temple University Press, 1973), ix–xxix; Ada María Isasi-Diaz, in Braude, *Transforming,* 87.

18. Call to Action, "Who We Are," http://www.cta-usa.org/whobishconference/bishindex.html.

19. *Daughters of Sarah,* November 1974, 1; Wes Michaelson, "Neither Male nor Female: The Thanksgiving Conference on Biblical Feminism," *Sojourners,* January 1976, 10–12.

20. Virginia Mollenkott, "Women and the Bible: A Challenge to Male Interpretation," *Sojourners,* February 1976, 21–25.

21. Virginia Ramey Mollenkott, in Braude, *Transforming,* 70; "Men, Women, and Biblical Equality," http://www.cbeinternational.org/files/u1/smwbe/english.pdf.

22. Jacquelyn Grant, "Black Theology and the Black Woman," in Wilmore and Cone, *Black Theology,* 418–33; Stacey M. Floyd-Thomas, "Womanist Theology," in Floyd-Thomas and Pinn, *Liberation Theologies,* 37–60; Delores Williams, in Braude, *Transforming,* 115–33.

23. Isasi-Díaz, in Braude, *Transforming,* 92–95; Isasi-Díaz and Tarango, *Hispanic Women;* Chung Hyun Kyung, *Struggle to Be Sun Again* (Maryknoll, NY: Orbis, 1990).

24. Schussler Fiorenza, in Braude, *Transforming,* 145, 151; Mudflower Collective, *God's Fierce Whimsy: Christian Feminism and Theological Education* (New York: Pilgrim, 1985); Letty Russell et al., *Inheriting Our Mothers' Gardens: Feminist Theology in Third World Perspective* (Philadelphia: Westminster, 1988); Ruether, in Braude, *Transforming,* 73–84; Ruether, *New Woman, New Earth: Sexist Ideologies and Human Liberation* (New York: Seabury, 1975); Ruether, *Sexism and God-Talk: Toward a Feminist Theology* (Boston: Beacon, 1983).

25. Rosemary Radford Ruether, "A Religion for Women," *Christianity & Crisis,* 10 December 1979, 307–9, reprinted in *WomanSpirit,* Summer Solstice 1980, 22–25; Z. Budapest, "Christian Feminist vs. Goddess Movement," *WomanSpirit,* Summer Solstice 1980, 26–27; Carol Christ, "Another Response to a Religion for Women," *WomanSpirit,* Summer Solstice 1980, 27–29; Carol Christ, "A Religion for Women: A Response to Rosemary Ruether, part II," *WomanSpirit,* Autumn Equinox 1980, 11–14.

26. "Reclaiming Principles of Unity," in Starhawk, *The Spiral Dance,* 6.

27. Starhawk, *Spiral Dance,* 1–24.

28. Barbara Epstein, *Political Protest and Cultural Revolution: Nonviolent Direct Action in the 1970s and 1980s* (Berkeley: University of California Press, 1991), 4.

29. Starhawk, "Consciousness, Politics, and Magic," in Spretnak, *Politics,* 172–84.

30. Ibid., 182.

Chapter 20. Resisting the Right

1. Phil M. Shenk, "An Ecumenical Outpouring," *Sojourners,* June 1981, 9–10.

2. Joyce Hollyday, "The Grandest of Bellicose Errors," *Sojourners,* January 1982, 5–6; Jim Wallis, "An Open Letter to President Reagan," *Sojourners,* April 1982, 3–4.

3. Mark Hulsether, *Building a Protestant Left: Christianity & Crisis Magazine, 1941–1993* (Knoxville: University of Tennessee Press, 1999), 201; Mark Zwick and Louise Zwick, "No Federal Funds—What Now?" *Houston Catholic Worker,* December 1996, http://www.cjd.org/paper/funds.html.

4. Robin Lorentzen, *Women in the Sanctuary Movement* (Philadelphia: Temple University Press, 1991), 4, 13–16; María Cristina García, " 'Dangerous Times Call for Risky Responses': Latino Immigration and Sanctuary, 1981–2001," in Espinosa, Elizondo, and Miranda, *Latino Religions,* 159.

5. "History: Highlights from Our First Twenty-Five Years," http://www.witnessforpeace.org/section.php?id=89; Swartz, "Left Behind," 564.

6. Wallis, "Open Letter"; "A Promise of Resistance," *Sojourners,* December 1983, 6.

7. "History," http://www.cpt.org/about/history.

8. "Kairos Document," http://www.sahistory.org.za/pages/library-resources/official%20docs/kairos-document.htm.

9. McKanan, *Catholic Worker,* 97–124; Ed Loring, "The Open Door Community: Purposes and Aims," in *A Work of Hospitality: The Open Door Reader, 1982–2002,* ed. Peter R. Gathje (Atlanta: Open Door Community, 2002), 17.

10. "The Challenge of Peace: God's Promise and Our Response," in O'Brien and Shannon, *Catholic Social Thought,* paragraphs 120, 188; "Economic Justice for All," in O'Brien and Shannon, *Catholic Social Thought,* paragraphs 13, 295–325.

11. Cited at http://sites.google.com/site/confrontingnuclearwar/8-the-role-of-religion-in-nuclear-disarmament.

12. Peter Maurin, "The C.P. and C.M.," in *Easy Essays,* at http://www.catholicworker.org/roundtable/easyessays.cfm#They%20And%20We.

13. William Stringfellow, "An Open Letter to Jimmy Carter," *Sojourners,* October 1976, 7–8; Swartz, "Left Behind," 510–12.

14. Joe Holland, "The Crisis of Family," *Sojourners,* May 1982, 26–29.

15. Michael Lerner, "Recapturing the Family Issue," *Nation,* February 6, 1982, 141–43; Michael Lerner, ed., *Tikkun Reader: Twentieth Anniversary* (Lanham, MD: Rowman & Littlefield, 2007), 5.

16. Jim Wallis, *The Soul of Politics: Beyond "Religious Right" and "Secular Left"* (San Diego: Harcourt Brace, 1995); Wallis, *God's Politics. Why the Right Gets It Wrong and the Left Doesn't Get It* (San Francisco: Harper, 2005); Michael Lerner, *The Politics of Meaning: Restoring Hope and Possibility in an Age of Cynicism* (Reading, MA: Addison-Wesley, 1996); Lerner, *The Left Hand of God: Taking Back Our Country from the Religious Right* (San Francisco: Harper, 2006), 1, 3; Jim Wallis, "Signs of the Times. Issues, Values, and the Rainbow Campaign in Election '88," *Sojourners,* November 1988, 15–20.

17. Danny Duncan Collum, "The '60s to the 1990s: Decades Turned Upside Down," *Sojourners,* January 1990, 18–24.

18. Lerner, *Politics of Meaning,* 124; Wallis, *God's Politics.*

19. Wallis, *God's Politics,* 19.

20. Wallis, "Signs of the Times"; Jim Wallis, "The Essence of Political Leadership," *Sojourners,* February 1989, 23–24.

Chapter 21. The Future of Radicalism

1. Daniel Berrigan, "Connecting the Altar to the Pentagon," *Fellowship,* November 1979.

2. David Halperin, *Saint Foucault: Towards a Gay Hagiography* (New York: Oxford University Press, 1995), 61; Victor Anderson, *Beyond Ontological Blackness: An Essay on African American Religious and Cultural Criticism* (New York: Continuum, 1995).

3. Michelangelo Signorile, "A Queer Manifesto," in McCarthy and McMillian, *Radical Reader,* 602.

4. William Stringfellow," "Jesus the Criminal," *Christianity & Crisis,* June 8, 1970, 119–22.

5. Swartz, "Left Behind," 96, 457–70.

6. John Howard Yoder, *The Politics of Jesus* (Grand Rapids, MI: Eerdmans, 1972); Mary Evelyn Jegen, "The Pacifist Vision," *Fellowship,* March–April 1980.

7. "12 Marks of a New Monasticism," http://www.newmonasticism.org/12marks.php.
8. Lynn White, "The Historical Roots of Our Ecologic Crisis," *Science,* March 10, 1967, 1203–7.
9. Richard R. Bohannon and Kevin J. O'Brien, "Saving the World (and the People in It, Too)," in *Inherited Land: The Changing Grounds of Religion and Ecology,* eds. Whitney Bauman, Richard R. Bohannon, and Kevin J. O'Brien (Eugene, OR: Pickwick, 2011); Stan McKay, "An Aboriginal Perspective on the Integrity of Creation," in *Liberating Faith: Religious Voices for Justice, Peace, & Ecological Wisdom,* ed. Roger S. Gottlieb (Lanham, MD: Rowman & Littlefield, 2003), 519; Brian Swimme and Thomas Berry, *The Universe Story: From the Primordial Flashing Forth to the Ecozoic Era* (San Francisco: Harper, 1992); Sallie McFague, *The Body of God: An Ecological Theology* (Minneapolis: Fortress, 1993).
10. Ruether, *New Woman, New Earth.*